CONDITIONS

Also available from Continuum:

Being and Event, Alain Badiou
Infinite Thought, Alain Badiou
Logics of Worlds, Alain Badiou
Theory of the Subject, Alain Badiou
After Finitude, Quentin Meillassoux
Politics of Aesthetics, Jacques Ranciere
Art and Fear, Paul Virilio
Negative Horizon, Paul Virilio
Desert Screen, Paul Virilio

CONDITIONS

Alain Badiou

Translated by Steven Corcoran

continuum

Continuum International Publishing Group
The Tower Building   80 Maiden Lane
11 York Road   Suite 704
London SE1 7NX   New York NY 10038

www.continuumbooks.com

Originally published in French as *Conditions* © Editions du Seuil, 1992

This translation © Continuum 2008

British Library Cataloguing-in-Publication Data
A catalogue record for this book is available from the British Library.

ISBN-10: HB: 0-8264-9827-2
ISBN-13: HB: 978-0-8264-9827-4

Library of Congress Cataloging-in-Publication Data
Badiou, Alain.
[Conditions. English]
Conditions/Alain Badiou; translated by Steven Corcoran.
    p. cm.
ISBN-13: 978-0-8264-9827-4
ISBN-10: 0-8264-9827-2
1. Philosophy, French–20th century. I. Title.

B2430.B27113 2008
194--dc22   2008017483

Typeset by Newgen Imaging Systems Pvt Ltd, Chennai, India
Printed and bound in Great Britain by MPG Books Ltd, Bodmin, Cornwall

Contents

CONTENTS

The Subtractive

Preface by Francois Wahl

When we agreed to gather together the larger part of papers and interventions in colloquiums that Badiou has given since *Being and Event*,
texts that all make considerable advances and that for the interest of
each of them ought not remain scattered, we planned that I would introduce them with a preface. Even if this were only to mark twenty-five
years of collaborative work. I should strictly apologize for the length this
preface has taken. But there is nothing more futile that those 'introits'
that only cast a semblance of light, since they can only be understood
once the book has been read and worked-through. Further, philosophy
does not tolerate – should not tolerate – the 'extraction' of concepts; the
movement, articulation and deduction of a concept in a text is something whose course, whose wovenness, we either rejoin and assume, or
else we have nothing but the conversation the *café philosophique*. Last, a
number of the papers included here – of an apparently easy read –
present a particular difficulty in that they make reference to the termi-
nology, and therefore to the apparatus, of *Being and Event*, which means
that any reading of these texts is incomplete without bearing in mind
what we should, properly speaking, refer to as the system that forms
their background.

First up, then, I have resolved to go over the great work again, stopping along the way at the points that are here reprised, and indeed
re-elaborated. I therefore do not pretend not to have, on some points,
omitted parts of the revision. Second, I try to indicate the new contributions that the present essays make to the point that constitutes their

central theme: the relation of philosophy to its 'conditions'. Finally, prepared by years of exchanging objections and responses, I state at least one of the points on which Badiou has not totally convinced me, or, more seriously, on which he seems in difficulty. In consideration of which, I will have fulfilled the ternary plan he is so fond of.

I

Beyond academic inventories, there are two styles of definition of philosophy: one is *descriptive*, the other *foundational*. Gilles Deleuze has recently provided us with an example of the first, through a sort of laying bare of philosophical work, from which he draws out the features specific to philosophy itself[1]; Badiou[2] has taken on all the risks of the second, whereby philosophy exists only on the condition of a thinking of *being*, one constructed according a systematic process, that takes into account the contemporary developments in rationality, and that allows, at its end, a proclamation about the current moment of *truth*. The rapprochement might seem inappropriate: Deleuze saves Bergson *via* Nietzsche, Badiou saves Plato *via* Cantor. But such are the points of convergence, and such the contrasts, that a comparison would bring out in more than one place the kernel of Badiou's thought: it is such that by embracing it very closely, one would let escape what it is when first seen from a distance.

At a glance Deleuze and Badiou can be seen to proceed along parallel paths in opposition to what might be called a contemporary *koinè*. Their work counters the claim that we bear witness to an 'end' of philosophy: philosophy has always been and continues to be specified by its *operational procedures*, which distinguish it as radically from science (more generally, from the knowledge of states of affairs) as from art (and Badiou adds: from politics and from love). Deleuze attributed uniquely to philosophy 'the art of forming, inventing, fabricating concepts'[3]; Badiou, while denying it can create truths, vests it with securing the compossibility of the truths that these four produce, the only ones that can. These procedures, then, make up so many of philosophy's 'conditions'. For both thinkers, the operations specific to philosophy are *immanent*: they are uniquely immanent to thought, are grounded in what is 'presented' to it, and to the exclusion of anything situated below or above whose obscurity would cloak thought in darkness. More: philosophy cannot be construed as that which completes, with a supreme or transcendent gesture, the count of Ones in which experience is enveloped: this would be a disaster. The reason is that if what philosophy has to think is content, donation, or being, then the onus is on it to affirm multiplicity, that is the multiple of multiples, pure multiplicity, or the *without-one*. It is not true, then, to say that philosophy is under the condition of *language* conceived as a transcendental condition of thought: for Deleuze, this would mean that thought remains confined to arguing in propositions; and, for Badiou, to reflecting the state of the situation – that is to grasping it without remainder: language can only accede to the pure multiple when *forced*. So, although the philosopher does pass through language, it is displaced each time anew with the dice-throw of a non-derivable naming. Last, Truth cannot be said to be a matter of *reference*, of the object of knowledge: Truth proceeds on the basis of a decision, which constitutes an *event*, a supplementary and thrown act, and, but it is also (says Badiou) subtractive, because it deducts.

Thereupon, Deleuze and Badiou part company. Deleuze described a practice whose key-word is the *creation of concepts*, 'self-positing' but fluid concepts, condensing a plurality of components that are remodelled in accordance with each displacement in this practice's site of intensity; it is a creation for which the only image is that of 'a point of absolute survey at infinite speed'.[4] On this view, a philosopher is one who articulates consistent concepts. This construction, however, is an art in which concepts comprise '"non-discursive" centres of vibration'[5], and in which 'deciding' between concepts is impossible inasmuch as the crossroads of problems to which they attempt to respond differ. Concepts, to be sure, are distributed on – but without coinciding with a diagramme or a plane – that is traversed by curved movements and the comings and goings of thought. This plane is a 'reserve of purely conceptual events'[6], which, although not situated outside of philosophy – for which reason it is called a 'plane of immanence' – is pre-philosophical, intuitive and avers that 'concepts themselves refer to a non-conceptual comprehension'.[7] Deleuze's work is very clearly an attempt to describe the process of philosophical work, to maintain thought in the *movement* – another key word – of its elaboration; as a result of which, Deleuze had clearly to model 'the philosophical' on the factuality of its production, configure what thought creates in the movement of its practice, and raise its 'trajectory' to the level of its 'project'.

Badiou's key-word is *Truth*: which is to say that, though he also endeavours to articulate the procedures by which it is produced, these latter have nothing to learn from thought's movement; in question is what is able to be established as true *discourse*, the conditions by which it can come to pass, through the putting to work of an operator of deduction. And inasmuch as he does here agree with Deleuze to oppose truth to referential knowledge, he argues that it can only be accomplished by a radical recasting: the objective is to determine *rational* procedures for truth-statements that no longer owe anything to the categories of epistemology: for the acquisition of a discernment. This is an objective for which Badiou will demonstrate that – this is his entire enterprise in a nutshell – it is necessary to forge two branches of a paradoxical pincer: a *matheme of the indiscernible*.

Matheme is used in the strictest sense of the word. If there is a 'before' of philosophy, a pre-philosophical moment that from the outside holds forth in the interior of philosophy, then it is ontology: for Badiou the science of being prior to every quality, the science of being *qua* being, has always been – that is, since Plato – and only ever will be *mathematics*. And mathematics, in its set-theoretic re-foundation, admits only of the *bottomless* multiple, the multiple of multiples. On this basis Badiou claims that being is the pure multiple 'such as it emerges in presentation'[8]; it is *'inconsistent'* with regard to everything that consists, or that is counted for One. But the pure multiple, if, in turn, it 'in-consists', if it is of itself unpresentable (since only structures, or multiples counted-for-one, can be presented), it can consist in no more than a weaving of the nothing and of the count: that is a weaving of the *empty* set, the set to which nothing belongs, or which is not a multiple of any thing. Hence we must freshly conclude – an axiom of ontology – that a situation is sutured to its being through the void; and further that, as it is everywhere included, 'the void is the proper name of being'.[9] Symmetrically, it would be regressive to postulate, along with the whole onto-theological tradition, the existence of a 'single' infinite: the theory of multiplicity admits only an *infinity* of infinities in the form, radically new, of 'non-successive' ordinals, which are 'Other, in that [they] can never be the still-one-more which succeed an other'.[10] They are axiomatically different from finite sets, but it is through them that the power of repetition expresses itself, whence this spectacular inversion: as concept, finitude comes after the infinite, since it is developed in the retroaction of the latter. It follows logically – a second axiom of ontology – that being is infinite, and is uniquely that.

This first exposition (outlined in broad strokes) leaves no room for doubt as to what philosophy consists in for Badiou: not relying on anything pre-given, it must *be* founded, and this essential act of foundation can only be attempted by ontology. That ontology, in its turn, has no base on which to found itself other than mathematics entails a twofold consequence: on the one hand, it falls to the philosopher to state the 'ontological dignity'[11] of what mathematicians content themselves with putting to work; on the other hand, the order of the mathematical imposes a 'base of rationality'[12] from which the philosopher may not stray, while forcing a confrontation with the extreme intricacies of the rational.

Above all, this entails – a law of every consequential ontology – a rigorous exploration of the intricacies of the multiple itself: that is, of what composes it. Now, regarding this, we know that the elements of a set – elements that are said to 'belong' to it – are themselves composed of subsets (or 'included' parts). These subsets obey this same transitive law in their turn, working into an altogether homogenous and stable tissue. This is at least the case for 'normal' multiples or *ordinals*, a 'concept [that] literally provides the backbone of the whole of ontology'[13]; but the philosopher cannot be content to remain within the confines of this beautiful order; since, by an effect of dissymmetry that is not without consequences, the set of the parts of a set turns out to be 'larger' than, or in excess of, the set itself. In addition, multiples can also take the form of *a-normal*, or exceptional, or unstable subsets, sets that contain certain elements that do not themselves constitute a subset, or that contain parts not presented as elements: from these we have objects of a 'typology of being', a new 'latent' figure of the void and a condition for everything that the philosopher, now across the barrier (*la barre*) of the 'there is', must manage to ground. Last, you'll observe that ontology fully deploys an axiomatics, which, as Badiou emphasizes, is each time also a decision, and so a responsibility of thought with regard to the systematicity it constructs.

Hence, between Deleuze's plea for the mobility of concepts in which that of thought is imaged, and Badiou's taking foothold in the reason of set theory as that in which the Real for thought is deployed (with all the attendant deadlocks), we have more than a contrast between two uncertain definitions of philosophical discourse: Badiou ties philosophy as ontology to the original form of rational discourse, and does so at the precise point that this discourse is in the process of recasting itself, to *reopen* itself – to make a 'hole' – via the void, the exception and the infinite.

The points of cross-over between the two thinkers are acutely interesting. Both dismiss the One and the structure by which a situation (to use Badiou's language) is placed under the regime of the count. However, for Deleuze, the pure multiple is a synonym of chaos, whereas for Badiou it is *organized* between zero and the empty set that incessantly fills it out, and the infinite set that expresses the specific power – exceeding simple succession – of repetition. In an a-theological gesture, both assert the immanence of the infinite; whereas Deleuze argued that in this immanence nothing would present itself were there no encounter between two multiples that are necessarily already given, Badiou claims to *unfold* being, *qua* the presentation of all presentation, uniquely through the implementation of set-theory axioms. Above all, Deleuze clearly posited an infinite that is without other, that circulates infinitely in the interior of itself, that is, as it were, *full*; whereas Badiou's articulation of a matheme of being involves two ontological axioms that work by indexing the multiple of the void and by locating the infinite in an exception to succession, and in so doing effect – a theme that will be with us from now on – a *double subtraction*.

None of this is better illustrated than by their respective readings of Spinoza. For Deleuze, Spinoza is the 'infinite becoming-philosopher'.[14] Why? Because he maintained thought entirely within the plane of immanence as 'One-All', and had the virtue to describe it as 'traversed by movements of the infinite, *filled* with intensive ordinates'. For Badiou, however, though he was well aware that only multiples of multiples exist, Spinoza could not help but reintroduce the One – in the metastructure of substance – because he *'foreclosed the void'*.[15] Spinoza attested despite himself to the fact that it is not possible to think the multiple without also thinking the errancy of the void, which is manifest in the impossibility of completing the passage from the infinite (substance and infinite modes) to the finite singular modes. So, even in Spinoza's work, 'the void [proves to be] ineluctable, like the stigmata of a split in

presentation between substantial being-qua-being and its finite immanent production'.[16] The fruit born by thinking the multiple with the
rigour of the matheme is thus double: it shows that there is only some
'there is' on condition of the void and that the infinite exists only on the
condition that it exists infinitely.

Philosophy properly speaking 'circulates' between ontology, which it
elevates to the level of thought, and the set of procedures that *produce*
truths. To reiterate: for Badiou there have only ever been four: science,
art, politics and love. These four procedures form a necessary and necessarily complete set for the post-event emergence of philosophy. They
then provide philosophy its stake: to 'configure, in a unique exercise of
thought, the epochal disposition [. . .] of the moment of truths'[17]; but we
must forthwith add that it cannot do so without revealing, by means
of a 'reflecting torsion',[18] Truth's type of *being*; and that if the truth–
procedures condition it, then they do so inasmuch as they are the site
of an epochal crisis of Truth. In point of fact, from the theory of the
multiple to psychoanalysis, including the post-Hölderlinian poem and
post-Marxist politics, everything that is advanced as truth patently occurs
in excess: in excess of knowledge, which is to say of the rule according
to which the multiples of a situation can all be discerned and classed
(and named: this is what Badiou calls the 'language of the situation')
under the concept of their properties. There is a crisis today – and so a
stake for philosophy – in that truth comes forward as that which knowledge prohibits: it is 'the "indeterminate", the unnameable part, the
conceptless link'.[19] In respect of which the excess returns, by making a
hole in knowledge.

The result of this is that, if there is a matheme of the Truth – which
must be understood as a matheme of that which specifies an operator of
truth *with regard to being* – then it has to be constructed in two stages.

In the first place, truths, since they create eras, belong to history; they
are dependent on *events*. Badiou therefore required a *concept* of the event,
and he elaborated one in striking fashion: for him, the event never occurs
globally in the situation in which it appears, it is 'local', and has a 'site'.[20]
It brings to pass in the situation – that is, it 'presents' – elements that
were not presented in it, other than in the opacity of its site. Hence, it
follows that 'a site is only "evental" [. . .] insofar as it is retroactively
qualified as such by the occurrence of an event'[21]: otherwise said, whether
an event is true is only something it can itself confirm: the advent of

the invisible in the visible depends on an act of *intervention*, an oblique wager that the evental multiple belongs to the situation, on the uncertain decision condensed in the choice of a *naming* that is supernumerary with regard to the language of the situation, and on the putting to work of an 'apparatus which separates out, within the set of presented multiples, those which depend on an event'[22] – that is what Badiou calls 'fidelity' to the event.

By thus articulating its concept, it then becomes possible to assign the condition of the event's *being*, paradoxical though it may be. As we've seen, since in a multiple that belongs to the situation the parts or subsets are normally included, it is easy to conceive – and can be demonstrated[23] – that terms exist that are in excess of norms, indecomposable terms whose parts cannot be apprehended. The site is a term of this type. The direct result is that the site reveals itself, as it were, to be eminently ontological, inasmuch as it opens onto the nothing, onto inconsistency. In sum, the site is *'on the edge of the void'*, and it is in its precariousness that being comes to pass. But the event is necessary to confirm this precariousness, and since it can only confirm itself, then it must be said – this is the second step – that evental multiplicities have *'the property of self-belonging'*.[24] This as we know is prohibited by the theory of multiplicity, and hence by ontology: of the event, being has nothing to say; it belongs to *'that which is not being qua being'*. But this is not to say that the event, as for it, has nothing to say about being. In one and the same movement it must be maintained both that the site opens onto being and its converse, that is, that the event in commanding the re-collecting of elements of the site through the filter of its supernumerary signifier 'exhibits the brilliance of the mark-of-one.'[25]

All that remains, then, is to construct the *matheme* of the event, just as we saw for the matheme of truth: 'The event is a one-multiple made up of all the multiples which belong to its site, and on the other, the event itself'.[26] Yet it is crucial to see that, as it is only ever in the future perfect, I can never say, as it were in advance, from within the situation, that the event belongs to the situation: the matheme of the event, it may fairly be said, is the matheme of an *undecidable*.

I will now compare this founding of the event, as 'illegality', and hence of history, with Deleuze's concept of the virtual, a concept to which all his other concepts are articulated, as it helps clarify what Badiou understands by both the constitution of *time* and that of the *Two*.

Having defined chaos 'not so much by its disorder as by the infinite speed with which every form dissipates taking place in it vanishes . . . a void is not a nothingness but a virtual',[27] Deleuze's work sets itself within the immanence of a becoming that thought can either only slow – which is precisely what science does through the construction of functions, whose arguments are made of independent variables – or that it can, on the contrary, aspire to return to, through an approximation of its speed, and which is what philosophy does: it 'retains infinite speeds while gaining consistency, by giving the virtual a consistency specific to it'.[28] This is what Deleuze somewhat enigmatically referred to as the 'event',[29] a 'pure sense that immediately runs through the components' and that, in retaining infinite movement, 'reconquers an immanent power of creation'.[30] We can see here how, on the continuum of actualizations of virtuals, time can only be configured by means of two *crosscuts*, by means of two vectors with contrary movements – one as close as possible to the actual, and another to the virtual – that continually pass into one another.

Badiou, however, because he has at his disposal both the *actuality* of the 'normal' multiple and the *paradoxical* character of the evental multiple, founds two *modes* of time of contrasting ontological status: that of *nature* and that of *history*. Nature being stable, consistent and composed of multiplies of subsets that can be infinitely counted-for-one,[31] it is of a time that does not concern the ontologist: it is simply 'coextensive to the structure'.[32] On the other hand, because the event attests to the fact that 'some newness [can arrive] in being',[33] because on each occasion it is a wager on being,[34] it invests history with an ontological dimension. Entailing an encounter with a site, intervention and fidelity, it cannot constitute an exception to time; but it is of a time that is specific to itself, that of a recurrence in which, once more, an event only supports by means of an event. This is because the intervention, which is an illegal decision, would become unthinkable had there *never* been an event, that is, testifiable consequences of other events (without first assignable). Intervention can only ever be 'a line drawn from one paradoxical multiple which is already circulating, to the circulation of another'.[35] In this way, 'the theory of intervention forms the kernel of any theory of time'[36] – it is a time punctuated with events, a time of series of gaps between the comings forth of being within the structure that counts the situation.

Here is where the problem of the Two comes in. For Deleuze, the two is a *pre-requisite*: 'There must be at least two multiplicities', since 'multiplicity is precisely what happens between the two'.[37] Were this not so, then, because every actualization arises on the base of mixture and connexion, nothing would occur. According to Deleuze, the pure multiplicity of ontology does not allow a description of the reign of differences, which institutes states of affairs as much as forms of thought, and in which 'concept' and 'function' are defined, in turn, only by the contrariety of their movement.[38]

Badiou is required to draw the Two not from the anonymity of the multiple but from the exception of the event's being. In doing so, he recognizes in it a decisive function in the foundation of the subtractive. For it so happens that, because the matheme of the event registers its belonging to itself, it must be counted *twice*. Not, as is said, because there are two times One, but because it 'interposes' – it interposes its supernumerary nomination – between the site and itself[39]; 'an event is an *interval* rather than a term: it establishes itself [. . .] between the empty anonymity bordered on by the site, and the addition of a name'.[40] Each event, as an event of being and as suspended from an interiority of events, is decided at the cost of a duplication. The event is founded upon 'the maxim "there is Twoness"'.[41] This could also be expressed: there is no history except insofar as, in the absence of any One, the Two is decided.

In the second place: since a truth is the 'result' of an evental procedure, its *definition* has to respond to a fourfold requisite: first, that it is always the truth of *a situation*, one in which the event has its site; second, that it is not an exact, perfect designation, a construction guided by the structure, and for which names happen to be available – a reminder that it is *subtracted from knowledge*, which it 'traverses'; third, that truth is a '*singular* production',[42] one pertaining to an encounter that is pursued in fidelity to an intervention, and that has by definition to consist in the production of a *multiple*, failing which it could have nothing to say about being and would itself be lacking in being; and fourth, that – this is its decisive characteristic – this multiple is by essence *indiscernible* in the situation, ceasing to be only on pain of falling back into knowledge: as truth of the situation, a truth is said to be *generic* because it gathers terms that have nothing in common between them, save their belonging to the situation.

In the last instance, this presumes that Truth is 'the truth of *being qua being*'[43]; since what is brought into play here is the crucial theorem of the multiple – its law and its deadlock: that which gives it its status as real – which states the unassignable excess of a set's subsets over its elements, that is, the principle of *'errant excess'*. Thus, the generic is nothing other than the consistent putting to work of the excess, the faithful investigation into the respect in which being 'evasively'[44] supplements all encyclopaedic determinations of the knowledge of the situation: it is a procedure equal to being. 'A truth is that minimal consistency (a subset, a conceptless immanence) which certifies in the situation the inconsistency from which its being is made'.[45]

Next, in order to construct Truth's matheme, we must master the following oxymoron: 'a *discernible* concept of what is an indiscernible multiplicity'.[46] Here what is at issue is the compatibility of the philosophical concept of Truth with mathematical ontology: we already know that the latter can only prohibit the generic procedure *qua* evental procedure; but the very possibility of speaking, from the vantage point of the multiple, 'of an indiscernible part of any multiple'[47] has at a minimum to be secured. There does happen to be a construction showing this,[48] and it is important to note that what we once again encounter in it, this time in the domain specific to mathematics, is the schema of the event: the 'situation' can be construed as a denumerable multiple; language of the situation is logically designated by discernible multiplicities; the intervention is denoted by the choosing of a name, of a letter, for the possible indiscernible (the reader of this collection will soon understand why Badiou has chosen the ideogram of femininity by way of a letter); the Two recurs, since a new multiple bound to the first – to the situation – can be discerned that at once forms the substance, the *stuff*, of the indiscernible – of which it is a part – and by its structure provides information about the *conditions* with which the indiscernible will need comply insofar as it is indiscernible; fidelity takes the form of an ordered investigation into these conditions, which dominate – that is, include and verify – each other; and so the structure of the generic set appears: it is the one that has no discerning properties because it has 'at least one element in common with every *domination*', even as these dominations are mutually exclusive.[49] The generic set is indiscernible in that it contains 'a little of everything'.

What remains to be shown is that this indiscernible set, which is established inasmuch as it can be thought, really *belongs* to the situation; or, to put it in the language of ontology, that it *exists*. Badiou refers to this as the ontological argument of the indiscernible. We know that because it was not presented in it, the indiscernible set does not belong to the denumerable multiple that comprises the initial situation; as such the set must of necessity belong to a new situation that is created by its adjunction to the first and that can be called a *'generic extension'*. Once more, the operators of the procedure are names. In the denumerable situation, these names – which are multiplicities like any other – can be assigned to designate the hypothetical elements of the extension formed by the indiscernible: the only means to achieve this is to combine them to one of the indiscernible's conditions; in this way they come to refer to this latter and will come to refer, taken all together, to each multiple of the indiscernible adjunction – this occurs, of course, without it being possible to say each time which. It is not that these names make up 'a language for the unnameable',[50] but that they belong *at once* to the discernible situation *and* to its extension formed by the indiscernible: so, without having lost anything of its evasiveness, the existence of the indiscernible is grounded within the very heart of that to which it is joined. Let us translate: *within being*, the Truth, that is, the generic, is prohibited because it depends on a supernumerary signifier, but *its own being* is itself henceforth possible insofar as its existence can be, as it were, 'indiscerned'[51] in the situation.

It was necessary to take this difficult passage through the matheme – which Badiou considers the kernel of his endeavour – because, by legitimating their procedures, it alone authorizes truths to say something about being; that is, to say the errant excess of being, which once more shows its subtractive character.

In the course of this debate, Badiou has resolved two memorable and related questions, contrasting him with Cantor and Leibniz, respectively. The first decisively demonstrated that all multiplicities can be designated via their ordered construction on the basis of the empty set, but then fell to the illusion that it is possible to resolve the problem of the *continuous*: to the contrary, it has been established that the type of multiplicity pertaining to the relation between the elements of a set and the set of its parts cannot be 'prescribed'.[52] Though ontology leaves us at an impasse at this point, there is a matheme of this impasse, that of the indiscernible. As for Leibniz, basing himself on the existence of God *qua* 'the complete language',[53] he asserted that 'in nature there are never two real beings that are absolutely indiscernible'. However, the doctrine of the generic proves not only that there can be no complete language ('constructivism' is refuted), but that the *indiscernible* can be thought, and that it can 'exist'.[54]

Once again, Badiou's theoretical decisions are clarified by comparison with Deleuze's, and this time there is open discussion. Though Deleuze, as we have repeatedly seen, is a thinker of the continuous, this continuous is, as Badiou qualifies it, 'organicist' (as opposed to mathematical)[55]: that is, an elastic whole of intension-based extensions and contractions. Instead, Badiou argues, ontology only postulates the continuous *qua* supplement, which, although anonymous and nondescript, is homogeneous to the composition of the multiple. This supplement is one that can be understood in the terms of the theory of the multiple: it is at once written into its principle by the theorem of the point of excess and is rejoined by thought on condition that it is paradoxically dependent – as a statement not of knowledge, but of truth – on the act of the Two.

Deleuze, even in *The Fold*, was averse to employing the very metaphysical concept of the indiscernible, and instead used that of the 'singular'. His work clearly argues for the claim that the concept–event is an incorporeal singularity, each component of which must, in its turn, 'be understood not a general or particular but as a pure and simple singularity [. . .] that is generalized or particularized'.[56] And also for the claim that, in their slowness, scientific functions are designated as references-actualizations that make up as many material individuations: that is, 'singularities insofar as they enter into coordinates'.[57] Both of these designations of singularity are effectively, and in very Leibnizian fashion, points of view, the former 'conceptual personae', the latter 'partial observers'.[58] Badiou's take on the matter of states of affairs or things is revealing: it can be rigorously shown in this matter, he argues, that 'in general the train of the world exhibits only *generality*'.[59] Instead, what is positively singular and as such distinguishes itself is a generic procedure: not as the point of concentration of the whole, but as a hazardous supplementation of the multiple.

Last, are we to say that, since for Deleuze there always remains a dark ground of unactualized potential, a site of the *indiscernible* is thereby named? No, because at issue is only what has not come to be discerned, what has not yet found its point of view; and it is thus, by comparison, easier to grasp what in Badiou's work marks the scission of the concept of the indiscernible, *qua* that which is established in thought but as being's inherent impasse: this by no means signifies that it is not, but rather that it is grasped – it would be better to say unassigned – uniquely at the infinite risk of an intervention.

We are now in a position to see the point at which, for Badiou, the trace of the *subject* is inscribed, since needless to say without its authority there would be no intervention. Badiou speaks of 'trace' here, because the generic procedure is *alone* what attests to the subject: like it, with it, the subject is uncertain, rare, singular and qualified (in accordance with the procedure it supports: lover, poet, scientist or political activist). 'The law does not prescribe there being some subjects', it is a 'configuration *in excess* of the situation'.[60] Always 'local', it is the 'form [by] which a truth is supported'.[61] In practical terms, the act, or the subject–intervention of the investigation – rather than simply *the* subject – operates within the encounter with the evental site, a supernumerary name and a situation. The subject is a finite and hazardous but faithful investigation: it is a militant. It is the militant of a truth to come, whose knowledge it does not possess. This subject is 'at once the *real* of the procedure and the *hypothesis* that its unfinishable result will introduce some newness into presentation'.[62] Its name persists as the – non-signifying – signifier of the Two within which the adventure of truth proceeds.

Let us once more take the detachment that comparison brings: Deleuze would say that interiority – he was hardly one to speak of the subject – is a re-folding, the condensation of a multiple exterior, and essentially that which is 'equal to the world of which it is a point of view'.[63] Whence this formulation, striking in its double movement: 'It is the brain that says *I*, but *I* is an other'.[64] Badiou, in his Cartesian fidelity, deposes the subject of substance, since it is a category of knowledge, but restores to the subject the effectuation of an investigation that nothing – no law – could restrict, since what hangs in the balance is a decision: its figure is indissociable from the advent of truths.

Bearing this in mind, what *type of being* is to be ascribed to the subject? It is not possible any more than it is for the Truth for the subject to avoid ontology's prohibition on the event. As with Truth, however, we expect that the subject's existence cannot be incompatible with ontology. And further that, as with Truth, the key issue concerns the existence of conditions in the starting ontological situation that permit the subject to circulate in each generic production without the arbitrariness of knowledge: that is, that permit it to make a proclamation, *from the situation*, about the legitimacy – the veridicity – of that which will have been produced by its intervention. Let us say that, if the surmise is correct, we will by the same token have the 'ontological substructure'[65] of the subject. The question is therefore: under what conditions can a subject, as the finite instance of an infinite procedure, be certain from within knowledge that a statement of truth 'will have been' veridical? The response is: all it takes is the existence of a term in the situation whose relation to the statement of truth, once it has been produced, is, as for it, discernable. It can be said that this term has *forced* the statement to be veridical, to come to a decision on the status of the indiscernible from within the field of knowledge.

This concept of *forcing* will give rise, in a final development, to a modal theory of proof: 'one can *know*, in a situation in which a post-eventual generic procedure is being deployed, whether a statement of the subject-language has a chance of being veridical in the situation which adds to the initial situation of a truth of the latter'.[66] If it does not support a relation of forcing with any term of the situation, we can rule out its being veridical. If it supports a relation of forcing with all the terms of the situation, it will always be veridical: this essentially says, that, in this case, the generic will have returned to knowledge. If the statement is such that it supports the relation of forcing with such and such a term of the situation, but not with such and such another term, then this is because it is part of the hazards of investigation and the terms encountered as to whether or not it will be recognized as veridical; what this then goes to explain is the uncertain character of an essential part of what issues from history, that is, from the four truth procedures. If, last, a statement supports a *positive* relation of forcing with certain terms of the situation, and a *negative* one with others, then we can know – a crucial result – that it is *undecidable*.

In all cases, the exploration of forcing provides considerable theoretical and practical lessons about the properties of a truth statement – otherwise said, of an 'effect of the subject'.[67] Being connected by means of that which forces it in the situation, a truth statement may only supplement this situation *without suppressing anything in it*. It 'reflects' the nature of the situation, as it does, and above all, the axioms of multiplicity; it cannot hold anything to be inexistent that had not 'inexisted' within the situation. On the other hand, it can, without contradiction, decide the disqualification of a term that was only a determination of knowledge – as, for example, its hierarchical place.[68] Let us translate: though it concerns a non-descript set, the subject's decision is not simply any decision at all, but inheres in what connects it to the situation. Still more decisively: by means of forcing the veridicality of the errant excess is demonstrated; quantity, 'the fetish of objectivity' is in fact evasive',[69] since the cardinality of the parts of a set *arbitrarily* surpasses in a generic extension – an extension that, as we have seen, belongs to the situation – the cardinality of its elements. Therewith is the problem of the *continuous* resolved. We can now say more than that its thinkable 'quantity' is indiscernible; with is veridicality assured, we can also say that it *is*: that it is *as undecidable*. There is no need to foreclose the excess on the pretext that a well-made language could not say anything about it; and no need to fix the errancy by adjoining a transcendent Whole: the excess *is* and it is immanent, and 'the subject, who forces the undecidable in the place of the indiscernible, is the faithful process of that errancy'.[70]

Thus, by means of the veridicality of its procedures, we can know that the being of the subject is possible, or, as Badiou says, that 'the existence of a subject is compatible with ontology'.[71] The upshot is that the subject is, on the one hand, unable to claim the false glory of proclaiming itself 'contradictory to the general regime of being'[72]; and, on the other, it can be affirmed to *exist* qua 'symptom' of being.[73] It might be said: the subject has to have been in order that what of the indiscernible is undecidable comes to be decided. Or that: 'the impasse of being [. . .] is in truth the pass of the subject'.[74]

None of this deduction would have been possible if Badiou had not taken it upon himself to think the multiple as such. And it is here that we reach the essence of his disagreement with Deleuze, for whom the multiple corresponds to the multiple without-one, which is a definition that is considerably more qualitative than mathematical, an assignation of the 'substance' or of the inherent nature of things[75] and not the matter of an 'abstract' dialectic. Deleuze's is a substantive definition that is self-contained (*qui enferme*), whence proceed all the contrasts that we have observed. The rapprochement with Deleuze helps us to see how rigorously Badiou examines multiplicity in its axiomatic, its ordination and its intricacies, how he chases down all the aporia in its concept, and how, since philosophy cannot simply take only what it wants of mathematics, he is able to render explicit the respect in which it constitutes a law for thought. He thereby affirms himself as the Platonist of our times.

As we approach the end of this 'foundational' trajectory, what is further striking is that the decision on being is not simply a portal, but a site of anchorage to which all the terms are tied, one after the other in a continuous chain. With Badiou, we never leave the discourse of being – that is, of the multiple *qua* the discourse of being – yet at the same time also come to define and secure the concepts of 'event', 'truth' and 'subject'.

A no less striking feature: from the moment that ontology is given only to thinking inconsistent multiplicities, and that the void turns out to be the name of being, the foundation reveals itself to be subtractive: subtractive with respect to what structures experience and knowledge by counting them for one. And it reveals that it is subtractive, if we may say so, a little more each time, to the extent that history and the un-decidable, truth and the in-discernible, the in-finite process to which the subject is attached, are so many acts of making holes in direction of the point of real wherein the mathematical axiom itself fails: it can only be attained, as Badiou says here, via 'the folly of subtraction'. There is no knowledge of being: of it there is only truth, and truth *is* 'in the trial of subtraction'.

II

Badiou's thought is insatiable, its *libido operandi* is unceasingly relaunched by the desire to explore further the supporting it has constructed and fixed. All delivered in the course of a single year, the essays you are about to read – papers and interventions in colloquiums – put to work the concepts that we have just retraced. They comprise as many examinations and advances in the field of what philosophy has to say about its connection to the four generic procedures comprising its *conditions*: as a philosophy under conditions. This can be recapitulated in five major points:

1. Badiou sets in place a transhistorical pairing of the philosopher and the sophist. We must bear in mind that he does so only to produce

the – hitherto schematic – *philosophical* status of *the* Truth, which he succeeds in strictly delimiting.

The sophist (today's being Wittgenstein) reduces thought to the effects of a discourse regulated by plural conventions: to an irreducible diversity of language games. On this basis the concept of truth can only be an illusion, because only language then regulates what, via each occurrence of its 'grammar', can be stated. The philosopher – whose mistrust towards 'language' Badiou clarifies here for the first time – takes cognisance of what, on the contrary, love, science, the poem and politics each produce in its own register of truths that are supernumerary to what is stated about them in the language of knowledge; and he then undertakes – this is his proper task – to construct in their interval the current moment of Truth.

But this at once entails impugning, as disastrous, every confusion of the *philosophical category* of Truth with a procedure that engenders truths; the philosophical category is uniquely 'operational', constructed on the 'seizing' of truths, of a 'pinch' of truths, all of which are, and remain, anterior and external to it. It is an *empty* category, then, for the reason that, of itself, it *presents nothing*. It corresponds purely to an argumentative assemblage and to the designation of a site for the compossibility of truths: it is neither knowledge nor a specific 'object'; it is neither a point of survey nor a foundation. Its statements, however, do contain an essential feature, a sole one: not producing the truth of the situation that they nevertheless welcome, and distribute among others, they are immediately *subtractive*, subtractive with regard to every presentation or experience, which is also to say, with regard to every presencing of meaning. '*Disaster*', then, to which philosophy is no stranger, lies in substituting plenitude for the void, in claiming to assert and to secure a meaning, and thus in proclaiming that philosophy is capable of uttering the place and name of Truth. Philosophy thereby also obscures what ought, rightly, be made its ethics: that 'there is no Truth of the Truth'.

Let it be noted that, contrary to a persistent prejudice, the rigour of the matheme here dispenses with dogmatism. And also that this dismissal is another name for a violent reduction of philosophy's powers, for a strict reduction of the status of its statements. With a single act, Badiou wants both to restore philosophy and to limit it to a sort of 'superior' fiction of thought. This is also why we must not – I state it because the error has been made – confound the void that forms the ground of *being*, and that Badiou refers to as the proper name of being, with the void of the philosophical category of Truth, which is a non-ontological or purely *logical* void.

It is here that the sophist proves a necessary partner for the philosopher, as one whom must be 'suffered': the sophist's function is to recall, beyond the local existence of truths – which the philosopher brings to bear against him – that the category of Truth is, as for it, void and ought to be kept so. The risk of not doing so – this is what theory itself demonstrates – is that it fuels and justifies terror.

2. Badiou posits that philosophy's history is punctuated by a series of accidents in which it becomes 'sutured' to a single one of its conditions, a condition that then tries to justify putting limits on truth in all of its instances.[76] So, as Badiou has it, in the nineteenth century precisely because philosophy was sutured to science and to politics, either in turn or simultaneously, what was instituted in the margins, from Hölderlin onwards, was an 'age of poets', whose significance lay in proclaiming the *deposition of the object* as the ultimate form of the presentation of being.

Badiou intervenes here with a double act. He reproaches Heidegger for his attachment to the exclusive aspects of this age and for suturing them to philosophy, which is henceforth destined to convoke presence in the 'flesh of language': presence, that means *being* as blind to the subtractive, blind to the un-binding rigour of argumentative technique. Philosophy must be wrenched from the prestige of poetical 'sacredness' and the temptations of interpretation; the latter promise only to return truth to what, precisely, it makes holes in (holes 'without edges'), namely, *meaning*. That said, the poem is a condition for philosophy; seized as a generic procedure, what the poem today states, and was the first to do so, is what presence is *in truth*: it is neither a collection of objects, nor the expression of a subject, nor the exhibition (but the disorientation) of language. The poem testifies to a crisis in Truth insofar as it deploys an impersonal and non-totalizing thought in which the multiple is attested to in its fundamental inconsistency. It unlinks knowledge via the supplementation of a mark – a letter – that 'upholds the murmur of the indiscernible'.

It is crucial here to grasp *at once* that the poem works with its own specific operations *and* that its enigma, often un-known, resides in what it produces by way of truth: thus, in 'Mallarmé's' method, Badiou shows that the figures he calls 'separation', which cuts a consistent multiple (or scene) out of the continuity of experience, and 'isolation', which withdraws all of experience's contours to render it to the field of pure inconsistency, also work to form the support of a new name of being: the without-relation (*sans-rapports*), un-binding (*de-liaison*).

3. Badiou defines himself as a 'Platonist of the multiple',[77] as one for whom thinking *mathematics* – which is not, or not initially, number, that fetish of objectivity[78] – alone constitutes ontology's possibility, just as it is only by founding the joint compatibility of truth and the subject on the theory of multiplicity that grounds their legitimacy. This is where strategic intention of Badiou's approach and the categorial instruments it brings to philosophical argumentation become clear.

The intention is to have done with the sequela of romanticism, whereby *time* is made into the very substance of thought: this includes everything from the 'temporalization of the concept' to the axiom that 'true-being can only be apprehended in its own temporality'. Badiou, who has constructed a genuinely philosophical concept of the event, certainly does not foreclose history, but it is a non-linear history, one punctuated with *aleas*, and woven of the resource that one event finds in another – perhaps very distant – one; but he is no historicist. And for two reasons. The first is that the thought of the multiple – whether discernible or indiscernible – is in itself radically a-temporal. Its site of thought is *eternity*, and as this eternity is immanent, it is also secularized. Therein lies the second reason: to maintain thought within the incompleteness of historicity means fixing the *finitude* of being-there as its condition. But, for Badiou, the word finitude is never innocent: it is inevitably bound up with a pathos that, *nolens volens*, makes room on the horizon for a divine Infinite. 'So long as finitude continues to be the ultimate determination of being-there, God remains'. And philosophy slips back into disaster.

Hence, the first operator that mathematics furnishes philosophy is one whereby it 'really accomplishes [. . .] the programme of the death of God': the concept of the *infinite* – of infinities – as reconstructed by set theory. This infinity is no longer a superlative, limit-one, but instead it is 'disseminated [. . .] among the aura-less typology of multiplicities'. It is no longer something that negates finitude by virtue of its status as exception, but on the contrary the ordinary and positive form of the multiple, from which the finite is deduced 'by negation or limitation', as 'lacunary abstraction'.[79] Let us translate: if the pathos of finitude was in the end the pathos of death, it must be said that we are infinite multiplicities in lacunary presentation, that death restores to their 'natural' being. Which, it is true, due to an essential dissymmetry, entails a halting point at which mathematics remits to philosophy its other operator: the foundational concept of the empty set – of the void that 'presents nothing'.

An explanation of his motives thus provided, Badiou goes on the front foot, with a striking spiralling movement. The construction of the matheme of Truth within the framework of the theory of the multiple was based, in *Being and Event*, on the articulation of three categories. Badiou re-reads them here from the angle of *subtraction*, because they each separately and all together 'draw underneath' of the totalizing finitude of knowledge, and because they make up the infinite hole of truth that pronounces the void of being. Their reformulation yields then: an *undecidable of a statement* that is neither veridical nor erroneous, that is subtracted from every norm that would claim to evaluate it; an *indiscernible of two terms* whose permutation does not change the value of the statement, as they are subtracted from every mark of difference; and a *generic of a part* that cannot be constructed, as no identifying trait between its terms proves possible: it is subtracted from predication, by excess. At this point, Badiou introduces an important novelty, a fourth category: the *unnameable*. If there is a formula that names a term fixing a place it alone can occupy, if, otherwise said, there exists a 'schema of the proper name', then the unnameable is that which is unique in not being 'named by any formula'. That is, 'that which is subtracted from the proper name and is unique in so being'. In question here is to produce, in the formulaic language of the matheme, a marker for the *singular qua* that is subtracted even from the singularization of the name; or, following the prerequisites of ontology *qua* 'the weakening of the One of language by the point-like ground (*point-fond*) of being'. The concept of the singular according to the tradition, that of Ockham, predicates every element of presentation one to one, locking structure in by means of an exhaustive application of the principle according to which 'there is only Oneness' (with the generality of the one-name, in Ockham; by virtue of the completeness of the language of God, in Leibniz). Badiou inverts the proposition: the singular leads to an undermining of the structure, it manifests the impotence of the 'principle of One as it is established through language'. It has the generic come up against that which renders impossible the exhaustion of its trajectory. It completes the trial of truth by specifying that it cannot possibly be completed: the singular, wherever it is localized, is always the same – and it is such that there can be but one: it is inconsistency, the groundlessness (*sans-fond*) of being.

PREFACE

It is remarkable that a theory of *evil* reappears here, by means of an inversion in the value of forcing: forcing was what had alone made it possible to secure veridicality in the generic, through establishing the veridicality of the connexions of its conditions to the names of knowledge. Here it comes to a limit at a point where no connection is any longer possible. Because truth is an event, at the risk stressed by the first three categories, a risk by which it 'says little', it is always tempted in the process of its production – against the open thrust of its trajectory – to say it all, to 'force nomination', even of the unnameable. Hence, evil turns out to be 'the denial of subtraction', a denial of the being of the proper, or of the proper of being. A refiguration of disaster, evil announces itself *within the field of truth*: its 'radical condition' lies in the very process of truth, and this obliges truth to engage in an ethics of restraint. In the matter of truth, it is important to never forget the maxim: 'Do not subtract the ultimate subtraction'.

4. The thread of these *Conditions*, as it emerges step-by-step, consists in this: upon the articulating and disentwining of truths and knowledge, articulate and disentwine philosophy and the truth–procedures. And maintain philosophy within its own space, that of a discipline with no proper object, precisely, which receives from its conditions only subtractive objects. This is never more obvious than in the placement of philosophy with regard to *politics*.

The reason for this is that here confusion has been total, such that today, under the blow of a common failure, philosophy and politics are more or less universally proclaimed conjointly dead.

Badiou's first move consists in restoring politics to its place: politics resides in the indiscernible of a situation where institutions and traditions state the sense in which holes are to be made. A production of a truth is always of *a* situation, but it occurs at the point at which the situation is given as indefinable, unpredictable, *unknown*. A truth is a procedure born 'in the offering of the event', and is pursued in an intervention effected by means of the aleatoric recollection of singular statements in the faithful trajectory of operative subjectivities. This is why a political truth can, with regard to the nomenclature of the situation, only be emancipatory; the name of the generic, infinite multiple here is the *'collective'*, which is brought about via the procedure 'in the form of its coming forth'. Politics presumes, relative to its field of exercise, the precariousness of inconsistency: as encounter of action and Idea, what

politics produces by way of a truth of the collective, a collective immanent to politics, is a calculated wager on the de-linked, the subtractive.

It remains 'to think politics'[80]: this is where philosophy comes in. Not
in order to bind itself in to *one*, no matter which, of its conditions, of the
truths of the collective: that would result in disaster, and would also, if
this truth is saddled contrary to itself with the norms of necessity, result
in an onset of terror, the essence of which consists in 'uttering the ought-
not-to-be of what is'. Nor does philosophy, *qua* custodian of Truth,
authorize any foreclosure of the intervention as *impossible*, on admission
of some 'incontrovertible reality' or 'consensus' – which means only the
consistency – of the situation. What we have here instead is a new figure
of sophistry, which, to say it at once, it is possible to counter with truths
(which is also to say: with politics). Philosophy, for its part, must *name*
the Idea: that is, that which 'will have been' the being of a political process, and whose eternity its subject will have supported. Moreover, this
eternity itself never receives any expression outside of history: in the
sequence of the history whose truth we have to produce, what prescribes
a fidelity to the event – the political event but also the event of 'seizing'
in the crises of truths – goes by the name of *equality*, because it is maintained in the field of the multiple, of its infinity, and excludes all satura-
tion of meaning: in a nutshell, it places itself on a par with the generic.
'Only a politics which can be named as egalitarian in political philosophy
authorizes turning toward the eternal contemporary time in which that
politics proceeds.'

The gesture of disentangling the generic from knowledge – or
interpretation – and the excess of the political from the state – or
State – of the situation shows itself to be pertinent since it enables
Badiou to establish the contours of the problematic of *Right* (*Droit*): of the
State of Right and Human Rights. For Badiou, Right is a category of the
State, in both senses of the word. It is therefore a category of the structure,
that is, of the collective set, inasmuch as the state's 'rule of counting does
not elevate any particular part to the paradigm of part-being in general'.
The state gives privilege to no part; but nor does it privilege any individual, since it is unable to take into account an individual's concrete infinity,
which, by counting it as One, it apprehends as an element of a part. And
it is not to impugn Right that cognisance is taken of the fact that, as a rule,
Right or Law functions *on this side* of political truth: instead, it would be
an 'abolition of all truth in politics' to limit the latter to the rule of Law.

The act, as for it, of articulation–disentanglement by which philosophical 'seizing' is instituted – Badiou writes this with reference to Althusser – as 'an instance of immanent naming of the avatars of politics', will provide a further occasion to specify precisely in what the restrained operation of philosophy consists. In grasping truths external to it – Badiou always returns to its amphibology: philosophy does not seize them without being seized by them – 'philosophy's specificity is that the field of its intervention is the same one that conditions it'. This is what Badiou refers to as *its torsion*. Philosophical intervention declares the being of truths, that is, what they attest to of being through *naming*. Naming as such constitutes the second moment of the operation, at once daring and decisive, and it is never more so, it seems, than in the field of politics. In this way the purely philosophical category of Truth can be at once objectless and effective: it is in it that is thought, and that is pronounced, what truths there are. In this way, too, philosophy can, by making proclamations within its own discourse – in *immanence* – about the truths that are produced outside of it, announce the Truth of a time.

5. That *love* is a generic procedure, a producer of truths, and as such a condition for philosophy, is a proposition that may come as a surprise, even though on this point Badiou is in agreement with Plato. That love (and not desire) is the point at which philosophy encounters psychoanalysis is cause for further astonishment. The reason for which this forms a decisive issue in Badiou's strategy is something he makes explicit here for the first time: it is the site of his argument with Lacan.

Let us thus set out from the last pages of *Being and Event*, where Badiou embraces those things that lead him to concur with Lacan, while regretting that, by the constitutive place the latter accords to language, he 'continued' to think within the 'statist' space of the structure. What is the cause for agreement? It is that there is a subject, one moreover that can be written in the matheme; and that there are truths, truths that exist in making holes in knowledge. What is the cause for disagreement? For Lacan, if truth is to remain intact at the point at which it is stated, that is, in a signifying chain, then the subject, a 'point zero', must be eclipsed, lapsing each time in the interval between one signifier and the next; whereas, for Badiou, truth 'exists only insofar as it is indifferent' to language, that is, to the encyclopaedia, and the subject, as occurrence of the event, supports the indiscernible of truth of a finite approximation by means of a naming, which is supplementary, and by an uncertain and faithful trajectory. We can see here that the essential point of disagreement between Badiou and Lacan concerns *the place of the void*: does it reside in the subject or in being? According to Lacan, only an empty subject can be sutured to the discourse of science; whereas, according to Badiou, the void is rather what sutures the subject to being. In other words: Lacan has being come to presence, in speech; whereas Badiou grants the – rare – subject a 'little' being, but being can only be thought as subtractive.[81]

By situating the debate thus Badiou derives strategic advantages and theoretical advances.

Strategic advantages: he can show that the Lacanian formulas of sexuation do not go beyond the mode of the century, that of 'a meditation on finitude'. Since what is castration, if not that enjoyment is universally, for every speaking subject, 'cut out' (*'en découpe'*), and that, by the same token, the speaking being does not have the set of signifiers at its disposal? But it also happens to be the case that a feminine-position exists, and that this 'woman' is 'not-whole', that is, that enjoyment is not always and everywhere in the form of phallic enjoyment. Lacan also declared that this interruption in the reign of castration is of the order of the *infinite*. Woman is most definitely barred 'somewhere' by the function of castration, but there nonetheless remains 'a type of enjoyment that is properly the infinite elsewhere of this somewhere'.[82] It is an elsewhere that, from the vantage point of the masculine position, remains inaccessible.

Only – by an incomplete recourse to the theory of multiplicity – Lacan hits a snag in his recourse to the infinite, which he, says Badiou, 'invoked only to revoke', recognizing in it only the mark of something that is inaccessible to operations within finitude: which is why he only qualified it negatively, as unconstructible. Only – because the structure of desire gets elaborated within the *pass* of a failing – what Lacan retains of the inaccessible is not the going-beyond, but the 'fissure' that it opens up within the lawful course of an operation: hence, the infinite is returned to the recurring place in which the void–subject falls between two signifiers.

So, we can see what Badiou stands to gain from the discussion. He places the 'pre-Cantorian' Lacan in a head-to-head with the set theory axiom of the infinite because the latter sustains a judgement of existence, and also because in it the inaccessible exists via a decision: mathematics allows – at a minimum – for an infinite that is not a restriction.

At the same time, Badiou lays down the beginnings of a doctrine of feminine sexuality using his own categories: if there is something infinite about feminine enjoyment, is it not because it has the structure of an axiom? He construes the position of woman as that which has 'to decide the inaccessible as regards its existence', that is, to decide on a supplement beyond the reach of the phallic function. Further: if feminine enjoyment finds support solely in the fissure, is it not, even in Lacan's own terms, that of the pure subject, in its eclipse? It can then be said that, in subtraction from the phallic function, there exists a 'generic function' that is supported by the woman-position. Last, Badiou here has managed to circumvent, in the thinker to whom he sticks most closely, the persistence of the theme of finitude that he deems ruinous for whoever summons thought within a secularized eternity. Without denying that castration, *qua* trait of the real, makes holes in the speaking being, or prohibits totality – but the Cantorian matheme does not admit the idea of the Whole in any case. He has reintroduced genericity into the formulas of sexuation, with the declared aim of freeing them of all pathos.

It might be said that in this pointed discussion philosophy has verified its consistency through an effort to remain 'compatible with the concept of psychoanalysis'. All Badiou has now to show is why the amorous procedure is a condition for philosophy, that is, which *truths* it alone carries. These truths, it turns out, are not only compossible but profoundly homogenous with those we have already encountered: love forms a new figure of the *Two* and of *disjunction*.

Of the 'Two', because if the truths of love are suffocated under the veil of the imagination by some myth, this then results in the fusional conception, that of an 'ecstatic One' that, once more, would spell disaster, as an effect of suppressing the multiple. Love – *qua* sexuated situation – presents two positions; or: 'It is the Two [which] proceeds in the situation'. Let it be clear that this is not an observation, but what transpires in a process that patiently supplements the situation: 'It is love, and love alone, which allows us to state [. . .] retroactively' the existence of two positions.

And these positions are disjoint since they govern the entire experience, without either one position ever being able to possess knowledge of what the other is. Badiou contends that: '*Nothing* of the experience is the same for the masculine position and for the feminine position'. The disjunction is verified only by the event of the encounter, by its naming (the 'declaration' of love that is drawn from the void itself in which the disjunctive is announced), by the uncertain investigation undertaken 'on the supposition that there is Two', and by the 'interminable fidelity to the premier naming' – love can be said to contain all the traits of a generic procedure. But if humanity, obviously, only supports generic procedures, if it is the 'historical body of truths', what status are we to give, then, to two procedures that are so irreducibly disjunct that it seems humanity is itself disjoined in them? The response is that here the generic is precisely the disjunction.

We were able to gauge through this analysis how Badiou makes philosophy circulate between the proper of a procedure and the thinking of what it produces as truth. On the one hand, the ontology of the multiple does not advance unarmed and brings about the extraction of the 'numerical schema' of each procedure, and with it the subtractive, which here redoubles the Lacanian thesis of the lack of sexual relationship. On the other hand, thought entirely takes account of the concrete aspect of the event: in it sexual traits figure as the mark of the Two, of that which announces the fracture of the One. However, this is only so 'on the condition of the declaration of love', outside of which the disjunction remains unattested. Moreover, each of these positions can know something by way of truth – in the sense of an existing anticipation of the veridicity of an always incomplete generic statement: for the masculine position, this is the effraction of the One by the split of the two; and, for the feminine position, that there is nothing, nothing that is human, outside the Two.

It is worth noting that the philosophical 'torsion' here includes once more – in negative outline – a definition of evil. But it would be caricatural to reduce to it the supplementation of sexuality by love as a truth procedure. We are instead to understand that, in the field of sexuality, only love can be the place of a decision on the indiscernible and provide the generic with a space or the trajectory of a work. What the philosopher asserts here is the synonymy of the generic and the rareness of the human.

III

Badiou agreed to it in the course of a debate: philosophy is the reign of *Polemos*. How could it be otherwise inasmuch as it is conditioned by the history of truths – in respect of which it is historical – and as its operation of torsion has no other guarantee than the double rigour with which, on the one hand, it extracts truths from time, and, on the other hand, it argues the formalization and the compossibility of these extractions? I do not intend to make any objections against Badiou from a position other than his own, that is to say, to reduce philosophy to conversation; instead, I want to ask if Badiou's position satisfies all of its own requisites, that is, first, whether there are not in its exposition some blind spots whose occurrence is not incidental, and then, and above all, to ask whether it really 'seizes' all the truths of its time. There are some questions that Badiou has to be asked from the inside of what should well be called his system, that is, from the vantage point of its axiomatic. The uninterrupted debate that we have engaged in for many years means my approach here will not come as a total surprise.

A first question concerns the status of mathematics. Trivially – and this is not what I intend to do – it could be asked whether or not, by means of mathematics, Badiou does not 'suture' philosophy to science. It seems to me a distinction ought to be made between, on the one hand sciences, that is, the natural sciences (in which, incidentally, Badiou has – contrary to Deleuze – hardly shown any interest, and ought one day address the question of what philosophy has to 'seize' in them); and, on the other, mathematics, which remains a distinct *precondition* for ontology, at once establishing the norm of the matheme and the deployment of the multiple as the ground of every 'there is'. But it is perhaps further necessary to trace a division within mathematics itself; I once asked Badiou about the status of the axioms of the void and the infinite – the axioms of the subtractive – as regards truth. His response to this was to say that they are *'conditions'* for truth: this would imply, then, that a distinction be made between the fundaments of the theory of multiplicity – conditions as much for mathematics as for ontology – and what mathematics can, on this basis, produce by way of truths. We then back up a notch, and enter a space of decision whose status has yet to be resolved, since it already belongs as much to a philosophical operation – be it unknown – as to a choice internal to mathematics. This amounts to more than a mere remark, because the beautiful order that had so rigorously tiered truth procedures and philosophy is lost. One would not be on the lookout for an ontology in mathematics if mathematics had not always already come across a philosophy.[83]

At the other extremity of the system, it is not at all clear that philosophy has no proper 'object'. What Badiou writes of his debt to Althusser – that in philosophy 'nothing happens', that it 'designates no real' and operates in 'the void of an act', and that only 'practices' produce events – does not allay our doubts, since Althusser's twofold strategy to counter idealism and historical materialism is not the only operative one here. The force with which Badiou points out the ignorance of mathematicians with respect to everything they do, from the ontological reach of the theory of multiplicity to Cohen's 'unwitting' founding of decision in the field of the indiscernible (i.e., ignorance for the philosopher, and the point remains valid if, as I have said, they work implicitly within philosophy), as well as his admirable theory of love as a Two in disjunction, shows well that, at the very least, the philosopher does more than seize and 'twist'. When Badiou says that philosophy 'proposes a unified conceptual space in which the naming of events occurs', and 'outlines a general space in which thought accedes to time', how does the operation come to say what would have been unsaid without it? From the pure multiple to being, from truths to the Truth, what occurs, what is carried out under the name, never further explained, of 'circulating thought'?[84] We can grant Badiou that philosophy has no 'object', since none of the truth procedures do; but it is somewhat paradoxical to write that philosophy is an 'unactual veracity under the condition of the actuality of the true',[85] when it has been strictly shown that no truth is actual because it is dependent on an infinite procedure. The sole question would thus seem to be: presuming that some truth is produced in the locus of philosophy, is this truth open to being forced, capable of veridicality? I readily accept that philosophy does not seize any truth that it does not receive from its conditions; I would not be so certain that its operation would not *produce* any once the modalities of torsion have been described It seems to me that what that would bring to light is that the philosophical operation is itself an *event*: if not, then what is the encounter with the site that was for Badiou the 'continuous' in which knowledge founders? And what is the intervention by which Badiou decides to seek out what in the mathematics of the indiscernible is pronounced of the site? And what is naming, of the sort by which Badiou subtracts the concept of the subtractive from the Cantorian theory of multiplicity? What, moreover, is *Being and Event* if not a faithful investigation into whether the axioms of the subtractive are sufficient to found the discourse of being, truth and the subject? In addition, the disaster with which philosophy is threatened at each moment would be a trifling matter if it did not seal with a *supplement* the truths of the time. That this supplement necessitates, conversely, a theory of evil, is this not what 'forces' it and attests to its veridicality? The modesty of the philosopher, in his floating position, cannot be such that he would not have to 'indiscern' at least *one* truth – namely, that every truth makes a hole in knowledge – in the anticipation of making it a support for the being of *the* Truth.

That, on the one hand, philosophy is already operative within the truth procedures that condition it, and that, on the other, it is itself a truth procedure is not something I say 'in defence' of Badiou – for little matter – but so that it be clearly recognized that what operates in philosophy is the *subject–language*. And how could it be so, if, by its language, the referent was not 'suspended from the infinite becoming of a truth'?[86] Moreover, by the same gesture with which he lays claim to be a descendant of Descartes, can Badiou deny, even if today it means displacing its site and reformulating its concept, that it is the province of philosophy *alone* to proclaim the subject? And how could it do so unless it was supported by its operation? Would it not hence be necessary to write that the subject of the political or amorous procedure, such as Badiou has analysed their procedures, is already the subject of philosophy, and can only be?

A blind spot or unexplained point: it is impossible, on each reading, not to be struck by the elementary nature of the description of evental *investigation*, which is reduced to the registering of negative or positive encounters that confirm or refute the anticipated outcome of the intervention. Here we come across a schematism that contrasts oddly with the complexity of the procedure's construction as a whole. An investigation would surely show itself to be especially complex and eventful, if only thanks to the constant recurrence of new encounters, of new namings, of incessant detours, of supplementary decisions – an event is woven of events, and through the chance of what they are; Badiou is – provisionally – right to say that the progression of a psychoanalysis would furnish a good example of it. This point would certainly remain marginal if it did not lead to another: for what is left in impasse by the formalism Badiou proposes is the intervention of the subject, of 'a' subject, of each singular subject, insofar as its own, limiting constitution – I did not say its empirical aspect – determines the investigation it conducts, and in this sense affects it with contingency, meaning by this the effects of recurrence, and not of 'pure' *aleas*. In a nutshell, the investigation would be simple if it led only to findings; but it continually finds more. This is a simple marker, for a point to which I shall return.

Regarding the seizing of the truths of our times, there is, in the refusal to take into account the constitutive dimension of *language* for thought – and, therefore, for the subject as for truth, a preconceived bias that seems untenable. The reasons for it are fairly clear: on the one hand, the plurality and disparity of language games is what fuels the scepticism of Wittgenstein and the analytic philosopher; on the other, since language is a structure, it indeed establishes itself as the formal type of the 'state' of the situation, a blocked state in which everything is discerned, in which the void is un-presented, the ultimate figure of the count: a meta-count, a consolidation of the One. This can be granted, but truth does itself pass via a supernumerary naming, and the unnameable itself gives a name to what alone has none. One is able to carry oneself to the limits of the structure, and 'force' it; force it, for example, to express the void: it is impossible, then, to deny that languages utterly organizes, and in advance, the space of thought, without there lacking any sites open to being supplemented. Indeed, what in particular does the poetic act consist in, if not such forcing? Within the system itself there is no reason to distinguish, as to their ontological status, between 'the language of the situation' and knowledge; and, if it is in the consistency of knowledge that – by means of a process whose importance we have noted – truth's possibility and being is certified, it follows that the consistency of language is also what provides the guarantee for the hazardous uttering of a truth that subtracts the latter from its order.

It is true that the consistency of language is also equally that of *sense*. As it is that one of Badiou's initial decisions was to wrench the trinomial of being–subject–truth from the games of interpretation: it is imperative to make a decision between the latter and the matheme, or between conversation and science. That is exactly what formulaic language, with its 'little letters' and its symbols, is: an exception to sense. Pure donation is prior to sense, being-qua-being is the void of sense, and the subject and the truth only make sense by means of a procedure that they support or whose result they announce; and these latter *are* only in the theory of the multiple and by virtue of the place it gives them as one of its moments. It is in this . . . sense that at the start of *Being and Event* Badiou could write: 'The thesis that I support [. . .] is not a thesis about the world but about discourse. It affirms that mathematics [. . .] pronounces what is expressible of being *qua* being'.[87] I shall be careful not to object to this, except to say that we have escaped from meaning and interpretation only to return to it, and that were this point forgotten the lengthy detour through the matheme would lapse into 'angelism'; apropos, as Badiou says convincingly, the debate on the sex of angels is crucial, because it pronounces the disjunction – and what he says about this demonstrates well that it is not devoid of effects of sense. Is the dazzling essay on the fictional apparatus of the generic in Beckett an interpretation? Yes, when an argument is made of the 'black–grey' or of the four categories of 'searchers'; no, or otherwise than expected, when these latter are read respectively as the 'localization of being' and as 'maxims of the subject'. It goes without saying that we cannot fail to pass through sense; the singular force of Badiou resides in the way that he 'sublates' it by the matheme, 'forcing' it always to say being (*au dire de l'être*). Badiou's is less a condemnation than the initiation of a new doctrine of interpretation 'in torsion'. Indeed, it is one that might furnish the criterion to distinguish between a psychoanalytical procedure and a 'philosophical' operation: for clearly in psychoanalysis the matheme is what secures the passage from one situation of sense to another, even if it were only one in which 'ab-sense' is pronounced; whereas philosophy's appointed end, then, would be the isolated affirmation of the matheme as such.

We are not yet done with language, we are not yet even at the point at which it comprises the place of a crucial discussion on the void, because we have not yet examined the site of the *subtractive*, according to its utterance. Badiou is averse to using the term 'signifier' and only comes to do so when sorting out his position on Lacan, despite enthusing over the fact that, due to the bar that separates signifier from signified, 'thought is only authorized by the void that separates it from realities'. His resistance bears on the concept of the 'signifying chain' in that it includes, between one signifier and the next, a void interval into which the subject falls. Moreover, using a second of Lacan's formulations, one much more like to his own, he argues: 'There is a hole there, and this hole is called the Other [. . .] *qua* locus in which speech, being deposited, [. . .] founds truth'.[88] According to Badiou, this statement contains two different conceptualizations – and two epochs – that he designates as 'the linear doctrine of the signifier' and the 'doctrine of the Other in holes', the first being algebraic, the second topic. In question here is what occurs in the place of the void in discourse: the subject or truth? Badiou means to show that in Lacan's own work the solution results in two different constructions of discourse and two different determinations of the void. If the subject is eclipsed 'in the gap between signifiers in which the metonymy of its being proceeds', discourse, which comes to comprise a metaphor of this being, is not, or not in the last instance, a pure *aléa* of the multiple: what this means is that what knots the subject to its being is that its being, in having to state itself in this way, is not, strictly speaking, undecidable; that what the trajectory of discourse makes emerge as chasm is not the nothing without limits but a singular lack, which is discerned by its limits: a differentiated loss in which the subject finds its marker, and on this side of which it is indeed strictly void. If, on the contrary, the Other makes a hole in 'everyday language' – like truth does in knowledge – what is thereby averred is the existence in discourse of a site at the edge of the void, of the void such as it is conceived 'intrinsically', which is to say, without any limits that singularize it, a perfectly subtractive void, exactly the same as that deemed to be generic, and whose process the subject comes to support. Badiou believes he discerns in Lacan's work a wavering between two concepts of the void, one embedded in the signifying structure, another that is excluded from it by means of de-liaison, and that this wavering is symmetrical to that concerning the infinite. So, Badiou contends: 'The "intercalary" category does not hold up, and Lacan knew it'. Lacan is, then, to have quibbled with himself because he knew that in the field of truth 'there is only one void', and that it is the set of the same name.

First, it ought to be remarked that, if in Lacan's work there is a twofold statement about the void, which I shall refer to as the *bounded* void and the *unbounded* void, then the second is not proven by an abandonment of the first – which would be entirely unthinkable: we are left with an open question, one that disallows Badiou from advancing that 'the only ontology compatible with Lacan's is [his]'. As it happens, there would a compatibility, albeit limited, had Lacan spoken of the void: but he spoke of the 'hole' where the place of the Other appears, and not once did he say about this Other – which does not belong to the register of 'existence' – that it expresses the void that yields the name of being[89]; instead, the Other fills in for everything that, in discourse, creates dehiscence, as is born out by the phrase given earlier from *Encore* that Badiou interrupts:

'truth, and with it the pact which makes up for the non-existence of the sexual relationship'. Wherever there is a hole, the Other fills it in, and the truth as a saying of the Other is a saying that takes a different signifying chain, one that supplements the first at the point of its lack. Parentheses, chasms, split, cleavage, loss, not-all: Lacan tracks down everything that attests to a cut *in* the experience of *parlêtre*. However, he does not do so with the aim of tying it to a foundational void, but instead to record ruptures *in the text* and, without closing them up, to read another letter in them, another statement (*énoncé*). And, in its turn, this statement (*enunciation*) also comes up against the impossible; but the Real, to say it again, is not the void: that is rather – these are the markers Jean-Claude Milner suggests – indistinct, dispersed, chaotic. Instead, the void is too full, full of signifiers in the wheels of the *automaton*. In Badiou's categories, Lacan is Democritean, and the effort to pass from what one could strictly designate as the at-the-edge of *a* void of truth to the truth *of the* void fails.

The point of all this, of course, is not to question the pertinence of the category of the void as Badiou uses it, but rather to say that it is not closely connected to psychoanalysis, which proceeds under the constraints of a 'bounded' void, a void enveloping a multiplicity that is not nondescript. This is not a merely local restriction, since what it bears on is the determination of the subject.

At this point, the decision to 'avoid' the constitutive function of language is complemented by another, no less problematic one: the attempt to avoid all predicative definitions of the *subject* yields, in order to attest to it, only its 'point of application', that of the 'errancy of the excess'; only 'its trace at the jointure of forcing'. The subject *is*, because it 'alone has a power of indiscernment'. Further, what comes to be announced here is the being of the Subject, not of 'a' subject.[90] Of the subject, and of its 'power', there is nothing to say, no specific form that ontology would specify, and that would destine it to decide on the indiscernible. There is here, in this refusal to say, a legitimate mistrust as regards everything that might call forth an ego-substance, a refusal of the pathos of finitude, and once more an avoidance of every retreat into structure. It is a deceptive gesture, whose rigour is unmistakable, and whose example ought to be followed in avoiding every referent of knowledge.

But it is a gesture that, it must be said, reaches an impasse on the question of what has been produced – by Freud and further still Lacan, and as we shall see this question is pressing enough for Badiou to attempt to overcome the impasse by maintaining his categories under the very condition of Lacan's – as *truth*: that is, the recurrent and *constituted opacity* of a site relative to the subject itself. Site, because an opaque part there pulls 'underneath' every utterance (*énoncé*). Part, because it is not possible to foreclose – or suture – the subject–support from the utterance in which it is included. It is an opaque but constituted part, because it is 'scanded'[91] by places that limit its 'indiscerned' aspect. We succeed in avoiding talk about 'structure', then, since what is in question is only a subtractive *constitution*, whose places do not define predicates; but there ought be no compromise on putting the generic under the *constraint* of a form, of the impassable place of the subject. Let us, because it cannot be avoided, turn again to linear algebrism: this place can be written using a four-lettered matheme – S1, S2, *a*, $ – but this does *not* make it mathematical. Truth here is in a position of *cause*, the signifiers of lack that express the subject's cipher are *already there*, and the subject occurs here solely as lacking an *object* (*décomplété d'un objet*). In other terms, psychoanalysis does not serve itself of an empty part by which to gather together the disjoint elements of the situation, but of a topic constitution that it strives to bring to light. If there is a signifying chain, this is because the metonymy of desire insists in it; if there is desire, this is because the object is in a position of exteriority internal to the subject; if there is a subject, then it is under the mark of the signifiers with which it comes to be identified. And this constitution of the subject, which implies that it has no *being* unless 'split', cannot be simply assumed to belong to the specific procedures of the clinic. It crops up under every procedure. As Lacan said, the 'great Necessity is no other than that which is exercised *in* the Logos', 'the division of the subject [is] the fate of scientific man'[92]; this is also why the truth is only 'half-said'.

In several of the texts gathered here, Badiou displaces the terrain of the discussion, takes the '*castrated structure*' of the subject as given, but undertakes to demonstrate that under this same condition all the evental traits of truth are there in the course of psychoanalytic work: it turns out to be immanent (which does not in fact create a problem), generic, infinite and it encounters the unnameable. It 'originates in a disappearing'; it testifies to an included part in the analytic situation, a part so 'nondescript' that 'its components could never be totalised by any predicate'; it can only be infinite – incompletable – in the anticipation of its veridicality; and it comes up against an impossible, 'unforceable' point, the Real of enjoyment. Now, this demonstration is relevant only *in the limits of the subject's constitution*, where not only is the chasm not indeterminate but is regulated by an immutable structure (*articulation*); but also where the infinite of the work consists in an investigation into a determinate disappearing that is written in the signifier; and where the unnameable is not without the markers that it receives from an object. There is no truth of the subject apart from that *constrained* by its constitution, which 'forces' the truth. The subject that finds its support in a truth is not transparent to it, and nothing will come into the true except on condition of its being, which, in being split, is no less constituted.

Badiou takes note that castration further signifies *finitude* for every *parlêtre* – that is, that language is not whole for the subject (even if he contests that there is anything more at issue here than a bar across the All, and not across the infinite, which remains implicitly open to the multiple); he admits, in the same movement, that, by the determination it imposes on the subject, the object *a* marks the latter with finitude. In the subject split by the *Logos*, at least one signifier is missing from its place in the Symbolic, and one partial, lost object, in the Real. But how can this *definite* subtraction, fitted out with edges and places, be articulated with an ontology of the multiple? I do not see how his concept of the subject could as such be maintained within it; it is a concept that, of course, is already a finite instance of an infinite truth, but in the support of that sole truth, so that, to the contrary, by means of what writes its finitude, its fidelity will necessarily also be a *constrained* fidelity, insofar as its condition determines it. It cannot easily be seen how the subject of the generic, in integrating the object (*a*), would not stumble as one stumbles when on passes from love to desire: the field in which truth induces an exploration of the situation as a *situation of the subject* is articulated around a recurrent vacuole that is specific for each procedure of discourse. It may well be advanced that the philosopher's desire is a desire for truth; it remains that this desire does not inhabit the anonymous field of what is thought as its object. The objection crops up again when Badiou identifies the enjoyment and the obstacle of truth; is what is touched on here the void of being or of the object? It may well be granted that it is being in the form of the object; but one cannot create an exception to the form, nor easily merge loss with an encounter with the void. When Kant and de Sade encounter the site in which they produce equality as truth, shall we say that it is due to the hazards of the investigation that the former names it law, the latter enjoyment and that Marx names it work? The subject of what will have been 'its' truth is on the cross of what is specific to the lack in its discourse. And the generic consists only within the limits fixed for it by the subject's constitution.

Last, Badiou is right to remind us that Lacan claimed to be an antiphilosopher – if the philosopher is one who posits that being and thinking are the same; but from the vantage point of the subject, such as it is determined in its constitution, Lacan could only ever be, and for the same reasons, an anti-mathematician. The matheme of the subject *resists* any simple inscription in the field of the multiple. Badiou is further right to recall Lacan's insistence on truth's impotence. But this powerlessness is only ontological because it is *localized*: 'The love of truth, [. . .] is the love of this: that the truth conceals, and this is called castration'.[93] Moreover this localization has a *reverse-side*: 'There is only truth of what desire conceals, of its lack'[94]; the place of truth is that of enjoyment – of the Other.[95] It is no accident if Lacan himself came up against this the day that he tried to master what he had produced in the disjunction of the three instances – to borrow from the best deduction of it, Jean-Claude Milner's: there is Oneness (that discerns), there is Sameness (the similar and the dissimilar) and there is (chaos) – in figuring it through the knot of three circles that cannot be superposed, not one of which can ever be accessed from the vantage point of either of the two others, but which all intersect, or 'get jammed' (*se coincent*), and, finally, which all overlap only at the locus of the object (*a*). Topology makes it possible to formalize this knot and the effects of its undoing; but formalization, once more, comes up against an irreducible, structural manifold, a hiatus on the very plane of the 'there is'. By this means, the passage from the matheme to the knot – as a return of the three instances – attests to nothing other than the first's getting stuck (*coinçage*), to the extent that – I adopt once more Jean-Claude Milner's expression – not being able to say, there is no other solution than to show: to show, it should be added, where it enjoys (*où ça jouit*). Let me not be read as saying that this is a sign of failure: the exemplary price of Lacan's last seminars is that in them we see him in a desperate struggle against the deadlock of finding an adequate matheme for the one-disjunction of the subject.[96]

From start to end, the discussion will have revolved around the evanescent – or itself 'evasive' – definition Badiou gives the subject. It is a concept of which we must at once maintain that – like those of being and the truth – it is everywhere it is proven to operate, a signature of philosophy, and that, in having a constitution, in being set in motion by the metonymy of a lack, it works to restrict – to restrict what it thereby conditions – the open field of the generic. Perhaps what the discussion will have ushered in is this concept of constraint. It indeed seems here that Badiou remains in thrall of the very thing he is struggling against in the philosophical tradition. To open the subject to the subtractive, to seize it in the deduction of the One (*au dé-compte de l'Un*), it is, in a nutshell, necessary to decide it from the vantage point of the indiscernible: from the indiscernible in general, from any indiscernible whatsoever. However – as Badiou repeatedly emphasizes – there is only ever truth of 'a' situation, each time; and there is no – as he says, rare – occurrence of the subject outside of what then re-emerges as a situation of the subject; the subtractive truth of which can be pronounced, if one endures the encounter with it. Which is, as he likes to remind us, a matter of courage.

Acknowledgements

A number of the following essays have already been translated by others and published elsewhere. These translations have all been immensely valuable.

Norman Madarasz, as the translator of the English version of *Manifesto for Philosophy*, translated 'The (re)turn of philosophy *itself*' and 'Definition of philosophy'. The latter was also published in Oliver Feltham's and Justin Clemens' *Infinite Thought*, together with 'The Philosophical Recourse to the Poem'.

Alberto Toscano and Ray Brassier, to whose translations I remain very close, translated 'Philosophy and Mathematics', 'On Subtraction' and 'Truth: forcing and unnameable', all of which are to be found in *Theoretical Writings*.

Lastly, 'What is Love?' was published in Umbr(a) no. 1 1996 by Justin Clemens and 'What is a Philosophical Institution?' by A. J. Barlett in *Cosmos and History* vol. 1, 2006.

I would also like to thank Alain Badiou himself for agreeing to the project, and the editorial staff at Continuum for their helpfulness and patience. Finally many thanks are due to Brian Corcoran and Lia Tajcnar for their abiding support and enthusiasm.

PART I
Philosophy Itself

CHAPTER ONE
The (Re)Turn of Philosophy *Itself*

I shall call my inaugural statement 'thesis 1', in homage to the affirmative style of my masters and especially of Louis Althusser. The form it takes is nevertheless negative in its evaluation.

THESIS 1. PHILOSOPHY TODAY IS PARALYSED BY ITS RELATION TO ITS OWN HISTORY

This paralysis results from the fact that, after submitting the history of philosophy to philosophical examination, almost all our contemporaries agree to say that this history has entered the – perhaps interminable – era of its closure. Philosophy is thus affected by malaise and what I shall term a delocalization: it no longer knows if it has a proper place. As a result, it either strives to graft itself onto established activities – art, poetry, science, political action, psychoanalysis and so on – or *merely* passes over into its own history, becoming a museum of itself. This going back and forth between historiography and delocalization is what I mean by philosophy's 'paralysis'. This paralysis, to be sure, is closely linked to philosophy's ongoing and pessimistic relation to its glorious metaphysical past. The prevailing idea is that metaphysics is historically depleted, but that what lies beyond this depletion is as yet unavailable to us. That is how I understand the statement of Heidegger's, in his testimonial interview, that states *'Only a God can save us'*.[1] Heidegger was certainly not waiting for a new religion. He meant that the salvation of thought will not come by continuing on with previous philosophical efforts. *Something* must, of necessity, *happen*, and the word 'God' designates this unheard-of, incalculable event, an event that is henceforth the only thing that can render thought to its original destination. Philosophy then gets caught between the depletion of its historical possibility and the coming without concept of a salvational turnabout (*retournement salvateur*). Contemporary philosophy combines a deconstruction of its past with an empty wait for its future.

My basic intention is to break with this diagnostic. The difficulty in doing so lies in avoiding the neoclassical style, the conventionalist (*pompier*) style of those who hope to fill in the chasm with meagre reflections on ethics.

We must grasp things at the root, and this root is the reflexive – almost parasitic – knot between philosophy and historiography. My thesis thus takes a second form, a form of rupture, which I shall call thesis 2.

THESIS 2. PHILOSOPHY MUST BREAK, FROM WITHIN ITSELF, WITH HISTORICISM

Break with historicism – what is the meaning of this injunction? It means that philosophical presentation must initially determine itself in the absence of any reference to its history. Philosophy has to have the audacity to present its concepts without first arraigning them before the tribunal of their historical moment.

In essence, Hegel's famous formula still weighs on us: 'World history is a court of judgement.' The history of philosophy is today more than ever its own court, and the verdict handed down by this court is almost always one of capital punishment: a verdict of the closure or of the necessary deconstruction of the metaphysical past and present. On this point we can say that Nietzsche's genealogical method, just like Heidegger's hermeneutical method, were no more than variants of the Hegelian apparatus. For Nietzsche, as for Heidegger, all thought that claims to be philosophical must first of all be *evaluated* in a historical assemblage (*montage*); the mainspring of this historical assemblage is to be found with the Greeks; and the game is played, the consignment is sent, in what happens *between* the Presocratics and Plato. With this occurrence the initial destination of thought was lost and trumped, and this loss has governed our destiny.

I propose to wrest philosophy from this genealogical imperative. Heidegger thought that we were historically governed by the forgetting of being, and even by the forgetting of that forgetting. For my part, I shall propose a violent *forgetting of the history of philosophy*, thus a violent forgetting of every historical assemblage of the forgetting of being. A 'forget the forgetting of the forgetting'. This imperative to forget is a matter of method and of course not at all of ignorance of this history. Forget history: this means, above all, making *decisions of thought* without turning back towards a presupposed historical meaning that has been set for these decisions. It is a matter of breaking with historicism so that we may endeavour, like a Descartes or a Spinoza, to produce an autonomous legitimation of discourse. Philosophy ought to decide its axioms of thought and draw the consequences. Only after so doing, and on the basis of its immanent determination, should philosophy summon its history.

It is important that philosophy determine itself in such a way that it is *philosophy* itself that judges its history, and not its history that judges it.

An operation of forgetting history and of axiomatic invention presupposes that we are willing to *define* philosophy today. That is, that we are willing precisely to define it otherwise than by its history, otherwise than by the destiny and the decline of Western metaphysics. I shall therefore give my thesis a third, and this time resolutely affirmative, form.

THESIS 3. A DEFINITION OF PHILOSOPHY EXISTS

I should add that in my view this definition is a historical *invariant*. It is not a definition in the sense that it is a result or a production of a loss of sense (*sens*); this definition is intrinsic and enables us to distinguish philosophy from what it is not, and indeed from what it has not been ever since Plato. It enables us to distinguish philosophy from what it is not, but which resembles it, resembles it a lot, and which, since Plato, we call sophistry.

The question of sophistry is very important. From the outset, the sophist has been philosophy's enemy brother, its implacable twin. Deep in its historicist malaise, philosophy today is very weak against modern sophists. It is even most often the case that our great sophists – because there are great sophists – are regarded as great philosophers. It is exactly as if we were to maintain that the great philosophers of antiquity were not Plato and Aristotle but Gorgias and Protagoras. And this is indeed a thesis that modern historiographers of Antiquity increasingly defend, and often brilliantly.

Who are the modern sophists? Modern sophists are those who maintain, in the school of the great Wittgenstein, that thought is caught in the following alternative: that it either consists in effects of discourse, in language games, or that it consists in silent indication, in the pure 'showing' of that which is subtracted from language's grasp. Sophists are those for whom the fundamental opposition is not between truth and error, or errancy, but between speech and silence, that is, between that which can be said and that which it is impossible to say. Or again: between meaningful and meaningless statements.

In many regards, what is presented as being most contemporary in philosophy is a powerful sophistry. Sophistry ratifies the final statement of the *Tractatus* – 'Whereof one cannot speak, thereof one must be silent'; philosophy, however, only exists in maintaining, precisely, that it endeavours to say what cannot be said.

No doubt the objection will be raised that, in its essential movement, contemporary discourse itself also claims to break with historicism, at least in its humanist or Marxist form; that it goes against the ideas of progress and the avant-garde; and that, with Lyotard, it announces the end of the era of grand narratives. Certainly. However, all that this discourse's 'postmodernist' challenge results in is a kind of general equivalence of discourses, a rule of virtuosity and obliquity. It attempts to compromise the idea of truth in the demise of historical narratives. Its critique of Hegel in effect amounts to a critique of philosophy itself, carried out to the benefit of art, or Right, or of an immemorial and unutterable Law. It must therefore be said that, insofar as it does no more than simply adjust the multiplicity of registers of meaning to some silent correlate, this discourse is essentially no more than modern sophistry. That an otherwise virtuous and productive discourse is mistaken for philosophy demonstrates the philosopher's inability to enforce a strict, founding distinction between himself and the sophist.

The modern sophist attempts to replace the idea of truth with the idea of the rule. This is the most profound sense of Wittgenstein's otherwise ingenious endeavour. Wittgenstein is our Gorgias, and we respect him as such. The ancient sophist already replaced truth with a mixture of force and convention. The modern sophist seeks to contrast the force of the rule, and more generally, the modalities of language authority of the Law, with the revelation or the production of the true.

A recent avatar of this desire is evident in the requisitioning of Jewish epic. In the course of the last few years this epic has become a paradigm whose effects extend beyond the political sphere, and that today we must consider as a genuine philosopheme.

It is not clear that this epic's grandeur and tragedy are appropriate to the ends the discourse of modern sophistry pursues. But what 'the Jews' do, *nolens volens,* is lend contemporary discourse something it would be missing without 'them', something that is missing in every fragmentary sophistry: historical depth. Having left behind the arrogance of progressist discourse, which it not unreasonably deems complicit in the theme of redemption, postmodernity is inclined to contrast a Jewish wandering in the original authority of the law to a Christianity for which the truth is actually *come*. The Jewish apparatus is said, dangerously assuming its traditionally received form, to combine the law with interpretation, and is thereby set in opposition to a Christian framework said to marry faith and revelation.

I could not say that thinking the caesura separating Judaism and Christianity in this way is well-founded. First, because the universal signification of the signifier 'Jew' does not lend itself to representation in religious narrative, even when brought to its highest level of abstraction. Second, because the thought of the Jew Paul is located at the exact point where the nexus between faith and the law is to be decided and is otherwise complicated. Instead, what interests me most in this example is the *strategy* that modern sophistry engages in: it tacks onto an analysis of language a historical and preferentially paradoxical Subject, which *nevertheless* makes it possible for this sophistic negation of philosophy to glean something of the modern prestige of historicism. This operation, we ought to recognize, works to confer on contemporary discourse the cumulated powers of a hyper-critique of forms and of a majesty of destiny.

For philosophy, sophistry's postmodern adaptability entails an obligation. This is because restoring philosophy to itself through a forgetting of its history necessarily entails that we give ourselves the wherewithal to

distinguish clearly the philosopher from the sophist. This I shall put in
the form of a fourth thesis.

THESIS 4. EVERY DEFINITION OF PHILOSOPHY MUST
DISTINGUISH IT FROM SOPHISTRY

All in all, this thesis requires that we undertake to define philosophy
through the concept of truth. This is because what the sophist professes
to show, ancient and modern alike, is precisely that there is no truth, and
that its concept is useless and uncertain, because conventions, rules,
genres of discourse and language games are all that exist. I will thus put
forward a variant of the fourth thesis, which I call 4a.

*Thesis 4a. The central category of any possible philosophy is the category
of truth, regardless of the name it is given*

So, the requirement to define philosophy, as stipulated by thesis 2, also
further entails, in light of the conflict with the modern sophist, the need
to elucidate the intra-philosophical status of the category of truth.

Such an elucidation is presented – in the effect *activated* by the deployment of its axioms of thought – as a renewal of the imperative to *philoso-
phein* that stretches back to Parmenides and Plato. From this perspective,
it works against the current of this century's becoming, whose givens
philosophy has claimed to harbour.

What are we to retain from this century at its close? What should we
retain in considering it from a *point of survey*? No doubt, three dispositions
of History, three places and three ideological complexes with a philosophical dimension, or pretension.

The three dispositions are Stalinist bureaucratic socialism, the adventures
of various fascisms and the 'Western' deployment of parliamentarisms.

The three places are Russia, Germany and the United States.

The three complexes are dialectical materialism, that is, the philosophy
of Stalinist Marxism, Heidegger's thought in its militant national–socialist
dimension and the American academic philosophy issuing from the
logical positivism of the Vienna Circle.

Stalinist Marxism registered a fusion of dialectical materialism and the real movement of History. Heidegger believed to have discerned in Hitler's advent the moment at which thought had finally confronted the planetary reign of technology, or the moment, as he put it in his Rectoral Address, in which 'we submit[ted] to the distant command of the beginning of our spiritual–historical existence'. Last, Anglo-Saxon analytic philosophy finds in the examination of language and its rules a form of thinking that is compatible with democratic conversation.

A striking common feature of these three intellectual endeavours is that they are all violently opposed to the Platonist foundation of metaphysics.

For Stalinist Marxism, Plato names the birth of idealism, a quasi-invariant figure of the philosophy of oppressors.

For Heidegger, Plato named the moment of the launching (*envoi*) of metaphysics. Being, for the Presocratics, was 'este', or was deployed as *phusis*. But with Plato, it became subject to and obliterated by the *idea*. Being came to be (*advenir*) in the constancy of Presence, such that the authentic question and care of being could be replaced by the cross-cut problematic of the Supreme Being. What at the height of distress can open to a (re)commencement of thought must also turn us away from thought's Platonic consignment (*envoi*).

The moderate, analytic procedure of Anglo-Saxon philosophy appears completely contrary to the etymological and historical meditations of Heidegger's work. However, it, too, imputes to Plato a realist and obsolete vision of mathematical objects, an underestimation of the impact of forms of language on thought and a metaphysics of the super-sensible. In a certain sense, both Heidegger and Carnap undertook to ruin or close metaphysics, and both their procedures of critical thinking, despite their divergence of method, nonetheless designate Plato as the emblem of what is to be overcome in philosophy.

All in all, Nietzsche was correct in proclaiming that Europe would try to cure itself of what he called 'the Plato disease'. This is indeed the real content of contemporary statements about the end of philosophy, or the end of metaphysics. This content is: what Plato initiated historically has entered into the closure of its effect.

For my part, I believe that it is necessary to proclaim or state the end of this End.

CONDITIONS

To state the end of the End, of *this* End, inevitably comes down to reopening the Plato question. Not in order to restore the prescriptive figure from which modernity has wished to subtract itself, but to examine whether there is not *another* Platonic *act* on the basis of which the future of our thought must be supported.

In Plato's work, I have for a long time been struck by the dreadful reversal that occurs between *Socrates' Apology* and, let's say, Book X of the *Laws*. After all, Platonic meditation was rooted in the question of why Socrates was killed? But what it ends with is a sort of nocturnal terrorism, a repressive apparatus that clamps down on impiety and the corruption of youth – that is, on the two charges that led to Socrates' execution. It seems in the end as if Socrates was legitimately put to death. That the character who articulates these charges in the *Laws* is called the Athenian is truly significant. After Socrates – portrayed in the life of his thought – along comes the generic representative of the *Polis*, once again passing judgement against Socrates and making a plea for the implacable fixedness of criminal laws.

This reversal makes me think that in Plato's work there is not merely *one* foundation for philosophy, *one* inaugural act, as, for example, the metaphysical gesture. Instead, I think that there is an initial setting-up of the philosophical apparatus, one that is then accompanied, escorted, by a progressively excessive tension that *exposes* this apparatus to a sort of disaster.

I would therefore like to consider for a moment the following question: what is it that originally exposes philosophy, at its extremity, to this disastrous induction, which inverts its initial givens? We can also state this question as: what did Plato give ground on in the trajectory that led him from aporetic dialogues to criminal prescriptions?

To answer this question, we must to start with that element by which philosophy is instituted as a singular site of thought. The central category of 'classical' philosophy is of course the Truth. But what is the status of this category? An attentive examination of Plato, which I cannot retrace here,[2] results in the following theses:

1. *Before* philosophy – that is, in a 'before' that is non-temporal – there are *truths*. These truths are heterogeneous and occur in the real independently of philosophy. Plato called them 'right opinions', or, in the particular case of mathematics, statements 'from hypotheses'. These truths fall

within four possible registers, systematically explored by Plato. These four plural sites, in which some truth insists, are mathematics, art, politics and the amorous encounter. Such are the pre-reflexive, historical or factual conditions of philosophy.

2. Philosophy is a construction of thinking where, *counter to sophistry*, it is proclaimed that there are truths. But this central proclamation presupposes a specifically philosophical category, which is that of *the* Truth. What is expressed with this category is both that 'there are' truths and that these truths are compossible in their plurality, a plurality to which philosophy gives welcome and shelter. The Truth simultaneously designates a plural state of things (there are heterogeneous truths) and *the* unity of thought.

The statement 'there are truths' determines philosophy to the thinking of being.

The statement 'truths are, for thought, compossible' determines philosophy to think the unique time of thought, namely what Plato called 'the always of time', or eternity, a specifically philosophical concept that inevitably accompanies the putting into place of the category of Truth.

Let it be said in passing: the contemporary renunciation of the philosophical notion of eternity, the cult of time, being-for-death and finitude are patent effects of historicism. Renouncing eternity – a concept that is by no means religious in itself but is essential to philosophy, including and especially atheistic philosophy, since this concept alone warrants placing philosophy under the condition of the matheme – works only to lay the ground for the sophist's triumph, the one for whom value only ever lies in the finite act of enunciation, such as it involves one in the normless disparity of discourses.

3. By itself the philosophical category of Truth is *empty*. It operates but presents nothing. Philosophy is not a production of truth, but an operation carried out on the basis of truths, one that disposes the 'there is' of truths and their epochal compossibility.

In *Being and Event*[3] I established that an essential link exists between the void and being *qua* being. That the philosophical category of Truth is as such empty sheds light on the originary junction between philosophy and ontology, that is, on the ambiguous dialectic between philosophy and mathematics. It is very important to see that, as void, the category of Truth – with a capital T – *is not the void of being*. The reason for this is that

11

it is not a presented but an operational void. The only void that is presented in thought is the void that the mathematicians call the null set. As we shall see, the void of Truth is a simple *interval* by which philosophy operates on truths that are external to it. This void is therefore not ontological but purely logical.

4. What is the structure of this operation?

Philosophy proceeds universally to assemble its organic category – the Truth – in two different and overlapping ways.

- It relies on paradigms of sequential linking, argumentative style, definitions, refutations, proofs, conclusive force. Let us say that, in this case, it assembles the void of the category of Truth as the *reverse-side or inversion of a regulated succession*. This is, in Plato's work, the regime of the 'long detour', of dialectical developments whose procedures are the same as those of the sophists' against whom he fought. The rhetoric pertaining to succession does not make up any knowledge, since we know perfectly well that none of the 'proofs' generated have ever been able to establish any universally recognized theorem of philosophy. But such rhetoric does *resemble* knowledge, even though its destination is in reality constructive. What is at stake is not to establish anything, or to gain 'knowledge' of it, but to attain to a category in the clarity of its assembly. This assembling imitates knowledge to productive ends. This is why I shall call this procedure – one that we also see followed in Descartes' order of reasons, and in the Spinozist *more geometrico* – a *fiction of knowledge*. Truth is the un-known (*in-su*) of that fiction.
- Or else philosophy proceeds by metaphors, the power of images and persuasive rhetoric. What is involved this time is to indicate the void of category of Truth *qua limit-point*. Truth interrupts the chain, and is recapitulated over and above itself. It is, in Plato's work, the images, the myths and the comparisons the procedures of which are the same as those of the poets he fought against. This time art is called upon, not for its possible intrinsic worth, nor for any imitative or cathartic aim, but to elevate the void of the Truth to the point at which dialectical progression is suspended. Here again, at issue is by no means to 'make a work of art'; yet the text resembles one and will be bequeathed and perceived as one,

even if its destination is totally different. We might say that art is imitated in its ways with a view to producing a subjective site of the Truth. Let's call this treatment at the limit a *fiction of art*. The Truth is the inexpressible of this fiction.

Philosophy borrows from its two adversaries of origin: the sophists and the poets. But one can also just as well say that philosophy borrows from two of its truth procedures: mathematics, as paradigm of the proof; and art, as paradigm of subjectivating power.[4] Its specific attribute involves borrowing only in order to construct a categorical operation, and thereby to establish its place.

The philosophical operation of the category of Truth disposes a sort of pincer movement. One of the arms of the pincers presents itself as a regulating of successiveness by argument. The other, as a declaration at the limit. Truth both links together (*enchaîne*) and sublimates.

5. The pincers of Truth, which link together and sublimate, have the specific function of seizing truth*s*. The relation of (philosophical) Truth to truth*s* (of a scientific, political, artistic and amorous nature) is a relation of *seizing*. By seizing I mean capture, hold and also seizure, amazement, astonishment. Philosophy is the site of thought at which (non-philosophical) truths seize us and are seized as such.

The effect of seizing taken in its first sense aims at rendering the compossibility of plural truths in persuasive fashion. They let themselves be seized *together* in the pincers that philosophy has constructed under the name of Truth (or any other equivalent name; all that matters is the function of seizing). At issue here, between Truth and truths, is not a relation of absolute survey, of subsumption, of foundation or of guarantee. It is a relation of seizing: philosophy is a pinch of truths.

Taken in its second sense, the effect of seizing drives philosophy with a singular intensity. This intensity resembles love, but it is a love free of the quandaries bound up with the love object, of the enigmas of its difference.

More generally, philosophy, because its central category is empty, is essentially *subtractive*.[5] Philosophy must indeed subtract Truth from the labyrinth of meaning. At its core is a lack, a hole; is the fact that the category of Truth and its escort in time, that is, eternity, do not refer to anything in presentation (*dans la presentation*). Philosophy is not an interpretation of the sense of what is offered to experience; it consists in the operation of a category subtracted from the category of presence. And this operation of seizing truths indicates precisely that once seized, truths are distributed within that which interrupts the regime of meaning.

This point is to my mind essential. Philosophy is above all a rupture with both narrative and commentary on narrative. By the twofold effect of the pincers of Truth, by the argument that links together and the limit that sublimates, philosophy contrasts the effect of Truth to the effect of sense. Philosophy is distinct from religion because it breaks with hermeneutics.

All this leads me to give the following provisional definition of philosophy:

> Philosophy is the evocation, under the category of Truth, of a void that is located in accordance with the inversion of a succession and the other-side of a limit. To do so, philosophy constructs the superposition of a fiction of knowledge and a fiction of art. It constructs an apparatus to seize truths, which is to say: to state that there are truths, and to let itself be seized by this 'there are' – and thus to affirm the unity of thought. The seizing is driven by the intensity of a love without object, and draws up a persuasive strategy that has no stakes in power. The whole process is prescribed by the conditions that are art, science, love and politics in their evental figures. Last, this process is polarized by a specific adversary, namely, the sophist.

The rupture with historicism is to be accomplished, and a strict delineation between the philosopher and the modern sophist initiated, in the element of this definition.

The first task, obviously, is to begin to take stock of the current becoming of truths within the fourfold registers of science, and particularly of modern mathematics; of politics, and particularly of the end of the age of revolutions; of love, and particularly that which psychoanalysis introduces into it of light, or shadow; and of art, particularly poetry since Rimbaud and Mallarmé. The need to pursue this path is ever greater since contemporary discourse, bound to the insignia of the 'end of metaphysics', often prides itself – and this is also a typically sophistic trait – on being in step with the times, on being at one with the youth and with liquidating archaisms. It is essential that philosophy deals in its pincers with the most active, the most recent, even the most paradoxical material. But to make such identifications itself presupposes axioms of thought that are subtracted from the judgement of History, axioms that allow the construction of a category of Truth that is innovative and appropriate to our time.

From here it is possible, philosophically, to figure our determination of today's dominant 'philosophical' discourse as a modern sophistry, and, consequently, to figure a determination in which thought bears a just relation to the statements constituting the latter.

But before we turn to this determination, we must again take up a pressing question: why does philosophy, such as we have elucidated its concept, recurrently expose thought to disaster? What is it that leads philosophy from the aporias of the void of Truth to the legitimation of criminal prescriptions?

The key to this reversal is that philosophy is worked on the inside by a chronic temptation to bring the operation of the empty category of Truth level with the multiple procedures of production of truths. Or again: that philosophy, abdicating the operational singularity of seizing truths, presents *itself* as a truth procedure. This also means that it presents itself as an art, as a science, as a passion or as a politics. Nietzsche's poet–philosopher; Husserl's vow to make philosophy a rigorous science; Pascal and Kirkegaard's wish to see philosophy as intense existence; and Plato's naming of the philosopher–king: all are as many intra-philosophical schemes of the permanent possibility of disaster. These schemas are all governed by the filling-in of the void that sustains the exercise of the pincers of Truth.

A disaster, in philosophical thought, is in the making whenever philosophy presents itself as being not a seizing of truths but a *situation of truth*.

The effects of filling in the void, or of its coming to presence, result in giving ground on three points. First of all, by presenting itself as the fullness of Truth, philosophy cedes on the multiplicity of truths, on the heterogeneity of their procedures. It asserts that there is only one place of Truth and that philosophy itself establishes this place. It transforms the empty gap of its Truth pincers – which is 'what there is' between sequential linking and sublimation – into a spacing of being in which the Truth *is*.

Since only *one* place of Truth exists, the required metaphor is one about accessing this place. Reaching this place reveals it in all its dazzling unity. Philosophy comes to consist in an invitation, a path, a point of access to what, in the place of Truth, is brought out into the open. Therein is ultimately an *ecstasy* of place. This ecstasy is clearly manifest in the Platonic presentation of the intelligible place, *topos noètos*. The poetically imperative style of the myth of Er at the end of the *Republic* is an endeavour to transmit the ecstasy of acceding to the place of Truth.

Second, when philosophy lends itself to substantializing the category of Truth, it cedes on the multiplicity of *names* of truth, on the temporal and variable dimension of these names. Theorems, principles, declarations, imperative, beauty, laws: such are some of these names. But if the Truth is, then there is only one veritable name, and it is eternal. Of course, the category of Truth always has eternity as an attribute. But this attribute is only legitimate so long as the category is empty, since it is only an operation. If the category attests to a presence, then eternity is projected onto the diversity of names. It institutes a unique Name, and this Name is necessarily *sacred*. The sacralizing of a name is made to double the ecstasy of place.

In Plato's work, the idea of the Good is assuredly overdetermined by sacralization. There are two legitimate philosophical functions of the idea of the Good:

- a designation, beyond *ousia*, of the Truth *as limit*. It therefore names the second arm of the pincers of Truth (the first is the dianoetic one).
- a designation of this essential point: that there is no Truth of Truth. There is a halting point, an irreflexive point, an empty void.

But the idea of the Good has a third illegitimate, excessive and dubious function. We see it whenever it operates as the unique and sacred name from which all truth would be suspended. Here the rigour of the philosophical operation is violated, abused and subverted.

Third and finally, whenever it thinks it is productive of truth, philosophy faults on its moderation, on its critical virtue. It becomes an anguishing prescription, an obscure and tyrannical directive. Why? Because then philosophy declares that the category of Truth is come (*advenue*) to presence. And as this presence is that of *the* Truth, then whatever falls outside presence has an order issued for its annihilation.

Let us make the point clearer. Philosophy, drawn outside of its operation, says: 'The void of the Truth is presence'. To be sure. But this void is actually empty, since philosophy is not a truth procedure; it is not a science, or an art, or a politics or a love. So this real void returns in being but as that which, if, in the eyes of philosophy, Truth is presence, falls outside Truth. Something of being presents itself as outside Truth, and therefore something of being presents itself *as that which ought not be*. When philosophy is philosophy of the presence of Truth, a presence posited beyond truths, then it necessarily says: this, which is, ought not be. A law of death attends the supposed coming to presence of the void of Truth.

To state that this, which is, ought not be, or that this, which is presented, is in its being only nothingness, produces *terror*. The essence of terror is to pronounce the ought-not-be of 'this' which is. Philosophy, whenever it is disposed to go outside of its operation, in the temptation exercised on it by the idea that Truth is substance, produces terror, just as it produces the ecstasy of the place and the sacredness of the name.

It is specifically this knotted, threefold effect – of ecstasy, of sacredness and of terror – that I call *disaster*. At issue is the specific disaster *of thought*. But every empirical disaster originates in a disaster of thought. At the root of every disaster there lies a substantialization of Truth, that is, an 'illegal' passage from Truth as an empty operation to truth as the coming to presence of the void itself.

Philosophy thus leaves itself open to disaster. Reciprocally, every real disaster, particularly historical ones, contains a philosopheme that knots together ecstasy, sacredness and terror.

There are powerful and visible forms of such philosophemes. The new proletarian man of Stalinist Marxism, and the historically destined German people of National-Socialism were philosophemes that raised, to unprecedented levels, the terror inflicted upon something declared to have no right to be (the traitor to the cause, the Jew, the communist etc.), and that proclaimed the ecstasy of place (German Soil, the Socialist fatherland) as they did the sacredness of the Name (the Führer, the father of peoples).

But there are feeble and insidious forms. The civilized man of imperial parliamentary democracies is itself also a disastrous philosopheme. Therein a place is ecstatically proclaimed (the West), a name is sacralized as unique (the Market, Democracy) and terror is exercised against that which ought not be – the impoverished planet, the distant rebel, the non-Western and the immigrant nomad that radical abandonment drives towards enriched metropoles.

CONDITIONS

There we have empirical, historical destinations of disastrous philosophemes passed on for implementation.

But from what point, in philosophy itself, does this disastrous abuse of the categorical operation proceed? What internal tension carries philosophy away, as the place of thought in which the seizing of truths is carried out, towards a schema of the presence of Truth that exposes it to disaster?

The key to the problem resides in the nature and the measure of the conflictual relation between philosophy and sophistry.

From its beginnings to our times, the stakes of this conflict bear on the function of truth in the heterogeneity of discourses, or on the style of determination of thought by the rule of language. They do not consist, and indeed cannot unless thought is to be threatened by the greatest of dangers, in a war of annihilation. Nothing is more philosophically useful to us than contemporary sophistry. Philosophy ought never yield to anti-sophistry extremism. Whenever it harbours the dark desire to do away with the sophist *once and for all*, philosophy loses itself. This is precisely, in my view, what defines dogmatism: the claim that the sophist, because he is like the perverse double of the philosopher, *ought not to exist*. No, the sophist must instead be assigned to *his place*.

If it is true that the sophist is the singular adversary of philosophy – and the more *similar* is his rhetoric the more he is an adversary – then it is also true that philosophy is always going to have to put up with company and sarcasm from the sophist.

Because what does the sophist say?

- The sophist says that there are no truths, and that there are only techniques for making statements, and places of enunciation. It is philosophically legitimate to respond, with the operation of the empty category of Truth, that there are truths. It is no longer legitimate to say, like the dogmatist, that there is a single place of Truth, and that philosophy itself reveals this place. Such a riposte is excessive, overstrung and disastrous. It confounds the operational void of Truth with the givenness (*donation*) of being. It transforms philosophy from the rational operation it should be into a suspect rite of initiation. It fills the void of seizing with the ecstasy of a unique place in which truth comes forth in the veiling of its offering. It is an imposture. Philosophy can counter the sophist

18

with the local existence of truths; it goes astray in offering ecstasy at the place of Truth.

- The sophist says that there is a multiplicity of language games, that there is a plurality and heterogeneity of names. It is philosophically legitimate to respond by constructing, with the category of Truth, a place where thought points to the unity of its time. To show, by seizing them, that these truths are compossible. It is no longer legitimate to say that there is a sole name for truths. It is dogmatic and ruinous to confound the heterogeneous plurality of truths under the Name, thus inescapably sacred, that philosophy gives to Truth.
- The sophist says that being *qua* being is inaccessible to the concept and to thought. Philosophically it is legitimate to designate, and to think, the empty place of seizing of truths with the Truth-pincers. No longer is it legitimate to claim that, under the category of Truth, the void of being comes to pass in the unique thought of its act, or of its destiny. Philosophy must counter the sophists with the real of truth whose seizing it effectuates. It goes astray in offering the terrorist imperative of True-being as such.

The ethics of philosophy essentially inheres in retaining the sophist as adversary, in conserving the *polemos*, or dialectical conflict. The disastrous moment occurs when philosophy declares that the sophist *ought not be*, the moment when it decrees the annihilation of its Other.

In the genuinely philosophical dialogues, Plato *refuted* the sophists. He did so respectfully in the case of Protagoras, with a sort of violent comedy in the cases of Callicles and Thrasymacus. But the statements of the sophist were always included in the dialectic.

In *Book X* of the *Laws*, Plato, with sombre scheming knotted from ecstasy, the sacred and terror, ended up *banning* sophists. He thus ceded on the ethics of philosophy, and exposed his thought in its entirety to disaster.

The figure of the sophist is at all times required if philosophy is to maintain to its ethics. Because the sophist is the one that reminds us of the emptiness of the category of Truth. The sophist only does so, of course, in order to deny truths, for which he must be combated. But the combat must occur within the ethical norm that regulates it. Philosophical extremism, as the figure of disaster in thought, desires the sophist's annihilation. But it in fact contributes to and participates in his triumph.

19

Because if philosophy renounces its operation and its void, all there is left to establish the category of Truth is dogmatic terror. To counter this, sophists will always have an easy time of exposing the deal philosophical desire makes with tyranny.

This is the problem we face today in a nutshell. The idea of the End of philosophy is at the same time the idea of the end of the category of Truth. Its stakes, without any doubt, concern a balance-sheet of the century's disasters. Dogmatic terror took the form of the State. Philosophemes of dogmatism were taken so far as to be incorporated in police-work and extermination camps. Places were glorified, and psalms sung to sacred names. This disaster compromised philosophy. The provisional ruining of Marxism's credit and the 'Heidegger affair' were only avatars of this compromise. We see therein the price philosophy pays when it renounces its void and its eternity. When it renounces its operation. The price it pays to want to *realize* itself within time.

However, to claim that philosophy as at an end and the Truth is obsolete is an inherently *sophistic* assessment of the century. We are bearing witness to a second anti-Platonic requital, for contemporary 'philosophy' is a sort of generalized sophistry, which incidentally is lacking neither in talent nor in grandeur. Language games, deconstruction, weak thought, radical heterogeneity, *différend* and differences, the ruin of Reason, promotion of the fragment, discourse reduced to shreds: all this argues in favour of a sophistic line of thinking, and puts philosophy in a deadlock.

Let us simply say: after the sophistic or postmodern assessment of the disasters of the century the time of the anti-sophistic balance-sheet begins. And since these disasters are borne of philosophy's paroxystic desire to inscribe itself in History; since the catastrophes of Truth come from the fact that, obsessed by its past and its becoming, philosophy renounced the void and eternity, so, then, it is entirely legitimate to draw up a new philosophical balance-sheet *against* the authority of history, against historicism.

The central point consists in redeploying the category of Truth in its operation, in its capacity for seizing. This redeployment has to factor in and overrule the objection of the great modern sophist. Yes, the reconstruction of Truth's pincers must give a place to the laws of language, chance, the indiscernible, the event and singularity. Philosophy's central category must explicitly be kept empty. But it must also maintain that this void is a condition for a real operation. Philosophy must not give up either on logical linking, as instructed by a contemporary mathematics, or on sublimations and limits, as instructed by a contemporary poetics. The intensity of its love will receive clarification from the quibbles of psychoanalysis. Its persuasive strategy will receive clarification from the debate on politics and democracy.

This is the fifth variation of my thesis. It can be quite simply stated as given in thesis 5.

THESIS 5. PHILOSOPHY IS POSSIBLE

From this follows a variant on this variant, let's call it thesis 5a.

Thesis 5a. Philosophy is necessary

At issue here is not the history of philosophy. At issue here is not ideology. Nor is it question of aesthetics, of epistemology or of political sociology. It is not a question of examining the rules of language. It is a question of philosophy *itself* in its singular delimitation, in conformity with the definition I have put forward of it. It is a question of philosophy such as it was inaugurated by Plato.

We can, and we should, write new *Republics* and *Symposiums* for our contemporaries. Just as Plato wrote the *Gorgias* and *Protagoras* for the great sophists, we should write the *Nietzsche*[6] and the *Wittgenstein*. And, for the minor sophists, the *Vattimo* and the *Rorty*. Neither more nor less polemical, neither more nor less respectful.

Philosophy is possible; philosophy is necessary. And nevertheless, in order for it to be, it must be desired. Philippe Lacoue-Labarthe says that History – he has in mind Nazi barbarity – now forbids any desire for philosophy.[7] I cannot grant him this, since such a conviction immediately places philosophy in a position of weakness with regard to modern sophistry. There is another possible solution and that is to desire philosophy against history, to break with historicism. This would enable philosophy to re-emerge as what it is: the clearing (*éclaircie*) of a Godless and soulless eternity, due solely to its effort that grants us that there are truths. This is the orientation that I do not hesitate an instant to consider a *duty* for thought. And if I compare, as Mallarmé did, the eternal void of the philosophical Truth to a bed of ideal, and therefore inexistent, flowers, to Irises whose genus – 'the family of irises' – only exists in the philosopher's operation, I shall say with him, combining exaltation and prescription – just as Truth superimposes a fiction of art on a fiction of knowledge:

> Ideas, glory of long desire,
> all within me rejoiced to see
> the irid family aspire
> to this new responsibility,

(Stéphane Mallarmé, 'Prose (for des Esseintes)' in *Stéphane Mallarmé: Collected Poems and Other Verse*, trans. by E.H. and A.M. Blackmore, Oxford: Oxford University Press, 2006. p. 53)

Any such burgeoning, any such re-turn of affirmative thinking are likewise wagers. Mallarmé, again: 'Every thought emits a throw of the dice'. Let us throw the dice of philosophy. When the dice fall, there will still be time to discuss, with modern sophists, what Mallarmé called 'the total count in the making'.

CHAPTER TWO
Definition of Philosophy

Philosophy is prescribed by conditions that constitute types of truth- or generic-procedure. These types are science (more precisely, the matheme), art (more precisely, the poem), politics (more precisely, politics in interiority, or a politics of emancipation) and love (more precisely, the procedure that makes truth of the disjunction of sexuated positions).

Philosophy is the place of thought where the 'there is' (*il y a*) of these truths, and their compossibility, is stated. To achieve this, philosophy constructs an operational category, the Truth, which opens up an active void in thought. This void is located in conformity with the inversion of succession (its style of argumentative exposition) and the beyond of a limit (its style of persuasive or subjectivating exposition). Philosophy, as discourse, is thus an activity that constructs a fiction of knowledge and a fiction of art in superposition to one another.

Philosophy *seizes* truths in the void that is opened in the gap or interval of the two fictionings. This seizing is its act. It is this act by which philosophy declares that there are truths, and by which thought itself is seized by this 'there are'. This seizing by means of an act attests to the unity of thought.

As a fiction of knowledge, philosophy imitates the matheme. As a fiction of art, it imitates the poem. As the intensity of an act, it is like a love without object. Addressed to all so that all may be in seizing the existence of truths, it is like a political strategy with no stakes in power.

Through this fourfold discursive imitation, philosophy knots into itself the system of its conditions. This is the reason that *a* philosophy is homogeneous to the stylistics of its epoch. This continual contemporaneousness is, however, oriented not towards empirical time, but towards what Plato called 'the always of time', towards the intemporal essence of time, which philosophy names eternity. The philosophical seizing of truths exposes them to eternity; with Nietzsche, we might say that it exposes them to the eternity of their *return*. This eternal exposition is all the more real insofar as truths are seized in extreme urgency, in the extreme precariousness of their temporal trajectory.

The act of seizing, such as an eternity orients it, picks truths out from the dross of sense, *separating* them from the law of the world. Philosophy is subtractive in that it makes holes in sense, or causes an interruption in the circulation of sense, so that it may come that truths are said all together. Philosophy is a sense-less or mad (*insensé*) act, and by the same token rational.

Philosophy is never an interpretation of experience. It involves the act of Truth with regard to truths. And this act, deemed unproductive by the law of the world (it produces not a single truth), disposes an objectless subject, a subject open only to the truths that transit in its seizing and by which it is seized.

I propose to call 'religion' everything that presupposes that there is a continuity between truths and the circulation of meaning. We can thus say: philosophy is what, against every hermeneutics, against the religious law of meaning, assembles compossible truths on the basis of the void. Philosophy then subtracts thought from every presupposition of Presence.

The subtractive operations by which philosophy grasps truths 'outside of sense' fall under four modalities[1]: the undecidable, which relates to the event (a truth is not, it comes forth [*advient*]; the indiscernible, which relates to freedom (the trajectory of a truth is not constrained but hazardous); the generic, which relates to being (the being of a truth is made of an infinite set that is subtracted from knowledge predicates); and the unnameable, which relates to the Good (forcing the naming of an unnameable engenders disaster).

The schema connecting these four figures of the subtractive (the undecidable, the indiscernible, the generic and the unnameable) provides the outline for a philosophical doctrine of Truth. It disposes the thinking of the void as that on the basis on which truths are seized.

One specific adversary, the sophist, polarizes the whole philosophical process. As his operation also combines fictions of knowledge and fictions of art, the sophist is externally (or discursively) indiscernible from the philosopher. Nonetheless, the two are subjectively opposed, for the reason that the sophist's linguistic strategy aims to spare the expense of making positive assertions about truths. In this sense, philosophy could also be defined as the act by which indiscernible discourses nevertheless come to form an opposition; or as the act that separates it from its double. Philosophy is always the breaking of a mirror. This mirror is the surface of language, onto which the sophist reduces all the things that philosophy treats in its act. If the philosopher sets his gaze solely on this surface, his double, the sophist, will emerge, and he may take himself to be one.

Philosophy's relation to the sophist subjects it to an inner temptation, yielding to which will cause it to split yet again. For the desire to do get rid of the sophist *once and for all* hinders the seizing of truths: 'once and for all' necessarily entails that Truth annul the aleatoric nature of truths and that philosophy unduly declare itself productive of truths. The upshot of this is that a declaration of being true comes to stand in as the double of the *act* of Truth.

Philosophy's operation thus comes to be corrupted by a threefold effect of sacredness, ecstasy and terror, which may lead it from the aporetic void that sustains its act to criminal prescriptions. On this basis philosophy induces every disaster in thought.

Disaster is held at bay by an ethics of thought that consists in the *restraint* that philosophy exercises towards its sophistic double, a restraint thanks to which it is subtracted from the temptation to split into two (into the couple void/substance), leaving it to focus on the primary duplicity that founds it (sophist/philosopher).

The history of philosophy is the history of its ethics: it consists in the succession of violent gestures through which philosophy is withdrawn from the disaster of reduplication. To put it another way: in its history, philosophy consists uniquely in a process of desubstantializing Truth, a process that also forms its act's own self-liberation.

CHAPTER THREE
What is a Philosophical Institution?
Or Address, Transmission, Inscription

I would like to attempt here a kind of deduction of the destiny of every philosophical institution. I would like to explore the possibility of submitting our institutional intuition to the concept. The danger is easy to see. It is certainly less than that to which Saint-Just was exposed when he maintained that institutions alone could prevent the Revolution from ending in the event of its pure uprising. The risk I am taking consists only in this: in reversing a materialist order whose specific effect has been to immerse thought in the massiveness of the social and the organic, I posit that philosophy's own determination, as such, prescribes what kind of institution might be adequate to it. In short, the concern here is to draw a brief, and still uncertain, transcendental deduction of every possible philosophical institution. As for real institutions – of which the unique to the world *Collège international de philosophie* is at the forefront – I recognize that their problems, their concerns, their internal competitions and their elected instances are, as is reasonable, anything but transcendental.

Let us start with its negative dialectic. An institutional prescription for philosophy does not take a causal form. Nor that of an incarnation. An institution cannot claim to be an effect of philosophy, nor can it offer its body to philosophy, or turn philosophy into a body, into a Great Body, as the specialists of French institutional sociology would say. But neither can an institution for philosophy be of instrumental value, in the sense that it would allow philosophy to fulfil its aims. The basic reason for this, in my view, is that these aims do not exist. I am not saying that philosophy has no destination. But I do not think this destination falls within the realm of aims or finalities. Far from devising ends for itself, philosophy always purports, in one way or another, to have done with ends, and even to have done with *the* end. Philosophy's greatest virtue consists in the fact that, although not ceasing to conclude, it nevertheless attests to an interminable imperative of continuation. It does not therefore require any means for its abolished ends.

Neither effect, nor body, nor instrument. What then is a philosophical institution? We might obviously argue that there is no such institution; however, from the schools of ancient thought to the college that I celebrated a moment ago, the empirical evidence attests to the contrary. Neither do I intend to engage in an interminable process of deconstruction, so as to show that, at the limit of the concept, these empirical institutions have in reality organized a forgetting of their destination. No, these institutions exist, and have a proven connection with philosophy. But then what sort of connection is it?

I will maintain that what the institution treats of is not a *line* of causality; is not the *volume* of a body; and is not the *surface* of an operation that can be set to a plan. Rather, it treats of a knot, the institution's entire purpose being to make sure that it does not come undone; and this same institution's entire risk being that it get cut. A philosophical institution is a procedure of conserving a knot, a knot in danger of being cut, which would cause its components to disperse. A good institution is knotting, opaque and cannot be dissolved. A bad institution is segmentary, dispersive and parliamentary. The first, the good one, is serried and obscure. The second, a cause of peril, counts the votes and divides up the functions, which most often it only gathers together in the particularly unphilosophical form of the colloquium. The caretaking of a knot is hardly compatible with the occasionally prudent, occasionally violent, management of the balance of factions.

What is the knot in question? I announced it in the sub-title: it is a knot that ties together an address, a transmission, and an inscription. Each one of these strands – as occurs in a figure that my master Jacques Lacan taught us to meditate on – holds together the other two: what can be said of them?

First, what I call philosophy's address is not those to whom or that to which it is addressed, but the subjective position that is specific to it. What characterizes this position is that it is purely and simply *empty*. One possible definition of philosophy might be that it has no specifiable address. There is no real or virtual community in a *vis-à-vis* with philosophy. No statement of philosophy is addressed to anyone as such. This is the meaning of stressing that what matters for philosophers is the 'question'. Questioning is a simple name for the void of the address. The philosopher's famous 'misaddress' – his *maladresse* – has as its ultimate essence a non-address, an absence of address. Every philosophical text is in the *poste restante* and requires advance knowledge that it is there to be found, since it was not *sent* to you.

Next, what I call philosophy's transmission is an operation by which it propagates itself through the void of its address. It is well known that philosophy is propagated by the very small number of those who, against all evidence, decide that it is addressed to them. Those that thus endure in themselves the void of address create such a void in themselves. This small number never make up a public or an audience, because a public is precisely always that which answers or fulfils (*remplir*) an address. Philosophy cannot be transmitted through this fullness, this over-fulfilment. This explains why philosophy's transmission has never been tied to the extension of a public, but instead to the restrained and unfigurable (*infigurable*) figure of the disciple. A disciple is one who undertakes to endure to coincide with the void of address. A disciple is one who knows that he does not form a public or constitute an audience but supports a transmission.

Last, I call philosophy's 'inscription' everything that turns the void of the address into a subsisting mark, everything that philosophy writes. As empty address, philosophy is in itself subtracted from the written, yet it is not thereby destined for voice. Philosophy is that which, bound to the void of the address, obeys the temporalized injunction issued by the categories of being and event, and is on this side of voice and of the written. It is, besides, this being 'on-this-side' of voice and the written that we have always named thought, and it is that to which the void of the address accords. Inscription is the marking of this void, the interminable procedure of a subsisting suture with the subsistent, the effectivity, the void. The inscription is open and offered to all, where the address is, by contrast, empty, and transmission offered to some.

Note that it is always possible that the knot I speak of does not tie. If this is the case – henceforth undecidable – then there has perhaps been philosophy but not *a* philosophy. Only the knot confers historicity on philosophy's existence. Only it decides that philosophy is there, in the form of a particular philosophy.

The historicity of philosophy thus requires that there is an address (generally covered by the proper name of a philosopher), some disciples (generally covered by the proper names of other philosophers, who, when their time comes, and after having submitted to the place of the void, produce such a place) and books, which are generally covered by the public instance comprised by the procession of commentaries, editions and re-editions. These three instances are also that of the void (the address), that of the finite (disciples) and that of the infinite (the inscription of its gloss).

It is clear that this knot is Borromean in nature, and consequently we consider it founding of the *historicity* of philosophy. Without the knot, philosophy, being reduced to the void of the address, would only be the point of indistinction between thought and being. In effect, only inscription holds the address and transmission together in time, since it is only upon encountering a book, an inscription, that a new disciple can arrive at the empty place prescribed by this age-old address. A disciple encounters this book precisely insofar as it is offered to all, and therefore insofar as it accords with the infinity of a prescription. It is no less obvious that only the address holds together transmission and inscription, since it alone attests to what the disciple was a disciple of, the empty place that he occupied, whose inscription perpetuates its existence. It is thus the void that, here as elsewhere, sutures the finiteness of transmission to the infinity of inscription. And last, it is certain that only transmission holds together the address and inscription, since a book cannot be written *except from the disciple's standpoint*, even if for the occasion, the master, to write, becomes the disciple of himself. But every so often, as we know (look at Aristotle, or Hegel, or Kojève, or even Leibniz, or Nietzsche, or Husserl; look into the archives, the re-transcribed lessons, the reigning disorder of notes and papers), yes, very often it is disciples in their finitude that expose the void of the philosophical address to the infinity of prescription.

The whole point of a philosophical institution is to preserve the knot. A philosophical institution is the custodian not of philosophy but of its historicity. It is therefore the custodian of philosophie*s*, in the plural. It is the knotted plurality of philosophies as a resistance in time, which often amounts to saying: as resistance to time.

What secondary imperatives does this first entail? What are the functions and the limits of the institution for philosophy by which, in keeping with its destination, it preserves the Borromean knot of address, transmission and inscription – which is also to say the knot of the void, the finite and the infinite?

The first derived imperative is obviously that such an institution be involved in the detection and existence of the three strands of the knot taken separately. And that it does so, I might say, without separating them.

Concerning the address, in which the suture of philosophy to being consists, this is something for which the institution can do nothing. It is not because there are institutions that, as Parmenides said, 'the Same, indeed, is at once to think and to be'. This 'the same' that is also an 'at once' is without any doubt an empty point, and the void is precisely definable from the fact that its institution is impossible. Though we know it to be untrue that the void fills nature with horror, it certainly does institutions. Their incoercible tendency is towards a plenitude, which over-completes it (*trop-plein*), which is precisely what makes their bearing so very unnatural.

But what an institution can – and therefore must – do for philosophy is to protect philosophers from the misaddress that arises as a consequence of its void address. It must provide the void with an address; it must be the address of the void of address. This means that it must authorize that he that nothing recommends, and that, above all, is neither recommended nor recommendable, feels at home in it as if it were his home. How can one who claims to philosophize, and so to have no address – how can this 'one' be recognized by the institution? This institution for philosophy cannot recognize anyone; it can only address him. It must quite simply test this indiscernible, and say that it will furnish his address. Allow me to call this first function of an institution for philosophy its function as *poste restante*. It is an institution thanks to which, contrary to what happens at PTT,[1] unregistered (*non-recommandé*) letters have a chance of arriving at their destination.

Concerning transmission, this institution must obviously multiply the chances open to disciples to occupy the empty place of the address. It has to make disciples proliferate. The onus is therefore on it to be an open, vacant house through which those who are destined to the void of a singular address may pass. A 'general pass' demands there can be no

criteria for attendance, or, as is the rule at the *Collège international*, that
seminar attendance is absolutely open to all, that there be no *closed*
seminars. Allow me to call this second function of an institution for
philosophy its function as a *maison de passe*.[2]

Finally, concerning inscription, the resources of the ordinary edition
cannot suffice, because such an edition is conceived in terms of a public,
indeed in terms of publicity, and this does not conform to the essence of
philosophical inscription, the infinity of which is measured in terms of
centuries, and not by exhaustion of the first print run. In my view, it is
essential that an institution for philosophy print, edit and distribute
synopses, notes and books. And as it is a matter of publishing things that
are neither recommended nor recommendable, of distributing void
addresses and the obscure turmoil of disciples, and as the public of all this
is incalculable and shady, or so we should at least hope, you will permit
me to call this third function its underground printing press function.

An institution for philosophy thus organizes within it a *poste restante*, a
maison de passe and an underground printing press.

But its second major task is to keep the three strands tied together, to
tighten, but not cut – on the pretext that the functions it involves are
disparate – the Borromean knot of the historicity of philosophy. For this,
it is required that the custodians of the institution, those that constitute
its core, and they always exist, are able to circulate right throughout the
knot; that they have care and concern for its 'holding together'; that they
themselves are cognizant of the paradoxical connections of the address
and transmission, of inscription and the address, and of inscription and
transmission. That they know how to articulate not solely the finitude of
needs and opportunities but the triplet of the void, the finite and the
infinite. That their desire is genuinely to be, with neither visible discontinuity nor caesura, inspectors of the *poste restante*, managers of the
maison de passe and underground printers. The only thing I really foresee
for such a task is a sort of convention of philosophers, 'convention' in the
sense used by the people of the Revolution of 1792; that is, a collective
body seized by the seriousness or application of decision, which, as such,
is the place of decision, and which at the same time appoints large committees, investing them with wide powers, but in keeping a serious watch
over them. The law of such an assembly cannot be that of the majority,
because it is the law of the knot, of the historicity of philosophy, the law
of philosophy's *present*. A convention of philosophers can alone prevent

the knot from continually being cut, historicity from being lost, and avoid the risk that philosophy is *put in order* (*mise à plat*), in short that terrible and classic moment when the institution that was for philosophy becomes anti-philosophic. We know the name of this danger: it is liberalism. Liberalism is what seeks to undo everything, and thereby to leave everything at the mercy of dispersion, competition, opinion and the despotism of the public and publicity.

Nietzsche, on one of his good days, observed that laws are not made against wrongdoers but against innovators.

Doubtless the inspectors of a wayward *poste restante*, the managers of a *maison de passe* and underground printers are generally seen to be wrongdoers. With regard to a philosophical institution, these figures are called upon to be innovative, and so they will risk falling under the force of laws, including those that the institution believes essential to its safeguarding. But assuming the strict discipline of the convention – indeed the convent-like discipline – of an institution for philosophy to be good, related as it is to a knot that must be guarded, tightened and retied using new combinations of the void, the finite and the infinite, then let it, this cruel discipline, be put at the service of such innovators. Doubtless only chance can see to it. A good institution for philosophy will therefore be that which offers the wrongdoer, which for philosophy can only be the declared enemy of all thought, and therefore the declared enemy of being, the greatest power of chance, that is, the empty power of the void of the address.

I shall conclude, as you might expect, with a wish: that if ever a philosophical institution in the process of forming its convention and of regulating anew the custodianship of the knot, if ever philosophy finds itself put to the test of a collective decision, let us hope that no wrongdoer's dice throw will abolish the chance of this rare occurrence.

PART II
Philosophy and Poetry

CHAPTER FOUR
The Philosophical Recourse to the Poem

Every philosophical enterprise turns back towards its temporal conditions so as to take in hand their compossibility at a conceptual level. In Heidegger's work it is easy to discern four modes of this turning back.

1. The point of support found in the intimate *ek-stasis* of time, in effect, in experience such as it is filtered through the concern of a question guiding its metamorphosis. This is the existential–ontological analysis of *Sein und Zeit*.
2. National-Socialist politics, militantly practiced by Heidegger as the German occurrence of a resolute decision and of thought's frontal encounter with the nihilistic reign of technology, a confrontation rooted in the categories of soil, work, community and appropriation of site.
3. The hermeneutic and historical re-evaluation of the history of philosophy thought of as being's destiny in its coupling with the *logos*. We have here the brilliant analyses of Kant and Hegel, of Nietzsche and Leibniz, and the lessons taken from the Greeks, singularly from the pre-Socratics.
4. The great German poems, seized from 1935, in the course on Hölderlin, as privileged interlocutors for the thinker.

This fourth support still survives today despite everything that managed to affect the other three. Its audience in France, including poets – from René Char to Michel Deguy – is the strongest subsisting validation of Heidegger's success in philosophically *touching* an unnoticed point of thought detained in poetic language. It is therefore necessary, for whoever wants to go beyond the power of Heideggerian philosophy, to reconsider, in the terms of this philosophy, the couple formed by the saying of poets and the thought of thinkers. To reformulate that which joins together and separates out the poem and philosophical discursivity is an imperative to which Heidegger, regardless of the mishaps of his 'affair', obliges us to submit.

Let us start by recalling that, for Heidegger, there is an original *in*distinction between the two terms. In the pre-Socratic consignment (*envoi*) of thought, which is also the destinal consignment of being, the *logos* is poetic as such. It is the poem that stands in as guard for thought, as shown us in Parmenides' *Poem*, and in Heraclitus' maxims.

It is by a kind of axiomatic contestation of this point that I wish to begin the reconstruction of an *other relation*, or non-relation (*dé-rapport*), between poetry and philosophy.

When Parmenides places his poem under an invocation to a Goddess and begins it with the image of an initiatory cavalcade, we must maintain, I think, that we are not, that we are *not yet*, in philosophy. For any truth that accepts a position of dependency with regard to narrative and revelation is still gripped by mystery, whereas philosophy only exists through its desire to tear down mystery's veil.

With Parmenides, the poetic form is essential; its authority justifies leaving the proximity between discourse and the sacred intact. Philosophy, however, commences only with a desacralization: it establishes a regime of discourse that is its own inherent and earthly legitimation. Philosophy requires that the authority of *profound* utterance be interrupted by argumentative secularization.

On this very issue, incidentally, Parmenides forms a sort of pre-commencement of philosophy: that is, in his sketching, with regard to the question of non-being, of a *reductio ad absurdum*. This implicit recourse to an autonomous rule of consistency is, within the poem, an interruption of the collusion organized by the poem between truth and the sacred authority of the image or of the story.

It is essential to see that the basis of this interruption can only be of the order of the matheme, if we understand by this the discursive singularities of mathematics. Apagogical argument is doubtless the most significant matrix of an argumentation based on nothing other than the imperative of consistency, and that proves to be incompatible with any legitimation grounded in narrative or in the initiate status of the subject of enunciation. The matheme here is that which, causing the Speaker to disappear, removing any form of mysterious validation from its site, submits argumentation to a test of autonomy, and therefore to a critical, or dialogical, examination of its pertinence.

Philosophy began in Greece because it was the only place where the matheme warranted the interruption of the sacral exercise of validation by narrative (or as Lacoue-Labarthe would say, by the mytheme). Parmenides names the pre-moment – the moment still internal to sacred narrative and its poetic capture – of this interruption.

It is well known that Plato names this interruption himself, pushing reflection to a systematic distrust of anything reminiscent of the poem. Plato proposed to us a complete analysis of this gesture of interruption constitutive of philosophy's possibility:

- Everything concerning the poem's imitative capture, its seduction without concept, its legitimation without Idea, must be removed, must be banished from the space in which philosophical royalty operates. This rupture is a painful and interminable one (see Book X of the *Republic*) but it is a matter of philosophy's *existence*, and not solely its style.
- Mathematics, in the support it provides for the de-sacralization, or the de-poeticization, of truth, must be explicitly sanctioned, pedagogically by the crucial place assigned to arithmetic and geometry in political education, and ontologically by the intelligible dignity that makes mathematics an antechamber to the ultimate deployments of the dialectic.

For Aristotle – who is as minimal a poet as possible in his expository technique (Plato, on the other hand, and he recognized it, always remained susceptible to the charm of what he excluded) – the Poem was only one particular object offered to the dispositions of Knowledge; at the same time, incidentally, he divests mathematics of all the attributes of ontological dignity it had for Plato. 'Poetics' becomes a regional discipline of philosophical activity. With Aristotle, philosophy's inaugural debate is brought to a close, and so, stabilized in the connection of its parts, philosophy no longer turns back dramatically upon what conditions it.

CONDITIONS

So, as early as the Greeks, *three possible regimes of the relation between philosophy and the poem* are encountered and named.

> The first, which I shall call Parmenidian, produced a *fusion* between the poem's subjective authority and the validity of utterances deemed to be philosophical. Even when 'mathematical' interruptions figure in this fusion they are ultimately subordinated to the sacred *aura* of utterance, to its 'profound' value, to its enunciative legitimacy. Image, the equivocity of language, and metaphor, all escort and authorize the saying of the True. Authenticity resides in the flesh of language.

> The second, which I shall call Platonic, effected a *distance* between the poem and philosophy. The former is isolated as a debilitating fascination, a seduction diagonal to the True, while the latter must exclude the possibility that poetry might deal with what it deals with *in its stead*. Avulsing the prestige of poetic metaphor necessitates that a basis be found in that which, in language itself, contrasts with it, namely, the literal univocity of mathematics. Philosophy can only establish itself through the contrasting play of the poem and the matheme, which form its two primordial conditions (the poem, whose authority it must interrupt; and the matheme, whose dignity it must promote). We can also say that the Platonic relation to the poem is a (negative) relation of *condition*, one that presupposes other conditions (the matheme, politics, love).

> The third, which I shall call Aristotelian, organized the *inclusion* of a knowledge of the poem within philosophy, itself representable as Knowledge of the kinds of knowledge. The poem was no longer conceived of in the drama of its distance or in its intimate proximity; it was grasped *through the category of the object*, that is, through that which, being defined and reflected as such, came to delimit a regional discipline within philosophy. The poem's regionality founded what was to become Aesthetics.

We might also express these three possible relationships of philosophy (*qua* thought) to the poem as *identifying rivalry, argumentative distance* and *aesthetic regionality*. In the first philosophy envies the poem, in the second it excludes it and in the third it classifies it.

With regard to this threefold disposition, then, what is the essence of the Heideggerian method of thinking?

I will schematize it into three elements:

1. Heidegger quite legitimately re-established the poem in its autonomous function of thought. Or, more precisely, he sought to determine the site – a site that is itself withdrawn, or undetectable – from which to perceive the community of destiny shared by the conceptions of thinkers and the saying of poets. We can say that his sketch of a community of destiny essentially contrasts with the third type of relation, which is subsumed under an aesthetics of inclusion. Heidegger subtracted the poem from philosophical *knowledge* to render it to *truth*. And in so doing, he founded a radical critique of all aesthetics, of all determinations that construe the poem as a region of philosophy. This foundation is established as one of the pertinent traits of modernity (its non-Aristotelian character).

2. Heidegger showed the limits of a relation of condition in which the *only* thing that is brought to light is the distance of the poem to philosophical argument. In some particularly fine analyses, he established that over a lengthy period beginning with Hölderin the poem rallied round some essential philosophical themes; this was principally because over this period philosophy remained in thrall either to science (the positivisms) or to politics (the Marxisms). It remained in thrall to them in the same way that I said it was to the poem for Parmenides: it lacked the play within which to establish its own law with regard to these particular conditions of its existence. I have suggested calling this period the 'age of poets'.[1] Let us say that, investing this age with totally original philosophical means, Heidegger showed that it was neither always possible nor always just to establish a distance to poetry using the Platonic procedure of banishment. Philosophy is sometimes obliged to open up to the poem in a more dangerous fashion: it must think, for its own ends, the *operations* by which the poem sets a date with a truth of Time (for the period under consideration the principal truth that was poetically put to work was the destitution of the category of objectivity as a necessary form of ontological presentation. This explains the poetically crucial character of the theme of Presence, even when, as in Mallarmé's work, it comes in its inverted form, that is, as isolation or as Subtraction).

3. Unfortunately, since, in his historical montage, and, more particularly, in his evaluation of the Greek origins of philosophy, Heidegger

failed to validate the – itself originary – character of recourse to the matheme, he only managed to revoke the judgement of interruption and thus to restore, using many subtle and varied philosophical names, both the sacral authority of poetic utterance and the idea that 'the authentic' resides in the flesh of language. There is a unity between, on the one hand, his recourse to Parmenides and Heraclitus construed as delimiting a site of the pre-forgetting and the coming forth of Being, and, on the other hand, his ponderous and fallacious recourse to the sacred in the most contestable of his analyses of poems, specially those of Trakl. The Heideggerian miscomprehension of the true nature of the mathematical sense of the Idea (which is precisely what, in denaturalizing it, exposes the Idea to the with-drawal [*re-traite*] of Being), entails that instead of inventing a fourth relation between philosopher and poem – one that is neither fusional, nor distanced, nor aesthetic – Heidegger emptily prophesied a re-activation of the Sacred in an indecipherable coupling of the saying of poets and the thinking of thinkers.

I want to retain from Heidegger the devaluation of philosophical aesthetics and the critical limitation of the effects of the Platonic procedure of exclusion. On the other hand, I want to contest the idea that philosophy is, as is claimed, in conditions that are those of its end and that this end must be sutured to the authority, won without argument, of the poem. Philosophy continues inasmuch as the positivisms are exhausted, and the Marxisms eviscerated; but also inasmuch as, in its contemporary force, poetry itself enjoins us to unburden it of all identifying rivalry with philosophy, to undo the false couple of the saying of the poem and the thinking of the philosopher. Because this couple of saying and thinking – forgetful of the ontological subtraction inaugurally inscribed by the matheme – is in fact that formed by the sermon of the end of philosophy and the romantic myth of authenticity.

That philosophy continues frees the poem, as singular operation of truth. What will become of the poem after Heidegger, after the age of poets, in other words, in what will a post-romantic poem consist? The poets will tell us, and they actually already have, since to de-suture philosophy and poetry, to leave Heidegger behind without returning to aesthetics, is also to think otherwise that from which the poem proceeds, to think it in its operative distance, and not in its myth.

Here are merely two indications:

1. When Mallarmé wrote, 'The moment of the Notion of an object is therefore the moment of the reflection of its pure present in itself or its present purity', what programme did he outline for the poem, once it is attached to the *production* of the Notion? The issue here is to determine the operations internal to language – those of separation, and isolation[2] – by which a 'present purity' can be *brought forth*, the coldness of what is present only insofar as it no longer has any presentable link to reality. It could be argued that poetry *is* a thought of the presence of the present. And that this is precisely the reason for which it is not in rivalry with philosophy, which is concerned with the compossibility of Time, and not with pure presence. Only the poem gathers the means to think the outside-place (*hors-lieu*), or the beyond of any place, to think 'on some vacant and superior surface' that which of the present resists reduction to reality, and to summon the eternity of its presence: 'A Constellation, icy with forgetting and desuetude'. That is, a presence that, far from contradicting the matheme, also implies 'the unique number that cannot be another'.

2. When Celan tells us,

> Wurfscheibe, mit
> Vorgesichten besternt,
> wirf dich
> aus dir hinaus

which can be translated as

> Cast-disc, with
> Forseeings bestarred
> cast yourself
> out your outside

in what does the intimacy of this intimation consist in? I understand it as follows: when the situation is saturated by its own norm, when its self-calculation is relentlessly inscribed in the norm, and when there is no longer any void between knowledge and prediction, it is necessary to be ready, *poetically*, for the outside-of-self. Because naming an event, in the sense I give to the latter, that is, that which, being an undecidable supplementation, must be named for a being-faithful, and therefore a truth, to occur – this naming is *always* poetic: to name a supplement, a chance, something incalculable, it is necessary to draw from the void of sense, in the absence of established significations, and to the peril of language. One must therefore poeticize, and the poetic name of the event is that which throws us outside of ourselves, through the flaming rings of prediction.

The poem, freed from all philosophical poeticizing, will no doubt have always consisted in these two thoughts, these two givings (*donations*): the presence of the present in the transfixion of realities; and the name of the event in a leap outside of calculable interests.

Nonetheless, we can and we must, we philosophers, leave the poets to look after the future of poetry beyond all that the hermeneutic concern of the philosophy has pressed on it. From the standpoint of philosophy, our singular task is instead to rethink its liaison or its de-liaison with the poem, that is, to think this relation neither in terms of Platonic banishment, nor of Heideggerian suture, nor with the classificatory concern of an Aristotle or a Hegel. What is it that, in the act and style of thought pertaining to philosophy, was from the very start founded on condition of the poem, and, at the same time, of the matheme, or of politics or of love? This is our question.

The moderns, and the postmoderns even more so, have readily exposed the supposed wound inflicted on philosophy by the specific modes through which poetry, literature and indeed art in general have borne witness to our modernity. Art, it is alleged, has always presented a challenge to the concept, and on the basis of this challenge, of this wound, we are asked to interpret the Platonic gesture as philosophy's need to banish the poets in order to establish its own royalty.

To my mind, there is nothing in such a gesture that is specific to poetry or to literature. Plato had equally to hold philosophical love, *philo-sophia*, at a distance from real love, which is caught in the malaise of desire for an object. He also had to hold the real politics of Athenian democracy at a distance in order to forge the philosophical concept of *politeia*. He likewise had to assert the distance and supremacy of the dialectic with regard to mathematical *dianoia*. Poem, matheme, politics and love – all of them at once condition and offend philosophy. Condition and offence: that's how it is.

Philosophy wants to and must be established in this subtractive point where language, divested of the prestige, or mimetic incitement, of images, of fiction and of narrative, is consigned to thought; where the principle of amorous intensity is unlinked from the alterity of the object and is supported upon the law of the Same; where the illumination of the Principle pacifies the blind violence that is implicit in the axioms and hypotheses of mathematics; and where, finally, the collective is represented in its symbol, and not in the excessive real of political situations.

Philosophy *is* under the conditions of art, science, politics and love, but it is always gnawed at, wounded, indented by the eventual and singular character of its conditions. Nothing about this contingent occurrence pleases it. Why?

Explaining philosophy's displeasure at the reality of its conditions presumes that we hold that at the core of its disposition lies a distinction between truth and sense. Were philosophy only obliged to *interpret* its conditions, were its destiny hermeneutic, it would gain pleasure from turning back towards its conditions, and from saying, interminably: such is the sense of what occurs in poetic work, in the mathematical theorem, in the loving encounter and in political revolution. Philosophy would then consist in the tranquil aggregate of an aesthetics, an epistemology, an erotology and a political sociology. This temptation is very old, and when one yields to it, philosophy is placed in a section of what Lacan called the discourse of the University.

However 'philosophy' begins when this aggregate is proven inconsistent. When the stake is no longer to interpret the real procedures in which truth resides, but to found a unique place where, under the contemporary conditions of these procedures, is it stated how and why a truth is, not a sense but rather, a *hole in sense*. This 'how' and this 'why' – the foundations of a place for thinking under conditions – are only practical in the displeasure involved in refusing givenness and hermeneutics. They require the primordial defection of the givenness of sense, an absense, an abnegation regarding sense. Or again an indecency. They presuppose that the truth procedures be subtracted from the eventual singularity that weaves them in the real, and that knots them to sense in the mode of traversing the latter, of hollowing it out. They therefore presuppose that the truth procedures be disengaged from their subjective escort, including from the object–pleasure they afford.

CONDITIONS

As such philosophy will:

- Envisage love solely according to the truth that hatches on the Two of sexuation, and on the Two *tout court*. But without the tension of pleasure–displeasure kept in play by the love–object.
- Envisage politics as truth of the infinite of collective situations, as a treatment in truth of this infinite, but without the enthusiasm or sublimity of these situations themselves.
- Envisage mathematics as a truth of multiple-being in and through the letter, as a power of literalization, but without the intellectual beatitude of the resolved problem.
- And last envisage the poem as a truth of sensible presence lodged in rhythm and image but without the corporeal captation of rhythm and image.

What produces philosophy's constitutive displeasure with regard to its conditions, the poem and its other conditions alike, is to have to *depose*, along with sense, the enjoyment (*jouissance*) that is determined there, at the very point where a truth occurs as a hole in the sense-making of knowledge.

Regarding the particular case of the literary act, whose kernel is the poem; what is the ever offended and recalcitrant procedure of this deposition?

The relation is all the more closer as philosophy is an effect of language. The literary is specified for philosophy as fiction, as comparison, image or rhythm and as narrative.

The deposition here takes the figure of a *placement*.

Philosophy certainly makes use, within the texture of its exposition, of fictive incarnations.[3] Thus, we have the characters of Plato's dialogues and the staging of their encounter. Or the interview Malebranche staged between a Christian philosopher and an improbable Chinese philosopher. Or the epic and novelistic singularity of Nietzsche's Zarathustra, a work that is borne along by the fiction of a character to such an extent that, in a text that is perhaps a little too hermeneutic, Heidegger was able to ask: 'Who is Nietzsche's Zarathustra?'

Philosophy exploits image, comparison and rhythm. The image of the sun served to expose to the day something of the presence that is essentially *withdrawn* in the Idea of the Good. And who is not aware of the marvellous paragraph 67 of Leibniz's *Monadology*, filled with cadences and alliterations: 'each portion of matter may be conceived as a garden full of plants, and like a pond full of fish. But each branch of the plant, each member of the animal, each drop of its humours is again such a garden or such a pond'?

Philosophy, finally, exploits narrative, fable and parable. Plato concluded his *Republic* with the myth of Er. Hegel's *History of Philosophy* is in many respects a monumental narrative and recital of the major subjective entities named the 'Orient', 'Greece' and 'Rome'. And 'Zarathustra, dying, holds the earth embraced'.

However, these occurrences of the literary are, as such, under the jurisdiction of a principle of thought that they themselves do not constitute. They are localized at points where, to complete the establishment of the site in which it is stated how and why it is that truth hollows out sense and escapes interpretation, it is necessary, by a paradox of exposition, to suggest a fable, an image or a fiction, to interpretation itself.

In the truth-procedures conditioning it, philosophy subtracts from the *aura* of sense, from all trembling and all pathos, to seize the *proving of truth* as such. But there is a moment in which it falls on the radical underside of all sense, into the void of all possible presentation, into the hollowing of truth as a hole *without borders*. This is the moment at which the void and ab-sense, such as philosophy ineluctably encounters them in the point at which truth transpires, must themselves be presented and transmitted.

The poem occurs in philosophy when, in its will to universal address, in its vocation to have the place that it edifies inhabited by all, it is enjoined to suggest to sense and interpretation the latent void that sutures all truth to the being of that which it is the truth of. This presentation of the unpresentable void in language requires a deployment of literary resources. But this is on the condition that this deploying is carried out at this very point; and therefore under the general jurisdiction of a completely different style – a style of argumentation, of conceptual liaison or of the Idea.

The poem occurs in philosophy *at one of its points*, and this localization is never fixed by any poetic or literary principle. It depends on the moment at which the argument places the unpresentable, and at which, with a torsion prescribed by the argument, the nudity of operations of the true is only transmissible by an always immoderate return to the pleasure of sense, which is always also a pleasure of the senses. The literary in philosophy is the vectoring, in an effect of sense, of the fact that the relation of a truth to sense is a defective, emptied relation. It is this defectiveness that exposes philosophy to the imperative of a localized fiction. The moment at which argumentation fails (*défailler*), imitates, in the power of argument itself, this: that truth causes knowledge to fail (*en défaillance*).

It is hardly surprising that in these conditions the best-known philosophical poem is by an author for whom the Void as such is the original principle of every uncompromising materialism. I am, of course, referring to Lucretius. For Lucretius, all truth is established as a combination of marks, from a rain of letters, of atoms, in the pure unpresentable that is the void. It is a philosophy that is especially subtracted from sense, and is especially disappointing to the enjoyment of interpretation. Moreover, it is a philosophy that resists all attempts to incorporate it into the Heideggerian schema of metaphysics. There is nothing onto-theological about it; for Lucretius, there is no Supreme Being, the heavens are empty and the gods are indifferent. Is it not remarkable that the only thinker who also happens to be a great poet also causes the Heideggerian historical assemblage to falter, and takes the history of being through a disseminated multiplicity that is entirely foreign to what Heidegger told us about metaphysics after Plato? Is it not symptomatic that this singular fusion of the poem and philosophy, unique in history, is precisely and wholly foreign to the schema under which Heidegger conceived the correlation of poem and thought? Nevertheless, it is this materialist, neuter thought, one entirely oriented towards the deposition of the imaginary, and hostile to the unanalysed effect of presence, that requires the prestige of the poem in order to present itself.

Lucretius buttressed his philosophy right throughout with the poem, and for the very reason that would have seemingly had him engage in banishing it in the Platonic manner. This is because his sole principle is material dissemination. Because it exposes as place for the proving of the true the most radical de-fection of sacred bonds.

At the beginning of Book 4 of *De rerum natura*, which should be translated as 'Of the real of multiple-being', Lucretius undertook, *pace* Plato if you will, to argue that the poem was an expository imperative of his philosophy. What are his arguments? The three main ones are: First, the book treats, said Lucretius, of an 'obscure thing', and the presentation of this obscurity of being requires the light shed in and by language, by the luminosity of a poem's verses: '*obscura de re tam lucida pango carmina*'.

Next, Lucretius sets himself to disengage the mind from the tight bonds of religion. To bring about this unbinding, this subtraction from the sense with which religion is continually brimming over, what is needed is a power of saying, some sort of prestige, such as that lavished upon us by the graces of the Muse. Last, the bare truth, prior to the occupation of its place, appears essentially sad. For most people, the place of philosophy, the place of the proving of the true is, as seen *from afar*, melancholic. Its deposition of pleasure needs to be buttressed by a supernumerary and secondary pleasure, one coated, said Lucretius, in 'sweet poetic honey'.

The poem therefore occurs, this time, in order to reopen the entirety of philosophical exposition, the entire philosophical address *to* the universal occupation of its place. It does so under the triple injunction of the melancholy of truths as seen from afar, or, said Lucretius, 'as yet unpractised'; of the unbinding, or subtraction from sense, which obliterates religion; and, finally, of the obscure, the heart of which is the unpresentable void, that occurs within transmission via the razing light of its glorious linguistic body.

But that which maintains in these injunctions a firm gap between philosophy and poetry insists. For the position occupied by the charms of language and verse is purely supplemental. They escort its will to be transmitted. They are therefore always and forever localized, prescribed. The real law of the proposal is rational and constructive argument, such as Lucretius inherited it from Epicurus. Lucretius explained why – it's nearly an excuse – he had recourse to the poem, whose referent is the one being addressed, and who needs to be persuaded that the sadness of the true seen from afar transforms into the joy of being when seen from up close. When it is a question of Epicurus, what is required was no longer legitimation but pure and simple praise. The poem must be excused, the argument praised. The gap remains, essential.

The reason is that the poem is exhibited as an imperative in language, and in so doing it *produces* truths. By no means does philosophy produce them. It presupposes and subtractively distributes them according to their specific regime of separation from sense. Philosophy only calls on the poem for its own purposes when this separation has to show what the argument framing and bordering it can maintain only by returning to what it was that made it possible: the actual singularity of a truth procedure, a singularity that is immersed in the pool, is in the layers, in the springs of sense.

CONDITIONS

The poem is summoned by philosophy when it must *also* say, as Lucretius expressed it: 'I voyage through unvisited places in the domain of the Pierides, never before trodden, I love to go and draw water from virgin springs'.

The poem comes to mark the moment of the empty page at which the argument goes on, has gone on and will go on. This void, this empty page, is not 'all is thinkable'. On the contrary, under a rigorously circum-scribed poetic mark, it is a way of saying in philosophy that at least one truth, elsewhere, but real, exists, and to draw from this observation, against the melancholy of those who look at it from afar, the most joyous consequences.

CHAPTER FIVE
Mallarmé's Method: Subtraction and Isolation

1. *HUSHED TO THE CRUSHING CLOUD*
   [*A LA NUE ACCABLANTE TU*]

Mallarmé indicated, straight and to the point, that his method, his logic, are the things of which the poem inscribes the absence or hush. The poem is a 'stilled, melodic encipherment, of the combinations of motifs that compose a logic'. Let us say that the poem, as an exercise of thought, subtracts (and it is the *act* of this subtraction) the thought of this thought. Henceforth, the poem's complexity possesses two sources:

1. the unapparent character of what governs it;
2. the multiplicity of subtractive operations, which are by no means to be confounded with the (dialectical?) simplicity of negation. Indeed, I will show that Mallarmé's work contains *three* types of negation: vanishing, cancelling and foreclosure.

The guiding thread for clarification will be syntactic, and is not of the province of interpretation or of semantics. On this point, Mallarmé was formal: 'What pivot, in these contrasts, am I assuming for intelligibility? We need a guarantee. – Syntax'.

In appropriating the Mallarméan poem at a philosophical level, which presupposes that the absence be restituted (i.e., the thinking, under the sign of Truth, of the operations of a thought), I shall always begin with a 'translation', a sort of 'review from scratch', or punctuation, of the poem's syntactic unfolding.

CONDITIONS

Consider the following poem:

> Hushed to the crushing cloud
> Basalt and lava its form
> Even to echoes subdued
> By an ineffectual horn
>
> What shipwreck sepulchral has bowed
> (You know this, but slobber on, foam)
> The mast, supreme in a crowd
> Of flotsam and jetsam, though torn
>
> Or will that which in fury defaulted
> From some perdition exalted
> (The vain abyss outspread)
>
> Having stingily drowned in the swirl
> Of a white hair's trailing thread
> The flank of a young Siren girl.[1]

So, to start with, here is a reconstruction, for philosophy, a hypothesis guided by grammatical construction.

- That the 'tu' of the first line, rendered in English here by 'hushed', is the past participle of the verb 'taire' (to be silent), and is to be related to the shipwreck (what shipwreck, silent in the sea, has abolished the mast that lost its sails?).[2]
- That 'by an ineffectual horn' refers to the participle (what shipwreck was silenced in the sea as a result of an ineffectual horn?).
- That the second quatrain forms a question (what shipwreck . . .?).
- That in the tercets we should see a comma after fury, as well as after exalted (fury, defaulted from some perdition exalted, the vain abyss).
- That 'fury' describes the abyss, which is guilty of having drowned the young Siren as a result of its terror.

By submitting to these guidelines, the only ones that allow all the material to be integrated, we arrive at a first reconstruction in which the poem is withdrawn from poetry and rendered in its latent prose, enabling philosophy to *return* to it from prose for its own ends:

> What shipwreck, then, has engulfed even the mast and torn sails that were the last remnants of a ship? On the ocean we see the foam, which is the trace of this disaster, and which knows about it but says nothing. The ship's horn, which might have alerted us, could not make itself heard; it was powerless to do so on this low sky and sombre sea, which, the colour of volcanic rock, imprisoned the possible echo of a distress call.

> Unless, furious at not having had any ship to make disappear, the abyss (sky and sea) swallowed a Siren, of which the white foam would be no more than a trailing hair.

Everything begins with an attestation of difference: there is the place, the situation, a merging of sea and sky. And there is the foam, which is the trace (the name), in the place, of a having-taken-place (of an event). The poem has to *treat* the trace, has to remain faithful to it.

The trace (the foam) is a sort of name that knows ('you know this') but that obliterates this knowledge ('but slobber on'). The poem is therefore obliged to *name the name*, that is, to assert the name as an evental naming. It works towards this by means of two hypotheses that are separated by an 'or will that which': (i) the foam is the trace of the sinking of a ship in this place; (ii) and the foam is the trace of a siren's dive.

On the basis of the foam, which supplements the nudity of place, 'ship' and 'siren' become two vanishing terms. They leave the mark of the first subtractive operation, that of the event itself, insofar as it is only ever given as abolished. The foam is what occurs only so as to name this abolishing. The ship is implied by the sinking, the siren by the dive, or the drowning.

To underline that the name of the event can only be implied from its disappearance, Mallarmé then composes metonymic chains, built upon the vanishing term liable to give body to this disappearing, which pare the supposed body back to the edges of inexistence. The ship is evoked only by the abolition not even of it as a whole but of its mast, its last piece of wreckage, and by the hypothetical call of an inaudible horn. The siren is resolved into her own childhood tresses, which in the end is but a single, white hair.

CONDITIONS

If we agree to mark by crossing out with a stroke the subtractive action of the vanishing of the term deemed supernumerary to the place (the ship-event, the siren-event), then the two chains interrupted by the 'or will that which' can be presented as follows:

foam $\begin{cases} \text{~~ship~~ (bit of wreckage)} \to \text{~~mast~~ (torn and abolished)} \to \text{~~horn~~ (ineffectual)} \\ \text{~~siren~~ (drowned)} \to \text{hair} \end{cases}$

These vanishing terms possess all the characteristics of evental naming[3]:

- that there are two of them places them in the element of the undecidable (this, or else that);
- they convoke the void of the place or the situation, that is, its being *qua* being: the ship is sunk and the siren 'stingily' drowned, as if the terms maintained their effect in their resorption in the empty depths of the marine abyss, whose surface they are on in the undecidable foam, the disappearing delegation.

However, that there are *two* hypotheses, two vanishings to peg the trace (i.e., the foam) to the disappearing of the having-taken-place is not simply, for Mallarmé, a symbol of the undecidable. The introduction of the siren in fact presumes a second negation *that is not of the same type as the first*. To be sure, the ship, in the perhaps-not-having-taken-place of its sinking, supplements the place twice over: it is stripped of its sails by the sinking, and its horn is extinguished (which is already a siren, but a warning siren), so that even its last piece of wreckage is abolished; but afterwards the shipwreck itself (and not only the ship) is also put into question. Perhaps it was actually a siren. The first subtraction figures the vanishing of the supposed evental term under the foam that re-traces it. The second *cancels out this vanishing itself*. And, on the basis of this cancelling-out, the second and final vanishing term (the siren) springs up.

Thus the second term is inscribed through the absenting of the first, which constitutes a radical lack insofar as it bears, not on the term (the ship), but on its disappearance (the sinking, the ship). The 'Or will that which' proceeds to abolish the abolished, and thus marks the undecidability of the event by means of a scission that cancels its hypothesis.

If the event character of the event *is* its undecidable character, all vanishing (the first subtraction, the pure event given by the primitive name 'the foam') must also be suspended. This second subtraction, which is a sort of subtraction from subtraction itself, I shall term *cancelling*.

That which took place, the ship, must fail in its having-taken-place, that is if the poem is the thought of the event *as such*. Then, along comes the siren, as ideal, which is the event established in its evental character insofar as it has undergone the trial of the vanishing of its vanishing (*l'évanoui de son évanouir*). This is the only way in which the poem can give us the donation of the event *with its undecidability*. Last, to the vanishing subtraction of the event cancellation *adds* the need to decide its name. And how to stage this decision poetically other than to revoke the first supposed name, and to mark it syntactically ('or will that which') by a *choice*?

So, this poem thinks the thought of the event by placing a name that is still lacking in concept (the foam) – thus keeping us in the suspense of not knowing whether the void of the place was really convoked in its being – in support of a pure choice at an undecidable point between two vanishing terms, terms – here the ship and the siren – that are necessary in order to seize the having-taken-place. Cancelling is the crossing-out of evental vanishing with a choice that is entailed by the constitutive undecidability of that which, for the time a disappearing takes, came to supplement the atony of place.

2. *HER PURE NAILS ON HIGH* [*SES PURS ONGLES TRÈS HAUT*]

Subtraction will always have its emblem in a poem that Mallarmé was rather proud of, which he described both as a 'sonnet which was empty and reflecting itself in all possible ways' and as – this was the title of the first version – an 'allegorical sonnet of itself'.

This is because in 'Her pure nails on high', which is devoted as usual to thinking the pure event on the basis of its decided trace (*trace decidé*), each of the subtractive operations is deployed, and, as it thereby adds foreclosure to vanishing and cancellation, it brings us to the theme of the unnameable.[4]

CONDITIONS

Without going into the syntactical constraints, I have presented the poem here followed by its prose preparation to open it to a first *seizing*:

> With her pure nails offering their onyx high,
> lampbearer agony tonight sustains
> many a vesperal fantasy burned by
> the Phoenix, which no funerary urn contains
>
> on the empty room's credences: no ptyx,
> abolished bauble, sonorous inanity
> (Master has gone to draw tears from the Styx
> with that one thing, the Void's sole source of vanity).
>
> Yet near the vacant northward casement dies
> a gold possibly from the decorations
> of unicorns lashing a nymph with flame;
>
> dead, naked in the mirror she lies
> though the oblivion bounded by that frame
> now spans a fixed septet of scintillations.[5]

In an empty room, at midnight, agony alone prevails, fuelled by the disappearance of the light. Such is the torch in the form of raised hands, which bear only an extinguished flame, that the anguish of the void cannot be cured by any trace of the setting sun, not even by the ashes that might have been gathered in a funerary urn.

The poet, as master of places, has departed for the river of death, taking with him a signifier (the ptyx) which does not refer to any existing object.

However, near the window facing out to the north, the gilded frame of a mirror shines, very weakly, in which sculpted forms of unicorns chasing nymphs can be made out.

All of this disappears, as if the nymph was drowned in the water of the mirror, and then in its reflection the seven stars of The Plough suddenly appear.

The event suggested in the poem is obviously the setting of the sun, that 'vesperal dream' that is the most often used metaphor for disappearing as such in Mallarmé's work. The whole sonnet is devoted to finding and treating in the place itself (no longer the sea and sky but an empty room) the traces of this glorious vanishing, which I call the primitive names of the event, and which are themselves supports of the indecidable (as the foam was in the previous poem).

This time the poem's extreme complexity results from the fact that the two quatrains deal not with a given trace *but with the apparent absence of any* trace. Here we clearly see that there is no total power of naming a pure event, since this power falls under a restriction: concerning evental disappearing, it may be that there is something in the place or situation that is so *withdrawn* as to be simply unnameable.

We are already familiar with the underlying logic of vanishing and cancellation that is exhibited in the tercets. Let us start, then, with what follows the 'but' assigned to dissipate the anguish of the unnameable.

The setting sun is the event at the limits of day and of night. There is a first metaphorization of it within the situation (the empty room) in the division of the mirror: a gilded frame with unicorns on one side and a dark mirror on the other. The gilded frame is like the vanishing sun of which the mirror is the night. The agony of the frame's gold leads on to the nymph, which is a properly disappearing divisibility. Pursued by the flame of the unicorns from the frame, she plunges, this new siren, into the night of the mirror. In order to confirm the undecidability of the event, this exemplary vanishing in turn also ends up vanishing. The nymph would also have been totally done away with in the mirror ('dead naked'), were it not for the appearance of the reflection of a constellation, which is very classically introduced by 'though' (i.e., by using the cancellation method).

Limiting ourselves to the tercets, then, we have:

- The primitive support in which what is at stake is the naming of the sun-event, that is, the mirror.
- A first vanishing term, a first attempt at naming, that is, the nymph.
- A second term that is related to the first by the cancellation of its disappearing, and that from then on 'fixes' a possible nocturnal fidelity to the event: the constellation.
- In this way we are given the sun-event, which is supernumerary to the emptiness of the room, via the decision of the star, and this decision, which cancels that of the nymph, points to the undecidable.

CONDITIONS

On this basis what does the long preparation of the quatrains signify?

By contrast to the poems that immediately supplement the place for us with a primitive name (sea + foam), this sonnet starts with a fruitless inspection of the place, and only late in the piece is a mirror found, whereby it becomes possible to go beyond the objective nullity of the place. We clearly see that in their succession the urn (funerary), the master (at the Styx) and the (inexistent) ptyx create a sort of threefold 'ban' of the subtractive. The first contains only ashes, the second is dead and the third is a word that says no word. But, above all, *not one of them is there*, not one is attestable *within* the situation: there is 'no funerary urn', the 'Master is gone' and there is 'no ptyx'. These entities are the stuff of vanishing terms (or evental namings), since they only have being in designating non-being. Nevertheless, they are unable to vanish, since, as they are modified in the place by radical *absence*; they lack any nameable effect. In this they differ fundamentally both from the supposed boat, which was inferred from the foam, and from the mirror that can be made out in the penumbra. These entities *do not trace anything*; all they do is lack.

One cannot maintain that any of these terms are, like the nymph (or the ship), affected by cancellation. Because if a vanishing term is to be cancelled, and its subtraction is to serve to present the undecidable, it also needs to bear a relation to a trace (the foam, the mirror), the cancellation of which indicates that it supports *another* nominal advent, that is, the siren or the constellation.

The urn, the master and the ptyx – these terms have all the attributes of a vanishing term, with the exception of the supposed act of vanishing, which alone bestows on them a capacity to recall the event. They also have all the attributes of the cancelled-out term, except that what is cancelled out is only that which, at the point of the indecidable, might have been supposed to be a vanishing term.

Or again: by contrast to the siren that came to be in the place of the ship, and the constellation that came to be in the place of the nymph, no other term can come to be in the place of these terms. They have the property of being *unsubstitutable*.

These terms, then, must be assigned a totally different subtractive function, which is not that of vanishing, as echo of the event, nor that of cancellation by decision, as echo of undecidability. I put forward that what these terms perform is a foreclosure: they indicate *that the power of the truth distributed by the event in a situation does not exhaust all of this situation*. What is foreclosed from this power is that there is any such thing as the 'subtracted' per se, any unqualifiable lack, or even anything that the faithful marking of the event, the constellation that forms the trace of the sun-event, could ever visit and name.

If the primitive terms (foam, mirror) are the stakes of marking the event, of designating its site; if the first vanishing terms (ship, nymph) effectuate this marking itself in subtractive fashion; if, finally, the terms issuing from cancellation (siren, constellation) point to undecidability, and launch victorious thinking (i.e., truth), then the terms in foreclosure comprise a halting point; they exhibit, in the place *as absence to self*, a zone that is that *of the unnameable*.

It follows that in the poetic complexity of subtractive operations we must distinguish between:

- vanishing, whose value lies in marking;
- cancellation, which avers the undecidable and sustains the truth;
- foreclosure, which points to the unnameable, and fixes the uncrossable limit of a truth-process.

What does this poem tell us then regarding the 'content' of the unnameable, metaphorically rendered as radical lack (as that which is subtracted from seizure by any post-evental truth)?

The Master (the poet) is 'at the Styx', clearly indicating that, in the absence to self of the place, he is a figure of the subject's subtraction. That every poem, in establishing its place, is paid for by subtracting its subject is a veritable theorem in Mallarmé's work: 'The right to accomplish anything exceptional, or beyond the reach of the vulgar, is paid for by the omission of the doer, and of his death as so-and-so'. Foreclosure here declares that at the locus of the poem the poet will remain unnamed. And, more generally, that from the interior of a truth process the subject of this process is unnameable.

There is no 'funerary urn'. This time subtraction applies to death. The affirmative power of a truth, such as it is supported by the constellation on the vanished condition of the sun-event, comes up against death as that which is never *there*.

Last, the pytx is simultaneously an 'abolished bauble, [a] sonorous inanity', and thus a pure signifier without signification, and 'the Void's sole source of vanity', and thus a materiality without referent, an object without object. Here the point is clearly one about language itself, about the poetics of the poem, which has no guarantee apart from language itself, no attestable referent corresponding to its not-all, and comprises a Nothingness on which its gap is supported.

In this way, the foreclosed terms declare that the unnameable can be stated either as subject, as death or as language. Victorious as it may be in the mirror in which it rescues the situation from forgetting what came to be in it, a poetic truth cannot force the statement into saying either the subject that it infers (the poet), the cessation it prepares (death) or the material that it contracts (language 'in itself').

To conclude: that these terms cannot be substituted tells us that at the locus of the unnameable a singularity remains that no metaphor could ever sublate.

3. *PROSE (FOR DES ESSEINTES)*

These three subtractive operations (vanishing, cancellation and foreclosure) and these three objects of thought (the event, the undecidable and the unnameable) do not set the ultimate stakes of the poem but instead form its conditions (something must take place which is not the place) and its limits (not everything is incorporated within the statement [*dire*]). The final question is that of the truth, or of the Idea or Notion, whose advent supposes schemas of rupture and singularization that cannot be rendered solely by a negative dialectic.

Let us first dispel some misconceptions as to what is at stake in a poem. A poem does not at all involve doubling the world with ill-assorted, consoling imaginings: 'Modern man disdains the imagination', and the gesture of the poet, having attained the sojourn of truth, is to 'keep it from dream, that enemy of his trust'.

The idea that what the poem transmits is the Presence of a nature is also to be dismissed. 'Nature has taken place; it can't be added to', and 'the cool morning [. . .] no sound of water but my flute's outpourings murmurs' – these two phrases give us to understand that no natural ecstasy exists that stands up to the challenge of poetic production.

Last, Mallarmé's poetry has nothing of subjective confidings: this is because, as we have seen, the subject is in the position of unnameable.

Mallarmé's poetry is therefore neither elegiac, nor hymnic, nor lyrical. What does it stand up and deliver? Mallarmé said it explicitly: the stake of poetry is the Notion, the metaphor of which is also the Number. But what is a notion? 'The moment the notion of an object is [. . .] the moment of reflection of its pure present in itself or its present purity.' The characteristic attribute of the notion is its *purity*. The stake of poetry is to attain the pure; the poetic machine is subtractive only with a view to a purification.

The quotes that follow, chosen from among many others, stand in confirmation of the point:

- the Number of the dice throw, which only has a chance of being repeated if it is 'a product of the stars';
- '[t]he pure vase of any drink';
- '[t]he most pure sense' that the poet gives to the 'phrases of the crowd';
- the 'virgin hero of posthumous expectation';
- the 'sheer gleam' of the Swan;
- and in the notes for the last part of 'Igitur': 'With Nothingness gone, all that remains is the castle of purity'.

But what is purity? It consists, I would argue, in the composition of an Idea that as such is no longer retained in any bond. This is an idea that captures being's indifference to every relation, that captures its separated scintillation, its multiplicity without Whole. This is the idea's coldness ('cold with forgetting and desuetude'), its disjunction, the emblem of which is the sea that 'becomes disjoined, properly speaking, from nature', and its virginity, in the sense of a separating whiteness, of a probative cut, such as in the famous text where the pure Two of the white (before writing and after writing) provides the only proof of the Idea: 'It is a virginity which solitarily, before the transparency of an adequate look, divides all by itself into fragments of candour, nuptial proofs of the Idea'.

As assembled by the poem that brings it forth, the Notion's purity designates above all else the un-linked (*dé-liée*) aspect of being, the non-actual character of every law, of every pact that binds and re-binds. The poem states that the condition of being is not to be in relation with anything ('Nothing, this foam, virginal verse'). The heroism of the thought–poem can be put in three words: (i) the negation of all natural relations; (ii) the obstacle to be overcome, which is itself a subject revealed in its anguish at the non-relation; (iii) the victorious coming forth of the Idea. In three words which establish the verse's impress: 'solitude, reef, star'; 'night and despair and precious stone'; Diamond, star, swan, 'a rose in the dark'. . . Extirpated from the rule of the relation, subtracted as much from nature as from the pathos of consciousness, placed on a background of nothingness, facing the latent void of the pure multiple, being shines—distant, but measurable *in truth*. Seized by the poem's operation, the purity of being, like that of the dancer's gesture, yields 'the nudity of your concepts', and writes 'your vision' 'like a sign, which she is'.

This seizing presumes, in addition to the major subtractive operations that set out the evental conditions for all thought, the implementation of schemas of rupture, whose sum effect is to break with the links in which the poem's starting point is enchained, to undo the representational illusion of natural relations or conventional relationships.

There are two main schemas of this type: *separation* and *isolation*.

The first, separation, consists in cutting out, from within the apparent spatial and temporal continuity of experience, a multiple that is 'enclosed when manifest', a sort of scene in which all that belongs to it can be inventoried and enumerated. In this way we go from the hybrid consciousness of the relation to the purified consciousness of a simple enumeration, of a detotalized multiple.

The second, isolation, consists in bringing forth a contour of nothingness that extirpates the given from any nearness to that which it is not, from all relations of proximity. This enables us to pass from the counted or consistent multiple to pure multiple-being, to that which is subtracted from the count, inexistent, a power of ontological purity.

We might say that separation is a schema of algebraic rupture (it undoes the law of relation to yield a countable juxtaposition), while isolation is topological (it suppresses proximities and connections that work 'by contact', or simple succession).

Isolation (the numerical place, the multiple-scene of which is determined by separation) is the supreme operation of Mallarmean poetics, conceived as a project of truth. It is the operation that yields the Idea, and Mallarmé was perfectly aware of it: 'Poetry [. . .] attempts hidden chaste crises of isolation, while the other gestation takes place'. Isolation is what defines verse, which 'achieves that isolation of speech' and negates 'with a sovereign blow, the arbitrariness that remains in the terms'. After describing his poetry as 'a solemn stir of words [*that*] stay alive in the air', Mallarmé could not have given Gautier greater homage than by adding that it is what the 'diaphanous gaze [. . .] isolates in the hour and radiance of day'. And also for having clearly seen that what is thus isolated is nothing other than a truth: 'already within these true groves we stay'.

To succeed in isolating a 'fragment of candour' is what is required of the poem in the Idea's service.

I will now point out the related functions of separation and isolation as they are conveyed in that genuine Mallarmean poetical art that is *Prose (for des Esseintes)*. Here is the poem:

> Hyperbole! can you not rise
> from my memory triumph-crowned,
> today a magic scrawl which lies
> in a book that is iron-bound:
>
> for by my science I instil
> the hymn of spiritual hearts
> in the work of my patient will,
> atlases, herbals, sacred arts.
>
> Sister, we strolled and set our faces
> (we were two, so my mind declares)
> toward various scenic places,
> comparing your own charms with theirs.
>
> The reign of confidence grows troubled
> when, for no reason, it is stated
> of this noon region, which our doubled
> unconsciousness has penetrated,
>
> that its site, soil of hundredfold
> irises (was it real? how well
> they know) bears no name that the gold
> trumpet of Summertime can tell.
>
> Yes, in an isle the air had charged
> not with mere visions but with sight
> every flower spread out enlarged
> at no word that we could recite.

CONDITIONS

> And so immense they were, that each
> was usually garlanded
> with a clear contour, and this breach
> parted it from the garden bed.
>
> Ideas, glory of long desire,
> all within me rejoiced to see
> the irid family aspire
> to this new responsibility,
>
> but Sister, a wise comforter,
> carried her glance no further than
> a smile and, as if heeding her,
> I labour on my ancient plan.
>
> Let the litigious Spirit know,
> as we are silent at this season,
> the manifold lilies' stem would grow
> to a size far beyond our reason
>
> not as the shore in drearisome
> sport weeps when it is fraudulent,
> claiming abundance should have come
> in my initial wonderment
>
> hearing the heavens and map that gave
> endless evidence close at hand,
> by the very receding wave,
> that there was never such a land.
>
> The child, already dexterous
> in the ways, sheds her ecstasy
> and utters 'Anastasius!'
> born for scrolls of eternity
>
> before a sepulchre chuckles 'Ha!'
> beneath its forebear any sky
> to bear the name 'Pulcheria!'
> veiled by too tall gladioli.[6]

To open this poem to philosophical seizing before restoring it to the closed immanence of its operations, it will suffice by way of prosodic preparation to take a passage as is from Gardner Davies, who, in accordance with an expression he borrowed from Mallarmé, deployed its 'layer of intelligibility' (*couche suffisante d'intelligibilité*).[7] Here is his recapitulative summary:

In the first line, the poet calls upon hyperbole, a figure of discourse very familiar to him, to call forth from memory a cabalistic expression, one worthy of figuring in an old book of magic with metal binding. This is because the poet, in the patient labour that is his and that he likens to the compilation of an atlas, herbariums, and rituals, is applying himself scientifically to translating the exaltation of idealist elans. Here we have the statement announcing the poem's theme. Memory furnishes him with the reminiscence of a pleasant summertime walk that was had in the company of his younger sister in a lovely countryside of comparable beauty to the young woman's charms. They become anxious, those who claim to know everything and have authority over children, when they hear these latter say, in all innocence, that this place of innumerable flowers, which their imaginations have explored in unison, has no name and so cannot be put about by cheap publicity. But indeed, on this imaginary island, whose air favours the penetrating gaze to the flash of objects, each flower did grow to enormous proportions, coming to be surrounded by an aureole of light that made them distinct from any garden flower. In keeping with his long-standing desire to attain the level of Ideas, the poet rejoices to see the irises fulfil this new function. A wise comforter, the child continues to stare at him smiling, while the poet takes care to return the child a carefully measured, ingenuous look. The poet at once asserts, in anticipation of quibbling objections, that in this shared silence the stems of these supernatural flowers grew way beyond the limits of human reason. This growth, he adds, is not cumulative in the manner of waves crashing on the beach: such a monotonously repetitive game would never have been able to introduce the notion of magnitude into his mind, astonished at the endless appeals made to the heavens, maps, and even waves surrounding the island trying to prove it never existed. The young girl emerges from her ecstatic silence and, calling on all the science at her disposal, pronounces the word that is destined to take place in the pages of the eternal grimoire *Anastase* – resurrection. She makes this revelation before at any time there existed a tomb, not under any sky, that bore the inscription *Pulcherie* – the beauty from which she issues – which in any case is dissimulated by the symbolic presence of one of the giant flowers.

Thus reworked into pre-philosophical prose, we can return to the poem and open it up by way of five punctuations, all of which aim to discern the use of schemas of rupture – of separation and isolation – that break with the appearance of relations (*liens*) and bring forth the star of being.

1. At the start of the poem, whose programme is laid out in the first two stanzas, we come across a crucial distinction between science, which 'instils the hymn', and 'patience'. Patience is a kind of labour wherein ('in the work of my patient will') a revelation comes to pass.

Patience is rendered specially with an 'encyclopaedic' metaphor, making it that much easier to decipher it as knowledge (in opposition to what poetic science contains of truth): 'altases, herbals, sacred arts' designate lexical, classified knowledge, that is, multiples as bound and totalized. By contrast, the poetical truth of science is likened to the creative formulas of alchemy, to the grimoire. And, as we see at the poem's end, a single word, 'Anastase', suffices to rescue the pure Idea of beauty for eternity. This single term is separated out from a background of long-standing and entangled forms of knowledge; it cuts through their heavy liaisons, but it needs all the same to undertake the trajectory patiently. The sudden de-linking of being is in effect, even if chance is summoned, a *result*.

2. The experience resulting in the Idea requires a Two, which the poem defends against the implicit accusation of its uselessness ('(we were two, so my mind declares)') . It is clear that the Two is only actualized as an ecstatic and silent co-presence before the growth of the ideal flowers ('our doubled unconsciousness', 'at no word that we could recite', 'as we are silent this season', 'the child sheds her ecstasy'). For the poet, a subtle heightening of conscious impulse emerges ('all within me rejoiced') and, for the sister, a contemplative and smiling calmness ('carried no further than a smile'). It is, moreover, this taciturn calm that is the true path on which the purity of the Notion can be made to emerge, and the poet will have to exercise all his 'ancient care' if he is to follow his sister on this path. For, as we see in the Platonic analytic of love, the Two has no function other than to convoke the Idea on the basis of the sensible. Between the Two and the Idea there is no dialectic and no

debate. It is a dubious thing to rejoice, and vain to recite words, when, beyond all computational cognition, the infinite of the essential flower compels.

3. The passage from the 'scenic places' of the third stanza to the wholly established magical floral Place of the sixth puts both schemas of rupture to effect, specially that of separation. This transformation creates the multiple within which the star of being will come forth, suspended from the chance of an utterance. It prepares the isolation of the Idea.

The initial multiple, the memory of a childhood promenade, is vague, continuous, related and uncircumscribed. Moreover, it is bound, compared and commented: 'towards various scenic places, Sister, comparing your own charm with theirs'. The fifth stanza will circumscribe it and firmly number it ('soil of hundredfold'), at the same time as it subtracts it from all encyclopaedic access, from any seizure in terms of knowledge, because it deprives it of every known name, or at least of every pronounceable name ('no name that the gold trumpet of Summertime can tell'). The flowers, which fill out the whole site – and therefore mark out a stage where nothing is left in the shadows – err among names: 'iris', then 'every flower', then 'manifold lilies', then 'gladioli'. This is because at issue is to establish an intelligible Place, a pure multiple, naturally one drawn and composed in the light ('sight' and not 'visions'), but that is also not related, nor relatable, to any possible empirical configuration.

Here separation combines the resources of number ('a hundred irises', 'manifold lilies'), of the self-enclosed firmness of an outline and of the silence that annuls every commentary, and hence the equivocation of relation. It comes to a close in due course with the metaphor of the island, which, thanks to its border and its isolation, is like the extreme opposite of the 'charms of scenic places' whence we began.

4. The flowered island, the image of the Place of ideas, is explicitly presented as a multiple that is not a Whole, has no relation and no representable structure. The type of infinite pertaining to such a multiple is moreover subtracted from all measure and comparison. Prior even to the final act of isolation, the poem has denied relation any being.

What is convoked to the 'new duty' of the pure notion is not the place as such, or some instance of the One, it is 'the irid family', the multiple of ideas ('Ideas, glory of long desire'). Furthermore, this multiple is also un-linked in its very composition: each of the flowers is in fact isolated from all the others by a 'clear contour, and this breach parts it from the garden bed'. This aureole not only of light ('clear' or 'lucid') but also of the nothingness ('breach' or 'lacuna') that surrounds each ideal flower accomplishes a preliminary separation of the place through isolation.

Gardner Davies rightly emphasized that the flower's ideality is designated by its separation with, and by its subtraction from, empirical gardens, as in the famous 'absent from every bouquet'. But more radically still, even the hypothesis of an ideal garden, which might have established a link between flowers in the suprasensible realm, is destroyed by the lacuna. What we have here is the full effect of an operator of isolation, of the cancelling of proximities, of topological relations. The flowers are foreign to every totality, and, like Herodias, they would say 'yes, for myself alone I bloom, in isolation'. Separation affords the poet the sight of an untotalizable multiple, a juxtaposition of 'pure' flowers that have no concept.[8]

This is also why the 'growth' of these flowers, which themselves symbolize the infinity of the idea, do not yield any comparative relation, or calibrated quantification, by contrast to the additive movement of waves onto the shore (that 'monotonous game', in which, as something repeated *ad infinitum*, we can clearly recognize Hegel's false infinite). The genuine infinity of being, though it is related to the multiple, is not bound to any bonds (*liens*) of reckoning, and does not carry any relation. This is exactly what is meant in saying that the 'stem' of the flowers 'grew to a size far beyond our reason'. This pure *excess* of the size of being is incidentally also the point on which the poem ends: the 'too tall gladioli' is the ultimate symbol of being, isolated at last, a symbol that victoriously conceals that death, the 'sepulchre', is able to affect beauty – 'Pulcherie'. This is to say that the excessive salvation of the Idea depends on the operations of separation and isolation, operations that yield the lacunary multiple, without whole or relation.

5. Last, you will observe that it is also possible to count the inexistence of the intelligible Place among the schemas of rupture, not this time with the poem's point of departure (the memory of a promenade in the countryside), but with everything whose existence can be attested *by knowledge* – by atlases, herbals and sacred rites.

This inexistence is amply modulated. Its sceptical witnesses are 'the age of authority' and 'litigious Spirit', that is, the realists and the naturalists, both of whom demand that existence be proven, that it be shown. These witnesses are overcome with doubt by the fourth stanza, as they observe that the ideal site does not even have an indexed name. In the third last stanza, the whole arsenal of forms of knowledge (the sky of astral bearings, maps and even the direct inspection of marine sites) is mobilized to establish that 'there was never such a land'.

Yet it is at the precise moment when the scene of the ideal multiple is thus subtracted from all known existence that the sister renounces the taciturn voluptuousness of the true ('sheds her ecstasy'), and, consenting to knowledge ('already dexterous'), she utters the word 'Anatasia', that is, 'resurrection'. When applied to the inexistent, such a word rescues pure being for always. The implicit threat of death is therewith removed, and in the foreground, the too tall gladioli – a singularity that is linked to nothing not even itself – registers the intellectual victory of the poem.

This victory consists in the fact that the word, that is to say the poem, which is a total expansion of the letter, can finally be born 'for scrolls of eternity'. It must – and this is the poem's philosophical lesson – be won by separation and isolation, extracted from the tenacious illusion (that is *doxa* itself) of the bond, of the relation, of familiarity, of resemblance, of the near.

There is only truth when 'the infinite at last escapes the family'.

CHAPTER SIX
Rimbaud's Method: Interruption

Rimbaud's poetry obliterates the joy whose exposition it is. It renounces the possibility that it establishes. It gets impatient with the daybreak of thought to which it is devoted. And, more profoundly still, it puts shadow and opacity right where it had given transparency and grace.

A Rimbaldian poem is its own interruption. This very caesura is what it contrives, by means of which it makes, like 'woman' in the work of Claudel, a promise that cannot be kept. More harshly still, in the sense that Rimbaud welcomed all harshness – 'True, the new hour is nothing if not harsh' – poetry is a promise that *should* not be kept. Its essential inner lesson resides in this imperative.

By itself, this internal deception, this point of flight in which the poem escapes from the poetry of the poem, in which it slips away is as though a language contaminated by the plague, or as though a transparent water that had been caught in some ignoble sluice, explains why it is that we, in this centenary more than ever, go to seek a consolation for his poems in the sandy legend of his life.

Because the interruption is brutal, unequivocal. It splits the poem in two. Its operators are the 'nothing', the 'enough', the 'but' and the 'no'.

In the *Drunken Boat*, there is a flood of Parnassian rhetoric that verges on radiant promise – 'Million golden bird, o future Vigour' – and then there is this: 'But, in truth, I've wept too much! Dawns are heartbreaking. / Every moon is atrocious and every sun bitter', which is like the abolition, or the revenge, of a zero degree of desire.

There are also invectives announcing the total destruction of the order of power and history, as in 'Perish! power, justice, history, down with you! / This is our due Blood! blood! the golden flame!'; but these joys in time's disaster are followed by the calamitous event of a kind of cosmic inferno – 'Dark strangers what if we left! come! come! / Woe! woe! I feel myself tremble, the old earth, on me, more and more yours! the earth melts' – and by this: 'It is nothing! I am here! I am still here!', which gives us cause to think that the imperative of the march into hell, of what Rimbaud called the 'whirlwinds of furious fire', is totally empty, that we are not due anything, that there is a force of attraction governing being and the 'there', the fixity of *Dasein*, that acts as a catchment basin, absorbing everything that would seem to happen.

The same occurs in *A Season in Hell* where, after having described his return as some fierce adventurer, as he who has 'limbs of iron and dark skin and a furious look', he who is made of gold and is 'lazy and brutal', Rimbaud breaks it off dryly with the famous 'You cannot get away. Let me follow the road here again, burdened with my vice'.

What to say moreover of the terrible fall of *Michel and Christine*? There is a stormy flight, and a magnificent pastiche of Hugo: 'Black dog, brown shepherd whose cloak puffs in the wind'. There is a lunar passage of warriors. And here we again have the promise of a certain transparency: 'And will I see the yellow wood and the bright valley, / The blue-eyed Bride, the man with the red brow, – o Gaul, / And the white Paschal lamb, at their dear feet, / – Michel and Christine, – and Christ! . . .' Yet the end of this verse, which pivots on the crucially equivocating figure of Christ, of this Christ who is for Rimbaud a name for renunciation of the undecidable, interrupts the link made between the storm and love's dispensation of transparency by prosaically declaring an 'end of the Idyll'.

The abruptness of the fall or of the caesura is literally staged in the ironically titled *Comedy of Thirst*. In these poems, the part of the one called 'I' is to reply by heaping scorn on whatever is said in the preceding passage. Once again we encounter in them that non-dialectical negation, the 'no' that does not sublate anything, with which Rimbaud turns poetry away from its own opening. It is a negation that proceeds from the edge of a clearing (*éclaircie*), right when poetic simplification had seemed to open the possibility of stating, unreservedly, the world in its transparency. Thus, in the poem *The Spirit* we first read 'Eternal Water Sprites / Divide the clear water. / Venus, sister of azure, / Stir up the pure wave'. Which is followed by the vindictive 'I's' response: 'No, no more of these pure drinks, / These water flowers for glasses. / Neither legends nor faces / Slake my thirst'.

But it is perhaps in that genuinely sublime poem *Memory*, where what is told unfolds like the mystery in a timeless tale, that the interruptive function is dispensed with the most rigour. Because the poem heedlessly sets us within an imagery of joy, of what might be called an epiphany of whiteness:

> Clear Water; like the salt of childhood tears,
> the assault on the sun by the whiteness of women's bodies;
> the silk of banners, in masses and of pure lilies,
> under the walls a maid once defended;
> the play of angels;[1]

But then, immediately following this, in a meter established half-way between the fifth and the sixth feet by the muted closure of the word 'angel' – because in genuine interruption the order of saying is *also* disturbed – there is a brutal 'No', followed by three points of suspension. And suspended we are. Because this 'no' terminates the epiphany of whiteness, giving way to a heavy and sumptuous terrestrial donation:

> no . . . the golden current on its way,
> moves its arms, black, and heavy, and above all cool, with grass. She
> dark, before the blue Sky as a canopy, calls up
> for curtains the shadow of the hill and the arch.[2]

Further down, the innocence of a 'then', in the sense of 'and then . . .', forms an ellipsis, an interruption that in the *Drunken Boat* had been kind of trumpeted forth. In the latter Rimbaud separated flame from the gold of black and of cold. In *Memory*, the caesura is situated between the airy and the grey, between the breeze and motionlessness, between promises of gratuity and labour:

> the breath
> of the poplars above is the only breeze.
> After, there is the surface, without reflection, without springs, grey:
> an old man, dredger, in his motionless boat, labours.[3]

Thus, at the heart of Rimbaud's poetry there is a protocol, whose effects of abruptness and dissipation the artist refined simultaneously, of a crack between what being carries of the promise of presence and what, in the withdrawal that modifies it, it enforces, in the form of a law of return and motionlessness.

Looking at this oeuvre, so short in its entirety, it seems to me that this exhibition of being in its splitting, the poetic establishing of a contour of ruin (*bord de perte*), supposes the singular work of prose within the poem. I am not speaking here about the becoming-prose of the poem, about the – itself undecidable – status of the poetic affirmation in *Illuminations*. No, what I am talking about is the way Rimbaud established prose implicitly within the heart of the poem. There is a prose lying in wait in this poetics, a prose that is obtained by a reordering (*dérèglement*) of verse using lexical contrasts, would-be platitudes and a peremptory syntax. And in addition to the clear markers of its operation – that is, the 'nos', the 'enoughs' and the 'buts' – interruption consists in the brusque rise to the poem's surface of the ever possible prose it confines. We see this, for example, in his poem *Brussels* in which a decasyllable, veering off-course, causes the poem to soar, enclosing it in an angel's wing, as in – 'Then, since rose and fir tree of the sun / And tropical creeper have their play enclosed here'. However this movement (*deport*) thereby also contains the possibility of prose, since with it verse's intrinsic basis is removed, the sensible here is no longer captive to number. Seven lines later, we read: 'La Juliette, that reminds me of l'Henriette / A charming railway station'. It is as though Rimbaud wished to have the resources of prose in store within the poem in order to interrupt it. And so also a store of deception or disappointment.

Even in *Memory*, there are incises of prose that, anticipating the final state of fixity, pointing in the flesh of the poem to the impasse of presence, are engendered not only by means of metric instability, but above all by means of the instability of images, of their always evasive associations. Thus, in the fourth stanza:

> Purer than a louis, a yellow and warm eyelid
> the marsh marigold – your conjugal faith, o Spouse! –
> at prompt noon, from its dim mirror, vies
> with the dear rose Sphere in the sky grey with heat.[4]

In the unallied sliding of colours (yellow, rose, grey), in this finely worked epiphany that joins the noon to the mirror of water, the brusque mention of 'conjugal' acts as a reminder, by which to disrupt the image, that in the inmost depths of this slow charm there lies a prose as dry as a notary's report.

For interruption effectively aims to disappoint; it attests to the radical doubt that besets the epiphany. And this 'prose waiting in ambush' is, with respect to the poem, which due to its instability and its flight compresses and conserves it, the latent figure of this doubt.

We might say that prose impurifies presence.

Pure presence is breath and movement alone; it is the grace of what lifts off into clarity. As it happens, there is in Rimbaud's oeuvre one and only one poem where this breathing is maintained until the very end without interruption or repentance. The fact that this poem is, as one says, 'in prose' is only apparently paradoxical. This poem, unlike many others, contains precisely no latent prosaism. It is, on the contrary, a piece of prose that is thoroughly imbued with poetry. In question here is the text from *Illuminations* entitled *Genie*, which is something like the complete inhabiting of the French language by a principle of weightlessness, and which from beginning to end forms the figure of a visitation:

> He knew us all and loved us, may we, this winter night, from cape to cape, from the noisy pole to the castle, from the crowd to the beach, from vision to vision, our strength and our feelings tired, hail him and see him and send him away, and under tides and on the summit of snow deserts follow his eyes, – *his breathing* – his body, – his day.[5]

At the other extreme, when, prose-struck and doubt-stricken, presence is terminated, we are left with the situation as imperative. Let us say that the full force of the law, duty, the universal attraction of the already-there and the motionless, can only be experienced as an effect of interruption. The duty-to-be (*devoir-être*) is only being itself, insofar as it is what is left of vanished donation.

There is no doubt one poem, *The Crows*, in which Rimbaud rendered – under a sign of death that merges the debacle of the war of 1870 in with the worthlessness of its existence – this prescriptive reverse (*envers*) of an interrupted presence as is:

> But, saints of the sky, at the top of the oak,
> A mast lost in the enchanted evening,

> Leave alone the May warblers
> For those who, in the depths of the wood,
> In the grass from which there is no escape,
> Are enslaved by a defeat without future.[6]

In the May warblers, in the enchanted evening, there is no longer any epiphanic worth. There is no longer any trembling, breath, visitation. The warblers are the promise that one begs the saints of the sky to leave aside for those for whom the entire breadth of the possible is withdrawn.

The key words here are enslavement, defeat and the suppression of all temporal opening. And they trace, without any process of interruption, that which marks interruption downstream of its effect.

But, between *The Crows* and *Genie*, between the defeat of enslavement and inexhaustible breathing, Rimbaud's poems are most often devoted to interruption itself, to what it is that carries to language less the ecstasy of givenness or the unfigurable duty of being-there than an instantaneous see-sawing from one to the other. What captivated Rimbaud was the enigma of this point, and it is to make truth of it, like of a pure event for thought, that he had need of the resources of poetry.

This is why I would say that what Rimbaud attempted in the interruptive operation of the poem was a thought of the undecidable.

One should not understand by 'undecidable' here the banal adolescent dilemma between an open and working (*oeuvreants*) life and a life attached to family, mother and work (*le travail*). Even if – in the themes of race, work and rootedness – Rimbaud captured for all time – without, alas!, destroying it – what could be called the Petainist vision of the world, which he summed up thus, in the glancing light of his historical consciousness:

> Rather, let me keep away from justice. – The hard life, simple brutish-
> ness – let me lift up with a withered fist the coffin's lid, and sit down
> and Be stifled. Thus, no old age, no perils. Terror is not French.[7]

We see here that Rimbaud does not neglect to say that, for a Petainist vision of the world, Robespierre and Saint-Just – who for some, including myself, ground along with Rimbaud and Mallarmé, and Hugo and a few others, the only tolerable idea of France that exists – must be set apart from France's stinking and motionless being. And it is true that France, insofar as it exists, is not a being, but an event. France itself must be decided. Always in violent division.

However, nor is this undecidability one between what is played out abstractly between freedom and what ought to be. Nor it is even, as urgent as the metaphor of departure in Rimbaud's work is, a conflict between wandering and return, between Aden and Ardennes. Rimbaud's savoir-faire, of course, was always evident in his expressions, and it was no different in his rendering of that *fin-de-siècle* commonplace, the call of the open sea. Baudelaire, in 1857: 'Free man, you'll always love the sea'. Mallarmé, in 1865: 'Still, my soul, listen to the sailors sing'. Rimbaud, in 1871: 'Down below – alone, and lying on pieces of unbleached / Canvas, and violently announcing a sail!' There is, though, nothing productive about his irrigating of poetry with salty water. But nor is this poetry a poetry of the *nostos*, of an immemorial attraction of the original site that might offset the indistinction of the Ocean. Poetry's arbitration is not one between the sea and land, or colony and metropole.

The undecidable division of being itself, of being *qua* being, is distributed by the poem between its legal situation and the disappearing of the pure event. In Rimbaud's poetics, the undecidable comes with our being proposed, literally, and in all senses, two universes, and not only one. This composition is that of someone who stands before a sudden decision for which there is no norm. If the derangement of the senses (*dérèglement de tous les sens*) habituates one quite frankly to 'see a mosque in place of a factory, a school of drummers made up of angels, carriages on roads in the sky, a parlour at the bottom of the lake', then interruption is the undecidable divide in this seeing. And all the more so as such a seeing proceeds *frankly*.

Let us show, in an ill-authorized digression, the mundane prose that this dissembles in the terms of my own discourse. When Pierre Mauroy, who was Francois Mitterand's prime minister at the time, and the late Gaston Defferre, who was the minister of our interior, found nothing more to say before a massive strike of workers demanding a basic right than that it was the doing of inhabitants who were foreign to the reality of France, and subversive Shiites, it might be surmised that they, too, suddenly saw a mosque at the site of a factory. But this alchemy of governmental speech, which turns worker gold into immigrant lead, has not finished making us pay for the mindless return of sheer Le-Penist stupification, of that most inept Gaul on the earth. And the reason is quite simply that these governmental declarations contained neither vision nor divide. This in return allows us to understand what Rimbaud meant by the derangement of the senses (*dérèglement de tous les sens*), and that, by contrast to the criminal blunders of state opinion, involves the torsion of a method of truth.

Torsion, because it ruins being's unity, and because all description is immediately caught in the fierceness of a preliminary decision regarding a now twofold proposition, in a way that what is to be named is something that no longer has any guarantee, no longer any innocence, and that the poem, devoted to the notation of the sensible, to the sensible thought of the sensible, but devoid of any donated (*donatrice*) unity, is twisted in the gap in which it must decide.

Interruption consists in an act of a duplicitous description, of a juxtaposition that is almost unintelligible between two incompatible figures of being.

Let us name these two universes, since we have their extreme limits at our disposal, as though they were isolated, that of *Genie*, and that of *The Crows*.

Both the universe of *Genie* and that of the *Crows* are poetically composed of emblematic terms and operations, of characters and relations (*rapports*). These are characters and relations that knot a state – on this occasion a state of grace – for which the poem suggest names, names whose lightness, whose faintness of breath, ought not dissemble that in the matter at hand these names are sacred.

Of course, taken as pure signifiers, the characters of the first universe can of themselves figure in the other universe. Interruption traverses the names themselves. The most flagrant case is that of women.

The word woman recurs throughout Rimbaud's work as belonging to the first universe. The poem *Sensation* revolves almost entirely around the promise this word brings. The poem begins with the combination of pure light and departure that we also see in *Genie*: 'In the blue summer evenings, I will go along the paths'. Then it moves towards an ecstatic suppression of thought and the torment of language: 'I will not speak, I will have no thoughts: / But infinite love will mount in my soul'. And it closes with the words: 'joyous as if with a woman'.

The Blacksmith, a very Hugolian poem, proclaims as ideal a working life lived 'beneath the solemn smile / Of a woman we love with a noble love'.

And we know that one of the words for hell in *A Season in Hell* is to be denied the 'camaraderie of women'.

But women are actually also at the heart of the second universe, and in this sense Rimbaud's homosexuality itself is a figure of undecidability; woman are as much *crows* as they are *genies*. One naturally thinks of the furious diatribe of *My Little Lovers*:

> O my little lovers,
> How I hate you!
> Plaster with painful blisters
> Your ugly tits![8]

More profoundly, there is what I would like to call woman under interruption, the one that supports the dry 'no' whereby it is attested that the universe that woman seemed to authorize in its being is always, ultimately, abolished. There is, for example, that funerary exclamation in the *Sisters of Charity*, bearing in mind that, as bequeathed by Baudelaire, the word 'sisters' designates woman as the clearing (*éclaircie*) of existence:

> But, o Woman, heap of entrails, sweet pity,
> You are never the Sister of charity, never.[9]

Interruption, here marked by 'never', also divides woman, who is emblematic in that she co-belongs to both universes.

The other figure from the universe of *Genie* that I would like to consider a moment is rather more stable, and untainted by division, and that is the worker. The worker is a major poetic reference for Rimbaud. There is, of course, the worker of the Commune, of prophetic revolt, the one who says:

> We are Workers, Sire! Workers! We are
> For the great new times when men will want to know,
> When Man will forge from morning to night,
> A hunter of great effects, hunter of great causes,
> When, slowly victorious, he will tame things
> And mount Everything, as one mounts a horse.[10]

Then, in *Seven-year-old Poets*, there is the worker crowd, the black mass that marks the transition between the Mother's Christian imperative, who 'closes the exercise book', and the promise of 'the amorous pasture, where shining / Swells, natural perfumes, golden puberties / Move calmly and take flight!'. Workers here are the sensible force that undermines God:

> He did not love God; but the men whom, in the brown evening,
> Swarthy, in jackets, he saw going home to their quarters,
> Where town criers, with the three drum rolls
> Make the crowds laugh and roar over edicts.[11]

As close as possible to the allusive transparency of being stands the workers of the poem entitled *A Good Thought in the Morning*. This is the daybreak of being, the miraculous supplementation by which dawn makes an offering to the night of love:

> At four in the morning, in summer,
> The sleep of love still continues.
> Under the groves dawn evaporates
> The scent of the festive night.[12]

Then a 'But' is uttered in objection to this sleep . . . and the workers

> But yonder in the huge lumberyard
> Toward the sun of Hesperides,
> In shirtsleeves the carpenters
> Are already moving about.[13]

Nevertheless, this But, which might be taken as an interruption, and as a breaking of dawn's enchantment by the evocation of work, is only a feint. The word 'worker' – this is one of Rimbaud's poetic contributions – does not signal a rising of the poem's latent prose to its impatient surface. There is no prosaism, for Rimbaud, in the sonority of the worker. Workers blend in totally naturally with givenness of the first flush of morning; they revive the evening of love whose morning is like a salvation that natural being destines it to:

> Ah! For those charming Workers
> Subjects of a Babylonian king,
> Venus! leave Lovers for a little while,
> Whose souls are crowned.[14]

Here the uppercase letters given alike to the words 'Workers' and 'Lovers' places them, under the banner of a Goddess, within the unity of the ecstatic universe.

More, Love is also the decisive relationship in this universe. Rimbaud, as we know, made of love the active key to salvation, that is salvation understood in the sense it takes on in the famous 'I want freedom in salvation'. Salvation happens in accordance with the ultimate promise of the season in hell, to 'possess truth in one body and soul'. Since what comes into question in this maxim is the body. And it is no exaggeration to say that, for Rimbaud, what is at issue in the name of love is the body *in which* a truth lies.[15]

Love is the materiality of salvation. It is, Rimbaud said, 'the call of life and song of action'; love is what he, as poet, is called upon to express: 'Someone will speak of great Love / The thief of Somber Indulgences'. Love is the consumate form wherein the promise of being is stated: 'Ah! Let the time come / When hearts are enamoured'. Love is the passage of visitation, apparent in *Genie*: 'He is love, perfect and reinvented measure, miraculous, unforeseen reason'. Love is what 'we, erect in rage and boredom, see pass by in the sky of storms and the flags of ecstasy'.

Love bestows the exact state of being within a redeemed universe. Of the names Rimbaud assigns to this state, eternity is the supreme one. *Genie* ascribes an eternity to love from the outset: we might even say that this state is love, but Rimbaud added 'and eternity: [a] machine loved for its qualities of fate'.

But what is eternity? Eternity, to all appearances, is nothing other than the presence of the present. It is sensible givenness insofar as it is the indiscernible of the intelligible, pure movement insofar as it is the indiscernible of pure light. It is, precisely, what is said there for all time:

> It has been found again
> What? . . . Eternity
> It is the sea gone off
> With the sun.[16]

Eternity is indeed also 'the warm green mist of afternoon'. Or again 'the bath in the sea, at noon'. It is already in 'in those good September evenings when I felt drops / Of dew on my brow, like a strong wine'. Eternity is within reach, since it is, in time, time itself, or what Plato called the always of time. Eternity is what, in a figure brimming over with nostalgia, one salutes in what one will never see again, 'endless sandy shores covered with white rejoicing nations', while 'a great golden ship flutters many-coloured pennants in the morning breeze'.

But by the summer of 1873 it was all too late. Directly following the supreme evocation of white nations and golden ships Rimbaud declared: 'I have to bury my imagination and my memories'.

This is because the poem that proclaims eternity regained in the indivisible alliance of light and wave is contraposed with the question that insists in *A Season in Hell*, a question that precisely *is* hell: 'Oh! Poor dear soul – might eternity not be lost to us?'.

Between eternity rediscovered and eternity lost, there is, with a distance, an interruption that leads onto the world as such, onto this world that has an imperative form that Rimbaud, straight after asking 'Quick! Are there any other lives?', became resigned to proclaiming the only form acceptable: 'I am reborn in reason. The world is good. I will bless life. I will love my brothers. There are no longer childhood promises. Nor the hope of escaping old age and death'.

But this desire to decide, at the point of the undecidable, for the second universe, for the one that is always already there, so manifest in *A Season in Hell*; this desire to annul the promise, or at least to attenuate the little weight it has, was a long-standing one. Indeed, downstream of interruption, Rimbaud hatched a world of imperative, and of return and motionless, the force of which often offsets that of grace (but, as always, within the poem itself, and well before the famous silence) or else that suspends its effect, or even, and most often, decides against it.

We have already seen how the caesura strikes and mutilates all epiphanies. And how an emblem as decisive as that of woman is distributed between two universes, between *genie* and *crows*. The reason for this is that the composition of the universe of duty, the earth in question at the end of *A Season in Hell*, the earth to which, as Rimbaud said, 'I am sent back to seek some obligation, to wrap gnarled reality in my arms', is a composition spun of ancient powers.

Its central figure is the Christ, with which Rimbaud pursued a *différend* as radical as that which distinguishes the redeemer from Dionysus-Nietzsche.

There can be no question of delving into Paterne Berrichon's idle chatter about Rimbaud's becoming religious. Instead, let us pay heed – because the characteristic of this poet's act of declaring is precisely its *seriousness*, its totally unplayful lack of humour – to this declaration: 'I have never been one of you; I have never been Christian'. Christ is not a name of religious sentiment. As Jacques Rancière has forcefully stated, Christianity for Rimbaud is above all the already-there of salvation, which, because it has taken place, strikes the idea of a new Christianity with impossibility. As a result, I should say, Christ is the name of the already-there of being; it is the name of a situation that, even though what it names is a 'crippling misfortune', is nevertheless always *sublated*. In this sense the Christ is a name of Rimbaud's poetry, an immanent operator, one bound up in a complex series together with woman, worker, mother, virgin, madness, Orient, France and a few others.

In the first place, Christ designates that interruption familiar to poets who transpose the Greek gods into the dialectical and mediating God of the West. He traces the entrenched path of our thought, but this path is, as Rimbaud said, 'Oh! the path is bitter / [Ever s]ince the other God harnessed us to his cross'.

But, above all, the Christ is the name of what prohibits us from keeping the choice of universes open indefinitely, of maintaining the tension of the undecidable. Since, for this opening, we have need of undiminished force, of an energy that exposes us to eternity. When Rimbaud exclaimed: 'Christ! O Christ, eternal thief of energy', he designated the power of powerlessness, or the temptation to seek *consolation*. Christ is less the name of what inclines us toward the universe of *Crows* than a name that claims that the already-there of being is sufficient to life, which is said to carry its principle of consolation within itself, and, consequently, which works to divert us from every abiding exposure to what the matinal surprise of the event admits of by way of truth.

The Christ names being to the extent that a solace is found in something's being simply no more than it is.

The victim of Christ is not the believer. It is someone who has been vanquished, someone who has been vanquished but who persists in drawing enjoyment from this defeat. It is the infant about whom the poet spoke in *Seven-year-old Poets*: '[. . .] In summer / Especially, overcome, stupified he was bent / On shutting himself up in the coolness of the outhouse'.

But, as with every poetic emblem, Christ would be powerless were it not possible to read in his name a long-standing affirmation. The truth is that what these latrines designate for Rimbaud is the *other place* of his desire and thought, a dark paradise that is on a par with the exquisite whitenesses of eternity. This is a paradise whose literary fortunes would continue until Guyotat's *Eden, Eden, Eden*. It is a paradise of rottenness and black water, of mud and urine. Underneath the force of duty, of science, of the rough reality to embrace, there is that Christ-like temptation of abandonment, not at all to lust or to the alchemy of the word, which are preliminary operations for eternity, but to the motionless flotsam of existence in a harsh place, and with no accrual of prestige, where existence becomes absolutely nondescript.

This is clearly the meaning of the peroration of *The Drunken Boat*:

> If I want a water of Europe, it is the black
> Cold puddle where in the sweet-smelling twilight
> A squatting child full of sadness releases
> A boat as fragile as a May butterfly.[17]

It is also the meaning of the I's response to the supposed 'friends' after they vaunt 'the wines which go to the beaches and the waves by the millions':

> I would as soon, or even prefer,
> To rot in the pond,
> Under the horrible scum,
> Near floating pieces of wood.[18]

And it is also the meaning, in *Memory*, of that suspect 'Joy / of abandoned boatyards, a prey / to August nights which made rotting things germinate'.

We know for sure that the power of this desire is itself undecidable, inasmuch as it is situated between abjection and saintliness. With it Rimbaud initiated a powerful literary figure that extends as far as Genet and Guyotat, and throws light on Proust and Beckett from below, a figure that finds the sublime of spirit in excrement, in the anonymous sodomized and trampled body.

Rimbaud knew precisely that the first universe, that of the ethereal sun and visitation, finds support in madness (*l'insensé*) and self-destruction. Again in *A Season in Hell*, he evokes in the past tense this foundational link that exists between obscure desire and the light of being: 'I dragged myself through stinking alleys and with my eyes closed I offered myself to the sun, the god of fire'. He evokes the correlation in thought between sewers and the transparent fire of the sky: 'Oh! the little fly drunk at the urinal of a country inn, in love with rotting weeds, a ray of light dissolves him!'. To speak like Patrice Loraux[19], this 'Oh', which bears an 'h', is all the same suggestive of laying oneself open to the offering of the little radiant fly up above the urinal.

In fact, this undecidable coupling of the epiphany and a desire for soilure had already been given its grotesque form as an interruption without marker in the exclamation: 'The Lilies, clysters of ecstasy!'.

It must nevertheless be admitted that, be it in the terms of sublime abjection, this desire is bound to the word of Christianity. And also that this desire further pushes the undecidable in the direction of the operator of 'Christ'. For as violent and asocial as it may appear, this desire is internally eaten away by the logic of a salvation already present within it. It speaks like the infernal spouse, the sexual seducer:

> When you no longer feel my arms around your shoulders, nor my heart beneath you, nor this mouth on your eyes. Because I will have to go away someday, far away. Besides, I've got to help out others too: that's what I'm here for. Although I won't really like it . . . dear heart . . .[20]

What is given expression here, against which Verlaine could do no more than brandish a vain revolver, is, following his 'penetrating caress', the Christ of disgusting duty, the one whose kiss, as we are told in a poem, is 'putrid'. Urine, sex, caress, excrement – if ever they appeal to thought, they only resolve, alas, in favour of the dead God.

Interruptive force, consolatory temptation, the termination of eternity – I understand their secret source less as residing in a privilege accorded to the simple duty of living than in this latent and muddied figure, this disgusting sublime that makes poetry *aspire* to the enchainment of being, this time given as non-being, or as an in some way *ruined* instance of presence. It is of course with this enchainment that *Memory* is concluded:

> Ah! Dust of the willows shaken by a wing!
> The roses of the reeds devoured long ago!
> My boat still stationary; and its chain caught
> In the bottom of this rimless eye of water, – in what mud?[21]

But before the moment of yielding to the attraction of perplexity, which here interrupts the poetic attempt thoroughly, depriving it of object; before the universe of realism, with the deep silt of that force named Christ, prohibits Rimbaud from even understanding what he had wanted to achieve under the injunction of the sea gone off with the sun, there is the undecidable itself, the absolute core of thought:

> Toy of this sad eye, I cannot pluck,
> o! motionless boat! O! arms too short! neither this
> nor the other flower: neither the yellow one which bothers me,
> there; nor the friendly blue one in the ash-coloured water.[22]

Neither one flower nor the other: what the poem, halting between the two, on the threshold of yellow and blue, summons us to is the event that it issues only to interrupt. Poetry existed, for Rimbaud, inasmuch as the division of being between the ash blue of its identity and the bothersome yellow of its supplementation by love was left unresolved.

Doubtless thereafter all that remained was the science of which he dreamt while in Africa: geography and surveying, strict commerce, accounts and photographs, minerals and unknown peoples, all of which had to be described with precision. This was the kind of science with which he associated work.

But science, brought into poetry, was unable to come to a decision at the point of the undecidable. And this was so, in Rimbaud's view, for an essential reason, namely its *slowness*.

Jacques Rancière sees in science's slowness a motif of merely second-ary importance.[23] I would object that Rimbaud asserted exactly that. However, slowness, above all, is not an external attribute, a simple given of history. That for which science is too slow is the poem; because the poem must prepare for the interruption through a sudden appearing. The promise of science is monumental, and can only be captured in the gigantic poetic arch of a Hugo. The headlong rush of Rimbaud's poetry towards the question of the event and the caesura is not made for raising monuments to the progress of spirit.

However, his poems almost from the outset contain a hypothesis about a possible conversion to the joint disciplines of science and work. It is a hypothesis that conforms to the burlesque figure of inter-ruption in *What is Said to the Poet Concerning Flowers*. The suave figure of the young poet, beholden to lilies and roses, and described as usual in the white of his matinal ingenuity – O white Hunter, who run without stockings / Through the Panic pastures' – is here broken, knocked about by the prosaic injunction of knowledge and commerce.

> Merchant! colonial! Medium!
> Your Rhyme will rise up, rose or white,
> Like a ray of sodium,
> Like a bleeding rubber-tree![24]

But what gradually becomes obvious is the relationship, which is out of keeping with the *aléas* of first morning and joy, between science and patience. This is expressed in *A Season in Hell*, which, as with everything it expresses, does so in the simplicity of the explicit: 'Labour I know; and science is too slow'. The poem had, though, been begun with a hymn:

> Ah! Science! [. . .] And royal entertainments and games that kings forbid! Geography, cosmography, mechanics, chemistry! . . . Science, the new nobility! Progress. The world moves! Why shouldn't it? We have visions of numbers.[25]

We could almost think that 'visions of numbers' appear above some splendour of the universe, that they relay the dawn, that they yield being in a composition that has broken loose of Christic siltation. This effectively appears to me to be the case. But it is not so for Rimbaud, who once again interrupts the – supposedly progressive, or progressist – donation by declaring the return of 'pagan blood'. Yet another return completed by the irremissible:

> Careful, mind. Don't rush madly after salvation. Train yourself!
> – Ah! science never goes fast enough for us![26]

In fact, Rimbaud's poetic linking of science to patience, through the attraction of their finales, occurs well before *A Season in Hell*. 'Patience' is a true word for the undecidable. There are four poems that are placed under the general title of *Feasts of Patience*, and this title alone inscribes patience within the order of that which works to prepare the coming of daybreak. Thus:

> I have endured to long
> That I have forgotten everything;

> Fear and suffering
> Have flown to the skies.[27]

But patience switches abruptly into the other universe, that of perpetuation without eternity, of repetition without presence. Patience then becomes something that must be overcome, by means of the suddenness of some drama:

> Being patient and being bored
> Are too simple. To the devil with my cares.
> I want dramatic summer
> To bind me to its chariot of fortune.[28]

In its coupling with science, patience advances in a disenchanted universe: 'Knowledge and fortitude, / Torture is certain'.

In this way the word patience is traversed by interruption, including in the poem celebrating its feast.

Hence, it has to be argued that, for Rimbaud, the science implied in patience is exactly a non-science, not science, which is also an impatience, an impatience for science. An impatience *tout court*. Impatience *itself*.

For Jacques Rancière, Rimbaud's impatience is, although attested, of the order of the vulgate, of pious discourse. It explains nothing. This is also my view, for the impatience of which I speak does not pertain to explanation. To be sure, as impatient as Rimbaud may have been, this impatience is not a character trait, a capricious impulse. It is a category *of thought*.

To understand it, the impatience in question ought not be seen as a subjective relation to time. It is a relation to truth. And as truth issues from an event and weaves a fidelity; as truth is thus a flash, or lighting up as well as labour; as it founds a time, and yet is eternal, it prescribes to a subject whose stuff it is, the irresolvable conflict between an impatience and a patience.

Among the multiple workers of a truth, irrespective of which, it is seldom the same workers that truth assigns to the patience and to the impatience it requires. Rimbaud knew perfectly well that he was doomed to impatience, or that his poetic task was, as he said – and what patience could ever do it? – to 'record the inexpressible', or to 'describe frenzies'.

Impatience *in* truth, in and for a truth, is exactly that: fixation, notation. Patience is deduction and fidelity.

CONDITIONS

Rimbaud's poetry is both completed by means of and brought to an end by impatience. And this is so not only for poetry, but for all that I refer to as truth procedures. We have already encountered the impatience of science. There is also the impatience that has been inscribed in politics since the crushing of the Commune. And there is the impatience of love since Rimbaud's passion for Verlaine. When Rimbaud concluded *A Season in Hell* by declaring, 'For I can say that victory is mine', there can be no mistaking that what is at issue is a victory over the patient operation that every truth involves. This is why, with a final pirouette, he announced that the truth is something he shall be permitted to possess. But if Rimbaud knew perfectly well that, in the guise of the unexpected opening of a universe, if he knew, if he feared, that the only way in which we can become the subjects of a truth is by deciding for the patience of its infinity, then he also knew that truth is most certainly something that we can never *possess*, since it is truth that transfixes us.

It must be accepted: the bitter 'victory' of *A Season in Hell* is a victory against the undecidable. Rimbaud may well have observed that 'We are not in the world', or that 'Real life is absent'. But it was only to ask, prematurely: 'Quick! Are there other lives?' Why 'quick', if not because in forging life's forces with the appeal of mud and latrines, as in the poems of moveless and ruined being, there is an injunction to impatience?

It is the undecidable itself that he attacked in stating: 'A hard night! Dried blood smokes on my face, and nothing lies behind me but that repulsive little tree'. The tree of Good and Evil, no doubt, but first and foremost the tree that simultaneously carries – without our being able to decide impatiently between them – the yellow flower and the blue flower, the tree that carries being as surprise and supplement, and being as configuration and vacuity.

Rimbaud in essence decided that, and it is here that the poem as capture of the undecidable served him personally, if truth is not *all* given in the daybreak of its event, if it requires the patience and fidelity of a labour or an incompletable series of hazardous attempts, then it is better to suppose that it does not exist. Rimbaud dreamt of a truth that would be coextensive to the entirety of a situation. To pursue thought according to the directives of a predicateless infinitive, to trace, in keeping with the rule of the evanesced surprise, its pure singularity, did not touch any desire in him.

So, when detached from every supposition concerning the truth of an event, there is nothing actually left but to do one's work, (the law of which is established by the situation). And when subtracted from anticipations of truth, all that is left is to devote oneself to the practical virtues of knowledge. Along the way, one will repent, like weary revolutionaries, for having supposed that the world could be other than it is, or that eternity might appear in the violent lack of the times. As Rimbaud said (and it is admittedly not what I like most about him): 'Well, I shall ask forgiveness for having lived on lies. And that's that.'.

The interruption in his poems is an impatience applied to seizing and suspending the undecidable. That is where Rimbaud's genius lay. But interruption is self-combusting; interruption is an impatience with *this* impatience, so that ultimately it is what decides. And what it decides is that nothing was ever undecidable.

Hence, what I seek at the very site at which Rimbaud interrupts himself, or interrupts his genius of the interruption, is the figure of Mallarmé. The absolutely *patient* figure of Mallarmé.

Both were poet–thinkers of the event and of its undecidability. Both sought, in the lifeless period following the crushing of the workers of the Paris Commune, to preserve a sudden appearing in the thought of the poem, to preserve the trace and light, if only a secondary light, of a pure presentation. Both discovered the origin of the poem in the visitation of a having-taken-place heterogeneous to the opaque and voiceless spread of being. But Mallarmé's chief purpose was to declare, using a schema not of interruption but of exception, that unremitting thought keeps eternity *at a distance*. It may well be that nothing takes place but the place, other than that the undecidable of the dice-throw brings forth a Constellation. Icy with forgetting and desuetude, this is precisely what Rimbaud caught a glimpse of and terminated: the vision of being in the Number. And it is conquered by means of a lengthily calculated supputation, which treats of the undecidable in the element of its abolition.

Rimbaud found this distance exasperating, since what obsessed him was a sort of instantaneous diffusion of the True throughout the entire expanse of experience, the choice of a universe in which pure presentation overcomes representation. It is quite true that, for Rimbaud, if life, or what is called life, is left unchanged, then the appropriation by thought of being as suspended between its fixity and its donation is lost to all desire. Better, then, to speak in favour of the indeterminate, anonymity and commerce, as if one were mimicking, in exchange for one's body, a fictive genericity of the whole actually existing universe.

Mallarmé, for his part, upheld that it is as patient singularity that a truth will turn out to be veridical, in the isolation of its procedure, without its ever fusing with the situation in which it insists. The province of poetry is a restrained action, one that changes thought, and leaves undecided an undecidability that metaphorizes that of the event, no matter the extent to which it affects situated being.

Rimbaud – it is the law of impatience as intellectual gesture – could not be satisfied with restrained action. Either truth transfigures being as given, or then only one restriction can be placed on it, that which excises impoverished objects from desire for a subject that nothing any longer distinguishes, an honest trader for whom poetry, at a sidereal distance, is really no more than what *Season* already says it is: one of his 'follies'.

Thus we are in turn summoned to the undecidable choice between the patience of the concept and of the generic becoming of a truth, and the impatience of whoever, assigned by eternity to the sensible form of time, making the idea tremble in the imminence of what is mortal, exposes himself to disappearing in its interruption. Between Mallarmé and Rimbaud.

Poetry has always propped itself up on exactly this undecidability, because for our education and joy it separates out the poets of incitement and the poets of composition, the tropes of interruption and those of the exception. On the one hand, there is the 'enough!' of impatience, the abrupt 'nos' and 'buts' of de-liaison. On the other, there are the 'excepts', the 'otherwises' and the 'thoughs', which rescue thought from being engulfed in the nullity of the site through a patient exposition of the void. In Rimbaud's work, there is a power of unprecedented, evanescent grace, which brings me to say that, yes, as a 'pure poet', in those moments in which he avowed to be 'touched' by language, he went further in his inventions than is possible with Mallarméan labour. In Mallarmé's work, however, there is such a strongly articulated process that, though occasionally a little self-enclosed, nonetheless will eventually yield the Idea. To love poetry is to love not being able to choose.

However, the philosopher, I mean the philosopher in the constraints of our time, with its confusion and its atomism, cannot hesitate in me. However radiant and brutal is the poetics of interruption, however persuasive its ultimate desire (and which I see in myself, let us say the desire to have a post in an administrative centre in a canton of the rural south-west, since here at least restraint and patience are merely a rule of the situation), it betokens the same mimetic temptation – which acts as if because truth was supposedly missing, it is spread out a little all over – that Plato, from the beginning, rebelled against. The only poets to escape his condemnation are those, like Mallarmé, whose subtractive patience dispenses with corporeal mimesis, with pursuing the burden of the sensible, and who know that there is truth only in an onerous exception.

Contestable as is the will to maintain, almost eviscerated, in increasingly complex and misunderstood operations, a fidelity to an original disappearing, it is only thus that today the imperative of philosophical seizing can be upheld (but tomorrow perhaps it will demand impatience, and Rimbaud). Life's polymorphous impatience is provisionally of no use to us.

More, Rimbaud might well have said that the philosopher's endeavour is too slow. His impatience carried him to the Orient, which is for him the site of non-philosophy. 'I expected to return to the Orient and to original, eternal wisdom'. This is something, he added – with the lucidity that drove him to canvass all the possible names of impatience – in which philosophers can only see 'a dream of depraved laziness'. Rimbaud's retort to this: 'Philosophers, you are part and parcel of your Western world'.

And perhaps Rimbaud was out to interrupt the West. But it was in not seeing that what was stirring before his eyes, and in which he proceeded, ordinary and mortal, to participate, consisted – fortunately for thinking and contrary to the use once made of this category with the compass rose – in the pure and simple disappearance of that West, its dissipation in monetary abstraction. The anticipatory response to which, in the poem itself, and not in its abandonment, consisted in what Mallarmé called 'the disappearance of the poet speaking'.

If the historical poem, *the* poem of poets, need not choose between interruption and disappearance, insofar as in it being is given to expressing, in every instance, the lacuna and the un-presented, philosophical seizing, as for it, when like today it re-seizes its power, will inhere in the relation without relation of eventual disappearing and generic exception.

The centenary of Rimbaud's death ought to be seen as a hijacking of what these times require of us. What is that massive panegyric, presented under the thus sullied names of Mozart and Rimbaud, of the radical, wayward and brilliant adolescent? Would anyone with their wits about them not be mistrustful, in these times in which each day is an ambush of the worst, of a tee-shirt plastered with the face of a rebel genius? Who does not see to what a slaughterhouse of concepts and real action we are led by the noisy parade for life and impatience, for plenitude and the fire of sun, and for youth, when what alone is needed to save thought is the idea and patience, the void and the cold Constellation, an ageless tenacity?

From the depths of Harrar where this stifling centenary tracks him down to no avail, Rimbaud, I am persuaded, because his impatience disposed him to think the moon was made of green cheese, says to us: 'Careful! In your current situation, you have no need of me! No wayfarers, great as they may be. The era of wayfarers is over. Now you need Mallarmé'.

PART III
Philosophy and Mathematics

CHAPTER SEVEN
Philosophy and Mathematics

What are we to make of the relation between philosophy and mathematics? Is it to be thought of as a difference? An influence? A boundary? Or perhaps an indifference? It is none of these. I understand it as follows: thinking this relation means determining the modalities according to which mathematics has been, ever since its Greek origins, a *condition* for philosophy. What is required is to think the figures by which, historically, mathematics has been entwined in the determination of the space proper to philosophy.

From a perspective that is still descriptive, it is possible to identify three of these modalities or figures:

1. From the standpoint of philosophy, the first modality determines mathematics as an approximation of, or preliminary pedagogy for, questions that otherwise fall to philosophy. Mathematics is recognized as having a certain capacity for thinking 'first principles', or for the knowledge of being and of truth, philosophy being the perfected form of this capacity. We shall call this determination the *ontological* modality of the relationship of philosophy to mathematics.

2. The second modality is one that treats mathematics as a regional discipline, a section of knowing in general. Philosophy then sets out to examine what it is that founds the regionality of mathematics. It at once classifies mathematics in a table of forms of knowledge and reflects on the guarantees (of truth or of correctness) of the discipline so classified. We shall call this determination the *epistemological* modality.

3. Last, the third modality posits that mathematics is entirely separate from the questions, or questioning, proper to philosophy. In this vision

of things, mathematics is a register of language games, a formal type or a singular grammar. In any case, mathematics does not *think* anything.

The most radical form of this orientation consists in subsuming mathematics within the general concept of technic, of the unthought manipulation of being, of its annihilating levelling as pure *standing-reserve* (*disponibilité*). This I shall call the *critical* modality, since it performs a critical disjunction between, on the one hand, the field specific to mathematics, and, on the other, a thinking of what is at stake in philosophy.

So, the question that I would like to ask is the following: where do we currently stand as regards the articulation of these three modalities? How is philosophy's mathematical condition to be situated from within philosophy itself? The thesis that I wish to put forward takes the form of a gesture, a gesture that involves re-entwining mathematics into the innermost structure of philosophy, from which it has in actuality been excluded.[1] Today's task consists in a new conditioning of philosophy by mathematics, a conditioning that we are doubly *late* in putting into place. We are late both with respect to what mathematics itself has pointed out, and with respect to the minimal requirements necessary for the continuation of philosophy. What is essentially at stake is a crucially urgent question, which threatens to exhaust us: how can we emerge from, *finally* emerge from, our subjection to romanticism?

1. THE DISJUNCTION WITH MATHEMATICS AS PHILOSOPHICALLY CONSTITUTIVE OF ROMANTICISM

Up to and including Kant, mathematics and philosophy were so entwined that Kant (following Descartes, Leibniz, Spinoza and many others) still saw in the mythical name of Thales a congenial origin of mathematics and of knowing in general. For all these philosophers, it seemed patently obvious that it was mathematics alone that had enabled the inaugural break with superstition and ignorance. For them, mathematics was the singular form of thought that had *interrupted the sovereignty of myth,* and that had given us the first form of self-sufficient thinking, one independent of any sacred posture of enunciation; in other words, mathematics was the first form of fully secularized thinking.

Now – and Hegel is decisive in this matter – romantic philosophy will proceed to almost entirely dis-entwine philosophy and mathematics. Romantic philosophy made possible the conviction that philosophy can and must deploy a thinking that at no point internalizes mathematics as a condition of that deployment. I maintain that this disentwining was the romantic speculative gesture par excellence, to the extent that it retroactively determined the classical age of philosophy as one in which, in various modalities, the philosophical text still internalized its mathematical conditioning.

Empiricist and positivist attitudes, which have been highly influential for the last two centuries, merely *invert* the Romantic speculative gesture. The claim that science constitutes the one and only paradigm of the positivity of knowledge can only be made from within a complete disentwining of science and philosophy. The anti-philosophical verdict of positivisms reverses the anti-scientific verdict of romantic philosophy, but without altering its fundamental principles. It is striking that Heidegger and Carnap disagreed about everything, except about the idea that it is incumbent upon us to inhabit and practise the end of Metaphysics. The reason is that for both of them the name metaphysics designates the classical age of philosophy, an age in which mathematics and philosophy are still entwined in a general representation of the operations of thought. Carnap hoped to isolate the scientific operation, and Heidegger sought to oppose to science, as a nihilist avatar of metaphysics, a line of thinking that draws on the poem. In this sense, both of them are descended, although on different sides, from the romantic act of disentwining.

From here is possible to see why the positivisms, the empiricisms and the refined form of sophistry epitomized by Wittgenstein are so obviously incapable of determining mathematics *as a type of thinking*, even though determining it otherwise (as a game, a grammar, etc.) means going against all the available evidence and offending the sensibility of every mathematician. For, in their very kernel, what logical positivism and Anglo-Saxon linguistic sophistry basically claim – but without the romantic force of any knowledge of this claim – is that science is a technic of which mathematics is the grammar, or that mathematics is a game and the only important thing is to identify its rule. In neither case does mathematics constitute a type of thinking. The only major difference between the romantics, who inaugurated what I shall call the second modern era (the first being the classical age), and the positivists or language-sophists, is that the former preserve an ideal of thought (in either art or philosophy), while the latter only admit forms of knowledge.

One aspect of this issue is that, for a great sophist like Wittgenstein, it is pointless to *enter* into mathematics. More cavalier than Hegel, Wittgenstein proposes a simple 'brushing up', a glance cast from afar like one an artist might cast on chess players:

> The philosopher must twist and turn about so as to pass by mathematical problems, and not run up against one – which would have to be solved before he could go further.

> His labour in philosophy is, as it were, an idleness in mathematics.

> It is not that a new building has to be erected, or that a new bridge has to be built, but that the geography *as it is now*, has to be described. (Ludwig Wittgenstein, *Remarks on the Foundations of Mathematics* (Oxford: Basil Blackwell, 1978), §52, V—52–53, pp. 301–2).

But the trouble is that mathematics, as an exemplary *discipline* of thinking, does not lend itself to description, nor is it representable in terms of the cartographic metaphor of a country to which one pays a quick visit. Moreover, it is impossible to be lazy in mathematics. It is possibly the only form of thought in which the slightest wandering of attention results is in the pure and simple disappearance of what was being considered. This is why Wittgenstein was forever speaking about something *other than* mathematics. He spoke of the impression it had on him from afar, and, more significantly, of the symptom it represented in his own itinerary. But this descriptive and symptomatological treatment already presumes that philosophy can hold mathematics *at a distance*. It presumes precisely the general effect that the Romantic gesture of disentwining seeks to produce.

What is the crucial presupposition for the gesture whereby Hegel and his successors managed to effect this long-lasting disjunction between mathematics, on the one hand, and philosophical discourse, on the other? In my opinion, this presupposition is that of *historicism*, which is to say, the temporalization of the concept. It was the newfound certainty that infinite or true being could only be apprehended through its own temporality that led the Romantics to depose mathematics from its localization as a condition for philosophy. Thus the ideal and atemporal character of mathematical thinking figured as the central argument in this deposition. Romantic speculation opposes time and life as temporal ecstasis to the abstract and empty eternity of mathematics. If time is the 'being-there of the concept', then mathematics is unworthy of that concept.

It could also be said that German Romantic philosophy, which produced the philosophical means and the techniques of thought required for historicism, established the idea that genuine infinity only manifests itself as a horizonal structure *for the historicity of the finitude of existence*. Yet both the representation of the limit as a horizon and the theme of finitude are entirely foreign to mathematics, whose own concept of the limit is that of a present-point and whose thinking requires the presupposition of the infinity of its site. For historicism, of which Romanticism is the philosopheme, mathematics, which links the infinite to the bounded power of the letter and whose very acts break with any sense of time, could no longer retain its paradigmatic status, whether it be with regard to certainty or with regard to truth.

We will here call 'Romantic' any disposition of thinking which determines the infinite within the Open, or as horizonal correlate for a historicity of finitude. Today in particular, what essentially subsists of Romanticism is the theme of finitude. To re-entwine mathematics and philosophy is also, and perhaps above all, to have done with finitude, which is the principal contemporary residue of the Romantic speculative gesture.

2. ROMANTICISM CONTINUES TO BE THE SITE OF OUR THINKING TODAY, AND THIS CONTINUATION RENDERS THE THEME OF THE DEATH OF GOD INEFFECTUAL

The question of mathematics and of its localization by philosophy has the merit of giving us profound insight into the nature of our times. Beyond the more vain than heroic assertions of 'irreducible modernity' and 'a novelty still needing to be thought', and so on, the persistence of the disjunction between mathematics and philosophy indicates to us that the historicist kernel of romanticism continues to be the referential site of our thinking. The romantic gesture still governs at the very point where the Infinite is still detained in its function of opening (*ouverture*) and in its horizontal structure with regard to the historicity of finitude. Our modernity is romantic in that it is still bound up in a temporal identification of the concept. As a result, mathematics can only be represented as a condition of philosophy from within a radically disjunctive gesture, one that persists in opposing the historical life of the concept and thought to the formal and empty eternity of mathematics.

Basically, an examination of their respective statuses in Plato shows that, from Romanticism on, poetry and mathematics have exchanged their places as conditions. Plato sought to banish the poets and forbid entry to anyone that was not a geometer. Today it is the poem that forms the core of the philosophical disposition and the matheme is excluded. So, although philosophers receive it in its scientific or technical aspect, contemporary mathematics has been left to languish in exile. It is viewed either as no more than a grammatical vacuity for the language exercises of sophists or as a morose speciality of obdurate epistemologists. Yet – seemingly since Nietzsche but actually since Hegel – the aura of the poem continues to sparkle with all its brilliance. Nothing illuminates modern philosophy's fundamental anti-Platonism more vividly than this symmetrical reversal of the Platonic system of conditions for philosophy.

And as such we might say that the question of postmodernism is not our chief question. Instead, there have been two modern epochs, one classic, the other romantic, and the question we must tackle is rather one of post-romanticism. How do we leave romanticism behind other than via a neo-classical reaction? That is the true problem, and it becomes even more real when we observe that, behind the theme of the 'end of the avant-gardes', the postmodern alternative merely amounts to a classico-romantic eclecticism. The only royal way I know of to arrive at a more authentic formulation of the problem is to examine the link between mathematics and philosophy. It is from this point of attack that we accede straight to the heart of the matter, and this concerns the critique of finitude.

Ever since the collapse of Marxist politics and the ensuing spectacle – itself also quite romantic – of growing collusion between philosophy or what stands in its stead and religions of all sorts, the urgency for a such critique has only risen. Can we really be surprised at so-and-so's Rabbinic Judaism, or so-and-so's conversion to Islam, or another's thinly veiled Christian devotion when nothing is said that does not boil down to this: that we are 'consigned to finitude' and '*essentially* mortal'? As always, to crush the infamy of superstition, it is necessary to summon the solid secular eternity of the sciences. But how is this to be done *within philosophy* if all we are left with after the disentwining of mathematics and philosophy to spice up the mortality of our being is the Sacred and Presence?

The truth is that this disentwining renders the Nietzschean proclamation of the death of God ineffectual. Atheists, we lack the wherewithal to be so, so long as the theme of finitude governs our thinking.

In the deployment of its Romantic figure, the infinite becomes the Open for the temporalization of finitude and, because it is in thrall to History, it remains in thrall to the One. So long as the finite remains the ultimate determination of being-there, God remains. God remains as that whose disappearance continues to govern us under the form of the abandonment, the dereliction or the releasement of Being.

Thus, a very tenacious and profound link exists between the disentwining of mathematics and philosophy, and the preservation, under the inverted or diverted form of finitude, of an inappropriable or unnameable horizon of immortal divinity. 'Only a God can save us' said Heidegger courageously, but those who lack his courage still entertain a relation to a tacit God in the default of being that, with mathematics deposed, is opened by our being made coextensive with time.

Descartes was more of an atheist than we are, because he was not missing eternity. Little by little, generalized historicism is smothering us with a disgusting layer of sanctification.

If not in its proclamation, then at least in its effectualness, the contemporary quandary about the notion of the death of God must be referred to the fact that philosophy's abandoning of the mathematical thought of the infinite delivers the latter, in the medium of History, unto a new avatar of the One.

The only way to situate ourselves within a radical desecration is to return infinity to a neutral banality, to inscribe eternity uniquely in the matheme, and to abandon conjointly historicism and finitude. The finite, still beholden to ethical *aura*, grasped in the pathos of mortal-being, ought today be thought of simply as the differential clause of a truth in the banal fabric of the infinite.

CONDITIONS

The current requisite for a desecration of thought – we see on a daily basis how long we have to go – resides in a complete dismantling of the historicist schema. The infinite must be submitted to the simple and transparent deductive chains of the matheme, subtracted from the jurisdiction of the One, stripped of all correlation with the horizon of finitude and released from the metaphorics of the Open.

And it is at this extreme point of thought that we are summoned by mathematics. We are enjoined to forge a new modality of entwining mathematics and philosophy, a modality by which the romantic gesture that governs us to this day will be terminated.

Mathematics has, under its own steam, arrived at a deployment of the theme of the infinite in the austere figure of the indifferent multiple. Three features – the infinite's indifferentiation, its post-Cantorian treatment as a simple number and the pluralization of its concept (there are an infinity of different infinities) – have all combined to render the infinite banal, to terminate the pregnancy of finitude and to make possible the assumption that *every situation* (ourselves included) is infinite. This evental capacity of mathematical thinking obliges us finally to connect it together with the philosophical proposition.

This is the sense in which I have spoken of today's philosophical programme as being a 'Platonism of the multiple'.

'Platonism' is intended as a provocation or a banner by which to proclaim the closure of the Romantic gesture, that is, the current necessity of once again saying, 'Let no one enter who is not a geometer', that is, when the situation is such that the non-geometer is still being schooled in this romantic disjunction and the pathos of finitude.

'Multiple' signifies the *referral* of the infinite to the indifferent multiple, to the pure matter of Being.

The conjunction of these two terms announces the effectiveness of God's death in the absence of any dereliction, the unbinding of the infinite and the One, the end of historicism and the regaining, within time, of an Eternity that has no need of consecration.

Before launching such a programme, it is necessary to look back over the history of the question. I will punctuate this history at the two extremities of its arch: at one end there is Plato, who sends the poem into exile and promotes the matheme; and at the other stands Hegel, the inventor of the romantic gesture in philosophy, the thinker of mathematics' abasement.

3. PROCEEDING PHILOSOPHICALLY, PLATO ESTABLISHED MATHEMATICS AT THE FRONTIER BETWEEN THOUGHT AND THE FREEDOM OF THOUGHT

The figure who has most clearly deployed a fundamental entwining of philosophy and mathematics in all its ramifications was Plato. He produced a matrix for conditioning where the three modalities of the relationship between mathematics and philosophy with which I began are contained in virtual form.

The main reference source for this is the celebrated text of Book VI of the *Republic*. As this text speaks of the relationship between mathematics and philosophy it may be thought of as canonical for the question at hand.

I have provided an extract of it here. In this passage Socrates asks his interlocutor, Glaucon, if he has clearly understood the preceding discussion, and, in order to verify it, he requests a summary. After having, as is customary, said how difficult it all is, that he is not certain to have properly understood and so on, Glaucon complies, and his summary meets the master's approval. Here is the synopsis:

> The theorizing concerning being and the intelligible which is sustained by the science [*épistémè*] of the dialectic is clearer than that sustained by what are known as the sciences [*techné*]. It is certainly the case that those who theorize according to the sciences, which have hypotheses as their principles, are obliged to proceed discursively rather than empirically. But because their intuiting remains dependent on these hypotheses and has no means of accessing the principle, they do not seem to you to possess the intellection of what they theorize, which nevertheless, insofar as it is illuminated by the principle, concerns the intelligibility of the entity. It seems to me you characterize the procedures of geometers and their ilk as discursive [*dianoia*], which is not how you characterize intellection. This discursiveness lies midway between [*metaxu*] opinion [*doxa*] and intellect [*nous*].[2]

What is of significance for us in this text is the relationship of conjunction/disjunction between mathematics and philosophy. So, I will proceed by identifying the fundamental features that, as it were, unfold the matrix of every thinkable correlation between these two dispositions of thought.

CONDITIONS

1. For Plato, mathematics is a condition of thinking, or of theorizing in general, for the very reason that it constitutes a point of rupture with the *doxa*, with opinion. This is well-known. But what commands our attention here is the fact that mathematics *is the only point of rupture with doxa that is given as existent or constituted*. The absolute singularity of mathematics is basically its existence. Apart from mathematics, everything that exists remains under the sway of opinion. So the independent, effective, historical existence *yielded* the following paradigm: it is *possible* to break with opinion.

For Plato there is also, of course, a superior form of rupture with *doxa* that he called dialectical conversion. But dialectical conversion, which constitutes the essence of the philosophical disposition, cannot be said by anyone to *exist*. It sustains itself not as an existence but as a proposition or project. Dialectics is a programme or an initiation, while mathematics is a procedure that is existent and available. Dialectical conversion is the (possible) point at which the Platonic text touches the real. In the form of the already-there, mathematics and it alone constitutes the only point of external support for breaking with *doxa*.

Now, the singularity of mathematics does not, and cannot, fail to provoke opinion, that is, the reign of *doxa*. Hence the reason for the continual campaigns against the 'abstraction' of mathematics, against its 'inhumanity'. Mathematics constitutes a permanent form of recourse for anyone looking for a real, given point of support on which to base a thinking that breaks with all forms of opinion. The singularity of mathematics is therefore in essence consensual, since everyone acknowledges that there is not, that there cannot be, any sort of mathematical opinion (which does not rule out, on the contrary, there from being – generally depreciative – opinions *about* mathematics). Mathematics displays – this is also its 'aristocratic' aspect – an irremediable discontinuity with all the immediacy of *doxa*.

Conversely, it is legitimate to claim that any negative opinion about mathematics, whether masked or overt, is a defence of the rights of opinion, a plea for the immediate sovereignty of *doxa*. In my view romanticism is no exception to this. Its historicism is inevitably led to erect the opinions of an era into the truth of that era. And its temporalizing of the concept immerses the latter in the immediacy of historicized representations. If the romantic project implies the destitution of mathematics, then, it is because one of its facets involves *rendering philosophy homogeneous to the historical power of opinions*. Construed as conceptual capture of the 'spirit of the times', philosophy is unable to encompass any a-temporal break with the regime of established discourses.

By contrast, what Plato prized in mathematics is precisely its capacity to effectuate a real break with the circulating immediacy of *doxa*.

2. After praising mathematics, Plato came to his quibbles. What he undertook to explain to us was that, as radical as the break with opinion may appear, the limitation of mathematics is that it is a *forced* break. Those who practise these sciences are 'forced' to proceed according to the intelligible, and not the sensible or *doxa*. They are forced: this implies that the break with opinion is in a certain fashion involuntary, unapparent to itself, and above all lacking in freedom.

That mathematics is a hypothetical discipline, that it makes use of axioms it cannot legitimate is the outward sign of what one could call its forced commandeering by the intelligible. The mathematical break is carried out under the constraint of deductive chains that themselves depend upon a fixed point specified in authoritarian fashion.

There is, in the Platonic conception of mathematics, something indistinctly violent, something that sets it in opposition to the contemplative serenity of the dialectic. Mathematics does not establish thought in its proper disposition of sovereign liberty. Plato thought, or experimented, as I do, with the possibility that every break with opinion, every founding discontinuity of thought can, and doubtless must, have recourse to mathematics, but also that this recourse also has something violent and opaque about it.

The philosophical localizing of mathematics conjoins the permanent paradigmatic availability of a discontinuity, an establishing of thought outside of opinion, *and* a constrained obscurity that cannot be appropriated or elucidated from within mathematics itself.

3. Since this mathematical break – which has the advantage of grounding its support in an historical real ('there are mathematical statements and mathematicians') – comes with the drawback of being obscure and forced, the elucidation of this break with opinion requires *a second break*. For Plato, this second rupture, which *traverses* the ineluctable opacity of the first, is constituted by access to the principle, the name

of which is 'dialectics'. In Plato's theoretical apparatus, we are thereby led to an opposition between 'hypothesis' (that which is presupposed or assumed in an authoritarian gesture) and 'principle' (that which is at once originary or a commencement and an elucidating authority or commandment).

Finally, dialectics or philosophy consists in the light shed on the opacity of the first break by a second break whose point of contact with the real is mathematics. If we can succeed in illuminating the hypothesis by the principle, then we shall come, including *in mathematics* itself, to enjoy thought's freedom or mobility with regard to its own break with opinion.

So, even though mathematics actually concentrates the discontinuity with *doxa*, only philosophy can orient thought according to the principle of this discontinuity. Philosophy lifts the violence of the mathematical break. It founds a peace of the discontinuous.

4. Mathematics is consequently *metaxu*: its topology, the site of its thought situates it in an intermediary position. This theme will prove hugely influential throughout classical philosophy (which preserves the Platonic entwining of philosophy and mathematics). Mathematics will be regarded as simultaneously eminent (through its given capacity to break with the immediacy of opinions) and insufficient (thanks to the constrictive character imposed on it by its obscure violence). Mathematics is here a truth *that fails to achieve the form of wisdom*.

In a first approximation, and this is what is usually retained, mathematics is a *metaxu* because it breaks with opinion without reaching the serenity of the principle. In this sense, mathematics is situated between opinion and intellection, or between the immediacy of *doxa* and the unconditioned (i.e., the principle) of the dialectic. More fundamentally, perhaps, mathematics is said to be an in-between in thought itself, to be that which plots a gap situated beyond even the rupture with opinion. This gap is one that separates the general requirement of discontinuity from the elucidation of this requirement.

It is certain that every elucidation of a discontinuity serves to establish the idea of a continuity. If mathematics is animated by an obscure violence, this is because, with regard to opinion, its sole virtue is its discontinuity. Dialectics, which grasps intelligibility *in its entirety*, and not only the discontinuous edge that separates it from the sensible, integrates mathematics within a superior continuity. The position of mathematics as *metaxu* is, in a certain sense, the in-between for the thinking of the discontinuous and the continuous. Mathematics emerges at the point where what demands to be thought is, on the one hand, the relation between that which is violently discontinuous within thought as such, and, on the other, the sovereign freedom that elucidates and incorporates this very violence.

Mathematics is the in-between of the truth and the freedom of truth

Mathematics is the truth as still beholden to an unfreedom required by the violent gesture of repudiating the immediate. It belongs to truth, but to a still constrained figure of truth. Above and beyond this constrained figure of truth is the free figure that elucidates the discontinuity, and that is philosophy.

Mathematics' insertion at the precise point at which the truth and freedom of truth enter into relation will historically determine the entwining of philosophy and mathematics for centuries to come.

Mathematics has paradigmatic value because it *cannot* submit anything to the regime of opinion. But the impossibility of this insubordination also means that mathematics is unable to shed any light on its own paradigmatic value. That it falls to philosophy to *ground* mathematics always means: philosophy has to name and think the paradigmatic nature of the paradigm, to establish, at the moment of discontinuity, the illumination of the continuous, when what mathematics disposes is only a stubborn blindness in not being able to propose anything else than the intelligible and the break.

Within this perspective, classical philosophy will continuously oscillate between the recognition of mathematics' salutary function as to the destiny of truth (this is the ontological mode of conditioning) and the obligation of grounding the essence of this function elsewhere, that is, in philosophy (this is the epistemological mode). This oscillation's centre of gravity can be stated as follows: mathematics is too violently true to be free, or it is too violently free (that is to say, discontinuous) to be absolutely true.

Plato initiated this apparatus. The difficulty of the matter is that Hegel seems not to have said anything different.

4. HEGEL DEPOSED MATHEMATICS BECAUSE
HE INITIATED A RIVALRY BETWEEN IT AND
PHILOSOPHY WITH REGARD TO THE SAME CONCEPT,
THE INFINITE

Hegel discusses the relationship between philosophy and mathematics in the massive Remark that follows the account of the infinity of the quantum in *The Science of Logic*, and he does so in a detailed and technically informed manner. Although Hegel's conceptual technique is far removed from Plato's, a look at some passages immediately suffices to show that the oscillation set in motion by the Greek thinker (mathematics engenders a break, but does not clarify this break) continues to govern Hegel's text:

> But in a philosophical perspective the mathematical infinite is important because underlying it, in fact, is the notion of the genuine infinite and it is far superior to the ordinary so-called metaphysical infinite on which are based the objections to the *mathematical infinite* . . .

> It is worthwhile considering more closely the mathematical concept of the infinite together with the most noteworthy of the attempts aimed at justifying its use and eliminating the difficulty with which the method feels itself burdened. The consideration of these justifications and characteristics of the mathematical infinite which I shall undertake at some length in this Remark will at the same time throw the best light on the nature of the true Notion itself and show how this latter was vaguely present as a basis for those procedures.[3]

The four features we identified in Plato's text are basically all to be found in Hegel's analytical programme.

1. The mathematical concept of the infinite was historically decisive in the break with the ordinary metaphysical concept. As for Hegel every rupture consists in a sublation or an overcoming (*Aufhebung*), he means to tell us that the mathematical concept of the infinite effectively sublates the metaphysical concept, that is to say, the concept pertaining to dogmatic theology.

It is in any case entirely legitimate to consider 'metaphysical' as pointing to a zone of opinion *within philosophy itself*, that is, to a *doxa* that Hegel declared to be untrue (it does not have the true concept of infinity). Similarly to Plato, mathematics for Hegel positively breaks with the untrue concept of dogmatic opinion. Mathematics constitutes the effectiveness of a break-overcoming on the question of the infinite.

2. But this break is blind; it is not illuminated by its own operation. At the start of his Remark, Hegel said:

> The mathematical infinite has a twofold interest. On the one hand, its introduction into mathematics has led to an expansion of the science and to important results; but on the other hand it is remarkable that mathematics has not yet succeeded in justifying its use of this infinite by the Notion . . .[4]

This is the Platonic theme to a tee: in its success, in its 'great results', we can recognize mathematics' force of existence, the fully deployed availability of a break. But this success is immediately counter-balanced by an absence of justification and so by an essential obscurity.

As Hegel put it a little later on in the text: 'Success does not justify by itself the style of procedure'.[5] The existence of a mathematics of the infinite has all the real force of a genuine success. All the same, there is an issue that is higher than that of success, which is that of the 'style of the procedure' used to achieve it. Only philosophy is in a position to illuminate this procedure. But the 'dialectic' in Plato's sense, was it not already a question of style? Of the style of thinking?

3. We can therefore be assured that, just as for Plato access to the principle, which requires the dialectical style, must dispel the violent usage of hypotheses, so also for Hegel a veritable concept of infinity must sublate and ground the mathematical concept, which is armed solely by its success.

4. Finally, as regards the concept of the infinite, mathematics is in an intermediary or mediating position; it is *metaxu*.

- On the one hand, mathematics provides the paradigm for this concept because it 'throws the best light on the nature of the true Notion itself'.
- But, on the other hand, it is still necessary 'to justify its use and eliminate its difficulties' because mathematics is unable to do so

itself. Philosophy thus takes on its traditional function as a sort of mechanic of mathematics: mathematics works but unaware of why it works it must be dismantled and taken in for an overhaul. It is almost certain that the engine will need replacing. This is because mathematics is situated between the metaphysical or dogmatic concept of the infinite, determined by modernity as a simply concept of opinion, and the true concept, the thought of which only the dialectic (in the Hegelian sense) can establish.

But if the four characteristics that singularize the couple mathematics/philosophy in Plato are to be found in Hegel, then what changes? Why does the effect of the Hegelian text, which founds the 'technic' of the romantic gesture of disentwining, of a philosophical abasement of mathematics, run counter to that of the Platonic text, which for centuries had guaranteed its paradigmatic value? How is it, then, that this great Remark, which is at once attentive and documentary, that is, which is *still* informed (there is a learnedness here that Heidegger and Nietzsche felt they could forgo), effectively gives mathematics its notice, and does not yield any new positive form of its entwining with philosophy? Why do we feel or know that after Hegel and his meticulousness the romantic submerging of our era in the temporalization of the concept will leave mathematics to its own specialization?

Well, what has changed is that, for Hegel, the centre of gravity of mathematics, the reason for which it merits philosophical examination, cannot be represented as a domain of objects, *but as a concept*, the concept of the infinite.

For Plato, mathematics means geometry and arithmetic, the objects of which are numbers and figures. This is why, to designate these types of thought, these 'sciences', Plato could use the word *technè*, that is, exercises of thought that have a determinate object. Because the field of its exercise is singular, the break with opinion is *localizable*.

For Hegel, mathematics is not acknowledged as the singular thinking of a domain of objects, but as the determination of a concept, and even, one could say, as the determination of *the* romantic concept *par excellence*, the infinite.

The effects of this apparently innocent displacement are incalculable. Because of its objectal restraint, of its having to do with figures and numbers, and not with a generic concept without object, mathematics was for Plato an always singular figure of thought, a particular domain or procedure, which as such did not rival with the complete ambitions of philosophy.

Hegel, on the other hand, in positing that the paradigmatic essence of mathematics is linked to one of philosophy's central concepts (the concept of the infinite), is constrained to set up, not an always singular entwining, but a rivalry between philosophy and mathematics before the tribunal of the True. And as the true concept of the infinite is the philosophical concept, and as this concept contains and grounds whatever is acceptable in its mathematical counterpart, philosophy ultimately proclaims that the mathematical concept is useless for thought.

True, classical thinkers were inclined to say that mathematics was a partly useless activity, since it dealt with objects, such as figures, that did not have much 'worth'. But this depreciation, which operated indirectly through an evaluation of the singular objects of mathematics, did not call into question the extent of the mathematical break with opinion. It merely indicated its local character. The uselessness of mathematics was relative, since, once mathematical thought was established within the narrow realm of objects in question, it remained absolutely true that the break with *doxa* had paradigmatic worth.

Hegel turned a judgement of mathematics' uselessness into an *instrinsic* one. For, once we are instructed by philosophy in the true concept of the infinite, it becomes clear that the mathematical concept is only a futile and crude approximation. This is the price to pay for temporalizing the concept: all that is to be traversed and sublated from then on becomes *dead* to thought. For Plato, on the other hand, mathematics and dialectics are two juxtaposable, albeit hierarchized, relations in an eternal configuration of Being.

If romantic philosophy after Hegel succeeded in radically disentwining mathematics and philosophy, it is because it declared that philosophy and mathematics deal *with the same thing*. The romantic gesture is not based on a differentiation, but on an identification. Hegelian philosophy, in the medium of the concept of the infinite, has the pretensions of being a superior mathematics, that is to say, a mathematics that has sublated, exceeded and abandoned its own restrained mathematicity and produced the ultimate philosophemes of its concept (of infinity).

5. THE RE-ENTWINING OF MATHEMATICS AND PHILOSOPHY AIMS AT A DISSOLUTION OF THE ROMANTIC CONCEPT OF FINITUDE AND AT THE ESTABLISHMENT OF AN EVENTAL PHILOSOPHY OF TRUTH

Ultimately, it may be said that what is at stake in the complete disjunction, as instituted by the romantic gesture, between philosophy and mathematics is *the localization of the infinite*.

Romantic philosophy localizes the infinite in the temporalization of the concept *qua* historical envelopment of finitude.

At the same time, mathematics followed a parallel but separate and neglected career, in which it came to localize infinities in the indifference of the pure multiple. It came to deal with the actual infinite in the banality of the cardinal number. It neutralized and wholly deconsecrated the infinite, subtracting it from every metaphor of tendency, of becoming, and of horizon, and wrested it from the reign of the One to disseminate it – whether in the infinitely large or in the infinitely small – in a typology of multiplicities that is free of any *aura*. By inaugurating a thinking in which the infinite is irreversibly separated from every instance of the One, mathematics has in its own field successfully accomplished the programme of the death of God.

The concept of the finite is then treated by mathematics as a particular case that is derived from the infinite. The infinite thereby ceases to be a sacred exception that orchestrates an excess over the finite, a negation, a sublation of finitude. For contemporary mathematics, the infinite is instead that which, representing the ordinary form of multiplicities, admits of a simple and positive definition, while the finite is that which derives from the latter by means of negation or limitation. If philosophy is held under the condition of such a mathematics, it becomes impossible to maintain a discourse of finitude. Just like every multiple situation, 'we' are infinite, and the finite a lacunary abstraction. Death itself only inscribes us in the *natural* form of infinite being-multiple, that of the *limit* ordinal, which phrases the sum of our infinity in a pure, external 'dying'.

Such, then, is the current standing of things. On the one hand, there is the ethical pathos of the finite, placed under the sign of death, which presupposes the infinite through temporalization and is unable to free itself of representations that are sacred, precarious and defensive with regard to promises of the coming of a God who will *cauterize* the indifferent wound that the world inflicts on the Romantic trembling of the Open. And, on the other, an ontology of indifferent multiplicity that can withstand the disjunction and abasement brought about by Hegel; one that secularizes and disperses the infinite, that grasps us humans in terms of this dispersion and that advances the prospect of a world evacuated of every tutelary figure of the One.

This gap forms the scene of our question: how to find a way out of Romanticism and attain a real post-Romanticism, to disperse the theme of finitude, and to gain rigorous acceptance of the infinity of every situation? The re-entwining of mathematics within philosophy is the necessary operation for anyone who wants to have done with the power of myths, of any and every myth, such as the myth of errancy and of the Law, and the myth of the Immemorial, not to mention the myth – since, as Hegel would have said, it is the style of procedure that counts – of the painful absence of myths.

To practise in thought a decisive rupture with romanticism (and the issue here is also political, since in revolutionary politics an historicist, and therefore romantic, element existed), we cannot do without any recourse – which is perhaps once again blind, or stamped with constraint, or violence – to the injunctions of mathematics. We philosophers, whose duty is to think this era beyond that which has devastated it, we must submit to its condition.

As the reader will have surmised, the terms of the proposition by which I am suggesting we re-entwine mathematics and philosophy cannot be characterized by the caution proper to the epistemological modality. It is of crucial importance to cut straight to the ontological destiny of mathematics. So, my proposition asserts at the outset: there is only the infinite multiple, which presents the infinite multiple, and the unique stopping point of this presentation presents nothing. Ultimately at issue is the void, and not the One. God is dead, at the heart of the presentation.

But, as mathematics has clearly had a century's head start in its secularizing of the infinite, as the only thought available of multiplicity as infinitely weaving the void of its own inconsistency is the one that mathematics, after Cantor, claims as its specific site, I shall make the provocative and therapeutic claim that mathematics *is* ontology, and in the strict sense, which is to say that mathematics is the infinite development of what can be said of being *qua* being.

Finally, if, in order to traverse and have done with historicism, the Heideggerian historial framework included, we must side with Cantor and Dedekind on the issue of the finite–infinite dialectic against Hegel; if the statement 'mathematics is ontology' is the contemporary way to put philosophy under the condition of mathematics, then our question becomes: what is the status of truth?

Will it consist in a dialectic, as it did for Plato and Hegel? Will there be (but this can no longer be a matter for ontology) a superior, founding, illuminating mode of intellection, one appropriate to the brutality of such a break? Is there anything that *supplements* the multiple indifference of being? All these questions belong to another order; they are questions that will drive the continuation of philosophy, and bring it to prevail over the morose theme of its 'end' into which it is forced by the exhausted romanticism involved in the thematic of finitude. Subject to its mathematical condition, the core of such philosophical propositions will consist in structuring truths around evental localizations, and in subtracting them from the sophistic tyranny of language.

However we look at it, we are called upon to bring historicism to a close and dispel all the myths engendered by temporalizing the concept. To achieve this, we cannot do without recourse to the courageous, solitary existence of the concept, since, in deposing all sacredness and the absence of every God, mathematics is nothing other than the human history of eternity.

CHAPTER EIGHT
On Subtraction

Invited here before you for whom silence and speech are the chief concerns to honour that which subtracts itself from their alternation, it is to Mallarmé that I turn to shelter my solitude.

So, by way of an epigraph to my address, I have chosen this fragment from the fourth scholium of *Igitur*:

> I alone – I alone – am going to know the void. You, you return to your amalgam.
>
> I proffer speech, the better to re-immerse it in its own inanity . . .
>
> This, no doubt, constitutes an act – it is my duty to proclaim it: this madness exists.
>
> You were right to manifest it: do not think I am going to re-immerse you in the void.

Concerning the compactness of your amalgam, I have come here with the duty of proclaiming that the madness of subtraction constitutes an act. Better: that it is the act *par excellence*, the act of a truth, one by which I come to know the only thing that one may ever know in the element of the real, and that is the void of being as such.

If speech, via an act of truth, is plunged back into its inanity, do not think it will plunge *you* back into it, you who hold the reason behind what is manifest. Quite to the contrary, we shall grant each other – I in the duty to speak, you in the duty to render my speech manifest – that the folly of the act of a truth exists.

CONDITIONS

Nothing can be granted existence – I mean the kind of existence that a truth presupposes at its origin – without being put to the test of its subtraction.

To subtract is not straightforward. Sub-traction, that which draws under, is too often conflated with ex-traction, that which draws from or forth, that which mines and yields the coal of knowledge.

Subtraction is plural. Allegations about its lack of effect, or causality, work to dissimulate operations that are irreducible to one another.

These operations are four in number: the undecidable, the indiscernible, the generic and the unnameable. These are the four generic figures that form the cross of being whenever it enters the trajectory, or comes across the obstacle, of a truth. Of a truth whereof it would be too much to say it is half-said (*mi-dite*), since, as we shall see, it is rarely said, not to mention almost never said, traversed as it is by the incommensurable unbinding between its own infinity and the finitude of forms of knowledge it makes holes in.

Let us start with pure formalism.

Take any norm for evaluating statements in a given situation of language. The most common of these norms is the distinction between veridical and erroneous statements. Were this language rigorously divided we could take the distinction between provable and falsifiable statements as another norm. But all that matters here is that such a norm exists. Thus, any statement that subtracts itself from the norm we can call undecidable. That is, an undecidable is a statement that cannot be inscribed in any of the classes into which the norm of evaluation is supposed to be able to distribute all possible statements.

The undecidable is therefore that which is subtracted from a supposedly exhaustive classification of statements realized according to a norm that allots statements values. The undecidable statement cannot be ascribed any value, although the norm of attribution only exists on the assumption of its complete efficacy. The undecidable statement is properly valueless, but that is the price that enables it to contravene the laws prescribed by a classical economy.

Gödel's theorem shows that in the language situation known as first-order formalized arithmetic in which the norm of evaluation is that a given thing has to be proved, there exists at least one statement that is undecidable in a precise sense: neither it nor its negation can be proved.

Formalized arithmetic therefore does not come within a classical economy of statements.

For a long time, the undecidability of Gödel's statement was seen as having the form of the liar's paradox, of a statement that proclaims its own indemonstrability; or a statement subtracted from the norm simply because it states that it is negatively affected by it. Today, we know that the link between undecidability and paradox is contingent. In 1977, Jeff Paris showed that there was an undecidable statement that he claimed was in no way paradoxical, but, and I quote him, 'a reasonably natural theorem of a finite combinatorial'. The subtraction involved here comprises an intrinsic operation, and is not the consequence of the paradoxical structure of a statement with respect to the norm from which it is subtracted.

Now, let's take, as before, a language situation in which there exists a norm for evaluating statements. Given any two presented terms, let's say a_1 and a_2, consider expressions of that language with two placeholders, such as 'x is bigger than y'; for example, expressions of the kind $F(x,y)$. When the value of the statement $F(a_1,a_2)$ differs from the value of the statement $F(a_2,a_1)$ we can say that the formula *discerns* the terms a_1 and a_2.

If, for example, a_1 is actually bigger than a_2, the expression 'x is bigger than y' discerns a_1 and a_2, since the value of statement 'a_1 is bigger than a_2' is 'true', while the value of the statement 'a_2 is bigger than a_1' is 'false'.

You can see that a formula discerns two terms if, by exchanging their places, that is, if, by the permutation of terms in the expression, the value of the statement changes.

Two terms are *indiscernible*, then, if, in the language situation in question, no formula exists with which to discern the two terms. So, in a hypothetical language reduced to the single expression 'x is bigger than y', if each of the terms a_1 and a_2 are equal, they are indiscernible. For, clearly, the expression 'a_1 is bigger than a_2' is false, and so too is the expression 'a_2 is bigger than a_1'.

Two given terms, then, are said to be indiscernible with regard to a language situation if no two-place formula in the language exists that can mark their difference through a permutation of terms that changes the value of the statement originally obtained by inscribing them in the places prescribed.

The indiscernible is something that is subtracted from the marking of difference through evaluating the effects of permutation. Two terms are indiscernible when you permute them *to no effect*. These two terms are two only in the pure presentation of their being. Nothing in language can ascribe their duality any differential value. They are two, to be sure, but not such that one could re-mark that they are. The indiscernible thus subtracts difference as such from any remarking (*remarque*). The indiscernible subtracts the two from duality.

In algebra the question of the indiscernible was encountered very early on thanks to the work of Lagrange. Let us then take as our language polynomials with several variables and rational coefficients. Next, we shall fix the norm of evaluation: thus, if, when determinate real numbers are substituted for the variables, the polynomial cancels itself out, the value can be said to be V_1. If the polynomial does not cancel itself out, the value is V_2.

Under these conditions, any polynomial with two variables, $P(x,y)$, clearly constitutes a discerning expression. It is then easy to demonstrate, for example, that the two real numbers +2 and −2 are indiscernible: since for any polynomial $P(x,y)$, the value of $P(+2,−2)$ is the same as the value of the polynomial $P(−2,+2)$: both the first polynomial – when x takes the value +2 and y −2 – and the second – in which x takes the value −2 and y + 2 – cancel themselves out. The principle of differential evaluation, then, fails for every permutation of the two numbers +2 and −2.

Little wonder, then, that it was by studying permutation groups that Galois came to develop the theoretical space in which the problem of resolving equations by means of radicals first took on meaning. In fact, Galois' invention amounts to a calculus of the indiscernible. This point carries some far-reaching conceptual consequences that are to be deployed in a forthcoming book by a contemporary thinker and mathematician René Guitart, who does so, it should be noted, using several Lacanian categories.

From this, we can deduce that while the undecidable is subtraction from a norm, the indiscernible is subtraction from a mark.

Now, take a language situation for which there is always a norm of evaluation. And take a fixed set of terms, or of objects, let's call it U. We shall call U a universe for the language situation. Let's take an object from U, which we'll call a_1. And let's take a single-place expression of that language, for instance $F(x)$. If in the place marked by x you put the object a_1 you obtain a statement $F(a_1)$ to which the norm will ascribe a certain value, that is, true or false, or any other value determined by a principle of evaluation. For example, let a_2 be a fixed object in the universe U. Now, suppose our language situation allows for the expression 'x is bigger than a_2'. If a_1 is actually bigger than a_2, we obtain the value 'true' for the statement 'a_1 is bigger than a_2' – the statement in which a_1 has come to occupy the place marked by x.

Let's imagine now that we take all the terms in U that are bigger than a_2. We thereby obtain a subset of U. This is the subset of all the objects a that, when substituted for x, give the value 'true' to the statement 'a is bigger than a_2'. We shall say that a subset is *constructed* in the universe U by the formula 'x is bigger than a_2'.

Generally, we shall say that a subset of the universe U is constructed by a formula $F(x)$ if this subset is exclusively composed of all the terms a of U that, when substituted for x, give the statement $F(a)$ a value fixed in advance. That is, all the terms that are such that the formula $F(a)$ is evaluated in the same way.

A subset of the universe U will be called *constructible* if in the language there exists a formula $F(x)$ that constructs it.

The generic is, then, a subset of U that is not *constructible*. No formula $F(x)$ of the language can be evaluated in the same way by the terms that compose a generic subset. You will see that a generic subset is subtracted from any identification by the predicates of the language. No one predicative trait can group the terms that make it up.

Observe that this means that for every formula $F(x)$, there are terms of the generic set that, substituted for x, yield a statement having a certain value, and that there exist other terms of the same set that, substituted for x, yield a statement having a different value. The generic subset is such that, precisely, for every formula $F(x)$ it is subtracted from the construction and selection authorized by that formula in the universe U. The generic subset contains, so to say, a bit of everything, such that no predicate can ever group all the terms. The generic subset is subtracted from predication *by excess*. Its multifariousness and predicative superabundance mean that there is nothing gathering it together that depends upon the power of a state or the identity of its evaluation. Language fails to construct its contour or gathering. The generic subset is a pure multiple of the universe; it is evasive and indefinable by any linguistic construction at all. It indicates that the power of being of the multiple exceeds that which such constructions are capable of fixing according to the unity of an evaluation. The generic is exactly that instance of multiple-being that is subtracted from the power of the One as it is contained in language.

It is easy to establish that, for every language having a relation of equality and of disjunction, in other words for nearly every language situation, a generic subset is necessarily infinite.

For let us suppose that a generic subset is finite.

Its terms would then compose a finite list, for instance, a_1, a_2, and so on until a_n.

Consider then the formula 'x = a_1 or x = a_2, etc., up to x = a_n'. This is a formula of the type $F(x)$, since the terms a_1, a_2, and so on are fixed terms, which therefore do not indicate any 'empty' place. It is clear that the set made up of a_1, a_2 . . . a_n is constructed by this formula, since only these terms can validate an equality of the type '$x_3 = a_j$' where j goes from 1 to n. Being thus constructible, a finite set cannot be generic.

The generic is therefore a subtraction from the predicative constructions of a language authorized, in the Universe, by its own infinity. The generic is, at bottom, the superabundance of being such as it evades the hold of language, when an excess of determinations brings about an effect of indetermination.

The proof there exist in very robust language situations, such as that of set theory, Universes in which generic multiples are presented was produced by Cohen in 1963. And since, as Lacan repeatedly stated, mathematics is the science of the real, we can thus be sure that this singular subtraction from the marking of the pure multiple by the effect of One of the language is genuinely real.

I have said that the undecidable is a subtraction from a norm of evaluation and that the indiscernible is a subtraction from the mark of a difference. Let's add that the generic is an infinite subtraction from any subsumption of the multiple within the One of the concept.

And last, let's take a language situation and its principles of evaluation. Once again let's consider one-place formulas of the type $F(x)$. Among the accepted values for statements, such as, true, false, possible, and so on, let's select one and only one and call it the value of nomination. We shall then say that a formula $F(x)$ *names* a term a_1 of the universe if that term is the only one that, when substituted for x, gives the statement $F(a_1)$ the value of nomination.

For example, let's take as our universe two terms a_1 and a_2. Our language allows the formula 'x is bigger than a_2'. Let's posit that the nominating value is the true value. If a_1 is actually bigger than a_2 then the formula 'x is bigger than a_2' names the term a_1. In fact, 'a_1 is bigger than a_2' is, as the nominating value, true, while 'a_2 is bigger than a_2' is false, which is not the nominating value. And the Universe only contains a_1 and a_2. So, a_1 is the only term in the Universe that, substituted for x, yields a statement having the value of nomination.

That a formula names a term means in fact that it is the schema of the proper name of this term. The 'proper', as always, is dependent on the unique. The named term is in effect unique in coming to give the formula that names it the fixed value of a nomination.

The unnameable will then be a term in the Universe, *if it is the unique one in the Universe not to be named by any formula.*

One should be attentive here to the redoubling of the unique. A term is named only in being the unique term that gives a formula the nominating value. A term is unnameable, then, only in being the unique term that is subtracted from that uniqueness.

The unnameable is that which is subtracted from the proper name, and which is alone subtracted from it. The unnameable is therefore the proper of the proper – so singular that it cannot even tolerate having a proper name. It is so singular in its singularity that it is the only instance not to have a proper name.

We are here bordering on paradox. For, as the only one not to have a proper name, it appears that the unnameable falls under the name – specific to it – of the anonymous. 'The one which has no name', is that not the name of the unnameable? This indeed seems to be the case, since it is the only one to perform this subtraction.

It follows from this redoubling of uniqueness that one form of uniqueness spells the ruin of the other. It is impossible to be subtracted from the proper name if this unique subtraction provides a support for the propriety of a name.

As a result, there would seem to be no proper of the proper, that is, no singularity of that which is subtracted from all self-doubling in the name of its singularity.

But this is only the case so long as the formula 'having no proper name' is a possible formula of the language situation in which one is operating. Or again, if the formula 'there exists no formula F(x) to which the unnameable term is the only one to provide with a nominating value' can itself be a formula of the language. For only this formula about

119

the formulas can serve to name the unnameable, which thus completes the paradox.

Yet it is generally not the case that a formula can refer to the totality of possible formulas of the language. The not-all here presents an obstacle to the deployment of the apparent paradox. Because, if you say 'there exists no formula F(x) such that this or that' you are in fact presupposing, albeit negatively, that all of the language can be inscribed in the unity of an expression. This would involve the language situation in a powerful folding back on itself and form a meta-language that would only engender an even more radical paradox than the one we already have.

Moreover, the mathematician Furkhen established in 1968 that the unnameable can be consistently admitted. He presents us with a fairly simple language situation – a sort of fragment from the theory of the arithmetical successor, plus a small morsel of set theory – such as is allowed by a model wherein one and only one term remains nameless (*sans nomination*). So this gives us a model in which the unnameable really exists, in which there exists a subtractive reduplication of uniqueness, or of the proper of the proper.

Let us recapitulate. We have the undecidable as subtraction from the norms of evaluation, or subtraction from the Law. We have the indiscernible as subtraction from the marking of difference, or subtraction from sex. We have the generic as infinite and excessive subtraction from the concept, the pure multiple or subtraction from the One. And we have the unnameable as subtraction from the proper name, or as singularity subtracted from singularization. These are the analytic figures of being such as it is brought forth in the failure of language to capture it.

We have now only to link topologically their dialectic. The framework of this linkage is set out in the gamma diagram shown in Figure 8.1.

It should be clear that we are now entering into philosophy, since the preceding section was part way between philosophy and mathematics, and therefore between philosophy and ontology.

Let us say in passing that Lacan was given to saying that ontology is a sort of disgrace. It is a disgrace of sense, or of the senses; I would add that it is a culinary disgrace, a familial disgrace for philosophy, not the perfect housewife but the disgraceful housewife. For me, however, 'ontology' is only another name for mathematics – or, more precisely, 'mathematics' is the name of ontology as a language situation. I thereby evade the disgrace of the household and this time perform a subtraction of all ontol-

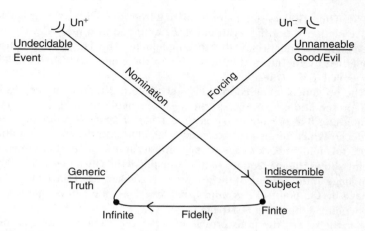

Figure 8.1

ogy from philosophy, which is nothing more than the language situation in which truths, in their plural procedures, are utterable as Truth, in the singularity of its inscription (*pointage*).

I come now to the gamma diagram.

The gamma diagram represents the trajectory of a truth, of whatever type. You are perhaps aware that I maintain that there exist four types of truths: scientific, artistic, political and amorous. This diagram is philosophical since it compossibilizes the types of truths through a formal concept of Truth.

Notice how the four figures of subtraction are distributed according to the register of pure multiplicity. Pure multiplicity also designates the latent being of these acts.

The undecidable and the unnameable are related insofar as they presuppose the One. In the case of the undecidable the one presupposed is a statement, and in the case of the unnameable it is the uniqueness of that which evades the proper name. The position of the One within each of these subtractive effects is nevertheless not the same.

The undecidable statement, subtracted from the effect of a norm of evaluation, lies outside the bounds of what may be inscribed, insofar as the very possibility of inscription requires precisely falling within the norm. Thus, Gödel's statement is missing from the field of the provable, since neither it nor its negation can be admitted into this field. Of this statement we might say that it supplements the language situation governed by the norm. I indicate this in the diagram by the plus sign appended to the One.

The unnameable, by contrast, is embedded in the intimate depths of the presentation. It testifies to the flesh of singularity, and it is thereby something like the point-like ground (*fond en forme de point*) of every order in which terms are presented. This radical underside of nomination, this folding back of the proper onto itself designates that which of being shows the inadequacy of the principle of the One as established by language in the naming of the proper. This weakening of the One of language by the point-like ground [*point-fond*] of being I have marked by appending a minus sign to the One.

For their part, the indiscernible and the generic are related as they both presuppose the multiple. Indiscernibility is said of at least two terms, since it is a difference without concept. And the generic, as we have seen, requires the infinite spreading of the terms of the Universe, since it is the diagram of a subset subtracted from every predicative unity.

Once more, however, the kind of multiple involved is not the same in both cases. The multiple implied by the indiscernible has at its criterion the marked places in a formula of discernment. As every actual formula of a language situation is finite, the multiple of the indiscernible is necessarily finite. On the contrary, the generic necessitates the infinite.

The gamma diagram thus superimposes the logical figures of subtraction onto a ontological distribution. There is a quadripartite division between the one-more, the one-less, the finite and the infinite. A truth circulates within this exhaustive quadripartite structure of the givenness of being, at the same time as its trajectory is pinned together by the entire logic of subtraction.

Now let's go over this trajectory.

In order for the process of a truth to begin, something must happen. It is necessary, as Mallarmé would say, that it is not the case that nothing takes place except the place. Since the place as such, or the structure, only ever gives us repetition and the knowledge that is known or unknown within it, that is, knowledge as it is in the finitude of its being. The advent, the pure supplement, the incalculable and the disconcerting, this is what I call the 'event'. It is, to cite the poet once again, that which has 'sprung from the croup and the flight'. A truth arises in its novelty – and every truth is a novelty – because a hazardous supplement interrupts repetition. As indistinct, a truth begins by surging forth.

But this surging forth directly sustains the undecidable. For the norm of evaluation that governs the situation, or structure, cannot be applied to the statement 'this event belongs to the situation'. Were such a statement decidable, the event would clearly comply in advance with the norms of repetition, and would not be evental. There is an intrinsic undecidability to every statement involving the nomination of an event. And no assessment, no exhibition (*monstration*) can here make up for the shortcomings of the norm. For barely has the event appeared than it has disappeared. It is no more than the flash of a supplementation. Its empirical character is that of an eclipse. That is why it will always be necessary to say that it took place, that it was given in the situation and that this unverifiable statement, subtracted from the norm of evaluation, is a genuine supplementation with regard to the field of what language decides: it is exactly in the one-more in which undecidability is played out.

The leap of a truth, then, involves a wager on the supplement. It involves upholding the statement 'an event has taken place', which comes to deciding the undecidable. But, of course, since the undecidable is subtracted from the norm of evaluation, this decision is an axiom. Nothing founds it, bar the assumed evanescence of the event. Every truth thereby passes through the pure wager placed on what has being only in its disappearing. The axiom of truth, which always takes the form 'this has taken place, this which I can neither calculate nor exhibit' is the simple, affirmative obverse of the subtraction of the undecidable.

With this the infinite procedure of verifying the true begins, or, that is, the examination in the situation of the consequences of the axiom. This examination, in turn, is not guided by any established law. Nothing can govern its trajectory, since the axiom sustaining it is decided independently of any appeal to the norms of evaluation. The trajectory involved is a hazardous one, lacking in concept. The successive choices of verification do not have any aim that might be representable as an object, or supported by a principle of objectivity.

But what is a pure choice, a choice without concept? It is obviously a choice between two indiscernible terms. If no formula exists that can discern two terms of the situation, it is clear that the decision to proceed with verification via one term rather than the other cannot be based in the objectivity of their difference. It is an absolutely pure choice, one free from any presupposition other than that of having, in the absence of any distinguishing mark in the presented terms, to choose the one through which the verification of the consequences of the axiom will first proceed.

In philosophy, this situation is clearly identified under the name 'freedom of indifference'. This freedom is a freedom that, confronting the indiscernible, is not governed by any identifiable norm of difference. If there is no value that discriminates things that you have to choose between, then your freedom as such constitutes the norm and merges with chance. The indiscernible is the subtraction that establishes a point of coincidence between chance and freedom. The likes of Descartes made this point of coincidence the prerogative of God. We know that he went so far as to say that the axiom of divine liberty is such that the choice of 4 rather than 5 as the answer to the sum of $2 + 2$ is a choice between two indiscernibles. In this case, the norm of addition comprises a norm from which God is subtracted. It is his pure choice that will retroactively constitute it, that is to say verify it, in the active sense of 'turn into truth'.

Putting God aside, the indiscernible will be held to organize the pure point of the Subject in the process of verification. A subject is that which disappears between two indiscernibles, that which is eclipsed in the subtraction of a difference without concept. This subject is the throw of the dice that does not abolish chance but that realizes it as a verification of the axiom that founds it. What was decided at the point of the undecidable event will pass via *this* term, in which the local act of a truth is represented – without reason or marked difference, and indiscernible from its other. As a fragment of chance, the subject crosses the distance-less gap that the subtraction of the indiscernible inscribes between two terms. In this regard the subject of a truth is genuinely in-different: it is the indifferent lover.

The act of the subject is, as you see, essentially finite, as is the presentation of indiscernibles in its being. However, the verifying trajectory continues investing the situation through successive indifferentiations in such a way that what is accumulated with these acts gradually comes to draw the contours of a subset of the situation, or of the universe in which the evental axiom verifies its effects. Clearly this subset is both infinite and incompletable. Nevertheless, it is possible to state that, were it completed, it would ineluctably form a generic subset.

How, indeed, could a series of pure choices engender a subset that could be unified by means of a predicate? This would entail that the subset was secretly governed by a concept, or that the indiscernibles in which the subject is dissipated in its act are actually discerned by some superior understanding. This is what Leibniz thought, for whom the impossibilities of indiscernibles resulted from God's computational intellect. But if there is no God who computes the situation, if the indiscernibles really are such, then the trajectory of a truth cannot coincide in the infinite with any truth. And, consequently, the verified terms compose, or rather, assuming their infinite totalization, will have composed, a generic subset of the Universe. Indiscernible in its act or as Subject, a truth is generic in its result or in its being. It is subtracted from every recollection of the multiple in the One of a designation.

There are thus two reasons, and not one, for saying that a truth is little-said.

The first is that, as infinite in its being, a truth can only be represented in the future perfect. It will have taken place as a generic infinity. Its taking-place, which is also its localized effects on knowledge, is given in the finite act of a Subject. Between the finite of its act and the infinity of its being, there is no measure. This lack of measure (*de-mesure*) is also that which relates the verifying exposition of the evental axiom to the infinite hypothesis of its completion; or what relates the indiscernible subtraction, founding of the subject, to the generic subtraction wherein is anticipated the truth of which the subject is a subject. This relation goes from almost nothing, the finite, to almost everything, the infinite. Whence the little-said of every truth, since what thereof is said is always of the local order of verification.

The second reason is intrinsic. As a truth is a generic subset of the Universe, it cannot then be covered by any predicate or constructed by any formula. This is the nub of the matter: there is no formula for truth. Whence the reason a truth is little-said, since ultimately the impossibility of a formulaic construction boils down to this that what we *know* of truth is only that we know of it, being that which is disposed, as always finite, behind pure choices.

That a truth is little-said in fact expresses the relationship, governed by an undecidable axiom, that exists between the indiscernible and the generic.

That said, the generic or subtractive power of a truth can be anticipated as such. The generic being of a truth is never presented, but we can know, formally, that a truth will always have taken place as a generic infinity. Whence the possibility of a fictive disposition (*fictionnement*) of the effects of its having-taken-place. From the vantage point of the subject, it is always possible to hypothesize a universe in which this truth in which the subject is constituted will have completed its generic total- ization. What consequences would such a hypothesis on the Universe have in which the truth proceeds to infinity? You'll observe that the axiom, which decides the undecidable based on the event, is succeeded by the hypothesis, which supports in fiction a Universe supplemented by the generic subset of which the subject, through the trial of the indis- cernible, supports local and finite delineations.

Is there anything that would obstruct such a hypothesis? Anything that might pose a limit to the generic power of a truth engaged in the fiction of its completion, and therefore of its being wholly said? Such an obstacle exists, to my mind, and it is none other than that of the unnameable.

Regarding the generic being of a truth, an anticipatory hypothesis obviously constitutes a *forcing* of the little-said. This forcing creates the fiction of a wholly said from the vantage point of an infinite and generic truth. The temptation is therefore great to exercise this forcing on the most intimate and most subtracted point of the situation, on that which attests to its singularity, on that which has even no proper name, on the proper of the proper, on the anonym for which not even 'anonym' is an adequate name.

Let's say that the forcing, which represents the infinite genericity of a truth in the future perfect, is most radically tested in its power to say-all in truth, when it attempts to give even the unnameable a name.

From the constraint exercised by the infinite, or by the subtractive excess of the generic, over the weakness of the One at the unnameable point, the desire can emerge to name the unnameable, to appropriate the proper of the proper in a nomination.

What I decipher in this desire, which every truth puts on the agenda, is the very figure of Evil. For the forcing of a nomination of the unname- able is tantamount to the denial of singularity as such, it is the moment in which, in the name of the infinite genericity of a truth, the resistance of what there is that is absolutely singular in a singularity, that is, the part of being of the proper that is subtracted from nomination, appears as an obstacle to the deployment of a truth seeking to ensure its dominion over the situation. The even-worse (*en-pire*) (in two words) of a truth is to force, in the name of generic subtraction, the subtraction of the unnameable to vanish into the day of nomination.

We shall call this a disaster. Evil is the disaster of a truth, one that comes when the desire to force the nomination of the unnameable is unleashed in fiction.

It is commonly said that Evil is the negation of what is present and affirmed, that it is murder and death, that it is opposed to life. I should rather say that it is the denial of a subtraction. What Evil affects is not that which is self-affirming, but rather that which is withdrawn from and anonymous to the weakness of the One. Evil is not the non-respect of the name of the Other; it is much more the desire to name *at any price*.

It is commonly said that Evil is mendacity, ignorance and murderous stupidity. But, alas, it is rather the case that Evil has as its radical condition the process of a truth. There is only ever Evil insofar as there is a truth axiom at the point of the undecidable, a trajectory of truth at the point of the indiscernible, an anticipation of the being of truth at the point of the generic and the forcing into truth of a nomination at the point of the unnameable.

If the forcing of the unnameable subtraction is a disaster, then it is because it affects the entire situation, by chasing singularity as such from it, of which the unnameable is the emblem. In this sense, the desire in fiction to suppress the fourth subtractive operation unleashes a capacity of destruction that is latent in every truth, in the very sense in which Mallarmé wrote 'Destruction was my Beatrice'.

The ethics of a truth consists then wholly in a sort of restraint with regard to its powers. It is important that the combined effect of the undecidable, the indiscernible and the generic, or that is of the event, the subject, and truth, accepts as the principled limitation of its trajectory that unnameable that Samuel Beckett made the title of a book.

Samuel Beckett was certainly not blind to the latent ravage that the desire for truth inflicts on the subtraction of the proper. He even saw in it the ineluctable violence of thought, as, for instance, when he said in his *Unnamable* that 'I only think . . . once a certain degree of terror has been exceeded'. But he also knew that the ultimate guarantee for the possibility of a peace among truths is rooted in the reserve of non-saying;

in the limit of the voice vis-à-vis that which shows itself; in that which is subtracted from the absolute imperative to speak the truth. This is also what he intended when in *Molloy* he reminded us that 'to restore silence is the role of objects' and when in *How It Is* he rejoiced over the fact that 'the voice being so ordered I quote that of our total life it states only three quarters'.

Subtracting is that on the basis of which every truth proceeds. But subtraction is what, in the guise of the unnameable, provides the norm and sets a limit for the subtractive subject. There is only one maxim in the ethics of a truth: do not subtract the ultimate subtraction.

This is exactly what Mallarmé, with whom I shall conclude, said in *Prose (for des Esseintes)*.

The danger is that a truth, errant and incomplete as it may be, takes itself, in the words of the poet, as an 'age of authority'. It thus desires for everything to be triumphantly named, in the Summer of revelation. But the core of what is, the 'southland' of our unconsciousness of being, does not and must not have a name. The site of the true, subtractively edified, or again, as the poet says, 'the flower that a contour of absence has separated from every garden', itself remains in its intimate depth, subtracted from the proper name. The sky and the map reveal that this country did not exist. But it does exist, and that is what troubles authoritarian truth, for which only that which is named in the power of the generic exists. This trouble must be made more profound in safeguarding the proper and the nameless. Let us conclude, then, with the following, in which everything I've said is said as a scintillation.

> The age of authority wears thin
> When, without reason, it is stated
> Of this southland which our twin
> Unconsciousness has penetrated
>
> That, soil of a hundred irises, its site,
> They know if it was really born:
> It bears no name that one could cite,
> Sounded by summer's golden horn.

(Stéphane Mallarmé, 'Prose (for des Esseintes)' in *Collected Poems*, translated and with a commentary by Henry Weinfield, Berkeley: University of California Press 1994, p. 46. Translation modified.)

CHAPTER NINE
Truth: Forcing and the Unnameable

Is it not natural – of a 'naturalness' that etymology justifies with a most extensive artifice – that, concerning truth, the philosopher states his declarations from the bias of love? The Platonic gesture, no doubt, as it was registered and acclaimed throughout the centuries prior to its vilification, is intent on seeing in *philosophia* – a friendship taken in wisdom – the connotation of a superior intensity, since, in the shelter of wisdom, what one discovers is the enigma of truth, and consequently – in the calm of friendship – the storm of love. Through this transference, in all senses of the word, philosophy – as Lacan showed us in his strange appropriation of a sort of real *Symposium* – presents itself as 'the love of truth'.

So, when Lacan stressed that a psychoanalyst's stance is certainly not to love the truth, we should be in no doubt he is pursuing a line of thought he came to call anti-philosophy.

As anti-philosopher, clearly, Lacan appointed himself as the educator of all future philosophers. A contemporary philosopher, for me, is indeed someone who has the unfaltering courage to work through Lacan's anti-philosophy. There are not many of them. It is as one of them, however, that I shall endeavour to explain what I declare is the return of truth. We might say that I speak here as a philosopher–subject supposed to know of anti-philosophy; and, hence, also as a lover of truth supposed to know what little credence can be granted to protests made in the name of such a love.

Lacan established the concept of truth in a seminar entitled *The Other Side of Psychoanalysis*, which has recently been published in an edition that I am simply taking as is, without entering into the controversies that invariably attend the inscription of the living word into the dead letter.

Lacan's basic contention consists in maintaining that, truth primordially being a kind of powerlessness, a weakness, it is as such necessary, if a love of truth exists, that this love is the love of that powerlessness, of that weakness. In this matter, you will observe, Lacan is for once consonant with Nietzsche, for whom the truth is in some sense the powerless form of power, or the power, as it is called in order to conceal it, of the powerless.

Yet, no sooner did Lacan do this than he distanced himself from the Dionysian preacher. Since, for Lacan, the root of the weakness in which truth lies is by no means of the order of revenge or *ressentiment*. Rather, what affects truth with an insurmountable restriction is, plainly, castration. Truth is a veil thrown over the impossibility of saying it all. It is at once something that can only be half-said and that conceals this acute powerlessness restricting access to saying – in an act of pretence, whereby it transforms itself into an image of itself as total. Truth is the mask of its own weakness. This time Lacan is consonant with Heidegger, for whom truth is the very veiling of being in its withdrawal (*retraite*). Except that Lacan distanced himself completely from the pathos with which Heidegger characterizes the becoming-distress of the veil and the forgetting. This is because castration is structural or it is the structure itself: which means that for Lacan there can be no place for the pre-castrated primordials that poets and pre-Socratic thinkers (ultimately) constitute for Heidegger.

As regards the authority of structure, what did Lacan argue the love of truth consists in? The logical consequence of what we have said is quite simply that the love of truth is the *love of castration*.

We are so used to thinking the horror of castration that it can only be astonishing to see a formula that expresses love for it. Nevertheless, this is exactly what Lacan pressed ahead with in a seminar dated 14 January 1970, in which we read: 'The love of truth is the love of that weakness whose veil we have lifted; it is the love of that which is hidden by truth, and which is called castration'.[1]

Thus truth, in the guise of the love one bears for it, affects castration with a veiling, whereby castration becomes stripped of the horror that it inspires as pure structural effect.

For the philosopher, this is stated: the truth is only tolerable for thought, that is to say, only philosophically lovable, inasmuch as one sets one's sights not on its plenitude or complete saying but on the resources of its *subtractive* dimension.

So, I shall attempt – not without the necessary approximation entailed, not only by a wish for concision, but also by the desire to consider as precisely as possible the indispensable mathematical parallels – to weigh truth in the scales of its power and its powerlessness, of its process and its limit, in its affirmative infinity and its essential subtraction.

I shall assemble the scales of my weighing up through a fourfold disjunction.

1. That of transcendence and immanence. Truth is not of the order of something that stands above the givenness (*donation*) of experience; rather it proceeds from the latter, or it insists in it as a singular figure of immanence.

2. That of the predicable and the non-predicable. There exists no single predicative trait capable of subsuming and totalizing the components of a truth. That is why a truth will be said to be nondescript or generic.

3. That of the infinite and the finite. Conceived in its incompletable being (as something that cannot be completed) a truth is an infinite multiple.

4. That of the nameable and the unnameable. The capacity of a truth to spread itself as judgement on knowledge is restricted by an unnameable point, one that cannot be forced without inducing disaster.

Thus, a truth is subtracted fourfold from the exhibition of its being. It is neither a *supremum* visible in the flash of its self-sufficiency, nor anything specified by a knowledge predicate, nor subject to the familiarity of finitude, nor a limitless power as regards it potential for knowledge.

To love truth is not solely to love castration, but to love the four figures in which its horror dissipates: immanence, genericity, the infinite and the unnameable.

Let us go through them in order.

That truth, at least *our* truth, is purely immanent was one of Freud's at once simple and fundamental intuitions. He defended the principle of immanence in an uncompromising fashion, especially against Jung. It is no exaggeration to say that one of Lacan's primary motivations was to keep this flame alive, bringing him to oppose the scientific and moralizing objectivism of the Chicago school.

CONDITIONS

I will use the word 'situation' – the most nondescript word imaginable – to designate the multiple of circumstances, of language, of objects, in which a truth proceeds. I shall say that this operation is *in* the situation and as such is neither its term, nor its norm, nor its destiny. In the psychoanalytic situation itself, the experience of the psychoanalyst, wherein a truth contrives (*machiner*) the subject, and singularly his suffering, things are clearly similar: the existence of the truth that emerges in the course of successive operations cannot ever be said to constitute a pre-given norm for what is being observed. Nor is the concern to discover or uncover the truth as if it were a secret entity buried, if I may say, in the deep exteriority of the situation. This is the point in a nutshell: that there is no depth, and that depth is only another name, one dear to hermeneuts, of transcendence.

But, then, if its process it strictly immanent, and if it is no longer there in the situation as a deep secret or intimate essence, where does a truth come from? How can it advance in the situation without always already having been in it? Lacan's genius lay in seeing that, as with Columbus's egg, the response is contained in the question. If a truth cannot come from the given (*une donation*), it is because it originates in a disappearance. This original disappearance, which came, for the time of a flash, to supplement the situation, and which is not localized within the latter except insofar as nothing of it subsists, and which insists *in truth* precisely insofar as it cannot be repeated as presence – this is what I call an 'event'. The event in philosophy is clearly analogous to what Freud called the primal scene, which since it only has a force of truth in its abolition, or since it has no site except the disappearance of the having-taken-place, means that it is pointless to ask, within the realist categories of the situation, whether it was real or invented. This question is, in the properly logical sense of the word, undecidable. The effect of truth consists in retroactively validating the fact that at the point of this undecidable there was the disappearance – acutely real and henceforth immanent to the situation – not only of the undecidable, but of the very question of the undecidable.

Such is the first subtractive dimension of truth, whose immanence depends upon the undecidability of what that immanence retraces.

What then is a truth the truth of? It can only be the truth of the situation itself, in which it insists, since there is nothing transcendent to the situation that is given to us, and nothing transcendent that truth would permit us to gain an apprehension of. This means that, since a situation, grasped in its pure being, is only a particular multiple, a truth will never be anything but a subset of this multiple, a subset of this set called 'situation'. This is the ontological requirement of immanence in all its rigour. Since a truth advances in a situation, that to which it attests does not at all exceed the situation itself. We could say that a truth is *included* in that of which it is the truth.

Here I shall open a careful parenthesis. Careful, because, I must admit, I am not nor have I ever been nor will I most likely ever be either an analyst, or an analysand, or analysed. I am 'unanalysed'. Can someone unanalysed say anything about psychoanalysis. You will be the judges of that. Now, from what I've just said it seems to follow that, to the extent that what is at stake in psychoanalysis involves a truth, it is not so much a truth of the subject as it is *a truth of the analytic situation itself,* a truth that the analysand will no doubt henceforth need to take on board, but of which it would be one-sided to say that it belongs to him or her alone. Psychoanalysis seems to me to be a situation in which the analysand is given the painful opportunity to encounter a truth, to cross a truth along the way. And it is from this crossing that he emerges either armed or disarmed. And perhaps it is in seeing things this way that we might throw some light on the mysteries of what Lacan, who clearly considered the real to be an impasse, called, precisely, 'the pass'.

So, let us look at the dimension of impasse. We will say that a truth only comes to the end of its process as a subset of the situation-set. Now we know that a situation specifies any number of subsets. This in fact gives us the broadest possible definition of knowledge. Knowledge is what names a situation's subsets. The language of the situation has the precise function of gathering, under a predicative trait, the elements of the situation, and thereby of constituting a concept's extensional correlate. A subset, such as, for example, one in a perceptual situation of dogs or cats, or in an analytic situation of traits and hysterical or obsessional symptoms, is captured in concepts of the language, on the basis of indices of recognition attributable to all the terms or elements that fall under the concept. I call this nominal and conceptual swarming of forms of knowledge the encyclopaedia of the situation. The encyclopaedia is a classifier of subsets, and the multiform entanglement of forms of knowledge that language continually elicits.

But if a truth is only a subset of the situation, then how is it distinguished from a rubric of knowledge? The question is philosophically crucial. The issue is to know if the price we pay for immanence is not the pure and simple reduction of truth to knowledge. If it were, this would grant a decisive concession to all variants of positivism. And, more significantly, to forms of neoclassical regression, which would involve abandoning the impetus that Kant gave, and Heidegger later renewed, to the crucial distinction between truth and knowledge, which is also that between thought and knowledge. Exaggerating the matter slightly, this neoclassical version would come down to saying that as soon as a given analysand's *case* is identified as being hysterical or obsessional or phobic, as soon as the patient's predicative trait is established, and he is inscribed in the analytic situation, the crux of the work is done. All that remains is to *draw the consequences*.

In his specific conception of fidelity to Freud, Lacan categorically rejected this nosological vision of the analytic situation. Instead, he took up and projected across the analytic field, the modernity of a non-conceptual gap between truth and forms of knowledge. Not only did he distinguish between them, but he pointed out that a truth is essentially unknown, that it is literally a *hole* in forms of knowledge.

In so doing – and to my mind this is a point whose consequences we are yet to grasp – Lacan has proclaimed that psychoanalysis is not a type of knowledge but a type of thought.

However, despite what is announced by those who variously aim at theological recuperation, that is, by those who are always hard at work trying to turn pig-feed into hosts, and who thus proffer mouth-watering speculations on the transcendence of the Big Other, Lacan was never prepared to compromise the immanence of truth.

He therefore had to force our impasse and establish that, even though it can be reduced to an insubstantial subset of the situation, a truth of the situation nevertheless remains heterogeneous to those subsets listed by forms of knowledge.

That is what is essentially expressed by the maxim concerning the 'half-said' nature of truth. That a truth is not all-said signifies that its plenitude, the subset that it constitutes in the situation, cannot be captured by a predicative trait that would make of it a subsection of the encyclopaedia. The truth at stake in the psychoanalysis of such and such a woman can in no way be assimilated to the fact that this woman is, so to say, a hysteric. Granted, there will be numerous components of the truth at work in such a situation that possess distinctive traits of what goes by the name hysteria in the register of knowledge. But saying so is not to do anything *in truth*. For the truth in question necessarily arranges other components whose traits bear no relevance to the encyclopaedic concept of hysteria, and it is only insofar as these components subtract the set from the predicate of hysteria that a truth, not a form of knowledge, proceeds in its singularity. Hence, however confident one may be in a diagnosis of hysteria and the consequences to be drawn from it, it is not only not a statement of truth, but is not even a half-said truth, since, being registered in knowledge, the dimension of truth is *entirely* lacking.

A truth is a subset of the situation that is formed in such a way that its components cannot be totalized under a predicate of language however sophisticated that predicate may be. A truth is therefore a nondescript subset, and so also indeterminate since the way it brings its components together rules out their having any common trait that would enable this set to be identified in knowledge.

And it is obviously because it is included in the situation under the form of a singular indetermination in its concept, because it is subtracted from every classifying grip of encyclopaedic language, that such a subset is not the knowledge of such and such a regional particularity of the situation but a truth of the situation as such, an immanent production of its pure multiple-being, a truth of its being, *qua* being.

As it so often happens, mathematics comes to the aid of Lacan's intuition. At the beginning of the 1960s, a mathematician named Paul Cohen identified such subsets of a set. Cohen called a subset subtracted from every determination by a fixed formula of the language a *generic* subset. And Cohen demonstratively established that the supposition that such subsets exist is consistent.

Twenty years ago, Gödel had already provided a rigorous definition of the idea that a subset is named in knowledge. Such subsets are sets whose elements validate a fixed formula of the language. Gödel called them *constructible* subsets. Cohen's generic subsets, by contrast, are precisely non-constructible sets. They are too indeterminate to correspond to, or to be totalized by, a unique predicative expression.

There can be no doubt that the opposition between constructible sets and generic sets ontologically grounds the – purely immanent – support of being of the opposition between knowledge and truth. In this way, Cohen's demonstration of the fact that the existence of generic subsets is consistent is a genuinely modern proof of the fact that truths can exist, truths that are irreducible to any 'given' of the encyclopaedia. In the ontological radicality of the matheme, Cohen's theorem comes to complete what began with modernity in the Kantian distinction between thought and cognition.

That a truth is generic and not constructible – which, in the guise of the half-said, was Lacan's ingenious intuition – entails, and we now come to the third of our disjunctions, that a truth is infinite.

This point seems to constitute an objection to every philosophy of finitude, even as, by way of his thesis of the *objet petit a*, Lacan inscribed finitude at the heart of desire. All of the being by which such desire is supported resides, in effect, in this object, which is also its cause, and of which, as is indicated by its always being a partial object, finitude is constitutive.

In reality, the dialectic of the finite and the infinite in Lacan is extremely tortuous, and I dare say that the philosopher's eye detects at this point the limit, and therefore the real, of that which – thinking it as thought, in keeping with Lacan's approach – psychoanalysis is capable.

That a truth is infinite constitutes an objection to philosophical ruminations on finitude only if that truth is immanent, and hence only insofar as it touches on the real. If truth is transcendent, or supra-real, then it can, under the name of God or one akin to it such as the Other, abandon the integral destiny of the subject to finitude.

I said a moment ago that Lacan sided with the immanence of truth, but I added that he did this 'on the whole'. For, he only ever strictly observed the constraint of immanence concerning what could be called the primordial determinant of this thought. Elsewhere, Lacan oscillated considerably on this point, essentially as a result of his hesitation to cut ties with the hermeneutics of finitude, to which, alas, the majority of contemporary philosophy is reducible, and that is today reviving a form of pious discourse, a religiosity that elevates the small God of minimum transcendence suitable to our democratic conviviality, to which we are reassuringly told no conceivable alternative exists.

It is certainly thanks to Lacan's implacable knife, to the sure way he sliced between the logic of sense and the logic of truth, that we have the whole conceptual apparatus in which the abjection of pious discourse was made perceptible. And as for democratic conviviality: we know it was not Lacan's forte, and more that, as is daily evident, it is by no means a suitable ideal for those who lay claim to his legacy.

All the same, Lacan's equivocation is evident, as we can see in . . . *Or Worse*, where he is led to say (it is only one of many examples) that Cantor's non-denumerable transfinite cardinals represent 'an object that I would qualify as mythical'. I for my part do not believe that we can take one more step in pursuit of the consequences of the infinity of the true except if we hold non-denumerable cardinals as being – not myth, but – real.

If we are to go beyond Lacan, then perhaps we ought to be faithful to the master by putting our essential trust in the matheme. And, above all, we must insist on demonstratively establishing the fact that every truth is infinite.

Let us suppose that a truth is finite. As a finite subset of the situation, it is composed of the terms a^1, a^2, and so on, until a^3, where the number n fixes the intrinsic dimension of such a truth. We have then a truth in which n components are articulated. It follows directly that this subset can be assigned a predicate, and that, as it is inscribed in the encyclopaedia, it falls under knowledge. To be brief, let us say that a finite subset cannot be generic, but that it is necessarily constructible. Consider the predicate (which is always available in a language of the situation) 'identical with a^1, or identical with a^2, . . . or identical with a^n'. The composed set of terms in question, the terms a^1, a^2, so on up to a^n, is exactly covered by this predicate. This predicate constructs this subset, identifies it in language and rules out its being generic. So it cannot be a truth. QED.

A truth's infinity immediately entails that it is incompletable. For the subset that it constitutes, which is delineated on the basis of the eventual disappearance, is composed along a succession that founds a time, such as, for example, that unique time of the analytic cure. Regardless of the norm internal to the extension of such a time, this time is itself irremediably finite. And hence the truth that unfolds in it does not attain the complete composition of its infinite being. It was Freud's genius to recognize this point in the guise of the infinite dimension of psychoanalysis, which always leaves open, like a gaping chasm, the truth that slips into the time inaugurated by psychoanalysis.

This, I believe, brings us back to castration as that which the truth veils, thereby giving us the permission to love it.

For, if a truth continues to open onto the infinity of its being, what kind of power can it have? To say that it is half-said is not to say much. The relationship between the finiteness of the time of its composition, that is, the time founded by the event of a disappearance, and the infinity of its being, is a relationship without measure. We should rather say: a truth is little-said; or even: the truth is almost not spoken. Is it legitimate, then, to speak of a power of the truth, of a power necessary to found the concept of its possible powerlessness? In the seminar I cited at the start Lacan directly stated that 'it seems to be among analysts, and among them in particular, that, invoking certain taboo words with which their discourse is festooned, one never notices what truth – which is to say, powerlessness – is'. Certainly. But if we are to avoid being either like those festooned analysts, or simply jealous of the festooned, we shall have to think the powerlessness of truth, which presupposes that we are first able to conceive its power.

I have conceived this power – which Freud perhaps already named with the category of 'working through' – under the name of forcing, which I've taken directly from the mathematical work of Cohen. Forcing concerns the point at which, although incomplete, a truth authorizes anticipations of knowledge, not statements about what is, but about *what will have been if the truth reaches completion*.

What the dimension of anticipation requires is that the formulation of truth judgements be carried out in the future perfect. This means that, while almost nothing can be said about what a truth is, when it comes to what happens *on condition that that truth will have been*, there is a forcing that enables almost everything to be stated.

In this way, a truth works in the retroaction of an almost nothing and the anticipation of an almost everything.

The decisive point, which Paul Cohen has also resolved in the ontological domain, that is, in mathematics, is the following: it is certain that the elements of generic subset can (definitely) not be named, since a generic subset is simultaneously incomplete in its infinite composition, and subtracted from every predicate that would, in language, identify it in a single blow. But it can be maintained that *if* such and such an element of the situation *will have been* in the hypothetically completed generic subset under consideration, *then* such a statement, as rationally connectable to the element in question, is, or rather will have been, correct. Cohen called this method *forcing*, since it is a method that limits the correctness of statements *to the anticipatory condition of the composition of an infinite generic subset.*

If I say 'correct' or 'correctness' it is because onto the opposition between knowledge and truth, Lacan superimposed an opposition between the correct (*véridique*) and the true. You will observe that a statement caught up in a *forcing* cannot without serious confusion be said to be true. This is precisely because its value cannot be determined except under the condition of existence pertaining to a generic subset, therefore under the condition of truth.

For my part, I prefer the term *veridical (véridicité)*, because it at once indicates a gap with and a connection to truth. I shall therefore say, projecting what Cohen's matheme prescribes for the philosopher, this: a truth proceeds in situation, without power either to say itself or to complete itself. This is sense in which it is absolutely castrated, being almost not what it is. Yet, it does have the power, with regard to a given statement, to anticipate the following conditional judgement: if such and such a component figures in a truth that is presumed complete, then the statement in question will have been veridical (or erroneous). In the dimension of the future perfect, a truth's power resides, in the anticipation of its own existence, in legislating on what is veridically sayable. What is veridically sayable obviously pertains to knowledge, and the category of the veridical is a category of knowledge. It can therefore be said that, castrated with regard to its own immediate power, a truth is all-powerful with regard to possible forms of knowledge. The mark of castration does not pass between truth and knowledge. It separates truth from itself and, in the same movement, frees up its power of hypothetical anticipation from the encyclopaedic field of forms of knowledge. This power is the power of forcing.

Psychoanalytic experience, I maintain, is woven of such an observation (*constat*). That which, little by little, comes to say itself in a cure is not only what, in a finite and metered time, plots the incompletable infinity of the true, but also – and especially with regard to the rare interventions of the analyst – the anticipatory marking of that which will have be able to have been said veridically, insofar as such and such a sign, act or signifier will have been supposed to be a component of such and such a truth. This anticipatory marking, we know, depends upon the future perfect tense of the empirical completion of psychoanalysis, beyond which any supposition about the completion of truth becomes impossible, since the situation has been completed, and with it the forcing of the possible veridicality of judgements pertaining to it. At which point it turns out that a said veridicality is something that we can call knowledge, but it is knowledge *within truth*. As to what the knowledge obtained that is 'forced' through treatment really consists in, the analysand, operating a retroaction that comes to compensate the anticipation of forcing, is the only witness we have.

I am again going to don the hat of the prudent unanalysed to say that, as a result, it does not seem to me appropriate to call the act of psychoanalysis an interpretation. I would prefer, as scandalously authoritarian as the word may sound, to call it a forcing. For what is required is to intervene based on the suspended hypothesis of a truth that proceeds in the analytic situation.

I do not think I am going too far in observing the doubt that lingers on the question of interpretation in many of the dead master's texts. This should give us no cause for surprise, if it is recalled that hermeneuts of all colours have rushed into the breach opened up by the faithful Paul Ricoeur and sought to saddle the word 'interpretation' with the burden of connecting psychoanalysis to forms of revamped pious discourse. To put it bluntly, I do not think psychoanalysis can be a form of interpretation, because its rule is not meaning but truth. It is certainly not either a discovery of truth, which, since it is generic, we know is futile to hope shall be discovered. As such our only hope left is that psychoanalysis consist, in the game of a risked anticipation, in the forcing of knowledge in truth by which a generic truth in the course of emerging fragmentarily delivers a constructible knowledge.

Having weighed up the power of truth, are we to say that even under the wagered condition of its emergent multiplicity it can without exception extend to all the statements that circulate in the site in which it proceeds? Does the truth, despite and because of its being generic, possess the power of naming all imaginable veridicities?

This would amount to disregarding the return of castration, and of the love linking us to it by way of truth, in the terminal form of an absolute obstacle, of a term that, although given in the situation, is subtracted from the clutches of veridical evaluation. Of a point that is in one way or another unforceable. I call this point the unnameable, and, Lacan, in the field of psychoanalysis, called it enjoyment.

Consider a situation in which a truth proceeds as the course (*tracé*) of a vanished event. We then have a situation that has been supplemented in an immanent way by the becoming of its own truth. For, the paradox of a generic truth consists in just that: it is a purely internal anonymous supplement, an immanent addition. What can we say of the real of such a configuration?

First, we should rigorously distinguish between the real and being. Lacan applied this distinction from his very first seminar. On 30 June 1954, he stated that the three fundamental passions, that is, love, hate and ignorance, can be registered 'only in the realm of being, and not in that of the real'. So, if love of truth is a passion, then this love is certainly addressed to the being of truth, but falters upon encountering its real.

Earlier we established the concept of the being of a truth: this being is that of a generic multiplicity subtracted from constructions of knowledge. To love truth is to love the generic as such, and that is why, as with all love, it has something astray with it, has something that language cannot contain, and that is maintained in the errancy of an excess through the power of the forcings it permits.

However, the question remains as to the real that this errancy itself, and the power it founds, comes up against.

In this regard, I would say that, in the field determined by a situation and the generic becoming of its truth, a real is attested to by a term, a point, and only one, at which the power of truth is suspended. There is one term in relation to which no anticipatory hypothesis on the generic subset permits us to force a judgement. It is a genuinely unforceable term, one that cannot, no matter how advanced the process of truth, be prescribed in such a way that it would be conditioned by this truth. No matter how great the transformative resources proper to the immanent tracing of the true, no naming is appropriate for this term of the situation. That is why I call it unnameable. Unnameable is to be understood not in terms of the available resources of knowledge but in the precise sense in which it remains out of reach to the veridical anticipations founded on truth. It is not unnameable 'in itself', which is meaningless; it is unnameable with regard to the singular process of a truth. The unnameable only emerges in the field of truth.

This sheds light on the fact that in the situation of the analytical cure, which is precisely one of the places in which a truth is held to be at work, enjoyment is at once what that truth deploys in terms of the real and what remains forever subtracted from the veridical range of the sayable. With regard to analytic truth, or the truth of the situation of the cure, enjoyment is exactly the unnameable point that constitutes a stumbling block for the forcings permitted by this truth.

It must be emphasized that this point is *unique*. For a single truth there cannot be two or more unnameables. The Lacanian maxim 'there is oneness' is here fastened to the irreducible real, to what could be called 'the grain of the real' jamming the machinery of truth, whose power consists in being the machinery of forcings and hence the machinery for producing finite veridicalities from the vantage point of a truth that cannot be accomplished. Here, the jamming (*enrayage*) effected by the One-real is in opposition to the path opened up (*frayage*) by veridicality.

This effect of oneness in the real, brought about by the power of truth, constitutes truth's powerless obverse. The particular difficulty there is in *thinking* this effect indicates this immediately. How are we to think that which is subtracted from every veridical nomination? How are we to think in truth that which is excluded from the powers of truth? Is not thinking it necessarily to name it? And how to name the unnameable?

Lacan's response to the paradoxical appeal is never fully spelt out. When he dealt in his seminars with trans-phallic enjoyment, and second-ary enjoyment in particular, what arose was something about which the least that could be said is that it is truly anterior to the Freudian cut, and that was precisely the triangle of femininity, the infinite and the unsay-able. That feminine enjoyment links the infinite to the unsayable, and that we see evidence for it in mystical ecstasy is something I would say is a cultural topic, and something one senses neither Lacan nor anyone following him has as yet submitted to the radical test of the matheme.

Perhaps one source of Lacan's difficulties lay in the paradox of the unnameable, a paradox that I will formulate as follows: if the unname-able is unique to the field of truth, is it not precisely named by this property? For if what is not named is unique, the 'not being named' functions *as its proper name*. Would not the unnameable ultimately be the proper name of the real of a situation traversed by its truth? Would not unsayable enjoyment be the name of the real of the subject, as soon as it has to come to terms in the cure-situation with his truth, or with a truth?

But then the unnameable is named in truth, it is forced, and a truth's reserve of power is effectively boundless.

Here again mathematics steps up to aid us. In 1968, a logician named Furkhen showed that the uniqueness of the unnameable does not form an obstacle to its existence. He in effect created a mathematical situation in which the resources of language and its power of naming are clearly defined, and in which one term exists, and only one, which cannot receive a name, in the sense that it cannot be identified by a formula of the language.

It is therefore consistent, in the order of the matheme, to hold that one and only one term of a given situation remains unforceable from the standpoint of a generic truth. In a situation supplemented by a truth this is evinced by a supplement's real. No matter how powerful a truth, how capable of veridicality it proves to be, this power comes up against a unique term, which with a single blow effects the swing from all-powerfulness to powerlessness, displacing our love of truth from its appearance, the love of the generic, to its essence, the love of the unnameable.

I am not saying that the love of the generic is nothing. By itself, it is radically distinguished from the love of opinions, that is, the passion of ignorance, as it is from the fatal desire for complete constructibility. But love of the unnameable reaches further still, and it alone makes it possible to maintain a love of truth without disaster or dissolution affecting the veridical in its entirety. For in matters of truth, only by submitting to the test of its powerlessness can we find the ethics required for the adoption of its power.

The circumstances in which we find ourselves in this autumn of 1991 enjoin me to conclude, in an apparently incongruous manner, with Ilyich Ulyanov, also known as Lenin, whose statues it is nowadays fashionable to tear down.

Let us note in passing that if there were some Lacanian who was tempted to join in the zeal of these statue-removers, he ought to reflect on a paragraph from the seminar held on 20 March 1973, which begins: 'Marx and Lenin, Freud and Lacan are not coupled in being. It is via the letter they found in the Other that, as beings of knowledge, they proceed two by two, in a supposed Other'.

Thus the would-be Lacanian toppler of Lenin's statues has to explain why Lacan identified himself as Freud's Lenin.

Let us add that at a time in which many analysts are preoccupied, whether only in the monumental guise of Inland Revenue and the European Union, they would surely do better to consider Lenin's writings than those of the statue-topplers – supposing such writings exist.

CONDITIONS

Lenin felt obliged to write: 'Theory is all-powerful because it is true'. This is not incorrect, because forcing submits in anticipatory fashion the expanse of the situation to a potentially infinite network of veridical judgements But, once again, this is merely the half of it. We must add: 'Theory is powerless, because it is true'. This second half of the statement's correctness is supported by the forcing's being in the impasse of the unnameable. But, on its own, this second statement is no more able to avert disaster than the first.

Thus, Lenin seems to have had a relation of love for castration that veils the latter in that half of half that it founds. As for the statue-topplers, it is all too evident that they have, on the contrary, adopted a straight love of powerlessness, which works only to make the bed for situations without truth.

It this oscillation inevitable? I do not think so. Under the strict guarantee of the matheme, we can advance in this discovery in which the love of truth relates to castration, by the twofold means of power and powerlessness, of forcing and the unnameable. We need do no more than hold both to the veridical and to the incompletable. To finite analysis and to infinite analysis. Or, as Samuel Beckett put it in the last words of a book that is not called *The Unnamable* for nothing: 'You must go on, I can't go on, I'll go on'.

PART IV
Philosophy and Politics

Part IV
Philosophy and Politics

CHAPTER TEN
Philosophy and Politics

1. CLOSURE OF PHILOSOPHY AND RETREAT OF THE POLITICAL?

Has philosophy not entered the unachievable impurity of its closure? Has politics – at least the politics that matters to thought, that is emancipatory politics, once called revolutionary politics – not come to attest its disaster? How, then, can the link presumed by an 'and' make thought circulate between two terms that, in themselves and for us, are wholly undermined?

It is at once by means of its inner relation to itself, and by means of the form of its assertions, that, in the opening pages of *The Fiction of the Political*,[1] Philippe Lacoue-Labarthe suggests to us in what sense philosophy could no longer be, in his eyes, but in the element of its inherent impossibility.

Its inner relation to itself is affected because, for him, the desire for philosophy is stricken by the melancholy of History. More precisely, such desire, when it is presented as the continuity of a right to desire, is turned by the century's obscurities into obscene caricature.

The form is affected because it has become impossible, in philosophy, to uphold the imperative clarity of theses. The result is that philosophy then can do no more than oscillate between an intolerable mutism – that of Heidegger faced with Paul Celan[2] – and the almost desperate search for a prose of thought that would prepare thought's leave for the poem.

Lacoue-Labarthe and Nancy also refer to this impossibility – an impossibility that henceforth consists not so much in philosophy's standing as in its subjective element – as the retreat of the political. This is because at the core of their assessment, which impacts both on philosophy's desire and on its saying (*dire*), there is without any doubt a conviction about the, henceforth improbable, or *impossible to find*, link between philosophy and what, of politics, inscribes into History the destiny of a thought in the form of a clearing.

2. THE COMMUNITY AS THE INHERENT IMPOSSIBILITY OF OUR WORLD

This 'clearing's' philosophical name was originally 'community'. If nothing less, this name – itself a descendent of revolutionary fraternity – has governed the philosophical reception of the avatars of emancipatory politics since 1789. Community is that by means of which philosophy *understands* first the socialist, and then the communist, proposition.

Insofar as it is still implicit in the remnants of the communist idea, at the limit of its term, community is that through which the collective emerges in the form of a coming forth (*éclosion*) devoid of substance or founding narrative, of territory or borders, that is not so much subtracted from oppression and division as it is deployed beyond any such partition, is undivided but without self-fusion and accomplished but without closure, or, as Mallarmé said, such as it ends 'in a whole stream of subtle branches'.

It is a 'community' whose disposition of being is not available for discovery, and so is unsituated, or incapable of being promised to anyone who would have but a will for it. It is one that, without hearth or home, does not allow itself, any more than a community of love, to be entrusted or transmitted to what it is not. It is a community that we will therefore call, with Maurice Blanchot, unavowable.[3]

It is a 'community' that no institution can realize or serve to perpetuate, such that we can only hold ourselves in the embrace of its coming, in the offering of the event. It is a community that we will therefore call, with Jean-Luc Nancy, inoperative (*désoeuvrée*).

It is a community with no present or presence, merely gripped in its coming, such as the ravages of time have stripped its thematic bare, have exposed its fine displacements. It is a community that we will therefore call, with Giorgio Agamben, the coming community (*communauté qui vient*).[4]

The impalpable gift of community is the same that today's world tells us is a specific impossibility of the world, and of every world, inasmuch as a world finds support alone in consensual consistency. Community, communism: what has passed before our eyes is the would-be proof that these latter were criminal traversings of an inconsistency of world. Far more than the ease of enjoyment and transit, far more than self-contained egoism and consent to rapine, and to injustice and to freedom as a holiday from truth, what people are saying – with the market economy, the technical reign of politicians, war and indifference – or rather what everyone is saying to oneself in the anonymous element of the statement is this: that today, as always, in this world the community is an impossibility. Since reasonable management, capital and general equilibria are the only things that *exist*.

Or else communi*ties* exist. But nothing is more contrary to the Idea of community than the idea of communal substance, whether it be Jewish, Arab, French or Western. Nothing places the community in the difficulty of its impossibility more than the realist alliance between the economy and communitarian cultural territories. And consequently, the *real* of the world is precisely the community as impossibility.

Or else this: real politics, the one that is preached to us, debars every Idea. To be *of the* world consists in nothing other than making this impossibility one's own, which means, and such is the imperative of our times, preside over all your actions and all your thoughts in such a way that these actions and these thoughts attest the impossibility of community. Or again this: act in the absence of Idea.

3. BARREN AS IT IS, BE CONTEMPORARY WITH THE VERDICT OF THE WORLD

I shall argue that we ought to understand the truth of this imperative. More precisely, we ought to understand this imperative *in the element of a truth*. Which is to say, we ought to understand it in the same way that, in his *Manifesto*, Marx understood the capacity of capital to dissolve all the sacred links upon which it was believed the consistency of the world rested. We ought thus understand it as a horror with no truth that exhibits matter for a possible truth. This is to say, we ought to displace the barren imperative of our world. Simply displace it.

Within which space of places is it to be displaced? In my view, everything rests here on the link between community and truth, and therefore, ultimately, on the link between philosophy and politics. The displacement consists in this: the fatal aspect of the communist Idea was that it presupposed the co-belonging of the community and the truth of the collective. In communism, community became the coming realization, in politics, of the collective as truth.

That the collective in its act is the truth of what it is, philosophy has since the beginning called justice. Plato stated exactly this at the end of Book IV of *The Republic* when he said that justice by no means consists in an external norm, in a qualification of what is. Justice, he said, is said of action that touches on the order within oneself (*intériorité*), an action that is veridically (*aléthos*) relative to what is there of such inner order and that issues strictly from it. In the figure of community, justice is therefore not what can be said of the collective; it is the collective such as it occurs veridically, or as truth, in its own immanent disposition.

This presupposes, of course, that justice is disjoint from necessity, in whatever form it operates. The tragedy of the communist Idea in its secularized form is that it placed necessity in charge of its paradigm, which was also to say, it submitted politics to a sense of History. This Idea of communism named the community as beholden to its own real necessity.

Instead, we ought to, in the same terms as Plato, maintain that such a stance is sophistic. In Book VI of *The Republic* Plato gave a definition of the sophist that is seldom mentioned but that in my view is crucial. The sophist, he said, is the one who cannot see 'the extent to which the nature of the good and the nature of the necessary differ'. The subordination of political will to the notion of a necessity of the community as the figure of good in politics consigns will to the domain of sophistry. Little wonder, then, that today this will, which for so long had been represented as the will to justice, expends itself in the inverted form of sophistic reasoning dominating us, and that is: because the community is impossible, emancipatory politics does not represent a good. Again, and we hear this repeated from all quarters, in the idea of communism, and therefore in the givenness of the community, the essence of justice is injustice. The impossibility of the community, which is the real of the world, prevents politics from falling under an idea. It follows that every kind of politics essentially consists in managing necessity. Which can also be stated as: there is no emancipatory politics. What there is, is the regulated and natural development of liberal equilibria.

If, contrary to this verdict, we assume that it is possible for politics to exist in the element of thought, and therefore of justice – since 'justice' is only the philosophical name for politics as a form of thought – then a thesis suggests itself whose consequences I shall now attempt to deploy: the impossibility of community forms no objection to the imperative of emancipatory politics, whether we name it communism or otherwise.

4. EXISTENCE OF POLITICS AT THE POINT OF ITS APPARENT IMPOSSIBILITY

Incidentally, Plato's conviction was also that the community's impossibility does not constitute an objection to a politics of which this idea is a philosopheme. In *The Republic*, Socrates' interlocutors try to unsettle him at several points by saying that the ideal city that he 'mythologizes', as he puts it, has not the slightest chance of existing. But Socrates' response to this, in its crafty variations, essentially comes down to saying that when politics is taken as a form of thought[5] – and obviously only such a politics is of interest to philosophy – then the norm of politics does not lie in its *objective* possibility.

But we are nevertheless not speaking about some utopia: since, in its very impossibility, the politics that is described, the mythologized *politeia*, actually has a *real*. This real is that of subjective prescription, of a prescription that carries out with regard to the world not nothing at all but what it is possible to do (even if it is in accordance with the real law of the impossible). There are two related figures of this possible-commensurable-with-the-impossible:

– First, the figure of statements. A politics is already real insofar as its statements have succeeded in existing. Politics, if it comes within thought, is initially contained in prescriptive statements. Plato did not hesitate to maintain that, in any case, its practical execution, *praxis*, bears less truth within it than the statement, *lexis*. As a result, a political prescription has no need first to establish its possibility in terms of realization. Socrates asks: 'Do you think, then, that our words are any the less well spoken if we find ourselves unable to prove that it is possible for a state to be governed in accordance with our words?' At the end of the day, every emancipatory politics presupposes an unconditioned prescription. 'Unconditioned' here means that radical emancipatory politics does not set out from an examination of the world that aims to demonstrate its possibility. And also that a politics is not obliged to present itself as something that represents an objective social grouping. A politics of emancipation draws itself from the void that an event brings forth (*fait advenir*) as the latent inconsistency of the given world. These statements are the namings of this very void.

– Second, the statements of an emancipatory politics envelop a second real principle, which is the principle of political subjectivity. This forms the main theme of the end of Book IX of *The Republic*, where there is a renewed attack by the sceptical youth. The politician, Plato said, will take care of public affairs 'very much so in the society where he really belongs; but not, I think, in the society where he's born, unless some miracle happens'. 'Where he really belongs' – this 'he' refers to the political man, the opposite of the politician (in the usual sense), that is, to the militant of an unconditioned prescription, as he is in situation in the society where he is born, and in which he will act, in accordance with this prescription, under the injunction of the chance of events, without ever giving ground on the subjective norm he has adopted. And, Plato added, 'it doesn't matter whether it exists or ever will exist; in it alone, and in no other society, could he take part in public affairs'.

5. PHILOSOPHICAL NAMINGS AND POLITICAL CATEGORIES

But if in order to be just politics requires no form of proof in terms of necessary or possible existence, if in the first place it is a form of thinking that, through the persistent efforts of a subject, is brought into being with the body of statements that make up its prescription, then it follows that the community, that is, the supposition of a real being of justice in the form of a collective that makes of itself a truth, is never – either intrinsically or in its letter – a category of politics. At best, the community is what, *in philosophy*, is pronounced as the trace of a real political condition, which is itself woven solely of singular statements and active subjects.

Or further, a truth, as a political truth, is deployed *qua* the immanent thought of its prescription and its possible effects. Or, to use Sylvain Lazarus' expression, politics (emancipatory or revolutionary, but we'll leave other types of 'politics' to the human sciences) is a 'thinking in interiority' (*pensée en intériorité*). In philosophy, the name of community, for example, expresses that this thinking, or this truth, *will have been*, if it is pursued faithfully. But a philosophical statement about the being of a truth, a statement that delivers its being to the future perfect, cannot be fused with the procedure of a truth, let alone constitute its ideal or norm. There is no politics that can will the community, since this name community (or 'justice', which is the same thing) is alone produced, and on its own terms, by a philosophy that has been conditioned by the statements of a politics. And this name is neither a name of politics, nor a truth of politics. It is a philosophical name *to* indicate that the being of such a truth will have been, inasmuch as there will have been a subject of it. This name turns the real time pertaining to a politics, regardless of the extension of its activity, towards the nominal eternity of its being.

This point is a particularly delicate one, even though it comprises only one aspect of the philosophical act construed as the *seizing* of truths by the operation of the empty category of Truth. We are indeed unaccustomed to thinking (philosophically) of politics as a truth–procedure. The prevailing idea is rather that, in its determination of politics, and that is either of the order of practice or of passions, philosophy determines the truth (*fait vérité*) of what is at stake in politics. The consequence of this 'ordinary' vision of things is that purely philosophical names, names destined to grasp *in Truth* the reality of political truths, are regarded as if they were names of politics itself.

We shall also say that philosophy is designated as the site in which politics is thought. Although politics *is* a site of thought. And it is not even correct to say that philosophy is the thought of that thought, since from Saint-Just to Lenin or Mao, the concern of the major texts of political leaders is to *identify politics as thought from within political thought*. This relation between thought and the thought of thought is internal to politics *qua* singular procedure and bears no similarity to the relation between politics and philosophy. As Sylvain Lazarus' oeuvre[6] shows today with particular force, this relation constitutes the *inner* tension of every truth procedure.

A politics (of 'emancipation' or of 'justice', which are philosophical names; or 'in interiority', which is a name that Sylvain Lazarus would assign to politics itself) is a singularity in situation, dependent on an event affecting the collective, of which, in sequential fashion, it presents the truth (but 'truth' remains a philosophical name, since the effectuation of the procedure does not name itself as such). Politics disposes its own operators, which are operators of thought and enquiry. Philosophy (or a philosophy) endeavours to *seize* this truth and therefore to anticipate its being, which, as generic, *has* on principle *not yet taken place*: what exists is its (finite) subject, not its (eternal) being. To perform this seizing, philosophy will dispose its own names and its own operations.

In particular, every philosophy, in having to compossibilize the various disparate truths in its seizing of them, must *distinguish* the political procedure from the other procedures. It fixes the given of the situation (the collective as infinite), the numericity,[7] the specific unnameable,[8] and so on. This is to say that the approach by which philosophy is placed under the condition of politics *necessarily involves giving a philosophical definition of politics*.

Politics, as a form of thought, however, does not proceed in a definitional way. A singular sequence of politics never issues from a definition of politics. This is what Sylvain Lazarus means to say when, in a striking expression, he says *the Name is unnameable*. In politics, the name politics is neither named nor defined. In this sense, every naming or definition of the name politics is extra-political, and has actually nothing to do with politics insofar as it advances as thought and as a trial of thought. These definitions and namings are the province of philosophy. In addition, even as thought is at stake in each case, 'to do philosophy' is totally different from 'making politics'. Philosophy disposes its operations with a view to stating that, insofar as politics is concerned, there is truth. But the 'there is' does not imply a determining judgement, because the essence of any singular politics is not made up of the truth it constitutes. The essence of a singular politics lies in the pathway of its procedure, and whether it does in fact comprise a *truth* procedure is sayable only in the philosophical act, which, for politics itself, only ever constitutes a sort of inactive recognition.[9]

We must recognize that the discipline of enforcing distinctions here – which is easy to exercise in the case of art, self-evident with regard to love, and was hard won over the centuries in the case of science – still remains a programme for the couple philosophy/politics, as is made abundantly clear by the current vogue enjoyed by the syntagm 'political philosophy'. Nothing is more fashionable than to confuse the definitions and axioms by which philosophy constructs the seizing of a singular politics in Truth, thereby exposing it to the eternity to come of its being, with the current lot of politics itself as a real immanent process.

Yet, this is perhaps the – almost unnoticed – point on which this century's balance-sheet was staked. For, the idea that it is possible to merge philosophical definitions, definitions that through anticipation aim at the being of a truth, with the immanent names of a truth, names that support the process of a politics, is an idea for which the century itself bears a name: Stalin. Dialectical materialism, as the philosophy of the party, and eventually of the party-state, is precisely that: the supposed fusion of the philosophemes of communism or community and the names of politics. In this particular case, it resulted in a fusion and legitimation of a criminal present through the future perfect of its latent truth. That is, in the identification of oppression and devastation with the community *itself*.

This fusion necessarily organizes a disaster.[10]

6. CONFUSING PHILOSOPHICAL NAMINGS AND POLITICAL CATEGORIES ORGANIZES A DISASTER

What are the elements that constitute this kind of disastrous configuration? When a philosophical name that retraces on the condition of a real politics what this real will have had of truth is identified with the names of this same real, three consequences ensue. And these consequences can be seen from the movement that led Plato in *The Laws* to propose a criminal legislation (notably against impiety) that would with a doubt have sustained Socrates' sentence, and at the end of the road re-enacted the crime on the basis of which, and against which, Plato entered into philosophy.

The first consequence involves the return of the reign of the One to the immanent sites of politics. An emancipatory politics is singular and evental. Its prescription is at once faithful and contingent. The sites that are its own are variable and displaced anew with each attempt. Countries, assemblies, factories, classes, the popular army, the insurgent crowd: these are as many protocols of disparate localization, constituted through a prescription that nothing came to found. If these sites are saturated by a philosophical anticipation of their coming truth, if they are focused on the eternity proper to the categories of philosophy, then what inevitably appears, in a supposition concerning its political effectiveness, is the substance of a unique site, a site that will be made the home of truth. This appropriation of a locality – for example, France the land of freedom, the millenary Reich, the homeland of socialism or the red base of the world revolution – entails a metaphor of access and imitation. Politics comes to be presented as thought's access to what unfolds in the unique site of truth, and as a mimesis of what took place there, a site that is not just any site but *the* site in which the taking-place is immemorial. As many a traveller and subservient organization can attest, what then comes to pass is an ecstasy of the site.

Incidentally, I am speaking here less of a particular politics than of a sort of configuration of the '1930s to 1950s', which constitutes a sort of formal historical schema of disaster whose essence lies in the rabatment of politics with philosophy. My description is therefore still philosophical (extract the 'forever of time') and ought not be confounded with what can be said about what these politics themselves involved from *within politics* itself. 'Disaster' is a philosophical concept that names the suturing of philosophy to politics. What is at stake, then, is what philosophy *sees*, is a seeing that is subordinated to the act of seizing.

We see, in these times, that this ecstatic dimension had its historical theatre in the staging of the site. It was staged, for itself, in those colossal gatherings at which the state's personnel displayed itself to the crowd, for a moment throwing back at it a perceptible sense of community, at once stable and furious. And it was staged, for the foreign pilgrim, in those joyous fetes that presented the site as magically peopled with young girls bearing bouquets, with workers whose pure act was already incorporated in the future and with leaders surrounded by a serene law of love.

There is no purpose served by simply laughing after the fact at these patiently staged scenes, or in foreclosing them as dishonest. There must instead be an in-depth investigation into what might be called the politico-statist style of the period. Because this theatre forms part of a singular relationship between politics, State and philosophy, a relationship that is crystallized in an obligation of ecstasy. And, we can in fact already clearly perceive this ecstatic dimension in Plato's solemn presentation of the *topos noétos*, the intelligible site. The myth of Er at the end of the Republic, which is rendered in a very imperatively poetic style, aims precisely to transmit the ecstasy of accessing the site of truth. The nodal point of this myth is that unfounded prescription, the pure decision at stake in every political procedure, is assigned to a site. There exists no other Greek text in which the perilous tension of the subjective as such resonates so strongly. In it Plato wrote of the choice of the fated future of wandering souls: '*Théos anaitios aitia élonénou*' a cause that is chosen, a God outside of all cause. At this point, a subject appears in radical subtraction from all divine influence. The text continues that this is '*o pas kindunos anthropô,*' or total peril for man. A magnificent statement about the un-founded nature of political prescription. But this un-founded nature comes to be localized in the eternal, and established and concentrated in the supreme beauty of the site, in which the light links up with the heavens, and through which the spindle of being turns on the knees of necessity, which is to say on the knees of the State. So, the conceptless transparency of the choice is thus invested and transfixed by the ecstasy of the site. This ecstatic dimension is the first face of disaster.

The second consequence of identifying the 'philosopheme' with the singularity of an emancipatory politics involves the reduction of the diversity of names of politics to a single and primordial name. As I have argued, every political sequence distributes the names specific to it. Virtue, terror, democracy, Soviets, communist party, liberated zone, councils, establishing of intellectuals in factories, resistance, popular committees, cells, congress: the list is interminable. All of these names share a temporal dimension and a variation that links them to the invented naming of one or more events. But if these names get sutured to the potential eternity of a philosopheme, it then comes to be that there is only one genuine name, and this name inevitably becomes the unique name of politics, the name of emancipation itself as it is presumed to have come to presence. As History has shown, such a name then becomes a *sacred* name. Almost always, moreover, because the uniqueness of a name can be guaranteed only in the proper that subtracts it from its equivoque, this name is indeed a proper name. The sacred name of emancipation is the name of an emancipator. In this sense, it has to be said that Stalin and Mao, considered in the eternal excess of their name over the variability of the names of politics, are creations, or creatures, of philosophy. In them and through them the sacredness of the name came to double the ecstasy of the site.

Last, if the contingent truths of politics are allowed to be directly not welcomed but subsumed by thought under a philosopheme, then these truths begin to take on the appearance of a despotic injunction. Why? Because then, in the presumption of its having come and its presence, the contingency of such a truth bears, in thought, a latent necessity. The incompleteness of every particular truth bears a closure clause. And so the something that is unnameable in the situation, which constitutes the limits and thus the real of the names of politics, is forced to disclose a name.

But if, in political law, truth is henceforth declared to be coextensive with the situation, and politics is said to carry total power as concerns the distribution of names, then that which in the real is excepted from the law, that which resists naming, and this always exists, is handed a death sentence. If emancipatory politics is the effectuation of its philosophical naming, the result is that something of being is presented as though it ought not be. In particular, when this community is actual, then its troubles, its dissidence, its ineluctable crack turn into mere remainders whose fictive being is a trick played on it by nothingness. When it is sutured to philosophy, politics ineluctably comes round to asserting that this, which is, has as its being that it ought-not-be. Annihilation, then, comes down to a simple implementation of the verdict of being, as abandoned to emancipatory political prescription.

To assert that what the law of being stipulates is that a part of what is presented is in reality nothing, is very simply the maxim of terror. This maxim is, moreover, examined and argued through in Book X of the *Laws*, in which Plato explained that the reason a re-offending disbeliever can and must be condemned to death is because in him the very ground of his possible being is lacking. The essence of terror consists in the annihilation of what is not. When the philosopheme of emancipation takes hold of the emancipatory political procedure, when it saturates the contingency of its statements, then terror completes the ecstasy of the site and the sacredness of the name.

This three-strand knot made up of the ecstasy of the site, the sacredness of the name and terror, is what I call a disaster. Philosophy is never innocent of such disaster, since disaster results from a confusion in thought between the philosophical reception of its political condition, that is, the mode through which it orients this condition towards eternity, and the immanent operations of politics itself.

7. IT CANNOT BE INFERRED FROM DISASTER THAT PHILOSOPHY MUST ABANDON ITS RECEPTION OF EMANCIPATORY POLITICS

Nevertheless, we ought to recognize that philosophy's guilt is relative to this: that a disaster is better than a lack of being (*mieux vaut un désastre qu'un désêtre*). However terrorist, sacralized and ecstatic it may be, because a politics sutured to philosophy at least falls under an idea, the philosopher will always prefer it – as ultimately, in the *élan* of the centuries, will *all of* humanity – to a politics that is evacuated of all thought, and whose excessive management calls only for the petty exacerbation of interests.

The way out, for us, is certainly not, under the pretence that the horrors of the century would compromise our principles, to renege on the theme of political emancipation. Every conversion to the prevailing state of lack of political being, or to 'democracy' in its market sense, leads philosophy to err in a desolate shadow, between art and a science that is melancholic and lost.

The task is a disjunctive one: *in order to* maintain the inevitable resurrection of communist forms of politics – irrespective of the names they receive – at the distance of a vital condition for philosophy, their notions and processes must be separated out from the names and acts of philosophy.

One facet of this century's balance-sheet, including the mindless crumbling of bureaucratic socialisms, therefore, is the need to de-suture philosophy and politics.

8. ALTHUSSER AS EXTREME LIMIT OF THE PHILOSOPHY/POLITICS SUTURE

The exemplary oeuvre of Louis Althusser permits us to better understand what is at stake when I speak of suturing and de-suturing. In an extremely short period of time, and with the power of a thought wholly condensed around its axioms, Althusser passed from a suture of philosophy to science (texts of 1965) to a suture of philosophy to politics, itself under the influence of Maoism ('put politics at the commanding post') and of the concomitant crisis of the PCF.[11]

Starting in 1968, in effect, Althusser construed philosophy as a figure of class struggle; philosophy is, as was his expression, class struggle in theory. Reflecting on Lenin reading Hegel in 1914–1915, Althusser said to us, 'is not erudition, it is philosophy, and as philosophy is politics in theory, *it is therefore doing politics*'.

What this expresses is a decisive rupture in the symmetry of philosophy's conditions. Politics comes henceforth to occupy a totally privileged position within the system of double torsion (as regards its conditions, and itself), which singularizes the act of thought we call philosophy. Politics maintains this privilege since, in addition to being a condition, it enters into the determination of philosophy's act.

I called this rupture of symmetry and determinant privileging of one of philosophy's conditions a *suture*. Philosophy is sutured whenever one of its conditions is called upon to determine the philosophical act of seizing and declaration. For example, when Althusser wrote 'Philosophy is a political practice of intervention which is exercised under the form of theory', he sutured philosophy to politics.

The trouble with sutures is that they makes their two edges, that is, both philosophy and the privileged condition, difficult to discern.

On the side of philosophy, the suture, which invests the philosophical act with a singular determination concerning its truth, destroys the categorial void necessary to the philosophical site as a site of thought by filling it in. To put it in Althusser's terms, we could say that, sutured to politics, philosophy in fact rediscovers one or more objects; as Althusser himself, however, had explained elsewhere, and very cogently, philosophy has no object. Althusser then came to state that philosophy intervenes politically in political practice and in scientific practice. But following Althusser himself, it can be shown that this is impossible. More Althusser, and with sound reason, never hesitated to promote a purely immanent conception of the effects of philosophy. He wrote, for example: 'Philosophy forms one [*fait un*] with its result, which constitutes the philosophy-effect'. And more clearly still: 'Philosophy intervenes in reality only by producing effects *in itself*'. But if the philosophy-effect is strictly immanent, then philosophy's (possible) external effects, for instance, its political effects, can only be completely opaque to philosophy itself. So philosophy as a supposed 'political practice' is at best an indirect and blind activity.

On the side of politics, the suture de-singularizes the process of truth. To be able to declare that philosophy is a political intervention, one must have an overly general and indeterminate concept of politics. For the rare sequential existence of what Sylvain Lazarus calls historical modes of politics, which alone constitute real conditions for philosophy, must be substituted a vision of politics that is porous to the philosopheme. Quite clearly, in Althusser's theory this role is played by his pure and simple identification of political practice with class struggle. Neither Marx nor Lenin ever declared that class struggle was by *itself* identifiable with political practice. Class struggle is a category of History and of the State, and only under entirely singular conditions does it constitute a *material* for politics. Wielded as the support of a suture between philosophy and politics, class struggle becomes in fact a simple category of philosophy, one of the names of the pure void where it occurs. This amounts, it must be admitted, to reneging on philosophical immanence.

But the ultimate difficulty can be seen in Althusser's insistence that philosophy is political intervention 'in theoretical form'. What is the formal principle that would distinguish philosophical intervention from the 'other forms' of politics? And what are these other forms? Are we to think that there is a 'theoretical form' of politics, which is philosophy, and a 'practical form', and which is what exactly? The French Communist party? The spontaneous movement of revolts? State activity? This distinction is untenable. In reality, emancipatory politics is itself a site of thought through and through. Trying to find in it a practical version and a theoretical version is simply futile. Its process, as with every truth process, is a process of thought that occurs under conditions that are evental, and in a material that bears the form of a situation.

Basically, what Althusser was missing, what *we* were missing between 1968 and, let's say, the beginning of the 1980s, and that we see today, was full recognition of the immanence to thought of *all* the conditions for philosophy. Indeed, there is that rule that sometimes Althusser did more than discern, and sometimes forgot, that is, that it is only

161

possible to think the immanence of the results and the effects of philosophy if one thinks the immanence of all the truth procedures that condition it, and singularly the immanence of politics.

Althusser indicated, if not developed, almost everything that we require to emancipate philosophy from both its academic repetition and from the morose idea of its end. Absence of object and the void, categorical invention, declaration and theses, placement under conditions, systematic rationality, torsion – all that, which still stands, is in his oeuvre. The paradox is that he invented this disposition within the framework of two successive logics that, because they were logics of suture, were entirely contrary to one another. But the lesson of the paradox is that we cannot escape theoreticism by way of politicism, nor, incidentally, by way of aesthetics or an ethics of the other.

De-suturing philosophy consists, in part, in abstracting a 'universal core' from the logic of Althusser's invention, and in being extremely careful never again to let any name (such as the 'class struggle' in Althusser's work) come to circulate between philosophy and politics.

9. AXIOMS OF SEPARATION BETWEEN PHILOSOPHY AND POLITICS

Some principles are required to enforce a strict delineation and evacuate the equivocal, and therefore disastrous, concepts that 'bind' philosophy to its political condition. I will posit the following:

1. That emancipatory politics exists through sequences,[12] under the evental chance that commands its prescription. It is never the incarnation or historical body of a trans-temporal philosophical category. It is not a descent of the Idea, nor a destinal figure of being. It is rather a singular pathing (*tracé*) in which the truth of a collective situation comes to light. But this pathing has no principle linking it to the traces that have preceded it. I will also put it that there is a history of States but no history of politics, in the plural.

For example, if we remain with the last two centuries, then, once again following Sylvain Lazarus' enquiries, we can clearly identify five sequences of political existence that are articulated around singular events and developed in intellectual systems connected to writings and proper names:

- The sequence of the montagnarde Convention between 1792 and 9 Thermidor, signed by Robespierre and Saint-Just.
- The sequence beginning with 1848 (correlation between the June of the French workers and Marx's *Manifesto*) and ending in 1871 (Paris Commune).
- The 'Bolshevik' sequence that is begun in 1902 with Lenin's *What is to be done?* – a work that contains the balance-sheet of the anterior sequence, particularly that of the Commune – is punctuated by the Russian 1905, and is brought to a close with the October Revolution.
- The sequence of the 'revolutionary war' that is begun with the first of Mao's writings about the Chingkangshan base (1928) and is brought to a close (perhaps, the enquiry needs doing) at the moment of the CCP's taking power in 1949.
- The sequence of the Cultural Revolution that began in 1965 and came to a close in the autumn of 1967.

These are complexes that Lazarus designates as some of the historical modes of politics. As for the first three, today there has been sufficient enquiry to establish their names. The first is the *revolutionary modality*, the second the *classist modality* and the third the *Bolshevik modality*. These modalities attest at once to the existence of emancipatory politics and to its sequential rareness. Let it be clear then that, when I maintain that philosophy is under the condition of politics, I am speaking precisely of such singular modalities, and in no way of the existence of states, which are themselves structural facts that have no particular philosophical bearing.

2. That, thus conceived, politics amounts to an immanent site of thought that disposes its nominations, its sites and its statements in accordance with the law of a specific fidelity to an event. In the sequence that is ours in France, then, there is really only one question: what politics is capable of closing the previous period without reneging on – is capable of freeing for its own ends – the universal kernel of the modalities that it identifies in history (singularly what is related to the names of Lenin and Mao), and

of establishing in thinking, as in the militant test to which it is submitted, the prescriptions and statements of a new modality? The evental referents that have been subjectively constituted, even if their names remain in suspense, are clear: the earlier mentioned sequence of the Cultural Revolution, and the years stretching from May 1968 to the end of 1975, and no doubt also the Polish movement beginning with the Gdansk strikes and ending in Jaruzelski's *coup d'état*.

People will ask: can such a politics be identified and pursued, given that it would surely set itself in opposition to the parliamentary figure of politics, to its Mitterandist version included, if only because Mitterandism has given shape – also on a subjective level – to what we might call a renegade's balance-sheet of May 1968? The response to such a question has to be formulated in the immanence of a continuation, and therefore from within the space opened by political prescription. There exists no analytical or external protocol of the process of this question. The existence of emancipatory politics does not proceed from an analysis of the situation, since by definition it is never transitive either to givenness (*donation*), or to the interests of social groups. It can therefore only ever presuppose its own existence. The question of existence here cannot be formulated except from the vantage point of a pre-existence. One can also say that it is impossible to infer the existence of a politics of emancipation from a position situated outside of its process. Emancipatory politics is not observed; it is *encountered*.

3. That philosophy as a site of thought is radically distinct from politics, but is placed under the condition of the evental figure of politics. It is therefore required, bearing the earlier mentioned data in mind, that philosophy, and therefore the philosopher, encounters politics as thought. On this basis, it could be said that philosophy, or rather a philosophy, seizes the singularity of a politics through generic names. The stakes of this seizure are to render the generic nomination of politics compossible to the other truth–procedures in the evental or faithful form of time. Thus, a thinking of time is attained that is turned towards eternity, since this time is grasped by thought only as the spacing in situation of truths. The philosophical question is, then: how to name a politics the referents and stakes of which are as stated, such that this naming is compossible with those of the modern poem, modern mathematics and the modern adventure of love?

10. THE PHILOSOPHICAL NAMING OF
AN EMANCIPATORY POLITICS AIMS AT
A TRUTH, AND IN NO WAY AT SENSE

It is exactly here that the following question arises: is community an acceptable name for the philosophical naming of a politics of our time? My response to it is, I must say, somewhat circumspect. The reason for doubt is clear: community, in the shape of communism, continues to bear within it the disastrous history of a suture. More precisely: through the name community philosophy worked to inject a sense of destiny into the heavy and cruel concepts of politics in its Marxist–Leninist age, an age whose passing was pronounced at least as early as the turn taken, in 1967, by the Cultural Revolution in China, and thereafter by the (rare) specifically political effects that came of the years 1968–1975.

Here some support must be sought in a chief operator of de-suturation. The statement in question is also, and it is not surprising, the most succinct maxim of modern atheism. This statement is: truths have no sense. Sequential, suspended from the chance an event, truths (including political truths) are the effects of a conceptless fidelity in a situation. They do not trace any general trajectory to which a sense could be ascribed. Truths occur in making-holes in, in the defection of sense. Because sense is only ever something the situation itself administers.

However, one of a suture's modalities, if not its essential modality, involves ascribing or infecting the defective neutrality of a truth with the weight of sense. In so doing, philosophy in fact exposes the singularity of a truth to a disaster of sense.

This is what makes thinking the destiny of communism so difficult, what makes its disaster so clearly devoid of thought. Since this disaster is universally presented as a disaster of sense. The communist enterprise is designated as criminal less than it is as absurd, or in other words: as devoid of sense. In this judgement sense is imputed to the naturality of the capitalist economy. The madness (*insensé*) of communism is that it aspired to subtract itself from the naturalness of sense, capitalist and parliamentary.

Yet, we must, contrary to this common opinion, argue exactly the opposite. Communism was exposed disaster because Stalinism saturated politics with philosophemes, and thus with a disastrous excess of sense;

which obliterated every truth, *because it presented sense itself as a truth*. The disaster was not a disaster of sense, but a disaster of truth through sense, under the effects of sense.

The supposedly natural character of the sense of modern, or Western, capitalo-parliamentarism is only in reality, as we are well aware, the efficaciousness of an absence of sense that carefully refrains from presenting itself as truth. Modern capitalism and its state political result, the consensual parliamentary State, contain neither sense nor truth. Or rather: they market this lack of truth and absenting of thought as 'natural sense'. Capitalo-parliamentarism shields itself from all confusion between sense and truth, upholding neither one nor the other. Its rule is only in its functioning, and is therefore a rule of exteriority. It requires nothing of the subject as political subject. It therefore quite naturally won out over the sutured and disastrous enterprise of real communism, which presented sense as if it were coextensive with a truth.

11. IS RIGHT A POLITICAL CATEGORY AND DOES IT PROVIDE MODERN PARLIAMENTARY POLITICS WITH ANY (PHILOSOPHICAL) SENSE?

No doubt we must do away with the recent topics by which a so-called political philosophy attempts to comes to terms with what it believes to be the triumph of capitalo-parliamentarism, which consist in an apology of right, of the State of Right and of human rights. Since what this apology explicitly aims to do is to provide the all-too-objectivist apparatus of the market economy and the electoral ritual with sense.

Were this simply an overtly propagandistic matter of opinion the question would not be worth going into. But it is clear that the category of right, as well as the more original one of the Law, are in the process of becoming obligatory through-passages for political philosophy – in reality, for modern sophistry.

Clearly, the apology of right and the Law presupposes a philosophical assessment of politics that confounds it with the state from the outset. Within such an apology, there can be no question of politics as a rare and sequential type of thinking. *From within* such a politics, 'right' can possibly take on a prescriptive sense, or a sense in consciousness, which has no relation to the state of right. This was the case around 1978 when the strikers at the Sonacrotra residences ran with the slogan 'French, immigrants, equal rights', and again in 1983 when the strikers at Talbot asserted 'workers' rights. In both cases, the question concerned a right without Right, a political prescription inaudible for absolutely any form of state right.

When our 'philosophers' speak of the State of Right, they have no way of taking stock of the right without right by which a political consciousness *is declared*. These philosophers speak of an institutional figure, and place philosophy, not under the condition of politics, but under the condition of the parliamentary state. Political philosophy as a philosophy of the state of right, grounds its own possibility in tying it to the existence of a particular form of State, and commits itself to opposing other states (the late 'totalitarian' State).

For the sake of argument, let us enter into the terrain – a terrain that, again, could never be ours (and has never been that of any genuine philosophy) – of political philosophy and ask: what is a state of right considered philosophically?

In the ontology of historical multiplicities I have proposed,[13] the State, *qua* the state of a situation, is what ensures the structural count of a situation's *parts*, a count of the situation that generally bears the a proper name of a particular 'nation'. To call such a state, that is such an operation of counting, a State 'of right', basically means that the rule of counting *does not hold forth any particular part as being paradigmatic of being-a-part in general*. To put it another way, no subset, whether it is the nobility, the working class, or the Party of class, or the 'rich', or the religious, and so on, is appointed any special function concerning the operation by which the other subsets are enumerated and treated. To put it still another way, in a state of right no *explicit privilege* codes the operations by which the State relates to the subsets delimited in the 'national' situation.

Because no paradigmatic part (or Party) validates the count of the State, it can only be validated by a set of *rules*, which are formal precisely in that they do not privilege, in the principle of their legitimacy, any particular subset, but are *said* to apply 'to all', which is to say to all the subsets registered by the State as being subsets of the situation.

The claim is often made that these rules hold for all 'individuals', and thus a contrast is made between the democratic reign of individual freedom and the totalitarian reign of a self-proclaimed fraction, the Party and its leaders. This is not at all the case: no state rule genuinely concerns the particular infinite situation we call a subject or an individual. The state only ever relates to parts or subsets. Even when it deals in appearance with an individual, it is not the individual in its concrete infinity that is concerned; instead, this infinity gets *reduced to the One of the count*, that is, to the subset of which the individual is an element, what the mathematicians call a *singleton*. The one who votes, who is imprisoned, who contributes to social security, and so on, is inventoried by a number, which is the name *of his singleton*, not his being taken into account as infinite multiplicity. What is meant in saying the state is a state of right is that its relation to the individual-counted-for-one is made according to a rule, and not on the basis of an evaluation of which a privileged subset constitutes the norm. A rule, regardless of which it is, cannot guarantee by itself an effect of truth, since no truth is reducible to formal analysis. Being at once singular and universal, every truth is, to be sure, a regulated process, but is never coextensive with its rule. To suppose, along with the Greek sophists and Wittgenstein, that rules constitute the 'ground' of thought, insofar as it is subject to language, necessarily entails discrediting the value of truth. That is, moreover, exactly the conclusion drawn by both these sophists and Wittgenstein: the force of the rule is incompatible with truth, which is itself then turned into a merely metaphysical Idea. For the sophists, there are only conventions and relations of force. And for Wittgenstein, only language games.

If the existence of a state of right – thus the state empire of rules – constitutes the essence of the *political* category of democracy, the crucial philosophical consequence is that *politics has no intrinsic relation to truth*.

This is, I reiterate, a philosophical consequence. Because only from a philosophical site can such a consequence be named. The state of right's sole *internal* legislation is to function. This functioning does not, on its own basis, state the relation that it either does or does not have to the philosophical category of Truth. Philosophy and only philosophy, since it is under the condition of politics, can state the current lot of politics as a truth procedure.

To state that the kernel of sense of a politics resides in Right inevitably entails that philosophical judgements about politics assert the radical exteriority of politics to the theme of truth. If the state of right is the ground of political aspiration, then politics is not a truth procedure.

This logical inference is substantiated by the empirical evidence. Parliamentary states of the West do not lay claim to any truth. Philosophically they are, if I may say so, relativist and sceptical states, not simply in an incidental or ideological way but intrinsically, inasmuch as their ground is the rule of right. This is the reason why these states readily present themselves as 'the least bad' rather than as the best. The 'least bad' signifies that, no matter what the case is, we inhabit the relative and the bad, or more exactly, that we inhabit a domain of statist functioning that bears no direct relation to any affirmative norm such as Truth or the Good.

It will be remarked that things were not the same with the terrorist and bureaucratic socialist states, which explicitly denounced the rule of right as 'purely formal' ('formal' freedoms, etc.). There can obviously be no question here of defending these police States. Philosophically, however, it is necessary to see that identifying these states with politics (class politics, communism) did not result in a cancellation of the truth function of politics. These states, which actually grounded the count of parts of the social whole in a paradigmatic subset, consequently held that this subset (the class or its Party) had a privileged relation with truth. A privilege *without rule* – which indeed was obviously very irregular – always involves a protocol of legitimation that bears on content and values. The privilege here is substantial not formal. Consequently, the states of the East always claimed to concentrate the reign of political truth in their police apparatuses. They were compatible with a philosophy according to which politics constitutes one of the sites from which truth proceeds.

In the parliamentarisms of the West, as in the despotic bureaucracies of the East, politics is in the last instance confounded with State management. But the philosophical effects of this confusion are opposed. In the first case, where politics ceases to come within the province of truth, the 'prevailing' philosophy is sceptical and relativist. In the second case, where politics prescribes a 'true State', the prevailing philosophy is monist and dogmatic.

This is what explains why in the parliamentary political societies of the West philosophy is regarded as a 'soulful supplement' whose prerogative it is to correct the regulated objectivity of opinions, an objectivity that is that of the laws of the market and financial capital, and on which a strong consensus is built. Meanwhile, the volontarist and police-like prerogatives of the political societies of the East were cast in the false necessity of a state philosophy – dialectical materialism.

In essence, Right comprises a sort of centre of symmetry, which disposes an alternation between the two terms of 'State' (when it is presumed to concentrate politics) and 'philosophy'. When right – that is, the force of the rule – is presented as a central category of politics, the parliamentary state or that is part*ies*-State, is indifferent to philosophy. Conversely, when the bureaucratic state, of the party-state, advocates a philosophy, in which its legitimacy is to reside, it will assuredly be a state of non-right. This inversion is the formalization, through the couple state/philosophy, of the contrary relations that the statement 'politics is realized in the state' entails as to the couple politics/truth, depending of whether the form of the state is pluralist and regulated, or unitary and party-based. In the first, the rule abolishes all truth of politics (dissolving it in the arbitrariness of number – voting), and in the other, the Party declares that it holds the whole of the truth, and thereby becomes indifferent to every circumstance that affects number, or the people.

Finally, opposed as the maxims are, the result of both impacts negatively upon philosophy, which with the first is engulfed in a pure supplement of opinion, and with the second, in an entirely empty state formalism.

We can be still more precise. The submission of politics to the theme of right entails that in parliamentary societies (i.e., societies regulated according to the ultimate imperative of financial capital) it becomes impossible to distinguish the philosopher from the sophist. This effect of indiscernibility is crucial: since, under the topic of right, philosophy's political condition is able to establish the rule as the essence of democratic discussion, so it becomes impossible to contrast sophistical logomachy (the virtuous game of conventions and powers) to philosophical dialectic (the dialogical detour of the Truth). As a result, quite generally, any old clever sophist may be deemed a profound philosopher, all the more so since the denials by which he rejects claims to truth are homogenous to the political condition as it is presented under the formal banner of right. Conversely, in bureaucratic socialist societies it is impossible to distinguish the philosopher from the functionary, or even from the policeman. The tendency is for philosophy to become nothing more than a general proposition of the tyrant. As no rule acts to code argument, pure assertion is placed in its stead, and ultimately it is the position of enunciation (i.e., proximity to the state) that acts to validate 'philosophical' statements. Thereby, any old state apparatchik or leader can pass for a philosophical oracle, since the place from which he speaks, that is, the party-state, is regarded as the point in which the whole political process of truth is concentrated.

It can therefore be argued that the effect *common* to regimes for which politics is embodied in a paradigmatic subset of the multiple-nation and to those that disseminate it in the reign of the rule is an effect of indiscernibility between philosophy and its rival 'doubles': on the one hand, the eclectic sophist; on the other, the dogmatic tyrant. Whether politics holds right as its organic category, or whether, in the name of the sense of History, it denies it any validity, the impact upon philosophy is one of indistinction, and ultimately of usurpation: it is the inaugural adversaries of the identity of philosophy, the sophist and the tyrant, or even the journalist and the policeman, that are declared philosophers on the public stage.

Every launching (*envoi*) of a politics signals an invention of thought, one that is immediately exposed to the hazardous effects of its rootedness in an event. Philosophy exists on the sole condition of this launching inasmuch as it, through seizing a truth that proceeds in it, makes this precariousness a dimension of eternity. Right, the Law, the State of Right, human rights are not part of any inventions today, and there is nothing in them to be philosophically seized. So, the effort that various 'political philosophies' have engaged in, to inject sense into the non-sense in which capitalo-parliamentarism deploys its non-truth, is a sophistic exercise that plays, for the philosopher, the simple role of a temporal marker and an adversity to be braved. We must be contemporaneous with its exercise. But there is no question of our becoming – it is rather what they guard us from, these 'professors who set a negative example' – purveyors of sense taken into the site of non-truth, or hermeneuts of state.

11. REASONS FOR WHICH THE WORD 'COMMUNITY' IS (PROVISIONALLY?) UNSUITABLE FOR PHILOSOPHICALLY SEIZING THE CONTEMPORARY STATE OF EMANCIPATORY POLITICS

The contemporary avatar of the 'return to right' and its counterpart, the 'return to ethics', situated as exercises in sense in the absence of all truth, enjoins us to advocate, on a philosophical level, the return of politics and its counterpart, the open rupture (*libre rupture*), as stakes of the seizing of truth in the absence of all sense.

Yet it is very important to say that 'community', even with the joint precautions concerning its inoperability and its coming, represents the truth of the collective as the exposition of a sense. I therefore think it difficult to submit it as the philosophical name of the short traces of political truth to which our situation can still bear witness.

Moreover, 'community' today is one of the names used in reactionary forms of politics. Every day I take a stand politically against the diverse forms of communitarism by which the parliamentary state seeks to divide and delimit latent popular zones from their inconsistency. In the use of expressions such as 'the Arab community', the 'Jewish community' or the 'protestant community', I see merely national, or even religious reaction. They are as many substantialist propositions that a political fidelity must imperatively undo. For what matters to us are not differences but truths.

Last, 'community' perpetuates sense, under the embrace of finitude. The coming forth of the collective in its own limits, the mortality of its assumption, the nostalgic echo of the Greek *polis* as a site of thought that is exposed: all that is there in the word 'community'.

Yet there is a philosophical statement that, in my view, gives shelter and welcome to what is most precious in a contemporary politics of emancipation. This is a statement that class logic and class antagonism had itself concealed in a sort of dialectical finitude. This statement is: the situations of politics are infinite. I would even say that, insofar as there is and there will be a post-Marxist–Leninist emancipatory politics, its purpose will be to *treat* exactly this point – by which it will take all its distance with regard to the State – that is to say, the ontological infinity of situations.

'Community' seems to me unable to stand as the name for this processing of the infinite.

13. TAKE 'EQUALITY' AS ELEMENTARY, AND DEVELOP IT IN A RIGOROUS LOGIC OF THE SAME

My conviction is that the best word for today is the old one of equality.

It is important to be rigorous here. 'Equality' as such is not to be taken as political name. Politics is given in always singular statements in situation, and there can be no question – that would amount to a suture – of saying that it consists in a desire for equality. But 'equality' can be a philosophical name *for* the compossibilization of emancipatory politics. Because equality neither designates nor presumes the advent of a totality. And because it has been possible ever since Cantor to think equality in the element of the infinite.[14]

The obvious objection to this is that it would have us tarry with the triad of 'liberty–fraternity–equality', the framework in which the French Revolution was philosophically seized. Quite so, for what we must recognize is that the era that was thus begun is not yet *philosophically* saturated. The temporal arch of philosophy does not coincide with any of the temporalities proper to its conditions, and no more so with political temporality than with any of the others. It turns out that the capacity of seizing inherent to the terms liberty, equality and fraternity remains intact, and that, in a recurrent fashion, philosophical polemic circulates between them.

Today, the concept of freedom contains no *immediate* value for seizing because it is ensnared in liberalism, in the doctrine of parliamentary and commercial freedoms. The word has been thoroughly besieged by opinion. This demands, then, the reconstruction of a philosophical concept of freedom through a point other than itself. A free use of the word 'freedom' requires its subordination to other words.[15]

The word fraternity has, for its part, been repeated and sublated by the word community, whose destiny we have already discussed.

The word equality must be secured in the absence of any economic connotations (equality of objective conditions, of status and of opportunity). Its subjective trenchancy must be restored: equality is something that opens onto a strict logic of the Same. Its advantage, then, lies in its abstraction. Equality neither presumes closure, nor qualifies the terms it embraces, nor prescribes a territory for its exercise. Equality is immediately prescriptive, and the current resolve to denounce its utopian character is a good sign, a sign that the word has recovered its force of rupture.

Let's say, then, that the philosophical embrace of emancipatory politics is to be carried out through the name of a radical politics of equality. Admittedly, this word would not include within it the theme of the social, or of redistribution, and less still that of solidarity, or State solicitude for differences. Equality here is a purely philosophical name. It is unhitched from every *programme*. It essentially designates this: only a politics that can, in philosophy, be named an egalitarian politics entitles one to turn towards the eternal of the contemporary times in which this politics proceeds. When no politics of the sort exists, when the reign of capitalo-parliamentarism encompasses the totality of the situation, our time is of no real *value*, and cannot survive its exposure to the eternal return.

The whole difficulty lies, once again, in subtracting the philosophical concept of equality from the economism that saturates it. At issue here is not the rich and poor, even if the existence of the rich and poor has since the Greeks (Aristotle sees in it the root of the intrinsically pathological character of real politics) been the matter of a sort of abstract scandal. In philosophical terms, it shall instead be said that the destination of politics, when, under the concept of equality, philosophy seizes it and exposes it to eternity, is not difference or sovereignty but the authority of the Same.

That philosophy can receive contemporary political truths under the name of equality essentially means that if communism exists, then it can only be a communism of singularities. And, further, that no one singularity can have any entitlement that would render it unequal to any other. This can also be said: the essence of a truth is generic,[16] that is, is without any differential trait that would allow it to be placed in a hierarchy on the basis of a predicate. And again: equality signifies that, from the vantage point of politics, what is presented has no need of being interpreted. What presents itself must be received in the nondescript nature and the egalitarian anonymity of its presentation as such. What presents itself in politics falls under what Alberto Caeiro, one of Pessoa's heteronyms, calls a thing. A thing is something that presents itself without being represented. A thing is not even representable in its difference. A thing allows no purchase for the interpretation of its difference; it is, very precisely, the same as every other. The 'same' does not mean that it can be identified under the element that singles out its predicate. A thing, in Caeiro's sense, has no need of belonging to a totality that can be qualified or differentiated as the same as another. *La chose politique*, or for politics, is outside the dialectic of the same and the other. It is the same without other; it presents itself as the same of the same. Neither is there any transcendent register such as Man or humanity from which the political thing would take a rule for identifying the same. In politics, things are entirely different: humanity exists only to the extent and in the precise measure that the same exists, the thing as same, which is also what Jean-Luc Nancy would call the thing itself,[17] and that is such that, under political prescription, it is its sameness itself.

I agree with Lacoue-Labarthe's radical thesis according to which Nazism was a humanism.[18] Since what Nazism actively did was to subordinate politics to a preliminary identification of man, of authentic man, of a man whose being only comes from difference and who embarks on his story by annihilating his subhuman, or differently human, other. Nazism is the criminal paroxysm of the dialectic of the same and the other, and it is impossible to decide whether it proceeds on the basis of a fanatical attention to the other or of a substantialist, culturalist and predicative conception of the same. Nazism teaches us where we are led when preliminary attention hones in on identity and difference, on territorial, racial and national communitarism, and on the living substance of the other. No dialectic, not even an anti-dialectic of the other, can avoid – as Hegel taught us once and for all – the figures of death and slavery. We cannot emerge from this by inverting the signs and delicately promoting respect for the other and differences. It is pointless to contrast the dark humanism of Nazism, which raises the deadly figures of Man to the summits of the State, with its elegiac and Western obverse, the well-off humanism of love for the other and respect of difference. No less foreign to thought is the cultural, the heavy sociological, idea of the impenetrable and respectable multiplicity of cultures. In politics, the thing itself is a-cultural, as is every thought and every truth. Comic, purely comic, is the theme of cultural politics, as is the theme of a political culture. Contrary to the other, the same in its sameness is in *no need of cultivation*.

Philosophically named, an emancipatory politics comes within an anti-humanism of the same. And it is from this anti-humanism, through which the same is supported only by the void of all difference in which to ground Man, that humanity issues. Humanity, prior to the real forms of egalitarian politics, simply does not exist, either as collective, or as truth, or as thought.

It is of this absolute same, that is prior to every idea of humanity, and out of which humanity issues: politics deals with the coming to light of the collective as truth of the same. This is why it excludes all interpretation, since, as the Parmenides translated by Beaufret said, 'the Same, is at once to think and to be'. To think and to be, but not sign and interpretation. Which is to say again that the thought of the same – and in the act relating it to the collective politics is such a thinking – excludes all hermeneutics of sense. Politics will be received by philosophy under the sign of the equal insofar as, attached to the void of the equal – accepting that a truth has no sense, not even an historical sense, that is, the donation of a sense to History – it also affirms that, as Caeiro puts it: 'to be a thing is to be subject to no interpretation'.

PART V
Philosophy and Love

CHAPTER ELEVEN
What is Love?

1. THE SEXES AND PHILOSOPHY

It has been claimed that philosophy as a will to systematization was edified by foreclosing sexual difference. It is true that, from Plato up to and including Nietzsche, the parts where this will makes an attempt to work this word into a concept are not the most consistent ones. But does this word have such a vocation? And does the word 'man', relieved of its generic consignment and delivered to sexuation, fare any better? Ought we conclude on this basis that philosophy indeed indifferenciates sexual difference? I believe nothing of the sort. There are too many indications to the contrary, provided one is aware that the ruse of such a difference, which is certainly subtler than that of Reason, makes the most of the fact that this difference foregrounds neither the word 'woman' nor the word 'man'. If only because it is philosophically admissible to transpose onto the sexes what Jean Genet said of races. He asked what a Negro was, adding: 'And first of all, what colour is he (or she)?' When asked what a man or a woman is, it would be a matter of legitimate philosophical prudence to ask: 'And first of all, what sex is he or she?' For we must admit that the initial obscurity is indeed the question of sex, whereas sexual difference can only be thought after paying the price of a laborious determination of the identity that sex sets to work.

Let us add that contemporary philosophy is, as we see everyday, addressed to women. It might even be suspected, and I lay myself open to this, of engaging, as discourse, in strategies of seduction.

CONDITIONS

All things considered, philosophy touches upon the sexes by means of love, to such an extent that it is indeed to Plato that a Lacan had to look for the means by which thought can gain hold over transferential love.

At this point, however, a more serious objection arises: bar precisely the Platonic inauguration, the genuine things that have been said about love – before psychoanalysis rattled its notion – have been said in the order of art, and more singularly in the art of novelistic prose. The coupling of art and the novel is essential. It is also clear that women have excelled in this art, that they have given it a critical impetus. Madame De La Fayette, Jane Austen, Virginia Woolf, Katherine Mansfield and many others. And, before all of them, writing in an eleventh century unimaginable for Western barbarians, there was Lady Murasaki Shikibu, the author of a key text in which what can be said about love in its masculine dimension is set out, *The Tale of Genji*.

May I not be instantly accused of having performed the classic move of confining women to the effects of sublimated passion and the dimension of narrative. To begin with, I will argue that the signifying link between 'women' and 'love' is of interest to humanity as a whole, and even legitimates its concept. More, I clearly acknowledge that women excel, and will continue to, in all domains, and are capable of re-establishing the field of every domain. The only problem, which is also one for men, is to know under which conditions, and what the price to pay for it is. Last, I consider novelistic prose to be an art of redoubtable, abstract complexity, and its masterpieces to be among the highest attestations of what, transfixed and constituted by truth, a subject is capable of.

From what point is it possible to observe the couplings of truth procedures such as the one that, as I said, exists between passion and the novel? From a place in which it so happens that love and art crossover or are compossible in time. This place is philosophy.

The word love here then shall be construed as a category of philosophy, something that is perfectly legitimate, as we see in the status accorded to eros in Plato.

The relation that this category maintains to love as it occurs in psychoanalysis – at the point of transference, for example – will no doubt remain problematic. I have adopted an implicit rule of external coherence: 'Specific as it is, make sure the philosophical category remains compatible with the analytic concept'. I shall not here, however, be able to enter into the details of that compatibility.

The relation that this category has the revelations of the art of the novel is going to remain indirect. Let us say that the general logic of love, as it is seized in the crack (*faille*) between (universal) truth and (sexuated) forms of knowledge, shall then be put to the test of singular fictions. The rule this time is one of subsumption: 'Ensure the philosophical category admits of the great love stories in the same way a syntax does its semantic fields'.

Finally, the relationship of the category of love to common evidences (because love is the truth procedure that, as compared with art, science or politics, although not necessarily the most common, is the most often *proposed*) is one of juxtaposition. There is a common sense from which departure cannot be taken without producing certain comic effects. This rule is stated: 'Paradoxical as its consequences are, ensure that the category remains in keeping with amorous intuition as it is socially bestowed'.

2. OF SOME DEFINITIONS OF LOVE THAT WILL NOT BE RETAINED

Philosophy, or a philosophy, establishes its place of thought by making *objections* and *declarations*. In general, objections are made to sophists, and declarations about the existence of truths. In the case concerning us here the following objections are seen.

1. An objection against the fusional conception of love. Love is not that which from a Two taken as structurally given creates a One of ecstasy. This objection is tantamount to an objection against being-for-death, for the ecstatic One can be inferred to be beyond the Two only as a *suppression of the multiple*. It is from the latter that we owe all the metaphors of night, of the obstinate sacralizing of the encounter, of the terror inflicted by the world. Wagner's *Tristan and Isolde* – in my categories, I call this a figure of disaster, as it is related to the generic amorous procedure. The disaster here is not even a disaster of love; it harks to a philosopheme, the philosopheme of the One.
2. An objection against the oblative conception of love. Love does not involve prostrating the Same before the alter of the Other. I will argue that love is not even an experience of the other, but an

experience *of the world*, or of the situation, under the postevental condition that there are Two. My aim is to subtract *Eros* from every dialectic of the *Eteros*.

3. An objection against the 'superstructural' or 'illusory' conception of love, so dear to the pessimistic tradition of French moralists. By this I mean the conception for which love is only ever an ornamental semblance via which the real of sex passes. Lacan came close to this idea on occasion as when, for example, he said that love is something that compensates for the lack of sexual relationship. But he also said the opposite as when, for example, he endowed love with an ontological vocation, that of giving access to being (*abord de l'être*). The point here is that, as I also believe, love does not compensate for anything. Love *supplements*, and that is something altogether different. Love can only consist in failure (*ratage*) on the fallacious assumption that it is a relationship. But it is not. It is a *production of truth*. The truth of what? The truth that the Two, not only the One, proceeds in the situation.

3. DISJUNCTION

I come now to the declarations, which are my attempt at an axiomatics of love. Why have I chosen this manner of proceeding? On the basis of an essential conviction, for which, moreover, there are already arguments in Plato: *love is by no means given in the immediate consciousness of the loving subject*. The relative poverty of all that philosophers have said about love, I am convinced, is because they have come at it either through either psychology or a theory of passions. But even though it involves the erring ways and torments of those in love, love does not by any means present its own identity in these experiences. Conversely, becoming subjects of love depends on the identity of love itself. Let us say that love is a process that arranges immediate experiences of the like, without the law of these experiences being decipherable from within them. We might also say: the experience of the loving subject, as the matter of love, does not constitute any *knowledge* of love. This is in fact a distinct feature of the amorous procedure (by contrast to science, art or politics): the thought that constitutes love is not the thought of itself. As an experience of thought, love does not think itself (*s'impense*). A familiarity with love certainly demands that the power of love has been experienced, and especially the power of its thinking. But it is also intransitive to that power.

All the pathos of passion, of error, of jealousy, of sex and of death must therefore be held at a distance. No theme requires more pure *logic* than that of love.

My first thesis is the following:

1. *There are two positions of the experience of love.* 'Experience' is construed in its broadest sense as the presentation as such of the situation. And there are two presentative positions. We can agree that these two positions are sexuated, and to call one woman, and the other man. The approach thus far is strictly nominalist: no empirical, biological or social distribution is acceptable here.

The fact that there will have been *two* positions can only be established retroactively. It is in effect love, and love alone, that permits us to state formally the existence of the two positions. Why? On the basis of a second, really fundamental thesis, according to which:

2. *The two positions are totally disjunct.* 'Totally' should be taken here very literally: *nothing* in the experience is the same from the position of man or from that of woman. Nothing. This means: the positions do not divide the experience between them; there is not one presentation allocated to woman and another to man, and then zones of overlap or intersection between them. *Everything* is presented in such a way that no coincidence can be attested between what affects one position and what affects the other.

I will call this state of things a *disjunction*. Sexed positions are disjunct as regards experience in general.

The disjunction is not observable; it cannot be the object of an experience or of an immediate piece of knowledge. This is because all such experiences or kinds of knowledge are themselves positioned within the disjunction and will never encounter anything attesting to the other position.

Were it possible to have any knowledge of the disjunction, that is, structural knowledge, a third position would be required. That would rule out the third thesis:

3. *There is no third position.* The idea of a third position engages the function of the imaginary: this involves the angel. The discussion about

the sex of angels is crucial insofar as what is at issue in it is the *announcement of the disjunction*. However, this can only be done from the vantage point of experience, or of the situation.

What makes it possible here for me, then, to announce this disjunction, that is, without having recourse to any angel, without acting as an angel? It is the requirement that the situation, which is not adequate in itself, is supplemented. Not by a third structural position but by a singular event. This event is what initiates the amorous procedure, and we might agree to call it an *encounter*.

4. CONDITIONS FOR THE EXISTENCE OF HUMANITY

Before we do this, however, we must, so to speak, let ourselves be carried way by the other extremity of the problem. This is the fourth thesis:

4. *There is only one humanity.* What does 'humanity' signify in a non-humanist sense? The term cannot be grounded in any objective predicative trait. That would make it into something ideal or empirical, and in any case inappropriate. By 'humanity' I mean that which provides support to the generic or truth procedures. There are four types of such procedures: science, politics, art and – precisely – love. Humanity can be attested if and only if there is (emancipatory) politics, (conceptual) science, (creative) art and love (not reduced to a mix of sentimentality and sexuality). Humanity is what sustains the infinite singularity of truths that fall within these types. Humanity is the historical body of truths.

Let us designate $H(x)$ the humanity function. This abbreviation indicates that whatever the term presented, it is supported by at least one generic procedure. An axiom of humanity indicates this: if a term x (let us say, in echo of the prevailing Kantianism, a noumenal human = x) is active, or more precisely *activated as Subject*, in a generic procedure, then it attests that the humanity function *exists*, as far as it admits this term x as an argument.

I insist on the point that the existence of humanity, that is, the effectiveness of its function, arises at a point x that a truth in process activates as the 'local verifying' that is the subject. In this sense, *indeterminate x's* constitute the domain, or the virtuality, of the humanity function, and as far as a truth procedure transfixes them, the humanity function localizes them in its turn. It is undecidable as to whether it is the term x that brings into being the humanity function that takes it as an argument, or whether it is the function that 'humanizes' the term x. This incertitude is suspended in the initiatory events of truth, of which the term x is a faithful operator (it is the same for whoever undergoes the tremendous duration that an encounter initiates as love: it falls to he or she to be, thereof famous solitude of lovers is a metonymy, localized as a proof that Humanity exists).

The term H as such (let us say: substantive humanity) appears as a virtual mixture of those four types of truth: politics (x militant), science (x scientist), art (x poet, painter, etc.) and love (x, 'elevated' in disjunction by Two lovers). The term H creates a knot of the four. As we shall see, the presentation of this knot is at the core of the disjunction between the positions of man and woman, in their relation to truth.

So, our fourth thesis, according to which there is only one humanity, comes to signify this: every truth is valid for *all* of its historical body. A truth, and it does not matter which one, is always indifferent to the predicative distribution of its support.

To make this point clearer, we could say that all terms x, as noumenal variables *of* the Humanity function, comprise a homogeneous class, one that is based on no other distribution than that induced by the subjective activations initiated by an event and thought through in a faithful procedure.

In particular, a truth is as such subtracted from every position. A truth is *trans-positional*. It is, moreover, the only thing that is, and this is why a truth shall be said to be generic. In *Being and Event*, I attempted to set out an ontology of this adjective.

5. LOVE AS THE TREATMENT OF A PARADOX

If we relate the consequences of the fourth thesis to the first three, we get a precise formulation of the problem now at hand: if there exist at least two positions, that is, man and woman, that are radically disjunct as regards experience in general, how can a truth come to be for all, or trans-positional?

CONDITIONS

We might expect the first three theses to entail the following statement: truths are sexuated. In other words, that there is a feminine science and a masculine science, just as once it was thought that there was a proletarian science and a bourgeois science. That there is a feminine art and a masculine art, a feminine political vision and a masculine political vision, and a feminine love (strategically homosexual, as certain feminist orientations have rigorously affirmed) and a masculine love. Obviously we might add that even if this were this the case, it would be impossible to *know* it.

But this is not the case in the space of thought I am trying to establish. I would like at once to posit the radicality of the disjunction, that is, the absence of any third position, and the idea that, as subtracted from every positional disjunction, the occurrence of truth is nevertheless generic.

Love is exactly the place where this paradox is dealt with.

Let us take the measure of this statement. First up, it means that love is an operation articulated around a paradox. Love does not relieve the paradox; it treats it. More precisely, it makes the truth of the paradox itself.

The famous curse according to which 'the two sexes will die each on their own side' is actually a non-paradoxical or apparent law of things. If we leave aside the eventful supplement and therefore pure chance, and remain with situations themselves, the two sexes *never cease to die each on their own side*. What is more, under the injunctions of Capital, which could not give a fig about sexual difference, social *roles* are 'in-discriminated'; the more the disjunctive law is stripped away, bereft of protocol or mediation, the more the sexes, almost undifferentiated, nevertheless die each on their own side. For this now invisible 'side' is all the more binding, as it is reflected in the total character of the disjunction. The staging of sexual roles, the registering of every term x into one of two supposed classes, let's say the *hx* and the *fx*, is in no way an expression of the disjunction; it is only a makeover or a cover-up (*maquillage*), an obscure mediation administered by all sorts of respective rites and rules of etiquette (*protocoles d'abord*). But Capital is much better suited by there being only *x*'s. Our societies, from thereon in, un-cover up (*démaquillent*) the disjunction, which again becomes invisible, and void of any mediating display. Through here the sexuated positions comes to pass in their apparent indiscernibility, which lets pass the disjunction *as* disjunction. This is a situation in which everyone feels as if it would kill the potential

186

humanity in him or her, the seizing of that x that one is through a veracious fidelity.

Love is then itself exposed in its function of resistance to the law of being. We begin to see that, far from 'naturally' regulating the supposed relation between the sexes, love is *what makes truth of their un-binding (dé-liaison)*.

6. LOVE AS THE SCENE OF TWO FORMS THE TRUTH OF THE DISJUNCTION AND GUARANTEES THE ONE OF HUMANITY

To understand this determination of love, and therefore to establish it as something that is ever renewed *in thought* – as the poet Alberto Caeiro put it *'to love is to think'* – we must return to the question of the disjunction. To say that it is total, to say that there is no neutral position of observation or third position, is to say that the two positions *cannot be counted as two*. Were it possible to count them, where could it be done? The two is not presented as such except in the three, in which is it presented as an element of the three.

We must carefully distinguish love from the 'couple'. The couple is what, of love, is visible to a third. The couple is therefore a two counted in a situation where there is a third. But no matter who it is, the 'third' in question does not embody a disjunct or third position. As such the two it counts is an indifferent two, a two that is entirely external to the Two of the disjunction. The phenomenal appearance of the couple, which is submitted to an external law of count, does not say anything about love. The couple names not love but the state (or the State) of love. It names not the presentation but the representation of love. It is not for love's sake that there are two counted from the vantage point of the third. In matters of love, the three is not (*n'est pas*), and the Two is subtracted from every count.

If the three does not exist, the first thesis must be otherwise stated. Strictly speaking, it is better to say:

6b. There is one position and another position. There is 'one' and 'one', which do not make two, as the one of each one is indiscernible, although totally disjunct, from the other. In particular, neither position includes the experience of the other, as this would amount to internalizing the two.

It is precisely this latter point that has always constituted the major deadlock for phenomenological approaches to love: since, if love is 'consciousness of the other as other', then the other is necessarily identifiable in consciousness as the same. Otherwise, how are we to understand that consciousness, which is the site of the identification of self as the same-as-self, might welcome or experience the other as such?

Phenomenology is thus left with two options:

- Either it can weaken alterity. In my language, this means that it detotalizes the disjunction and in fact reduces the schism man/woman to a division of the human, in which sexuation disappears as such;
- Or it can annihilate identity. This was the Sartrean way: consciousness is nothingness, and it is not its own position; it is consciousness (of) self, non-thetic consciousness of self. But, in the severity of this pure transparency, we know what love becomes for Sartre: an inescapable oscillation between sadism (turn the other into an in-itself) and masochism (turn oneself into an in-itself for the other). This means that the Two is only a machination of the One.

To maintain at once both the disjunction and the 'there is' of its truth, it is necessary to *set out from love as a process*, and not from amorous consciousness.

I will thus posit that love is precisely this: the advent of the Two as such, the scene of Two.

Care is required here: this scene of the Two is not a *being* of the Two, since that presupposes the three. This scene of the Two is work, a process. It only exists as a trajectory in the situation, *under the supposition that there are Two*. The Two is the hypothetical operator of an aleatoric enquiry, of such work, or such a trajectory.

The advent (*ad-venue*) of the hypothesis of a 'Two' is evental in origin. The event is that hazardous supplement we call an encounter. The event–encounter only consists in the form of its disappearance, of its eclipse. It is fixed only through a naming, and this naming constitutes a declaration, the declaration of love. The name it declares is drawn from the void of the site from which the encounter draws the little bit of being of its supplementation.

What is the void summoned here by the declaration of love? It is the void – un-known – of the disjunction. The declaration of love puts into circulation in the situation a term drawn from the null interval, a term that disjoins the positions man and woman. 'I love you' brackets side by side two pronouns, a 'you' and an 'I', that cannot be bracketed side by side as soon as they are referred to the disjunction. The declaration nominally fixes the encounter as that whose being resides in the void of the disjunction. A Two that proceeds amorously is specifically the name of the disjunct as apprehended in its disjunction.

Love is the interminable fidelity to a first naming. It is a material procedure that re-evaluates the totality of experience, passing fragment by fragment through the whole situation, according to its connection or disconnection with the nominal hypothesis of the Two.

This yields the specific *numerical schema* of the amorous procedure. What this schema expresses is that the Two fractures the One and meets with (*éprouve*) the infinity of the situation. Such is the numericity of the amorous procedure: One, Two, Infinity. This numericity structures the becoming of a generic truth. Of what is it the truth? Of the situation *such as two disjunct positions exist in it*. Love is nothing other than an exacting series of enquiries into the disjunction, into the Two, which, in the retroaction of the encounter, turns out to have always been one of the laws of the situation.

From the moment that *a* truth of the situation proceeds as disjunct, it also becomes clear why every truth is addressed to everyone and guarantees the uniqueness of the humanity function $H(x)$ in its effects. For, as soon as it is grasped in truth, it immediately re-establishes that there is only *one* situation. One situation, and not two. It is a situation in which this disjunction is not a form of being but a *law*. Truths are without exception all truths of *this* situation.

Love is that site where the disjunction happens not to separate the situation in its being. Or where the disjunction is effectively a law and not a substantial delineation. That is the scientific aspect of the amorous procedure.

Love fractures the One in accordance to the Two. And it is on this basis that it can be thought that, although worked over by the disjunction, the situation is exactly as if there is a One, and that it is through this One-multiple that all truth is assured.

In our world, love is the guardian of the universality of the true. It elucidates the possibility of universality, *because it makes truth of the disjunction*.

However, what is the cost of doing so?

7. LOVE AND DESIRE

As a post-eventual hypothesis, the Two must be materially *marked*. The
primary referents of its name have to be given. These referents, as we are
all aware, are bodies, insofar as they are marked by sexuation. The differential trait that bodies bear inscribes the Two in its naming. The sexual
is linked to the amorous procedure as the advent of the Two, in the twofold occurring of a name of the void (the declaration of love) and a material disposition (restricted to bodies as such). The amorous *operator* is
composed of both a name – drawn from the void of the disjunction – and
a differential marking of bodies.

This question of the advent of bodies in love must be carefully circum-
scribed, because it necessarily entails the severance of love and desire.

Desire is captive to its cause, a cause that is not the body as such, and
still less the 'other' as subject, but that is an object the body bears, an
object before which the subject, in its fantasmatic framing, comes forth
(*advenir*) in its own disappearing. Love obviously comes within the defile
of desire but it *does not have the object of desire as its cause*. The supposition
of the Two activated by love, which marks bodies *qua* materiality, can
neither elude the object cause of desire, nor arrange itself with it. This is
because love treats bodies from the bias of a disjunctive naming, whereas
desire relates to them as it does to the principle of being specific to a
divided subject.

Love is therefore always in the quandary if not of the sexual then of
the object that wanders there. Love fits through desire like a camel
through the eye of a needle. It must pass through it, but only insofar as
bodies in their keenness restitute the material markings of the disjunction, by which the declaration of love realizes the interior void.

Let us say that love does not deal with the same body as desire, even
as this body is precisely 'the same'.

In the night of bodies, love attempts to expand, to the extent of the
disjunction, the always particular character of the object of desire.

It attempts to overcome the limitations of stubborn narcissism by establishing (but it can only do so by first being limited to the object) that this body-subject is in the descent of an event, that, before the brilliance of the object of desire was unveiled there, this body (as supernumerary emblem of a truth to come) was *encountered*.

Furthermore, it is only in love that bodies have the purpose of marking the Two. The body of desire is the *corpus delicti*, the *delicti* of the self. It secures the One in the guise of the object. Only love marks the Two by a sort of letting-go (*dé-prise*) of the object, a letting-go that proceeds only because there was a hold exercised over it in the first place.

First, it is at the point of desire that love fractures the One in order that the Two occur in supposition.

Although there is something ridiculous about it – its smacks of a Church father credo – it must be assumed that differential sexual traits attest to the disjunction only when conditioned by the declaration of love. Outside this condition, *there is no Two*, and sexual marking is held *within* the disjunction, without being able to attest it. To put it somewhat bluntly: any sexual unveiling of bodies that is non-amorous is masturbatory in the strict sense; it has only to do with a position in its interiority. This is, moreover, no judgement, only a simple delineation, because masturbatory 'sexual' activity is a fully reasonable activity in each of the disjunct sexuated positions. Further, one is (retroactively) assured that there is nothing commonly shared in this activity when one passes – but can one 'pass'? – from one position to another.

Only love exhibits the sexual as a figure of the Two. It is therefore also the place where it is stated that there are two sexuated bodies and not only one. The amorous unveiling of the bodies is the proof that, under the unique name of the void of the disjunction, the marking of the disjunction itself is happening. This, which under its name is a faithful procedure of truth, conducts an investigation into having always been radically disjunct.

But this sexuated attestation of the disjunction under the post-evental name of its void does not abolish the disjunction. What is at stake is simply to force its truth. It is therefore quite true that there is no sexual relationship, because what love founds is the Two and not a relationship between the Ones in a Two. The two bodies do not present the two – which would require there be three, an outside-sex – they do no more than mark it.

8. THE UNITY OF AMOROUS TRUTH – SEXUATED CONFLICT OF KNOWLEDGES

This point is very delicate. What it requires is that we understand love makes truth of the disjunction under the emblem of the Two, but also that it does so *within the indestructible element of the disjunction*.

As unpresented, the Two is what proceeds in the situation as the complex of a name and a corporal marking. It serves to evaluate the situation through laborious enquiries, including enquiries into the thing that is both its accomplice and its misunderstanding: desire. Sexuality, but also living together, social representation, outings, speech, work, trips away, conflicts, children – all these constitute the materiality of the procedure, the trajectory of the truth in the situation. Yet these operations do not unify the partners. The Two proceeds *as disjunct*. There will have been a single truth of love in the situation, but the procedure of this unicity functions in the disjunction whose truth it makes.

The effects of this tension can be observed on two levels:

1. In the amorous procedure, where *functions* are grouped together that work to redefine the positions.
2. What the future of the one-truth authorizes by anticipation *in knowledge* is sexuated. Or again: foreclosed from truth, the positions return in knowledge.

The first point leads me to refer to an essay of mine (the last one in this book) that is based on the work of Samuel Beckett, 'The Writing of the Generic'. In it I establish that, for Beckett (which thereby brings me to what has the function, in the prose novel, of thinking the thought of love), the becoming of the amorous procedure demands there be the following.

– A function of *wandering* (*l'errance*), of randomness (*aléa*) and of chance voyage, which sustains the articulation of the Two and the infinite. This function works to expose the supposition of the Two to the infinite presentation of the world.
– A function of *motionlessness* (*immobilité*), which guards, which holds the premier naming, which ensures that the naming of the event is not engulfed by the event itself.

- A function of *imperative*: always continue, even within separation. Take absence itself as a modality of continuation.
- The *narrative* function, which, through a sort of archiving, inscribes when and as needed the becoming-truth of wandering.

It is possible to show that the disjunction can be reinscribed within this table of functions. 'Man' I shall define axiomatically as the amorous position that couples imperative and motionlessness, and 'woman' as the position that couples wandering and narrative. These axioms readily intersect with both crass and *précieux* clichés: man is he (or she) who does nothing, I mean nothing obvious for and in the name of love, because he considers that once something is won it stays won without having to be proved again. Woman is she (or he) who makes love voyage, and wants her word to be reiterated and renewed. Or, in the vocabulary of conflict: 'man' is silent and violent; 'woman' gossips and makes demands (*est revendicatif*). These are empirical matters relating to the work involved in enquiring into love, for there to be truth.

The second point is more complex.

In the first place, I shall object to the notion that it is possible, in love, for each of the sexes to learn anything *about the other*. I do not think this is at all correct. Love is an enquiry into the world from the vantage point of the Two, and not at all an enquiry about each term of the Two about the other. There is a real of the disjunction, which dictates precisely that no subject can occupy both positions at the same time and in the same respect. This impossibility lies at the site of love itself. It governs the question of love as a place of knowledge: what it is that, on the basis of love, can be known?

I shall now proceed to distinguish carefully between knowledge and truth. Love *produces* a truth of the situation in such a way that the disjunction is constituted as law. The truth composed by love proceeds to infinity. The disjunction is therefore never completely presented. All knowledge *relative to this truth* is formed in anticipation: if this truth that can never be completed will have taken place, then what judgements can be considered – not true but – veridical? That is the general form of knowledge as conditioned by a generic- or truth-procedure. For technical reasons I call it *forcing*.[1] One can *force* knowledge through a general hypothesis on the having-taken-place of a truth *in process* (*en cours*).

CONDITIONS

In the case of love, the process (*en-cours*) of truth bears on the disjunction. Each one can force certain knowledge about the sexuated disjunction from love through a hypothesis about its having-taken-place.

But the forcing occurs *within* the situation in which love proceeds. If the truth in question is genuine, forcing, and therefore knowledge, will be subject to the disjunction of positions. The knowledge man has about love, on the basis of love, and the knowledge woman has, remain disjunct. Or further: the veridical judgements that are made about the Two, on the supposition that it began in an event, cannot coincide. In particular, the forms of knowledge about sex are themselves irremediably sexuated. The two sexes do not ignore each other; they know veridically in disjunct fashion.

Love is that scene in which a truth proceeds, a truth about the sexuated positions through a conflict of knowledges for which there can be no compensation.

This is because truth is at the crux of the un-known (*in-su*). Knowledges are veridical and anticipatory but disjunct. Formally, this disjunction is representable in the instance of the Two. The position man supports the split of the Two, an in-between where the void of the disjunction is fixed. The position woman makes the Two endure in wandering. On a previous occasion, I put forward the following formula: 'man's' knowledge is made of judgements ordered around the nothing of the Two. And 'woman's' knowledge orders them around *nothing but* the Two. I might add here, then, that the sexuation of knowledge as regards love disjoins:

1. the following veridical masculine statement: 'What will have been true is that we were two and not at all one';
2. from the no less veridical feminine statement that: 'What will have been true is that two we were, and that otherwise we were not'.

The feminine statement targets being as such. That is her destination in love, and it is ontological. The masculine statement targets the changing of the number, the painful fracture (*effraction*) of the One by the supposition of the Two, and this is essentially logical.

The conflict of knowledge in love shows that the One of a truth is also exposed simultaneously as logical and as ontological. This point refers us to the *Book Gamma* of Aristotle's *Metaphysics* and to an admirable recent commentary of it published by Vrin under the title *The Decision of Sense*.

The enigma of Aristotle's text resides in the passage between the ontological position of a science of being *qua* being and the crucial position of the principle of identity as a purely logical principle. This passage, in general, is no more frequented than the passage from the position of women to that of man. In this commentary, the authors show that Aristotle passes 'by force' with the ardour of an intermediary style: that pertaining to the refutation of sophists. Between the ontological position and the logical position, all there is, is a medium of refutation. It is also thus for each of the positions engaged in love, where the *other* position only allows itself to be attained as if it were a sophistry to be refuted. Who has not experienced the exhausting fatigue these refutations bring about, which can ultimately be encapsulated in the deplorable syntagm 'You don't understand me'? We might say this is the enervated form of a love declaration. To love well is to understand poorly.

I think it no matter of mere coincidence that this commentary on Aristotle, which I have added to here in my own way, was written by a woman, Barbara Cassin, and a man, Michel Narcy.

9. THE FEMININE POSITION AND HUMANITY

I might have concluded with these words. But I shall add a postscript to return to where I left off.

The existence of love makes it retroactively appear that, in the disjunction, the position woman is singularly conveying of the relation between love and humanity. That is, humanity as I conceive it, as the function $H(x)$ that creates an implicative knot out of the truth procedures – science, politics, art and love.

Yet another trivial cliché, people will say. Woman is such as to think only about love; woman is the being-for-love.

Let us take some courage to work through this cliché.

I shall posit axiomatically that the woman position is such that the *subtraction* of love modifies it with inhumanity for itself. Or further, that the function $H(x)$ can only take on value insofar as the amorous generic procedure exists.

This axiom signifies that, for this position, the prescription for humanity has value only to the extent that the existence of love has been attested.

CONDITIONS

We should note in passing that this attestation does not necessarily take the form of an experience of love. It is possible to be 'seized' by the existence of a truth-procedure from an angle that is altogether different to that of its experimentation. Here, too, we must guard against the least psychologism: what matters is not any consciousness of love but that for, the term x, the proof of its existence has been produced.

I shall posit that woman is that term x that, as noumenal virtuality of the human and irrespective of its empirical sex, only activates the humanity function on the condition of such a proof. Thus woman is she (or he) for whom the particular subtraction of love *devalorizes* $H(x)$ in its other types, namely, science, politics and art. *A contrario*, the existence of love deploys $H(x)$ virtually in all of its types, especially the most connected, or interlinked ones. This undoubtedly sheds light on – providing it is granted that the writing of romance novels has to do with a 'feminized' term x, which must be investigated – women's excellence in writing novels.

For the man position, things proceed differently: each type of procedure by itself gives value to the $H(x)$ function, without taking into account the existence of the others.

I have thus progressively come to *define* the words man and woman through the point at which love cuts into the knot of the four types of truth-procedure. And further, referred to the humanity function, sexual difference can only be conceived (*n'est pensable*) in the exercise of love *qua* criterion of differentiation.

But if love, and love alone, makes truth of the disjunction how could it be otherwise? Desire is unable to found the thought of the Two, since it is in thrall to the demonstration of being-One that the object requires of it.

I further maintain that, independently of sexuation, desire is homosexual, whereas love, as gay as it may be, is principally heterosexual.

The passing of love through desire – I pointed earlier to its difficult dialectic – can further be stated as: to have the heterosexuality of love pass through the homosexuality of desire.

At the end of the day, and regardless of the sex of those a love encounter destines to a truth, woman and man only ever exist in the field of love.

Let us briefly return to Humanity. Stating that H is a virtual composition of the four types of truths also makes it possible to argue that, for the woman position, love type *knots the four together*, and that it is only as conditioned by love that H, that is, humanity, exists as a general

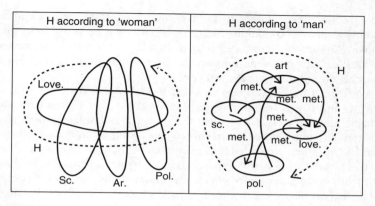

Figure 11.1

configuration. And that, for the male position, each type *metaphorizes the others*, this metaphor meriting the immanent affirmation, in each type, of humanity H.

This would result in the two schemas given in Figure 11.1.

These schemas clarify why the feminine representation of humanity is at once conditional and knotting, which authorizes a more complete perception and, should the case arise, a more direct right to inhumanity; whereas the masculine representation of humanity is at once symbolic and separative, which may incur some indifference, but also a greater ability to conclude.

Are we dealing with a restricted conception of femininity here? Even in a sophisticated form, does this cliché not refer back to a schema of domination that could be summarily put as: access to the symbolic and the universal is more immediate for man? Or, let us say, is less dependent on an encounter.

I could object by replying that the encounter is everywhere: *every* generic procedure is postevental.

But the essential point lies elsewhere. The essential point is that love is, as I've said, the guarantee of the universal because it alone makes the disjunction comprehensible as the simple law of *a* situation. That the value of the humanity function H(*x*) is dependent, for the woman-position, on the existence of love, can also be stated as: the woman-position

CONDITIONS

requires for H(x) a guarantee of universality. It knots the components of H only under this condition. The woman-position is sustained in its singular relation to love so it can be clear that for every x, H(x), no matter what the effects of the disjunction are (or disjunctions: since the sexual disjunction is *perhaps* not the only one).

With this I have given the Lacanian formulas of sexuation an extra turn of the screw. To put it very schematically: Lacan started with the phallic function Φ(x). He ascribed the universal quantifier to man (for every man), and defined woman through a combination of the existential and negation, which led him to say that woman is not-whole.

This position is in many respects classical. Hegel, proclaiming woman the irony of the community, effectively indicated this effect at the border of the existential by which a woman makes holes in the whole that men strive to consolidate.

But such occurs as a strict effect of exercising the Φ(x) function. The most obvious outcome of what I've just said is that *the humanity function H(x) does not coincide with the Φ(x) function*.

Regarding the function H(x), the feminine position in fact sustains its universal totality, and the masculine position metaphorically disseminates the virtualities of H's one-composition.

Love is that which, splitting H(x) from Φ(x), returns to women, within the complete range of truth procedures, the universal quantifier.

PART VI
Philosophy and Psychoanalysis

PART VI

Processing and Applications

CHAPTER TWELVE
Philosophy and Psychoanalysis

I intervene among you as someone, like the Eleatic Stranger from the *Sophist*, neither an analyst, nor an analysand, but an expatriate of a memorable and precarious place, someone who comes at your invitation put to your experience a doubting consideration.

Shall I, like the Stranger with regard to Parmenides, commit some sort of speculative parricide? What makes me likely to do so is that being the author of a *Manifesto for Philosophy*, I am no doubt placed as a son of philosophy, let's say to be brief, as a son of Plato, a son of parricide. This criminal heritage may determine a repeat-case. What shelters me from doing so is no doubt the fact that I object to the sermon of today announcing philosophy's end, that I modestly claim to take a single step forward, and thus that as the commonplace of today's thought is parricide, it is filial respect that forms a figure of singularity.

But to which my proximity to you will lead or carry me, you yourselves will be the judges.

The point that disposes philosophy and psychoanalysis is that of a – non-dialectical – law of compossibility between a *ressentiment* whose essence is seduction and a consent whose essence is reserve. I shall not again go over the textual and empirical sources.

The question organizing this field can be put as follows: what can we suppose about the bias by which a truth touches being? I propose to transform this question into another more precise but essentially identical question, which is: what is the localization of the void? For, we can, I think, agree to say that it is on the basis of its suture to the void that a text can support its claim to have other than a relation (*rapport*) to realities – or other than what Mallarmé called a 'universal reporting'.

We can agree *in principle* to repudiate doctrines of truth that posit a relation of correspondence between mind or statement and thing. We certainly cannot – on this philosopher and the psychoanalyst are not opposed – contravene a major axiom of every poet, which is that every thought emits a throw of the dice. Therewith thought exhibits between itself and the continuity of the place the void of a suspended act. Mallarmé called this void, as you know, Chance. Chance supports what Lacan in 1960 called – in a genuinely maximal expression – 'the only absolute statement', a statement made, he said, by 'someone of authority'. This statement, of course, is 'that no dice-throw in the signifier will ever abolish chance'. Since this statement is absolute, and is the only absolute statement; since it was made by that 'someone of authority' Mallarmé, it shall be the statement cementing our pact throughout what I have to say. You will allow me to translate it thus: thinking is made possible only by the void that separates it from realities.

So the whole question is: where is the void localized? What is the place of the void? If Mallarmé brings us together and absolutizes the question, this is because he contented himself with calling localization 'place'. Void is the essence of place, of every place; such that a truth, be it in his terms a Constellation, cold with forgetting and desuetude, emerges only within the spacing of an indeterminate place. A truth inscribes itself in the black of the sky if the non-place of the dice throw, separative and undecidable, blocks the repetition that in general determines that – outside of thought and act – 'nothing takes place but the place'.

We can also agree on the fact that philosophy and psychoanalysis make no sense without a desire for something to take place other than the place.

But philosophy and psychoanalysis each localize place differently. They are regimes of experience and thought that are specific, each one of which is subsumed by Mallarmé's absolute statement, and each one of which is conceivable not from place in general, but from its own place, a place fixed in destiny by its specific foundation: Freudian for one, Parmenidian for the other.

Yet these places are disjoint in their origins. The place at which philosophy localizes the void as the condition of thought is being, *qua* being.

The place at which psychoanalysis localizes the void is the Subject, *its* subject, the Subject as the unconscious that occupies the gap between signifiers in which the metonymy of its being proceeds.

Must we therefore end up in a disagreement and at an impasse?

In the seminar of 8 May 1973, Lacan explicitly stated that the place that founds the truth has the manner of the void. This void is the Big Other as hole: 'There is a hole there and that hole is called the Other [. . .], the Other *qua* locus in which speech, being deposited [. . .] founds truth'. But what matters to us here is that this localization is presented by way of contrast to the localization that Lacan attributes to philosophy. 'There is a hole *there*': what is this 'there'? What is this other place where the hole that founds truth occurs? The there or other place is a thought (une *pensée*) that can be inferred from thinking (le *penser*). That a thought exists that can be inferred from thinking amounts precisely to the supposition that being thinks. Because, if thinking (le *penser*) necessitates a place filled with a thought (une *pensée*), the reason is that being as such thinks. It is in the same place as this supposition of a full thinking being (*plein être pensant*) that Lacan localizes the foundation of truth as hole.

Now this supposition, and therefore this other place in which the big Other makes holes, is exactly the place of philosophy. And I quote: 'That being is presumed to think is what founds the philosophical tradition from Parmenides on'.

Philosophy thus establishes the place of its specific void, namely, being as the self-founding of thinking, at the place where psychoanalysis also establishes its own but as a radical ex-centering of the opening (*trouée*) in which it originates that a truth can be the cause of a Subject. The apparent identity of the place unknots, insofar as philosophy localizes its void at the point of the Same, as in Parmenides' declaration that 'the Same, indeed is at once to think and to be'; whereas it is at the point of the Other that psychoanalysis makes holes in it, that it 'de-supposes' (*désuppose*) the thought that philosophy infers from thinking (*au penser*). Hole of the Other or the nil gap of the Same: these instances of the void, which are joined as to the place, are incommensurable.

We can find no cause for consolation in the fact that Lacan immediately proceeded to concur with Heraclitus in opposition to Parmenides, because for Heraclitus being is neither given nor hidden; it signifies.

And because, in philosophy, this 'signifying' gave rise to a tradition that could not be further from psychoanalysis, and that is the tradition of hermeneutics. It is better to keep up the disagreement than to confuse philosophy with the interpretive custodianship of sacred texts.

If we move from thought and turn to the act, the situation is no better. Under the name of Kant, philosophy this time determines the void, that of practical reason, in the presupposition of the purely formal character of Imperative. The Law is without content, and it is its being evacuated of any assignable reference that constitutes it as command-ment. The capital result is that philosophy postulates the void *in* signifi-cation. The moral meaning of the act lies in the universally presentable nature of its signification, and the universality of signification is itself grounded in the formal void of the Law.

In the seminar of 6 July 1960, Lacan contrasted this localization with the three major premises of the Ethics of psychoanalysis:

> First, 'the only thing of which one can be guilty is of having given ground relative to one's desire'.
> Second, the ethical hero is the one who, having been betrayed, shows no tolerance of betrayal, since any reparative tolerance of betrayal rules on the side of the servicing of goods.
> Third, genuine Good, that which dispenses no service, is what serves to pay the price for access to desire, that is, to give access to the metonymy of our being.

Where, then, do these three propositions localize the void?

The importance of betrayal cannot be underestimated. Because by means of the act betrayal hollows out a point at which the peril of the servicing of goods is uncovered. The void is precisely that gap, this dis-covery of the servicing of goods, such as its scourge (*plaie*) is exposed in betrayal, and through which, so as not to cede on our desire, the meton-ymy of our being must pass – at a premium price. If it does not pass through this void proper, which at once reveals and makes an incision in the reposeful massivity of the servicing of goods, the metonymy of our being will forever be articulated with this servicing. Since, as Lacan said, 'beyond this limit, there is no return' .

A crucial consequence of this apparatus is that, this time, the void is not presupposed to lie within signification, by way of its universality.

It is presupposed to lie *beneath* significations, on their flipside, as the sliding, the threading, the rivulet, the channel of our being, in the un-presented that forms the lining of the signifying chain. I quote:

> The channel in which desire is located is not simply that of the modulation of the signifying chain, but that which flows beneath it as well; that is, properly speaking, what we are as well as what we are not, our being and our non-being – that which is signified in an act passes from one signifier of the chain to another beneath all the significations.

This time philosophy can be said to localize the void in the formal universality of signification by means of the act, whereas psychoanalysis situates it on the other side, in the duplication and doubling of all signification. For, according to Kant, the universality of the moral act, in the form of the void, opens onto being itself, *qua* being, what he called the supra-sensible; whereas, according to Lacan, ethics opens, singularly, in response to the discovery of betrayal, to our being, to that which, to use his own words, 'we are, and we are also not, our being and our non-being'.

Localization of the void in signification and in universality, or localization of the void on the other side (*revers*) of all signification and in the singularity of the occurrence. Localization of the void as an opening onto the supra-sensible, or localization of the void as 'channel' of our being: as we move from pure reason to practical reason, the dispute is displaced and intensified.

If, now, we examine the general form of the question of truth, we find that this opposition appertains, after Parmenides or Plato and Kant, to Hegel and the dialectic.

The point that psychoanalysis and philosophy have in common is that they both hold truth and error to be absolutely entwined. Lacan said it most rigorously in the seminar of 30 June 1954: 'So long as truth is not entirely revealed, that is to say in all likelihood until the end of time, its nature will be to propagate itself in the form of error'.

One can only agree to such a proposition. Yet, in the very same text, Lacan proceeded to distinguish between, on the one hand, what he called discourse, in which he included philosophy, singularly Hegelian philosophy, and, on the other hand, speech, which psychoanalysis certifies to be in excess of discourse.

CONDITIONS

What maxim does discourse, and hence philosophy, fall under? This maxim is that 'in discourse it is contradiction which sorts truth from error'. Let us say, then, that the void of difference between truth and error, granting that the latter presents the former, is localized in the negative, in explicit contradiction. Or, as Lacan put it, that 'error is demonstrated as such when, at a given moment, it results in a contradiction'. This also means that philosophical dialectic localizes the void separating error and truth at the point at which being *qua* being would as it were coincide exactly with non-being *qua* non-being. At this point the 'nothing' of being remains, as the ultimate proof of truth such as error exhibits it.

Now, with psychoanalysis it works differently. This is essentially expressed by saying: the unconscious ignores the principle of contradiction. And more subtly:

> The genuine speech that we are supposed to uncover through interpretation obeys laws other than those of discourse, which is subject to the condition of having to move within error up to the moment when it encounters contradiction. Authentic speech has other modes, other means, than everyday speech.

It follows that 'the Freudian innovation is the revelation, within the phenomenon, of these subjective, experienced moments, in which a speech emerges that surpasses the discoursing subject'.

If, therefore, dialectical philosophy localizes the void in contradiction, pushing it to a pure point at which being *qua* being cannot be maintained, then psychoanalysis localizes it in the excessive emergence of speech, which is such that the subject of discourse is disrupted, is interrupted.

Either a localization of the void in that which 'exorbitates' being from its self-identity, or a localization in the excess over self of the subject, in the rift of discourse and speech: you understand the insistence of the dispute.

And then again . . . Every truth emerges from having found a pass in the impasse, and no doubt it is also so with that truth that we aspire to say, and that is at stake empirically in the observation that neither has psychoanalysis interrupted philosophy nor has philosophy been able to deconstruct psychoanalysis.

I shall begin by indicating a difficult torsion in Lacan's text, taking every precaution, so as not to become immediately subsumed within the categories of discourse, not to speak of contradiction.

In the seminar of 20 March 1973, Lacan stated that if psychoanalysis is grounded in a presumption or ideal, it is 'that a knowledge about truth can be constituted on the basis of its experience'.

But, in the seminar of 15 May of the same year, in express opposition to Plato, he stated quite simply that the real essence of his teaching consists in determining the conditions for this statement: that 'there is some relationship of being that cannot be known'. He also put it as: 'Something true can still be said about what cannot be demonstrated'.

It takes quite a bit of work, I'm sure you'll agree, to be able to link these two theses together. And it was perhaps this difficult linking that led Lacan, in the immediate follow on, to express his uncertainty about how to approach truth.

How indeed can a knowledge of truth emerge whose whole being, or relation of being, consists in not knowing? Does determination of a knowledge of a truth of the unknown not presuppose that in the formula 'it thinks' it is said that ultimately being thinks, something that Lacan dismissed as a defect of philosophy's inaugural hypothesis? Against Plato, Lacan maintained that the approach (*abord*) to being is not reducible to the Idea construed as knowledge that fills being or as knowledge immanent to being. But does not the exception of an unknown relationship, as it is given *in truth* through psychoanalysis, lead us back to the very edge of knowledge, and so to the Idea?

Are there – this is the most pointed form of the question – any Ideas specific to psychoanalysis?

In my view, it is in the light, or in the shadow, of this question that Lacan, like Plato, summoned mathematics. Mathematics has always been the place-holder of the Idea as Idea, the Idea as Idea to which Lacan gave the name of matheme.

In 1954, Lacan referred to speech as that which is in a relation of excess to the Hegelian discourse of contradiction. In 1973, he expressly referred to mathematical formalization: 'Compared to a philosophy that culminates in Hegel's discourse . . . can't the formalization of mathematical logic serve us in the analytic process?'

It is remarkable that immediately after stating that 'mathematical formalization is our goal, our ideal', Lacan then goes on to discuss the backbone of his teaching, namely, the notion that 'I speak without knowing it'.

As we can already intimate, there is, then, an intrinsic link between three terms or functions.

CONDITIONS

- first, that the relationship of being is not reducible to knowledge
- second, that there is possible knowledge about the truth of this relationship;
- third, that mathematics is the locus of the Idea.

In this instance, we may therefore assume that the localization of the void lies in none other than the remainderlessness of the matheme; the matheme empties out all the scraps and conveys that which in experience touches the un-known of a truth. As it is presented in mathematizing literalization, the void is what separates truth and knowledge, each time psychoanalysis opens us up to some knowledge of a truth.

Lacan told us that Plato was wrong to fill being with knowledge. However, the matheme enables a completely different incompleteable filling-in: a filling up of the void, of the very void disjoining them, with the un-known and knowledge.

In this sense, there can be knowledge of an un-known truth at the point of the void. And, consequently, access to being would consist, just like in philosophy, in the presupposition of a void that only the little letters of formalization can nail down without remainder, therefore without total (*plein*).

This presupposes that being and the real are distinct, insofar as the real remains a function of the subject. Lacan had always insisted on this distinction. Discussing the three fundamental passions – love, hatred and ignorance – in the seminar of 30 June 1954, Lacan argued that they can only be registered 'in the dimension of being, and not in that of the real'. His view never changed on this point, despite the incessant re-elaborations to which he submitted the category of the real. On 26 June 1973, he again stated that 'it is love that approaches being as such in an encounter'.

Philosophy and psychoanalysis can be compossible, since the double paradoxical condition of mathematics and love cross over at the point where the void is localized in the disjunction of an un-known truth and a knowledge of that truth. This point, I maintain, is that of the Idea. Psychoanalysis and philosophy both ultimately demand that we adhere to Spinoza's unfounded and unfoundable maxim: 'Habemus enim ideam veram', we in effect have, but as an effect of nothing, as localization of the void, a true idea. One, at least.

At this point I should like to conclude. The conclusion can be stated in five theses, five philosophical theses, but theses that, I hope, will provide rules for our peaceful co-existence:

Thesis 1: Only mathematics is entitled to postulate that localization of the void takes place in being. There is no onto-logy than other genuine mathematics.

Thesis 2: A truth provides an access to being that is not demonstrated, that is not known, but that proceeds to infinity in the Chance of a trajectory. A truth is 'an indiscernible' of the place in which it proceeds.

Thesis 3: The inauguration of a truth-process is exactly what Lacan referred to as an 'encounter' when he said that in an encounter 'it is love that approaches being as such'. This inauguration, incidentally, is what Plato in his *Symposium* called *exaiphnès*, the 'sudden'. It is what I call 'event'. The event is undecidable.

Thesis 4: In its being the subject is nothing other than a truth grasped in its pure point; it is a vanishing quantity of truth, a differential eclipse of its incompletable infinity. This vanishing is the in-between of the event's undecidability and truth's indiscernibility.

Thesis 5: Philosophy and psychoanalysis have a common border to two procedures that are external to one another: mathematics, on the one hand, and love, on the other. The knot of these components forming the outer border of philosophy and psychoanalysis consists in the localization of the void in the link, or the relation, that might be supposed to 'hold together' the Idea and the thing, or being and the knowledge of being. Love undergoes the void of relation, because there is no sexual relationship. Mathematics undergoes it, because it exhausts it in pure literalization.

If, finally, the common border of psychoanalysis and philosophy is de-liaison, the localization of the void in the non-relatedness of every relation, the subjective category of this relation, you will tolerate my saying that its – unexpected – name is: 'courage'.

On 26 June 1973, Lacan said that 'love can only actualise, what, in a sort of poetic flight, in order to make myself understood, I called courage – courage with regard to this fatal destiny'. But twenty years earlier, on 19 May 1954, he had posed the following question: 'Do we have to extend analytical intervention as far as the fundamental dialogues on justice and courage, which we find in the great dialectical tradition?' As you will have noticed, we almost had here a psychoanalysis leading towards a modern Platonism. This remains a question. It is not easy to answer. And Lacan found it difficult (*penible*), since, as he said, 'contemporary man has become singularly unused to tackling these grand themes'.

This incapability persists, but it is to counter it that I have called on philosophy to accomplish one more step, to knot together once more being, truth and the subject, and to repudiate the feeble apologetic of its end. If the common border of our efforts, of our practice and thought, is as I claim, then, with total clarity, we can say to each other this single word, a word of pacifying severity that is only seemingly anachronistic: courage!

CHAPTER THIRTEEN
The Subject and Infinity

I would like to start with a passage from a text by Lacan, from page 94 of the canonical edition of the seminar entitled *Encore*. This text has troubled me for some time, and in what follows I aim to explain, on the basis of this trouble, what I understand of the paradoxes that it presents to thought.

Here is the passage:

> In that logic, on the basis of the fact that one can write 'not-every [pas-tout] x is inscribed in Φx', one deduces by way of implication that there is an x that contradicts it. But that is true on one sole condition, which is that, in the whole or the not-whole in question, we are dealing with the finite. Regarding that which is finite, there is not simply an implication but a strict equivalence. It is enough for there to be one that contradicts the universalising formula for us to have to abolish that formula and transform it into a particular. The not-whole becomes the equivalent of that which, in Aristotelian logic, is enunciated on the basis of the particular. There is an exception. But we could, on the contrary, be dealing with the infinite. Then it is no longer from the perspective of extension that we must take up the not-whole [pas-toute]. When I say that woman is not-whole and that that is why I cannot say Woman, it is precisely because I raise the question [je mets en question] of a jouissance that, with respect to everything that can be used in the function Φx, is in the realm of the infinite.
>
> Now, as soon as you are dealing with an infinite set, you cannot posit that the not-whole implies the existence of something that is

produced on the basis of a negation or contradiction. You can, at a pinch, posit it as an indeterminate existence. But, as we know from the extension of mathematical logic, from that mathematical logic which is qualified as intuitionist, to posit a 'there exists', one must also be able to construct it, that is, know how to find where that existence is.

This is not a marginal text. In fact, it sets out one of the basic conditions needed to validate the formulas of sexuation, and that is a condition of infinitude.

The formulas of sexuation are the logic by which Lacan maintains that sexuation is the key to the real of the differences of the sexes. It sets out from the function $\Phi(x)$, which expresses in an indeterminate fashion, as Lacan put it in his seminar entitled . . . *Or Worse*, that '*the sexual relationship raises a question for the speaking being*'. We are quite aware that, for Lacan, this is a radical question, because the said relation is properly without being. There *is no* sexual relationship. And why? Because the veritable sense of the function $\Phi(x)$, which formulates or formalizes the question of relation, is that access to sexual enjoyment is, for the speaking being, gained by way of castration. As Lacan also said, in the same seminar, '$\Phi(x)$, this means the function called castration'. Yet, this function of castration, even though every speaking being is necessarily a case of it, operates in two formally different ways. This formal difference results from the fact that once the function takes hold of a speaking being, it either can or cannot be of an absolutely universal scope.

Roughly speaking, we might put the matter as follows: the statement 'for every x, $\Phi(x)$', that is, the statement 'it is by means of the for all, of the universal, that the speaking being is formed in the process of castration', prescribes the position of man. Whereas the statement 'not every $x \Phi(x)$', which is the statement of a restriction to, or a partial subtraction from, the operation of the function, prescribes the position of woman. This is how we come to the famous expression according to which a woman is not-whole. Not-whole, that is, in phallic enjoyment, access to which presupposes the effect of the function Φ – of the function of castration.

The purely logical difficulty that Lacan was constantly trying to avoid is the following. In Aristotle's logic, the negation of a universal implies the affirmation of a particular. If we say 'not every man is mortal', this necessarily implies that 'some men are immortal'.

Modern predicate logic backs up Aristotle's viewpoint. The negation of a universal statement is equivalent to the affirmation of an existential statement. If you posit 'not for every x $\Phi(x)$' it can be shown that this is equivalent to positing 'there exists x such that not-$\Phi(x)$'.

As a result, in classical logic, if a woman is inferred from the statement 'not every x $\Phi(x)$' this means that she is inferred from the statement 'there exists x such that not-$\Phi(x)$'.

Yet Lacan does not at all want to accept that there might exist an x, and hence a speaking being that is radically subtracted from the function Φ. Castration is universal in that it affects access to enjoyment for every speaking being, regardless of position, woman or man. There exists, then, no x whose access to enjoyment is inferred from a not-$\Phi(x)$. It would be, this x, neither man nor woman. It would be an angel, and it is certainly not for nothing that the mode controlling angels' entry into enjoyment, were this of the contemplation of God, has been discussed *ad infinitum*. Lacan wanted his formulas of sexuation to be compatible with what I suggest be regarded as an axiom of utmost importance, axiom number 1, and that states: 'there is no angel'. This is essentially expressed by saying that castration is effective for every speaking being, hence for every thinking being, and that here we suppose, in conformity with canon law, that angels think. It follows that they are not. For the angel, this being subtracted from the whole operation of castration, the cogito is expressed as 'if I think, I am not'.

There is nothing in this that is surprising, since in numerous passages Lacan identified castration purely and simply with the action of language. For example, in . . . *Or Worse*, we find this: 'What is written as $\Phi(x)$, is that one can no longer have at one's disposal the totality of signifiers, and that this is perhaps a first approach to the whole question of castration'. Castration means that language is not-whole, precisely. If therefore the existence of a woman as not-whole means that there exists an x totally subtracted from castration, it would follow that, unsubdued by the real of language, this woman would not speak.

If 'not every $x\Phi(x)$' is equivalent, as is the case in classical logic, to 'there exists an x such that not-$\Phi(x)$', then a woman is silent. There is indeed a way of talking about incoherent babblings that says: 'And so your daughter is dumb'. Which is the point precisely. At issue in the inexistence of the sexual relationship, as we are well aware, is that there is a woman present who is not your daughter. We must thereby return to this logical problem: to which conditions does the Lacanian not-whole comply in order to avoid implying that 'there exists at least such a one that is not'?

The trouble plaguing me thus has a very clear cause. It is that, in order to resolve his problem, Lacan took two paths that are undoubtedly incompatible.

The first path consists in saying that the logic underlying the formulas of sexuation is not classical logic but a variation of intuitionist logic.

The second, basing itself on Cantor's set theory, introduces, outside the field of the Φ function, the abyss of actual infinity.

Now, intuitionism is defined, amongst other things, by a categorical rejection of actual infinity. We have a new and grave problem.

The two paths are mentioned in the passage from *Encore* that concerns us. The first paragraph explicitly invokes the infinity of feminine enjoyment, that is, that part of enjoyment subtracted from the operation of the function Φ. The second finds support in intuitionism for the requirement that all existence be constructed, which, incidentally, rules out the existence of any actual infinity.

Let us examine these two heterogeneous solutions in turn.

What leads Lacan into the neighbourhood of intuitionist logic is the sense content of the formula defining the woman position, that is, 'not-all $\Phi(x)$'. Lacan in effect explained that this formula is not to be taken in extension, that it is not to be taken as meaning that there are some who are subtracted from the action of the function Φ. It signifies that it is not from the vantage point of the whole that a woman supports its effect. The formula therefore only indicates a subtraction-from, or a making-a-hole-in, this effect. As a result, you cannot extract from the negative, or subtractive, formula 'not every $\Phi(x)$', an existential affirmation of the type 'there exists x such that not-$\Phi(x)$'. Lacan made this point very clearly in . . .*Or Worse*:

> What is this 'not-whole' [*pas toutes*]? It is very precisely something that deserves to be interrogated as a structure. Because, contrary – and this is the crucial point – to the function of the particular negative, namely, that 'there are some who are not', this affirmation cannot be deduced from the 'not-whole' [*pas-tout*]. It is the 'not-whole' to which it is reserved to indicate that somewhere it has a relation to the phallic function, and nothing more.

This passage is very clear: far from indicating that it is possible to extract an affirmation from it, such that 'one' exists whom is not under the effect of castration, the not-whole (*pas-toute*), on the contrary, points to a particular mode of that effect, namely, that it is 'somewhere' and not everywhere. The for-all (*pour-tout*) of the 'man' position is also an 'everywhere'. The somewhere, and not everywhere, of the 'woman' position is expressed: not-whole.

This logical point becomes essential as soon as, from the ostensible negation of the universal by the not-whole, it turns out to be impossible to deduce a negative existential affirmation. It is not true that from 'not every $\Phi(x)$' it follows that 'there exists an x such that not-$\Phi(x)$'.

Now, such is exactly the intuitionist position. In pure logic, this position ultimately boils down to a restricted handling of the powers of negation. This is how the intuitionists come to reject the principle of excluded middle, namely, by not accepting the principle p or *not-p*. Similarly, nor do they accept any equivalence between double negation and affirmation: for them, it is not possible to conclude from the truth of not-not-p as to the truth of p. And again, nor do they accept that the negation of a universal is equivalent to the affirmation of a negative existential. For an intuitionist, therefore, from the statement 'not for every x $\Phi(x)$' there is no reason to conclude that 'there exists x such that not-$\Phi(x)$'. On this point intuitionism coincides perfectly with Lacan's aim.

But from where do intuitionists draw their suspicion regarding the demonstrative powers of negation? To my mind, this suspicion stems from two principal determinations.

The first, which we shall return to, is a rejection of an actually existing infinity, considered as the effect of an uncontrolled negation of the finite, of which it lacks any clear concept.

The second, consists in the refusal of reasoning by the absurd. If you want to demonstrate statement p by means of the absurd, you posit not-p and draw a contradictory consequence from it. As a result, not-p is impossible. In classical logic, if not-p is false, it follows that not-not-p is true. And consequently, since not-not-p is equivalent to p, you have demonstrated p. An intuitionist will reject this conclusion on the grounds that not-not-p is not equivalent to p. But, above all, the intuitionist will say: I want a direct demonstration of p, which shows the truth of p in steps, and not this fictive and mindless detour that advances from not-p.

Only, Lacan did not actually accept either of these two determinations. Not only does Lacan permit himself use of reasoning by the absurd, but it could be shown that this very approach is implied at every moment of the symptom and its interpretation. And, as we shall see, Lacan also had recourse, at least in appearance, to Cantor's actually existing infinite, to the famous alephs, which he examined and interpreted, whereas intuitionists consider them mere fictions lacking in thought content.

Moreover, the conviction that Lacan thought within the parameters of intuitionist logic cannot be maintained for very long. And this is for the simple reason that real mathematics is not, and has never been, intuitionist, since some of its most crucial results have depended on the actually existing infinite and reasoning by the absurd. Well, especially in . . . *Or Worse* and in *Encore*, Lacan paid such mathematics quite a radical tribute. In . . . *Or Worse*, we should recall, he said things such as: 'There is no teaching other than mathematical, the rest is joking-about'. And in *Encore*, we find this: 'Mathematical formalization is our goal, our ideal'. So, fortuitous as the coincidence between the play of his formulas of sexuation and intuitionist restrictions may seem, I do not think Lacan was actually prepared to have his thought comply with these restrictions.

The real solution to the problem lies on the side of the infinite. But does the passage from *Encore* with which we started really shed light on this problem?

Lacan begins by saying that, if the field in which it operates is finite, the 'not-all' will actually lead us back to the proposition 'there exists one such that is not castrated', and hence to the dis-universalization of castration. Thus Lacan admits classical logic for the finite. Insofar as the finite is concerned, then, we can at least confirm that Lacan is not intuitionist.

We must therefore posit that the field in which the not-all proceeds is infinite, since the assertion that there exists an angel is untenable. But what is this field exactly? It is the field of feminine enjoyment. It must therefore be admitted that there is some infinite *(il y a de l'infini)* in feminine enjoyment. This infinity is such that what of it is affected, or barred, by the function of castration is 'somewhere', and not everywhere. Consequently, an enjoyment remains that is properly the infinite elsewhere pertaining to this somewhere, a some place that, before the infinite, fails to be everywhere. Of course, since castration is predicated on the basis of the finite availability of language, this enjoyment, which is of the order of the infinite, and which overflows the phallic *touché*, is properly dumb or speechless. Here the girl we have just mentioned appears again. It is the enjoyment of the dumb girl in a woman that subtracts that woman from the whole of castration, which, may I say, not-wholes her. Let us say of a girl that she infinitely 'not-wholes' a woman in the scission of enjoyment.

But have we come to the end of our troubles? Must we not conclude, regarding the example of this speechless girl who infinitely inhabits the finite enjoyment of a woman, that she at least, that she nevertheless, really exists in subtraction from the function Φ? A woman's supplementary enjoyment, feminine enjoyment, does it not silently attest to an *ek-sistance* outside of the effect of castration? In this matter, does the infinite not support in itself, in the not-all that is the not-everywhere, a situated negation of the somewhere in which the universality of the function of castration partially operates? After all, does not Lacan himself end up saying, in . . . *Or Worse*, and it actually really is the worst, that a woman is uncastratable?

On the basis of the not-whole, we shall then refer back once more to the inference as to the existence of an angelic negation of castration. Is a speechless girl an angel? Such is the question. Commenting on *Hamlet*, Lacan posits that *girl is Phallus*.[1] We are at the 'spinning wheel' of knowing whether, within the infinite arcana of feminine enjoyment, it is to be presupposed that our girl is an angel. This, logically, would give 'the phallus is an angel',[2] which is one way among others to resolve the pressing question of the sex of angels: they don't have any sex, because they are it.

But this is not where Lacan wished to come to. Hence the most tangled section of our passage:

> Now, as soon as you are dealing with an infinite set, you cannot posit that the not-whole implies the existence of something that is produced on the basis of a negation or contradiction. You can, at a pinch, posit it as an indeterminate existence.

It is clear that, driven on by despair, Lacan is struggling against allowing any existential consequences to flow from the not-whole. In sum, against allowing that a woman on the cross (which, as we see, is a crossroads) of her enjoyment might lead to the conclusion that there exists at least one angel. But what was Lacan really driving at? How can the infinite here be the ultimate condition of the universality of castration, in spite of the not-all?

Let us grasp the difficulty of the problem. When Lacan tells us that the infinity of the field of enjoyment presents an objection to negation, he means, I think, this: there is phallic enjoyment insofar as it is determined in an always finite fashion by the ineluctable effect of the function Φ. This enjoyment is somewhere, which also means that it is topologically determined as circumscribed, cut out (*en découpe*), which is another way of naming its finitude. And then there is the other enjoyment, through which the woman position is inferred from the not-all. But, as this alterity is of the order of the infinite, *it cannot be supposed to be an existence that would repudiate castration*. It is, as Lacan stated, too indeterminate to do that. Phallic enjoyment, finite and circumscribed, is predicated on the for-all, its for-all has a perimeter (*pourtour*). But the feminine supplement is not finite; it does not complement the first enjoyment as would a determinate set. It is without perimeter: there is no perimeter of the not-all. And this is why it includes no existence that would be a product of the negation of the first enjoyment.

In . . . *Or Worse* Lacan defines the not-whole as 'that which is not contained in the phallic function while nevertheless not being its negation'. Here we have a difference or an exteriority that is not a negation. The infinite alone enables this infringement of Hegelian logic. The infinite prohibits the relation between the two enjoyments from being dialectical, from being the unity of contraries, and ultimately from being a relation. The infinite is here a power of dissymmetry. The impossible relation of the for-all of man and the feminine not-all is inscribed in the division of enjoyment: neither can be actualized as the negation of the other, because actually the infinite is by no means the negation of the finite. It is its *inaccessible* determination.

This is a crucial adjective, both in set theory and in the logic of the formulas of sexuation. The enjoyment of the feminine not-whole is properly the inaccessible infinity in which castrated enjoyment is determined.

Last, we might posit this: if the feminine not-whole remains compatible with the functional universality of castration, and if it is in a non-relation with the masculine for-all, this is because the infinite does not allow for any determination, via negation, of an existence. The infinite is only a function of inaccessibility. Thus is not the symbol of feminine, or secondary, *jouissance* the perimeter of an infinite set, left remaining by subtraction from phallic enjoyment? Or again: secondary *jouissance* is the indeterminate silence in which the articulation of phallic *jouissance* proceeds, such that the former is like the first infinite cardinal, ω, is for whole numbers: that in which and towards which they insist, but forever incommensurable with it.

But as a result, we begin to see more clearly the reason why Lacan, contrary to us, saw no contradiction between recourse to the infinite and recourse to intuitionist logic. Lacan had no need for his argument of any actually *existing* infinite set. All he required is that there is a point that is inaccessible *to the finite*. The definition of the infinite as inaccessible to the given operations of the finite is certainly the one the intuitionist finds the most acceptable. It does not prove the actual existence of the infinite, but only its negative virtuality within the finite. The infinite is not a set, but a virtual point subtracted from the action of the finite. This gives us a good explanation as to why feminine enjoyment ultimately has the structure of a fiction: it is a fiction of the inaccessible. From here stems the organic relation between this enjoyment and God.

Ultimately, Lacan remained pre-Cantorian. He did not really accept – this disavowal is expressed in our passage – that the infinite can sustain a judgement of existence, or a real effect of separation. This classical refusal of the actual infinite is explicit in . . . *Or Worse*. In it Lacan declares the following:

> Set theory [. . .] yields what it calls the non-denumerable [. . .] but which, translating it into my vocabulary, I do not call the non-denumerable, an object I would unhesitatingly qualify as mythical, but the impossible to number [*dénombrer*].

So, it is clear that, in the case of the continuous, Lacan squarely held the actual infinite to be an imaginary object. He limited himself to the function of the impossible, which is itself referred back to operations, to the count. This confirms that Lacan had no concept of the infinite other than in terms of operational inaccessibility. And this is the reason for which the infinite does not uphold any judgement of existence, which, were we to bear out its consequences, would be the existence of a myth, such as, for example, of an angel – an existent subtracted in its entirety from castration.

A question thus arises: what precisely is the inaccessible?

In set theory, we know of two major operations that permit the construction of a new set on the basis of a given set.

CONDITIONS

The first operation is the passage to the set of parts. Take an original set E. The operation then yields a new set, notated as P(E), whose elements are the parts of the original set. And P(E) is of course called the set of the parts of E.

The second operation consists in the union of E, notated as U(E). The elements of U(E) this time are the elements of the elements of E. We can say that U(E) disseminates E, that it disperses its elements, and afterwards gathers together this dispersion.

The inaccessible can thus be simply defined. Basically, a set I – where I stands for infinity – is inaccessible if you cannot construct it by performing, as many times as desired, the two operations of passage to parts and of union on the basis of sets that are smaller than it.

What I have said here is neither precise nor rigorous, since I have in particular shed no light on what it means for one set to be smaller than another. But we must get to the heart of the matter, which resides in two points: to talk of inaccessibility we first require a starting domain, a collection of sets from which to proceed. And we require operations. Hence a set I is inaccessible *as regards the starting domain*, if – this is an important qualification – the repeated application of operations to the set of the starting domain does not allow the set I to be constructed. Otherwise said, given E, a set from the starting domain, the repeated application of operations of the type P(E) or U(E) never yields the set I. With these operations I cannot be attained from the starting domain, and the impossibility of operational attainment is what defines inaccessibility.

The classical example is the example of the cardinal set, ω, the smallest conceivable infinite set, with regard to the domain of natural whole numbers. Given a whole number n, that is, a finite set, it is easy to show that the set of part of n, that is P(n), is the whole number $2n$. We remain thus well and truly within the finite. As for the union of n, U(n), things are worse still: as union is equal to the number n-1, it is even smaller than the starting term. Hence it is clear that there is no way to construct an infinite set, not even 'ω' (the smallest of them), by starting out from whole numbers and repeating the operations of passage to parts and of union. Therefore, ω is inaccessible in relation to the total domain of whole finite numbers. Although whole numbers indefinitely approach ω as their limit, and although they insist in following on from one another in some way *in* ω, nevertheless the infinite is the inaccessible inherent to the successive insisting of numbers.

That the smallest infinite cardinal, ω, is out of reach for every operational procedure applied to whole finite numbers results in a major consequence: since the existence ω cannot be constructed, or operationally established, this existence can only be *decided*, that is, using that form of decision specific to mathematics – an axiom. At issue here is the axiom of the infinite, which states that ω exists without any operational mediation. The inaccessible's existence can only be axiomatic.

This warrants a parenthetical remark. Since feminine enjoyment is of the order of the infinite, does it not turn out that, rather than having the structure of a fiction, it has the structure of an axiom? A woman then would, as the condition of her enjoyment, have to decide the inaccessible as regards its existence. This axiomatic character of secondary enjoyment in no way contradicts its unutterable character. Granted, the axiom does state something, but the decision on this statement, the gesture by which it is inscribed are not all stated in the axiom itself. The axiom does not express its axiomatic dimension, and so the decision that it is remains tacit. Silently, in the infinite element of her enjoyment, a woman would have decided that with respect to primary or phallic enjoyment there exists an inaccessible point that supplements its effect, and determines her as not-whole with regard to the function Φ. It is properly this silent decision that would forever block the sexual relationship from existing. For, summoned to the place of enjoyment, the position 'man' and the position 'woman' would continue to be separated by that layer (*épaisseur*) without substance (*épaisseur*) not even of the axiom, but of the axiomatic, and thus instituting, dimension of this axiom. I shall close this parenthesis there.

When Lacan, in . . . *Or Worse*, undertook to clarify the identification he made between the 'infinite' and the 'inaccessible', he referred to the classic example of ω. He stated that the operations do not succeed in constructing it. 'This is', he said, 'precisely what is lacking and what, at the level of the aleph$_0$, reproduces that crack (*faille*) that I call inaccessibility'. And he continued:

There is properly speaking no number which, though one may use it in a process of indefinite addition with any, or even every one, of its successors, or take it to whatever degree one would like of exponentiation, one will ever reach the aleph.

What ought to retain our attention here is the mention of a crack (*faille*), of the inaccessible as crack. The image in fact seems incongruous.

CONDITIONS

Since, it is actually as a supplement to, or limit of, the effect of an operational repetition that the virtuality of the inaccessible appears. Of course we have seen that it is at the point of the inaccessible that operational activity fails. But the failure does not open any cracks in the activity. The inaccessible only exceeds – and, once again, an explicit decision is necessary – the impotent repetition of licit operations. The inaccessible is the infringing, or the crossing of a law, and not the opening within this same law, or in the field over which it rules, of the abyss of a crack.

We must therefore ask ourselves where Lacan went wrong, such that he lacked this crack. This is the question to which the extract of . . . *Or Worse* responds that I shall examine. It is an astounding passage, if however we can call such a transcription a passage.

[I am going to speak to you] about what we can say about whole numbers, concerning a property which is that of inaccessibility. Let us define it in such a way that a number is accessible inasmuch as it can be engendered either through the summation, or through the expo-nentiation, of numbers smaller than it. Thus, it can be shown there is inaccessibility in the starting numbers, and very precisely at the point of 2. This is of utmost interest to us, especially concerning this 2, since the relation from 1 to 0, well I have sufficiently underlined that 1 is engendered from the lack marked by the 0. Take 0 and 1, and whether you add them together, or put them together, or put 1 with itself, in an exponential relation, you will never reach 2. In the sense I have just posited, the test as to whether the number 2 can or not be engendered from smaller numbers either through addition or exponentiation proves negative: there is no 2 that can be engendered by means of 1 and of 0.

A remark of Gödel's is illuminating here, and it is precisely that the $aleph_0$, ω, namely the actual infinite, is an example of the same case, while for whole numbers after 2 it's quite different – let's start at 3: 3 results from 1 and 2, 4 can be made from 2 squared by itself, and so on. There is no number that cannot be engendered by one of these 2 operations on the basis of numbers that are smaller than it. This is precisely what is lacking and what, at the level of the $aleph_0$, repro-duces that crack that I call inaccessibility.

What is fascinating in this passage is the enthusiasm with which error is made a principle of organization of the thinkable.

Lacan began exactly by positing an operational domain (whole numbers) and operations (addition and exponentiation). It is from the failure of these operations to establish the existence of this or that number on the basis of smaller numbers that inaccessibility is determined.

But what is stupefying is that the example that serves as the guiding thread for this veridical thought of the inaccessible is the number 2. The majestic ω is only – Gödel is called in vain to the rescue – a repetition of what is already given, in its entirety, in the simple number 2.

The surprising consequence is the following: 2 is infinite. Indeed, the only true concept of the infinite is the inaccessible, so the number 2 is, according to Lacan, inaccessible.

That Lacan is manifestly not very particular about the way he arrives at this result indicates that he expects it will have considerable advantages. And considerable they are.

If, indeed, the inaccessible is already given *between* the 1 and the 2, then it is quite true that it has the structure of a crack. A crack between 1 and 2, and therefore, as we might expect, between S1 and S2, the signifying difference in which the subject comes inaugurally to be represented so as to fall. But if it is at this very point in the gap between signifiers that the inaccessible is given, then feminine enjoyment continues to remain homogenous with the primordial structuring of desire. More precisely, if the inaccessible is given in the rift that moves from 1 towards but without attaining 2, the infinite summoned to ground the differences of the sexes remains commensurable with the fundamental finite structure of desire, and therefore of the subject, such as it is articulated in the signifying chain.

All of this would yield a memorable consequence, which I state at my own risk, because Lacan does not chance it, even though it follows from the inaccessibility of 2: secondary enjoyment, feminine enjoyment, merely in being inferred as inaccessible, would be enjoyment of the pure subject, of the split subject as such, since it is in the point of the crack between its primordial signifiers that the inaccessible is established. The unutterable character of this enjoyment would then be nothing else than the always tacit eclipse of the subject in the interval of what it represents. To the insistent question 'what does a woman want?' it could be said: to enjoy the pure form, the naked form of the subject that she is. And the partner would serve only to put this finite law into play, a function of contour, of which the inaccessible is the going-beyond.

This would require that 2 were inaccessible. But it is not. It is inaccessible neither according to the operations of set theory nor according to those Lacan proposes, and that happen to be variants of the former.

In set theory, it can be easily shown that 2 is very exactly the set of the part $1,2 = P(1)$. The number 2 can therefore be attained on the basis of numbers smaller than it.

More, 2 is also accessible according to Lacan's own definition, which admits of sums. We know at least the equation $2 = 1 + 1$! The assertion according to which, in Lacan's own terms, 'the test as to whether the number 2 can or not be engendered from smaller numbers either through addition or exponentiation proves negative' contradicts elementary mathematics in provocative fashion.

The point is obviously not to play Lacan's supervisor. The point is to take stock of the symptom that this provocation by error forms and to propose an interpretation of it.

This symptom takes us back to something I remarked earlier: confined in the gap between 1 and 2, the infinite construed as the inaccessible remains compatible with the finite logic of the chain, of the succession of signifiers.

But, more profoundly, his haste in concluding, which takes error as the vehicle of a more profound supposition concerning truth, boils down to saying that, if determined purely from the operational field, thus sparing ourselves the cost of an axiom of existence, the infinite must in a certain sense be able to be thought as a modality of the finite.

A strict definition of the infinite by way of the inaccessible, which, you will recall, is necessary to block the inference whereby secondary enjoyment leads to an existence entirely subtracted from castration – necessary, then, to avoiding the not-all underwriting the existence of an angelic exception – this definition is restrained from the outset. It prepares the ground for a significant declaration according to which – as the fundamental albeit erroneous example of the 2 shows – the infinite, *qua* inaccessible, is equally finite.

This proves that Lacan is not Cantorian. Even in the logic of enjoyment, the real existence of the actual infinite is more of a hindrance than an aid. Lacan only summons the infinite to dismiss it. The infinite must remain an operational fiction, one that points to the abyss or the crack in which the subject is constituted, but that is only a secondary clarification. Consider this important remark from . . . *Or Worse*: 'What is constituted on the basis of 1 and 0 as the inaccessibility of 2 is only given at the level of the aleph zero, that is of the actual infinite'.

To be sure, mention is made here of the actual infinite. But its 'actuality' is not brought into play as such, since ω is only invoked to clarify, to render to thought an infinite of inaccessibility that is already entirely actual in the finitude of 2.

A propos of infinity, what would burdening ourselves with the weight of a judgement about real existence help us, if its whole effect is conceivable from the first segment of the sequence of finite numbers? As Leibniz said about indivisibles, all that is required is that ω amounts to a 'useful fiction', since it is only, in its possible essence, the repetition of zero or of two.

Ultimately, both the restriction of the concept of the infinite – such as it is at stake in the thinking of feminine enjoyment – to inaccessibility alone, and the application of this concept to the finitude of 2 converge towards a pre-Cantorian determination of the infinite as an imaginary letter. The Lacanian doctrine of the subject is essentially finite, to the extent that even the infinite has to show that its existence does not exceed that of the finite.

If we suppose that, following the announcement of the death of God, our century comprises a mediation on finitude, then Lacan is genuinely our contemporary.

But this is precisely what I cannot accept. Underneath the finitude that is registered in all of contemporary philosophy's various states, the century is secretly governed by the radical invention attached to the name Cantor. He secularized the infinite by means of a literalization whose boldness – an unheard-of transfixion of the religious veil of meaning – orients us within a thinking still to come that can be encapsulated in a single phrase: insofar as a number is its real, every situation is essentially infinite.

As a result, when Lacan sensed with his usual genius that questions pertaining to the differences of sexes cannot be dealt with without recourse to the infinite, but at the same time established finitude itself as the norm of that recourse, he ultimately had to slip up 'symptomally' and pay the price for inconsistency, as indicated here by the pseudo-inaccessibility of 2.

And this is not merely incidental, for who does not see that the 2 is clearly a numeration with an effect of real, since there happen to be, and this is a contingency that founds us, two sexes, and not one, or three, or an infinite number?

This restrained boldness, which establishes itself in the vicinity of Cantor only to renovate finitude, for the modernity of finitude, is very much, I would like to suggest, where the root of companionship lies between the Lacanian logic of the signifier and intuitionist logic.

But intuitionism is but a rearguard war, incidentally not without its effectiveness, that has been waged in logic against the incalculable effects of the genuine killing of God at work in mathematical literalization and effectivity of the infinite in Cantor's work and that of his successors.

Bound by his collusion with this defensive, Lacan's endeavour led him to defend the idea that feminine enjoyment is infinite solely as a fiction that is useful for defending a thought of the subject as finite; that it is, if I may say, an obscure clarity thrown on the finite structure of desire in its most paradoxical point. This profound relation between finitude and the sexual non-relation, therefore, between finitude and the infinitude of secondary enjoyment, is avowed by Lacan in . . . *Or Worse*. In it he talked about the point through which the enjoyment constitutive of the speaking being marks itself out from sexual enjoyment, and he went on to say of this demarcation that 'one only managed to draw up the catalogue on the basis of analytic discourse in the perfectly finite list of drives. Its finitude is related to the impossibility which is demonstrated in a genuine questioning of the sexual relation as such'. It is clear in this passage that the infinite mediation of feminine enjoyment, which seemed to imply the impossibility of a sexual relation, in the end turns out to be a consolidation of the finitude of the drives. It is therefore certain that, respectful as it may be, Lacan's invocation of Cantor, could only ever act as the support of a detour that leads back to the solid and – believed to be – modern ground of finitude.

But Cantor and the modern proclamation of mathematical infinity as a real letter can not serve as detours. They are actually rather the turn (*tour*) that truth takes us on, as forms of knowledge cling on tightly – sometimes in abjectness – to the archaic delirium of finitude.

So, all is to be begun again, but on the same paths that Lacan set out for us. This reworking is actually another story. Suffice it to outline the theoretical programme.

It has been established that the phallic function governs the sexuated division of enjoyment, and that this distribution touches the order of the infinite.

However, the infinite of inaccessibility is not adequate. What must be discovered is the affirmative force of the infinite, which is always lodged in some axiomatic decision.

Yet, giving full recognition to the existence of the infinite implies a modification of the Lacanian edifice on two decisive points.

The first is that it is not possible to account for the difference of the sexes, such as love makes truth of it, on the sole basis of the phallic function. A second function is required, the generic function, or humanity function.[3] And, as regards this function, quantifiers, the universal and the existential, the for-all and the not-all, are not distributed in the same way as they are for the function Φ, which takes all its importance in its own singular register, that of enjoyment. But this register must be doubled by another, that of disjunctive truth, whose logic is – or if you will, whose formulae are – in spite of Lacan's efforts, irreducible to the formulae of sexuation in their original presentation.

The second point is that the Two, the numericity 2, is without any doubt the crucial operator of the infinite becoming an amorous truth, therefore of a truth concerning the difference of the sexes. This operator is nevertheless not inaccessible from that which precedes it. Nor is its numerical accessibility adequate to establish it in the field of love. A particular operation is required: the Two arises through the 'effraction' of the One, effraction that immediately leads, without mediation, to the infinite.

I anticipate that I shall be forgiven for concluding in such elliptical fashion. I only meant to accompany Lacan, our master, to the point that he in some sense led us to, a point that, if we are to be faithful to him, we need to go beyond.

Lacan taught us of thought's composure, at the very point of its deadlock. He prevailed over phenomenological and dialectical pathos. He introduced the virtues of the matheme to a field outside that of its usual application. It is in this sense that he is truly our master, the one Mallarmé spoke of:

> The Master's piercing eye, wherever he would go
> Has calmed the unquiet marvels of Eden's wild delights.[4]

From the Eden of thought that Lacan opened up for us we shall not be banished. But we shall also, as has been attempted here, inquire into its marvel.

CHAPTER FOURTEEN
Anti-Philosophy: Plato and Lacan

From the 1960s, Lacan, who had so often quoted and commented on certain philosophers (chiefly Plato, Aristotle, Descartes, Kant, Hegel, Kierkegaard and Heidegger), began to foreground *anti-philosophy*, turning it into one of the nexuses of the analyst's discourse.

What is 'anti-philosophy'?

Lacan's basic claim is that as philosophy is an instance of the master's discourse, what opposes it is the ethics of the discourse of the analyst.

With regard to the thinking of being, although there are some of Lacan's late texts that led us to believe he welcomed its proximity to his own thinking (texts in which he spoke sarcastically of '*hontologie*'[1]), we must nonetheless recall that, as early as 1955, he contrasted it formally to the endeavours of Freud: 'the Freudian world is not a world of things, it is not a world of being, it's a world of desire as such'. This statement was later to be supplemented, and in more ontological, or 'hontological', style, with this: 'The *I* is not a being, but something attributed to that which speaks, a solitude by which a rupture of being leaves a trace'. Let us also note that Lacan's recourse to mathematical paradigms is expressly directed against philosophy's discursive style. Take, for example, this statement from 1973: 'compared to a philosophy that culminates in Hegel's discourse, cannot the formalization of mathematical logic serve us in the analytic process?' And the examples can easily be multiplied. Everything points toward the fact that, for Lacan, distinguishing psychoanalysis from philosophy – an aim that, in my wish to delimit philosophy, I would unhesitatingly grant him – is not sufficient. Psycho-analysis also has to provide a basis on which to judge philosophy in the illusions it propagates, illusions that in Lacan's eyes appeared unlikely to have a brilliant future ahead of them, and in any case a much less certain one than the illusions of the religious, which, for structural reasons, he held to be infinitely more tenacious.

To clarify the matter of Lacan's anti-philosophy, it is doubtless necessary to refer to 'the Plato symptom'.

The Plato symptom applies universally to every stance our contemporaries hold on what philosophy is.

Were we to place Nietzsche at the threshold of the contemporary, his diagnostic, we know, is that the century must be cured of the Plato sickness. His is very much an anti-philosophical diagnostic. Nietzsche's 'we free spirits' refers to those that have roused themselves from the philosophico-Christian jurisdiction originally contrived by Plato

On this point, as on many others, everything suggests that Nietzsche saw things correctly – which is not to say that he saw truly. Our whole century is anti-Platonic. Heidegger's hermeneutics, Anglo-Saxon grammarian analytics and official Marxism (or, if you will, fascism, parliamentary sophistry and Stalin, i.e., everything this century developed in terms of forms of State), all share a common feature – which is what constitutes anti-Platonism as a symptom – and this is that they regard Platonism not only as obsolete but as the apparatus of thought from which we must *finally* get free.

It was in this sense that our century well and truly declared, with the known consequences, that it would cure itself of the Plato sickness generally referred to as 'metaphysics'.

So, let us ask: *where* is Lacan placed in this century? What hold does the Plato symptom have over him? This question governs the status that Lacan accords to anti-philosophy.

I will say forthwith that the Plato symptom's seizure of Lacan appears rather comprehensive.

For starters, we can see this in that Lacan, together with all the others who are out to judge philosophy (or metaphysics), saddles the signifier 'Plato' with the accusation of the origin. The origin, of course, is a space of thought from which the utmost effort is to be made to escape.

The origin forms a system; it structures, as it were, the page of our thinking. As Lacan said, in 1954: 'Let us take Plato as an origin, in the sense in which we speak of the origin of coordinates'. Then, in 1960, he claimed that it was 'our friend' Plato who forged the 'mirage' of the

Sovereign Good. The friendship looks like it is in a little trouble. In the very same year, but from a more neutral viewpoint, he said of Socrates – the nuance, as we shall see, is important – that '[he] inaugurated this new being-in-the-world that I here call a subjectivity'. We need go no further. For it is already sufficient to show that the very order in which we explore all our problems, from the notion of Ethics to the theme of the Subject, was founded by Socrates–Plato. This is a great deal. It is a little too much.

Indeed, once this enviable posture is granted, it then appears capable of being refuted by Freud's theoretical invention; Freud's creation suspends Platonic jurisdiction.

In a move symptomatic of modernity, Lacan did not hesitate to formulate this in terms of a global opposition – appertaining to and disjoining basic orientations of thought – between Plato, or what originates with Plato, and the essential thrust of the Freudian invention. Let us quote an exemplary expression from 1955. Lacan had just contrasted psychoanalytical remembrance with Platonic reminiscence, and then claimed: 'this [contrast] is [only] one of the ways in which the Platonic and Freudian theories differ'. Only 'one of the ways' – here we are placed theory against theory, and Freud against Plato.

On closer examination, Lacan's grievances against Platonism range throughout the entire expanse of the philosophical field, and as Lacan considered Plato to have marked the whole field from the start, they suffice to give us a sense of his notion of anti-philosophy.

This grievances bear at once on the following points.

- The process of knowledge. Let us call these gnoselogical grievances.
- The question of speaking well (*bien dire*) and of the Good *tout court*. Let us call these ethical grievances.
- Last, the relation of knowledge to being, in the form of truth. Let us call these ontological grievances.

I shall begin by examining what is at stake in each of these three orders.

We know just how much Lacan owed to Saussure, and how he thought that Freud's discovery would only be made clear by foregrounding the fact that there is no relationship between signifier and signified. This is because this non-relationship indicates that something of the subject of enunciation escapes from the 'one' that the statement positions it as.

Now, it is Plato himself who is presented as showing an exemplary expression of contempt for this claim. As Lacan said, in 1973:

> The *Cratylus*, by none other than Plato, results from the endeavour to show that there must be a relationship and that the signifier in and of itself means something. This attempt, which we can qualify from our vantage point as desperate, is marked by failure, because another discourse, scientific discourse [. . .] gives us the following, that the signifier is posited only insofar as it has no relation to the signified.

We will come across further instances of the idea that 'none other than' Plato has been irreversibly discredited by scientific, or rather Galilean, discourse.

But is this trial led in forthright terms? Lacan himself was the first to recognize the properly comic genius that sparkles in Plato's dialogues. Are we to take the mind-blowing etymologies of the *Cratylus* literally? Is Plato's strategy really to save the signification of the signifier at any cost? Instead the central premise of the dialogue emerges when Socrates declares that we, we philosophers, we set out from things, and not from words. Etymology here is only a vector of an intellectual comedy involving a profound thesis on the *seriousness* of language, which is contrasted to the ludic surface that sophists of all ages want to reduce it. That language is able to latch onto the thing itself, and that philosophical thinking must be situated in the very point of this latch – that is what impassioned Plato.

To be sure, Lacan did note elsewhere the reality of this passion in Plato's work, albeit under the name of Socrates, and he did so from two angles:

The first consists in recognizing what can be deciphered in the philosopher of a desire for scientificity, or at least an ideal thereof. Take this declaration from 1960:

> Socrates demanded that we do not content ourselves with *doxa*, to which we have an innocent relation, but that we ask why, that we satisfy ourselves with no less than that certainty he called *episteme*, or science, namely that which gives an account of its reasons. This, Plato said, is the business of Socrates' *philosophein*.

What appeals to Socrates, Lacan added, is science. This being so, what the philosopher, that is, Plato, establishes is, including in the figure of his

desire, something that would seemingly come in the future to under-
mine him in the form of Ferdinand de Saussure.

The other angle relates to what I said about the statement made in the
Cratylus concerning philosophical passion for the thing itself. Lacan
approvingly noted the central point, via what of it is shown in the relation of the Subject to the formidable presupposition of its enjoyment, the
Thing, *das Ding*. I quote, again from 1960:

> In a short digression in letter VII, Plato told us what it is that the
> whole operation of the dialectic is after: it is quite simply the same
> thing that I had to take stock of last year in my remarks on ethics, and
> which I called 'The Thing', which is here called *to pragma*. You may
> understand by this, if you will, the great affair, the ultimate reality,
> that on which the very thought which confronts it, and discusses it,
> also depends, and which is, I might say, only one of the ways to prac-
> tice it. It is *to pragma*, the thing, the essential praxis. *Theoria* is itself the
> exercise of the power of *to pragma*, the great affair.

Here we see that Plato is recognized as having a certain paternity, and
a power of anticipation, which effectively counterbalances the properly
positivist verdict that would condemn Plato for having misrecognized
the possible avatars of scientific discourse.

Lacan was more rigorous in his attempt to refute the Platonic doctrine
of reminiscence, and of what constitutes its ontological underpinning,
that is, the theme of the participation of being in the supersensible realm
of Ideas.

Lacan's view of reminiscence was that it is essentially tantamount to
a game of mirrors that leads thought along an infinite regress via the
duplications (*doublons*) and doubles (*doublures*) of the imaginary, and
that has to provide for these similitudes an 'always-already-there' to
regulate (*normer*) their dizzying movement. Consider, for example, what
he said in 1955:

> Plato cannot conceive of the embodiment of ideas in any other
> way than in a series of endless reflections. Everything which
> happens and which is recognized is in the image of the idea. The
> image existing in itself is in its turn only an image of an idea existing
> in itself, is only an image in relation to another image. There is only
> reminiscence.

The specifically imaginary status of reminiscence at once holds it outside of genuine repetition and stops it shy of the creative power of the symbolic. Thereby was Lacan able, on the one hand, to set up a contrast between Plato and Kierkegaard, as when, in 1953, he noted 'the distance that separates out the reminiscence Plato presupposed for the advent of the idea from the exhaustion of being that is consummated in Kierkegaardian repetition'; and, on the other hand, to contrast the imaginary sterility of the similitudes of reminiscence against the real capacity for commencement implicit in the symbol. Once again the year is 1955 and immediately after what he said about reminiscence he stated:

'When we speak about the symbolic order, there are absolute beginnings, there is creation'.

Hence, the Platonic doctrine of reminiscence, in thrall to the endless reflections of the imaginary and to an illusory pre-givenness, thus finds itself deposed twice over, once by the true concept of the automatism of repetition, and again by the power of beginning inherent in the symbol.

There is in the background a more serious, albeit implicit, point which consists in identifying the Platonic Idea, *qua* recapitulative schema of imaginary errancy, with Jung's archetypes – an association that, it must be admitted, is none too pleasing.

We certainly could wonder whether Plato had not already alluded to the series of endless reflections that Lacan mentions in anticipating the third man argument, and in all the aporias that attend the theory of reminiscence. Since, in the unfolding of its presentation, reminiscence is formulated more as a sort of myth that refers to cycles of existence than as a concept with a regulated operation. Indeed, the immense construction of *the Republic* manages to avoid all mention of it until the final myth of Er, when it is merely alluded to in the example about the one who returns from among the dead.

Of course, it could be argued that the instances of myth in Plato precisely indicate points where the imaginary constrains thought to a law of pure resemblances, to analogies without concept. Are not Jung's archetypes constantly propped up on myths? Indeed, it could be argued. But this view on Plato's recourse to myths is not one that Lacan himself held. In fact, he very rightly pointed out that the instances of myth in the dialogues are always the result of a calculation that very accurately localizes the point at which it would be a little far-fetched to lead every 'truth-effect' back to the consistency of the signifier. In 1960, he said:

'Throughout the whole Platonic oeuvre, we see myths emerge at the required moment to fill in the chasm of what cannot be ensured dialectically'.

Hence for Lacan myth is less the mark of the imaginary than a laboured supplement to argumentative style, needed whenever conceptual compression reveals the crack of its incompleteness.

We might, incidentally, also take this as a useful way of approaching Lacan's own oeuvre, that is by picking out if not the myths then the fables which, as in Plato, fill in for discourse at the precise points where a signifying sequence is caught lacking.

There is, it seems to me, a more serious limitation of Lacan's critique of reminiscence and it is that, in the assumed infinite regress from the existent to ideas and also between ideas themselves, he failed to take into account the crucial function of the *halting point* that Plato called the Good. Indeed, if we extricate Plato's 'Good' from the theological dross with which the centuries have covered it, we see that its chief purpose is to designate the point of radical alterity at which all referrals (*renvoi*) and all relations come to be suspended. With Plato the Good serves as the place of the Other, which, ex-centered, places speech under the law of truth. This is the reason why Plato said that the Good is neither an Idea nor even *ousia* – that *ousia* that does not translate being neither substance nor essence – since we should rather say: it is what of being is exposed to the Idea. The Good is the very place in which the idea takes effect for that which is exposed there, and is consequently subtracted from both the Idea and from exposition, thus from *ousia*. It is exactly in this sense that Plato could say that the Good is 'that which prodigies the truth . . . and the capacity of the believer'. What prodigies is not prodigied. In Lacan's terms, we can express this as: there is no other of the other. And in Plato's as: the Good is neither the Idea nor what of being is exposed to the Idea.

In short, if reminiscence is not what Lacan says it is, that is because the endlessness of imaginary captation happens to be curbed by a point of excess, namely the Good, the chief purpose of which is to tell us that there is no truth of truth.

The same objection can more or less also be applied to Lacan's harsh critique of the theme of participation. This critique moreover is marked with a feature whose significance we shall come to below. Lacan's critique proceeds in such a way that it is as if Plato did not believe in his own arguments for a second, as if his elaborations concerning the participation of the sensible in the intelligible were no more than a sort of Platonic tall story, a farce for limited disciples. Witness this declaration from 1961:

> The Platonic idea that all that exists exists through its participation in some sort of intemporal essence reveals its fiction and its lure to the light of day, and it does so at the very point in the *Phaedo* where it is impossible not to say that we have any reason to think Plato believed in this lure anymore than we.

It may well be that participation is a lure, except if we are to suppose that the following is its sole question: what is the price to be paid in thought for introducing, with the symbolic, the thesis 'there is some Oneness', precisely at the point where the multiple is presented to us? That all horses pertain to Horseness is something to which we must give a name, whether participation or something else, to indicate that this is the case.

We all know the story about the cynic who said he saw horses, but never horseness. This road does not take us far, and it is certainly not the one Lacan was heading down. Because if the truth is to remain intact, nothing less than the radical transcendence of the Big Other is required, in which, to be brief, all human desire participates, because it at once finds there both the signifiers that articulate it (as that which belongs to it) and the object causing it (as what is included in it).

Now, regardless of whether Plato gradually abandoned the theme of participation, as Robin claims, or did no more than complete the apparatus, as Festugière argues, this theme was certainly not his last word about the mode in which the One occurs in the multiple. This last word is rather to be found in the doctrine of the 'greatest kinds' and their mixtures elaborated in both the *Sophist* and the *Philebus*, and also in that decisive handbook on the quibbles of the One, the *Parmenides*.

Lacan was well aware that in the end we cannot solve the paradoxes of the One with the initial image of it given in the concept of participation. For there are actually two paradoxes here, and Lacan commented on both of them.

The first is that the Platonic One is fragmented not only in the sensible manifold it is presumed to link together, but also in itself, and it is thereby dialectically subtracted from the unity of its own One. In 1973, Lacan remarked that 'there are as many ones as you would like – they are characterized by not resembling each other in anything, see the first hypothesis of the *Parmenides*'.

The second is that, just as the Good was beyond *ousia*, which it far exceeds, said Plato, in prestige and power, so is the Platonic One beyond being itself incompatible with being. In Lacan's terms, there is definitely some Oneness (*il y a de l'Un*), but it does not follow from this that the One is. The One's non-being separates it from itself, and links it to the Other in a constitutive torsion that only the event can support. Lacan knew that this paradoxical One, this One that is not, this One that is the Other as such, has its origins in the work of Plato. He put it clearly in *L'Etourdit*:

'It is the logic of the Eteros which has to be brought to notice, the remarkable thing here being that it was first spelled out in the Parmenides, on the basis of the One's compatibility with Being'.

What are we to conclude? If not that, on this point, anti-philosophy, pursued with lucid awareness, and with a constantly open sense of inventiveness towards what incites it, to which Lacan always attested, *nolens volens* undermines the anti-Platonism that the whole century had believed was the hallmark of its solemn novelty.

That Lacan proclaimed in his seminar . . . *Or Worse* that 'Plato is Lacanian' is not to be lightly brushed aside. It is a statement that adroitly weighs up recognition of the fact that Lacan himself is not Platonic with a recognition of their shared affinity in relation to the doctrine of the One, which clarifies why, with a distance of twenty-four centuries, which is not nothing, the discussion between them could not be stopped by anything – save death.

But since, after the balance-sheet of the horrors of the last century of this temporal gap, we are called from all sides to ethics – a word that I believe Lacan, in 1955, gave a place of honour before anyone else, and for less uncertain ends – let us see what this call says of Plato.

As we might surmise, it is Lacan's view that Plato's adopted posture is the obligatory posture of the philosopher, which is also an imposture, and which results from his holding, as subject and for others, the discourse of the master. There is in the seminar of 1960 a colourful expression about this, and which does not function by mortmain:

Plato, Lacan said, was a true master: a master at a time when the *polis* was decomposing, taken over by the democratic flurry, a prelude to the times of great imperial confluence. He was a sort of more comic version of de Sade.

I should imagine that, assuming he had the anachronistic parameters on hand to comprehend it, Plato would have been a little wondrous at his being called a 'more comic version of de Sade'.

All the same, the position of the master is not unequivocally contestable, far from it. On the basis of its authority, Lacan even attempted to make a distinction between modern or Galilean science and what the Greeks called 'science', *épistemè*. Accordingly, in 1964, he stated that 'what distinguishes modern science from science in its infancy, as discussed in the *Theatetus*, is that when science arises a master is always present.'. We might therefore be led to surmise that the absence of master is a sign of modernity. However Lacan ultimately concludes by placing Freud at Plato's side: 'Freud is certainly a master.' Mastery, then, is not in itself Greek or pre-Galilean. It conjoins every science 'which arises'; it is a sign of beginnings, both ancient and modern.

That said, the polemical point remains, against this de Sade touched by comic genius. But its most distinctive feature resides in that with which it is contrasted, and that is the figure of Socrates. A whole swathe of Lacan's critique of Plato can be made only on the condition of first making a radical distinction between Plato and he who nonetheless constitutes his central fiction, the character (or the person—therein lies the whole problem) of Socrates.

Lacan definitely was not the first to have engaged in making this distinction. Hegel, Kierkegaard, Nietzsche and many others preceded him. But in his work the distinction is made in accordance with the canon of discourses. He attributes to Plato the master's discourse, and, by means of an astounding historical twist, the analyst's to Socrates. Incidentally, this goes to show that for Lacan the ability to hold the analyst's discourse is very much independent of any reference not only to institutions and professions but even to Freud's theoretical invention. For, with the exception of Freud, the only analyst with whom Lacan could identify, I believe, was indeed Socrates.

In 1953 Lacan went so far as to ask us to feel 'in Socrates and his desire the still-intact enigma of the psychoanalyst'. Such was his expression. Better still, in 1960, in testimony to his almost naïve desire to convince us that the *Symposium* is not one of Plato's fictions but a genuine account,

Lacan endeavoured to read 'the *Symposium* as a sort of report of psycho-analytic sessions.'

I shall now provide all the reasons that make it possible to recognize in Socrates the first historical analyst; but, admittedly hostile to the distinction, I shall do so without taking away the credit from Plato, of whom Socrates is in my eyes a clarificatory fiction.

There are two main ones.

The first is that Socrates is presented as the subject-supposed-to-know about love. Lacan maintains that Socrates' position gets its authority through his maintaining ignorance about everything with the exception of eros. It is on this fundamental supposition, of having a familiarity with eros, that the transferential love that all have for Socrates is commanded. In some astonishing lectures in the seminar on transfer, Lacan showed how the transferential relationship of Alcibiades to Socrates, to this treasure, this *agalma*, of which Socrates is a holder, and which consists precisely in what he knew about love, is interpreted and diverted by Socrates onto Agathon. Socrates' analytic impassivity works wonders here, establishing that what Alcibiades asks from him, he could only have in identifying, in Agathon, the sparkle of his lack.

The second reason for qualifying Socrates as an analyst – and here there is no doubt we are talking about Plato – is that in the universe of discourses there is an entailment of truth. Socrates-Plato is the one who, beyond and against the sophists, ushered into history the idea that what is at issue in the logic of the signifier, once it is consistent and linked together, is the position of truth. From among many others, let us cite this passage from 1960:

> What Socrates called science was that which is necessarily imposed, on every interlocution, as a function of a specific manipulation, of a specific internal coherence that is linked, or so he believed, solely to the pure and simple reference to the signifier.

What Lacan is stressing here is that Socrates – and in this he is original – was not a humanist, that he was not one to refer man to man. For, as Lacan quite rightly noted out, the expression 'man is the measure of all things' is sophistic, not Socratic. The Socratic formula, so Lacan argued, instead involves 'refering the truth to discourse'.

We see the extent to which it is only by subtracting Socrates from Plato, by isolating this operative fiction from the philosophical tissue in which it occurs, that Lacan was able to attach to Plato the ironical distance that the master's discourse levies.

Instead, the truth is no doubt that, as much with regard to love as to the primacy of signifying consistency, Plato is inclined to occupy the position of analytic discourse *and* that of the master. If we put together again what Lacan separated for his own ends, we are handed a valuable lesson, which is that philosophy is always diagonal to the four discourses. Philosophy simultaneously retains – it 'compossibilises' in its exercise of thought – the master's injunction, the hysterics' loudly uttered interruption, the savant ratiocination of the University, and the analyst's subtraction. It is in this sense that Plato's dialogues found philosophy, via the free play they establish, under the shelter of literary form, between these disparate regimes of discourse.

Moreover philosophy's plasticity also enables it to instruct through the example of deadlock. Platonic *aporia* is attended by the *atopia* of his discourses. It is this a-topia that Lacan identified as indicating of Socrates' specificity, as we see it born out in Alcibiades' eulogy to him. Lacan seems also to have identified his own position with this diagonality of places. However, is this very site not that of the philosopher, whose conditions of emergence Plato already listed in a singular passage of Book VI of the *Republic*? Plato argues in this passage that philosophers only ever emerge on the basis of eccentric or, I would say, delocalizing, conditions, which he listed as follows: being in exile; being born in a small unknown city; having an ordinary metier before entering into philosophy by some properly inexplicable movement; being sick or in a precarious state of health; and possessing a divine sign. In short, there is nothing that is less 'normal' than the philosopher. So if he is a master, he is one a-normally, that is, in his withdrawal from, and negation of, the official disposition of things and discourses. This alone is what enabled him to undertake his subversive traversal of the registers of discourse, and to be one who, under the systematic law of the concept, both utters and interrupts, both ratiocinates and keeps silent.

Is this to say that we should recognize the office of philosophy as residing in such an ethical disposition? We know that Lacan did not subscribe to this view. Busy constructing the notion that Socrates and Plato occupy disjunct positions, Lacan located in Plato a sort of moral sentimentality, a *Schwärmerei*, allegedly leading him to abandon the pure requirement of signifying consistency and the encounter with the void it implies.

CONDITIONS

By contrast to Socrates, Lacan claimed, Plato was unable maintain the impassivity of the analyst, and that is the reason that Aristotle is, in ethical terms, superior to him. Consider these statements from 1960:

> What I have called Plato's *Schwärmerei* lies in his having projected onto what I call the impenetrable void the idea of the Sovereign Good. As for our own experience, I have undertaken in part what one can call an Aristotelian *conversion* in relation to Plato, who on the plane of ethics has without a doubt been surpassed.

What I said a moment ago about the function of the Good suffices for you to understand my reluctance to corroborate this assessment and deem Plato to have been irremediably surpassed in the order of Ethics. Because the twofold function of the Good, as ex-centred halting point in the recurrence of the real, and as that which slaps a ban on every truth of truth, does not call on us to engage in superstitious sentimentality. What Plato staged was rather of the order of the call to an avulsion, to a conversion, to a chance rupture with the serial dimension of the prevailing situation. As he wrote in Book VII of the *Republic*, we call true philosophy the turning of the soul from a sort of obscure day towards the real day, or the ascent towards the aspect of being that is exhibited in the Idea.

What I see as the subject in this 'turning' is what Lacan had claimed was excluded by the doctrine of reminiscence, namely an absolute beginning. It is true that to turn away from such a turning, to make do with the obscure day, to prosper in the established order, or in what Lacan calls the servicing of goods, is the basis of all villainy. If ethics involves not consenting to the villainy that consists in a simple appropriation of what presents itself, then 'true philosophy' in Plato's sense, that of a turning, is always of itself an ethical proposition.

Let us add to this, that what governs the possibility of such a turning is not the sovereign Good conceived as an imaginary projection onto the impenetrable void. It is much rather, as Plato was perfectly well aware, were it only after Socrates' death, the summoning of such a void by the paradoxes of the One, paradoxes I for my part name paradoxes of the Ultra-One, i.e. of an event, an encounter, an incalculable precipitating of what comes to pass. And this Ultra-One on which our conversion is dependent is exactly what Plato himself endeavoured to submit to systematic examination; this he did as early as the *Republic*, where he argued that the Good cannot be thought or named except by means of

ANTI-PHILOSOPHY

metaphorical language drawn from the void where thought confronts itself, but also later in the *Sophist* and in the *Parmenides*.

The problem is no doubt that on this point Lacan overly identified Plato with Parmenides, despite the parricide of the *Sophist*, a murder-of-the-father in which he might have found more to retain his interest. Therewith are we brought closer to the properly ontological dimension of the dispute.

In 1973, Lacan levelled at Parmenides the charge of having founded the philosophical tradition on the supposition that being thinks. And it is true that Parmenides' fragment says that 'the Same, indeed, is at once to think and to be'. Now, due to his conception of the Platonic idea, Lacan was led to discern in it an attempt at a sort of levelling out of knowledge and being, at producing an equivalence between the two. Again in 1973:

'In Plato's work, form is the knowledge that fills being . . . It is real in the sense that it holds being in its glass, but it is filled right to the brim. Form is the knowledge of being'.

Thus, for Lacan, philosophy insists on filling the glass of knowledge with being, of desiring that, so that it can establish its mastery, being fills knowledge right up to the brim. And this is what the Platonic Idea, which is the real being of a hypostatised knowledge, aimed at achieving.

According to Lacan, however, Freud's discovery locates being outside of knowledge; he discovered that between thought and being there is a discordance, a crack, in which the effect of the subject as such unfolds. Immediately following his remarks on Plato, Lacan expressed the point as follows:

'There is some relationship of being that cannot be known. It is that relationship whose structure I investigate in my teaching'.

The opposition is clear. It would seem to exclude psychoanalysis from operating under the sign of the Idea.

There are again good grounds for again questioning Lacan's interpretation here. Since the 'highest kinds' found in the *Sophist*, especially the Idea of the Other, attest that intellection is established as much in the position of non-being as such. Ideas in Plato's work do not fit into the simple schema of a completion of being by means of knowledge. The reason for this is that they are mixtures, whose key lies in that which, through the position of the Other, affects, or infects, being with

241

a paradoxical part of non-being. This is also the exact sense of the aporetic conclusion to the *Parmenides*: if the decisive figure of the One is to be reduced to knowledge alone, we come to the untenable, nihilistic conclusion that nothing is, neither the One, nor the other than One. This is to say, for Plato, another way is required, one that indeed assumes, to adopt Lacan's terms, that there is some relationship of being that cannot be known. Let us say that there needs be an experience, or an occurrence, the chance of which is irreducible to what can be known. And it is not unimportant to remark that in neither of these two fundamental dialogues is Socrates any longer the one who speaks; it is instead, respectively, the Eleaic Stranger, or an old Parmenides impro-bably portrayed in a disavowal, indeed in the non-being (*désêtre*), of his own thinking.

But, what I shall focus my attention on here is the surmise that, at the very point at which Lacan turns away from the Idea, the matheme then enters the stage.

In *L'Etourdit*, Lacan reprises the notion that owing to rigorous scientific developments Plato has been surpassed. This time at issue is Gödel's discovery of the language expressions of first-order formalized arith-metic, expressions that in the terms of its calculus are undecidable, despite being semantically true. In Lacan's view, this structural undecid-ability undermines Plato's surmise in the *Meno* concerning the innate-ness of mathematical ideas, as Socrates thought he encountered them in the slave in relation to the problem of the doubling of a square. For if mathematics consists in the form of the eternal Idea, and as such is regis-tered in the dianoetic part of our soul, then it must necessarily have always been *decided*. But Gödel's theorem, it seems, precludes one from maintaining this. As a result, said Lacan, it is possible to say that, 'with respect to the *Meno*', we have made progress 'on the question of what it is possible to teach'.

However, in a universe regulated by science, this progress has to be paid for as usual with a loss of faith in what can be granted to true opinion. Since, as Lacan continued, 'the true opinion to which Plato gave meaning in the *Meno* no longer has anything but an ab-sence of signification for us, which is confirmed if we refers ourselves to that of our *bien-pensants*'. This is, let it be said in passing, the very type of violent declaration that Lacan, that rebellious master, often uttered so as to shoot holes in the poor consistency of our epoch.

This loss – which, it must be stressed, results from the fact that science no longer supports the Idea in Plato's sense – is something that Lacan proposed to remedy by recourse to 'a matheme furnished to us by topology.' Recourse to the matheme is here introduced as an attempt to remedy.

Now, who is unaware that mathematics for Plato is an indispensable condition for remedying, by means of the Idea, the loss of truth that sophists expose us to? Does not the most Platonizing dimension of Lacan's work reside in the constancy of his references to that which bears no relation to reality and so is all the more apt to open onto the real? And is not mathematics, for both Plato and Lacan, the only available paradigm for such references?

Clearly, however, Plato and Lacan once more part company over what we might call the *placement* given to mathematics in their respective systems of thought. For Plato, as we know, mathematical thinking, or *dianoia*, is only the antechamber of the dialectic. It is *metaxu*, an in-between, mid-way between *doxa* and genuine *épistemè*. For Lacan, on the other hand, the type of access the logio-mathematical gives to the real makes it a supreme and improbable ideal for analytic discourse. He put it forcefully in Seminar 20, a veritably inexhaustible text: 'Mathematical formalization is our goal, our ideal. Why? Because there is no other matheme, in other words, it alone is capable of being integrally transmitted'.

We can thus say that for Plato mathematics is propaedeutic, while for Lacan the matheme is normative.

Let us further remark the differences between them concerning what they emphasize and retain about mathematics.

For Lacan, mathematics is a kind of formalization, that is to say it is the power of the letter. It is from this viewpoint that we can make sense of the particularly radical statement to be found in the same seminar, namely that 'only mathematization touches the real, and in this aspect it is compatible with our discourse, analytical discourse'. Only mathematization. This is a strong statement. And you will remark that mathematics has here shifted from the ideal position it occupied a moment ago with regard to the symbolic or transmission to a position of compatibility with regard to the real. For analytical discourse, mathematization is at once the ready ideal of integral transmission, and that real *qua* impasse of formalization with which what of the real occurs in the subject of analysis can and must coexist.

CONDITIONS

For Plato, the power of mathematics also lies in its attaining the real, a real to which Plato gave the name of intelligible, and that, similar to Lacan, he distinguished from reality, or what he termed the sensible. But, for him, formalization does not constitute this power. This power is constituted through axiomatic decision, through what Plato called hypotheses. Yet this axiomatic functioning does violence to thought; it has something constrained and blind about it. This is why it is only by means of re-ascending to the principle within dialectics that mathematics can be rendered in the clarity of its own power.

Does this leave us with an opposition between a modern formalizing conception of mathematics and a classical hypothetico-deductive conception? This would no doubt be to misrecognize the function of the axiom in Lacan, whose importance is such that we can maintain that the Subject in his work is less the effect of a cause than the consequence of an axiom. It would simultaneously to be to misrecognize the function in Plato's work of the letter and of the matheme, whose act is, as we see, the only way to resolve the paradoxes of the One. For, this supernumerary One that contains the void that it summons, and which I call event, is it not in the end reducible to the letter which names it? Is it not, with regard to the established alphabet of situations, that additional letter, one devoid of all signification, but one with which other words and unheard-of significations thus become possible, at the price of a strict fidelity to what has happened? It is a letter whose excess inscription, and only it, explains how the philosopher can be, as Plato indicated in *Book V* of the *Republic*, 'one for whom life is an awakening [*upar*] and not a dream [*onar*]'.

Let us take a step back from textual constraints and look at things from a distance, even if, as Lucretius maintained, truth seen from afar is melancholic. Which thinkers in the history of our thought have tried to join together in a unique disposition the subjective intensity that only love lavishes and the rigourous transmission of the matheme? Yes, which thinkers, if not Plato and Lacan, have taken the risk simultaneously to maintain that the process of truth cannot be accomplished without some sort of transference, to which the demand for love is key, and that it cannot be transmitted without a matheme, the form of which is the axiom? Which thinkers have been able to write on the door of their school – since both Plato and Lacan founded schools, and that of Lacan, under the name *La Cause Freudienne*, presses on, and we should hope it will continue to do so for at least as long as the Academy did, without being able to know who its Damascius will be – yes, which thinkers have been able to write the double maxim that none shall enter unless a geometer, or logician, or topologist, and that none shall enter unless ready to uphold, in the radical effects of an encounter, the atopic, asocial intensity of amorous *de-liaison*? Both Plato and Lacan, though from two different angles, worked towards identifying this strange complex of conditions for thinking, which obscurely joins the folly of passion and the beatitude of demonstration.

At the point of concluding, the idea strikes me that Lacan's convoluted and divided relations to Plato, which all the same exempt him from the philosophical anti-Platonic *doxa*, finds its symptom, which I'll now interpret, in his strange and restated conviction that Plato concealed his thought more than he presented it. We saw above Lacan's insinuation that in the *Pheado* Plato had been simply having his disciples on with all his talk about the 'empty' theme of participation. There is an even more singular text in which Lacan claimed that the whole political construction of the *Republic* – which he referred to as a sort of strategy for the breeding of well-behaved horses – was only presented by Plato to arouse a feeling of total horror. This perfect city was merely designed to drown in irony something that Plato himself abominated, a self-evident abomination that Lacan claimed we all share. This is stretching Plato's image as one who conceals his real thinking behind his explicit arguments pretty far. But such is Lacan's position. After an interview with Kojève Lacan once reported that they both shared the conviction that Plato had concealed what he thought. Lacan thereby felt he could ask for leniency:

> 'You should therefore not bear me a grudge if I do not give you Plato's last word, because Plato was very decided on not telling it to us'.

Having already separated the fiction Socrates from his master, this dissimulating Plato seems, does it not, like simply another way of enabling him to his maintain ambiguous stance in relation to philosophy? If the entirety of the *Republic* is an ironical imposture, how then are we to know whether we are speaking about what Plato thought or what he un-thought (*ce qu'il impense*)? About what he thought about philosophy or about its sophistic contrary? At any rate, quite independently of this, Socrates's placement within analytical discourse is enough to indicate that it had already been anticipated by philosophy.

CONDITIONS

I will posit, then, that, as regards what is said about Plato, anti-philosophy shows itself to be an apparatus of duplicity. This is not a judgement, since this duplicity is an operation. Inasmuch as it must be constituted as an independent figure of thought and act, psychoanalysis, like politics, or poetry, or love, or science, must explicitly distance itself from philosophy. Inasmuch as it touches the subject, being, truth and ethics, psychoanalysis must traverse and make holes in philosophy. In its Lacanian disposition, psychoanalysis is always a traverse of at least love and mathematics, both of which, as generic procedures, are conditions for philosophy. Lacan did not miss all that is opened in accessing these conditions from the standpoint of philosophy, albeit, if I may say, from the *other side* of these procedures. By 'the other side' I mean for whoever, like him, as he always said, draws everything from clinical experience.

Anti-philosophy designates the ambiguity of these two relations, the one of distance, the other of a traverse. Socrates and Plato, Plato the 'dissimulator' and Plato the 'sincere', distribute alternately, in praise and criticism, the two functions immanent to anti-philosophy, functions that are contrary to one another, and whose contrariness is seen in that the 'anti', as a function of distance, also supports the affirmation of 'philosophy', the function of traverse.

Lacan said somewhere, I'm certain of it, although for once I've not found where, that if some happen to believe that analysis is a continuation of the Platonic dialogues, they are mistaken. Which is duly noted, because it matters to me as much as to him that psychoanalysis is strictly distinguished from philosophy. But he also asked whether – and here I know exactly where, it is in the seminar of 19 May 1954 – 'we ought not to pursue the analytic intervention as far as the fundamental dialogues on justice and courage, in the great dialectical tradition'. Which is also duly noted. This time it is the Platonic dialogues that further analysis, or work to complete it. A torsion of the anti-philosophical schema.

One will see that, between its examination in the *Laches* and its discrete occurrences in Lacan, the word 'courage' in itself provides sufficient reason for having here experimented with coupling these two names, Plato and Lacan; since it is no doubt necessary to have a little courage in thought to stand, as I attempt to do, at the crossroads of all that these two names refer to that I consider essential. To stand in a crossing in torsion, without any unity of plane, between anti-philosophy and philosophy.

In a crossing basically implying a sole imperative that might be put as follows: Endeavour to apply yourself at a point in which at least one truth comes to pass. You will thereby emerge as the subject of that which this truth is the tissue of being. Not that you come from being, but on the contrary from that which has come forth, from an event or from transbeing. This is a coming forth whose having-taken-place will turn out only insofar as it will have taken place through your faithful activity.

Or again, and to conclude: Be willing to stay, suspended and hardworking, giving no ground, between the undecidability of the event and the indiscernibility of truth.

PART VII
The Writing of the Generic

CHAPTER FIFTEEN
The Writing of the Generic: Samuel Beckett

1. THE IMPERATIVE AND ITS DESTINATION

The opening attack: a *'vers de mirliton'*,[1] a *'mirlitonnade'* written by Beckett around 1976. It is a quite singular *mirlitonnade*, since as we see it couples the mirliton with Heraclitus the Obscure:

> Flux causes
> That every thing
> Even in being,
> Every thing,
> Thus this one here,
> Even this one here,
> Even in being
> Is not.
> Let's speak about it.[2]

For Beckett, speaking will always remain an imperative, but an imperative pertaining to the thing's undecidability or balancing. The thing is not withdrawn. It can be shown. It is *this* thing; however, upon being determined, it oscillates between being and non-being in accordance with its flux. Writing – the 'let's speak about it' – could then said to be situated in a space of decision relating to things in their being, a decision that – if only because its fitting form is that of *mirlitonnade* – no dialectic will ever sublate. That the thing can simultaneously be held in the place where it is and in the place where it is not is given in the image of flux;

this flux, however, is never the synthesis of being and non-being, and is not to be confused with Hegelian becoming.

Writing is established at the point where the thing, on the edge of disappearing, as is entailed by the non-being of its flux, is submitted to the undecidable question of its stability. This is precisely the reason why, as it is never destined by anything whose being is motionless, writing, with regard to the incertitude of the thing, takes on the form of an imperative.

What this interminable imperative must take stock of, if in all generality it is the beam oscillating between being and non-being, the balancing and the weighing of the thing, can also be also transformed into a certain number of *questions*.

Critique, in Kant's thinking, is organized around three questions: What can I know? What should I do? What can I hope? In Beckett's thinking there are also three questions, formulated in an ironic analogy that characterizes his relation to philosophy. These questions find clear expression in his *Texts for Nothing*. Here is one variant: 'Where would I go if I could go, who would I be, if I could be, what would I say, if I had a voice, who says this, saying it's me?' This threefold question concerns *going, being* and *saying*. This is the threefold instance of an 'I' that is transversal to questions, a subject caught in the interval between going, being and saying. Up until 1960, and a little beyond, in what is the best-known part of Beckett's work, the 'character' is, always and everywhere, a man of trajectory (going), of motionlessness (being) and of monologue (saying).

Given this trio of elementary situations pertaining to the subject, it is immediately possible to mark what I shall call the fundamental tendency in Beckett's work towards the *generic*. This 'generic' desire is to be understood as the reduction of the complexity of experience to a few major functions, as the treatment in writing of only that in which an essential determination inheres. For Beckett, writing was an act ruled by a strict principle of economy. In keeping with it, he was required, and to an ever greater degree, to subtract anything that figured as mere circumstantial ornamentation, any mere secondary amusements, since, if its destiny is to say generic humanity, writing can and must restrict itself to exhibiting, or to detaching, these rare functions. Initially, at the outset of this prodigious enquiry into humanity in which the art of Beckett consists, it is true that there are three of these functions: going, being and saying.

The internal metaphor in Beckett's work for this subtraction of ornaments inheres in the 'novels': throughout the text's progression, the characters that *accomplish* the fiction of generic writing shed all their inessential predicates – habits, objects, possessions, body pieces and fragments of language. Beckett often drew up the list of what needed to be lost for the generic functions to emerge. And he did not refrain from saddling these ornaments and vain possessions with unpleasant epithets, indicating that if the essence of generic humanity is to be apprehended, it can only be done by setting aside and dispelling these extraneous disasters. One is these lists is given in *Rough for Theatre, II*: 'Work, family, third fatherland, cunt, finances, art and nature, heart and conscience, health, housing conditions, God and man, so many disasters'. The subtraction of 'disasters', in prose, produces a fictional apparatus that lays bare or renders destitute. It is crucial, I think, to relate this apparatus to its function of thought, because those who have taken literally what is only a figuration have all too often interpreted it as a sign that humanity is, for Beckett, a condition of tragic devastation, of absurd abandonment. Yet, if I may say so, this perspective accepts the viewpoint of the proprietor, the one for whom possessions are the sole proof of meaning and being. Instead, in Beckett's work, when we are presented with a subject at its destitute end, it is someone who, *nolens volens*, has *managed* in the misadventures of experience to shed the disastrous ornaments of circumstance.

It is essential to repudiate every interpretation of Beckett that passes through the 'nihilist' mundanity of the metaphysical vagrant. Beckett spoke to us of something that had been far better *thought out* than this despair of the *salon*. Like Pascal's, what Beckett's work endeavoured to achieve was an intrinsic examination of humanity's functions, through a subtraction from the figure of humanity of everything that sidetracks it.

In the first place, the fictional apparatus of destitution is an operator enabling the *presentation* of a progressive purging of 'characters'. We see this process, clearly evident in the flesh of its prose, from the first to the last of Beckett's writings, and that where it led was to a sort of cracking point at which *prose is subordinated to a hidden poem*. This process further involved a paring down of metaphors to a finite stock of terms, which ultimately resulted, in their specific combination and recurrence, in an ensemble of thought.

The kind of economy that Beckett's texts were, little by little, to form is one that I am happy to call ancient, or categorial. The primitive functions of this economy, as we have seen, are movement, rest and logos. If one observes, and how not to, the gravitational shift that occurred, as of the 1960s, towards the question of the Same and the Other, and more particularly to that of the Other's existence, real or potential, we can maintain that throughout its course his work comes to plot the five 'supreme kinds' of Plato's *Sophist*. These kinds are the underlying concepts needed to grasp humanity's generic existence, and they underlie its prosodic destitution, as that on which a thinking of our destiny is predicated. We could say that these supreme kinds, Movement, Rest, the Same, the Other, the Logos – as displaced variants of Plato's proposal – constitute the reference points, or primitive terms, for an axiomatic of humanity as such.

On the basis of these axiomatic terms, it is possible to discern the specific questions that organize Beckett's work, questions that dispose a fiction of humanity, in which the functional reduction of humanity is exhibited and treated as something that is oriented towards essence, or Idea.

I shall restrict myself to discussing only four of these questions. At once theological and a-theological, Beckett's oeuvre is a summa, and its disposition cannot be exhausted here. These four questions are as follow.

1. That of the *site of being*, or more precisely, of the fiction of its truth. How does a truth of being enter the fiction of its site?
2. That of the *subject*, which, for Beckett, is essentially a question of identity. What are the processes by which the subject might hope to identify itself?
3. That of the 'what happens', the 'what arrives'. How to think the supplement to motionless-being we call the event? For Beckett this problem is closely related to that of the capacities of language. Is it possible to *name* what happens or arrives *insofar as* it arrives?
4. That of the *existence of the Two*, or the virtuality of the Other. This is the question that ultimately holds all of Beckett's work together. Is there any possibility of an actual Two that would go beyond solipsism? The question at issue might also be said to be the question of love.

2. THE BLACK–GREY AS THE SITE OF BEING

The originary axiomatics is an axiomatics of wandering, motionlessness and voice: is it possible on the basis of this triplet to grasp any truth whatsoever of what is insofar as it is? This operator of truth is not just

THE WRITING OF THE GENERIC

any operator. For Beckett, who is an artist, this operator is an apparatus of fictions, and in this apparatus the resulting question is one about a 'site'. Is there a site of being that can be presented in the apparatus of fiction so that the being of this site of being itself becomes transmissible?

Taking Beckett's *oeuvre* as a whole, we can in fact observe a sort of interweaving of two ontological localizations, which are seemingly contrary to one another.

The first localization is a closure: set up an enclosed space so that the site's set of traits are denumerable and exactly nameable. Here the aim is to make 'what is seen' coextensive with 'what is said', under the banner of the closed. The obvious examples are the play in which the characters of *Endgame* are enclosed; the room in which Malone dies (or does not die); and Mr. Knott's house in *Watt*, not to mention the cylindrical arena of *The Lost Ones*. There are many more examples of closure than these. In a text entitled *Closed Place*, Beckett wrote: 'Closed place. All needed to be known for say is known'.

Here we see the precise ambition of this apparatus of fiction concerning the question of the site of being, that is inasmuch the apparatus as one of closure: to create a strict reversibility between vision and diction in the register of knowledge. The type of localization required is particularly ascetic.

But there is a totally different apparatus, one that, on the contrary, is an open, geographical space, a space of trajectories, and of varieties of pathings (*parcours*). We see this in the countryside, plains, hills and forests through which Molloy pursues the search for his mother, and Moran the search for Molloy. We see this also in the city and the streets of *The Expelled*, and even, despite tending towards uniform abstraction, the underground of black mud in which, in *How It Is*, the larva of essential humanity crawl. We see it once again in the beautiful flower-covered Irish and Scottish hilltops, through which the old couple of *Enough* wanders in happiness.

In these spaces of wandering, just as in the closed spaces, Beckett's inclination is to work towards suppressing all descriptive ornamentation. The result is a screened image of the earth and sky, a space of wandering, of course, but a space that itself is a sort of motionless simplicity. We find the ultimate purging of the space of the trajectory, or of the possible space for all movement in a work called *Lessness*: 'Grey sky no cloud no sound no stir earth ash grey [*noir grise*] sand. Little body same grey as the earth sky ruins only upright. Ash grey all sides earth sky as one all sides endlessness'.

Once its fictive purification is attained, the space of being (or the apparatus that attests to the question of being in the form of the site) could be termed a 'black–grey'.[3] That might be enough.

What is the black–grey? It is a black that no light can be supposed to contrast with; it is an un-contrasted black. This black is sufficiently grey that no light can be opposed to it as its Other. Abstractly, the site of being is fictioned as a black–grey enough to be anti-dialectical, distinct from every contradiction with the light. The black–grey is a black that has to be taken in its own disposition and that forms no pair with anything else.

What is effectuated in this black–grey, in which the thinking of being is localized, is a progressive fusion of closure and of open, or errant, space. Little by little, in Beckett's poetics – this is one achievement of his prose – the enclosed and the open become merged together in the black–grey, and it turns out to be impossible to know whether it is destined to movement or rather to motionlessness. The figure that 'goes' and the figure that 'remains at rest' are superposed in the site of being. We see this superposition accomplished in *How It Is*, in which generic humanity's two major figures are presented as being voyage and fixity, two figures that nonetheless inhere *in the same space*, whereas these metaphors of localization, wandering and closure, remain disjunct between *Molloy*, which is the novel of the trajectory, and *Malone Dies*, which is the site of saying fixed in the point of death.

This final and unique site, the anti-dialectical black–grey, does not come within the realm of clear and distinct ideas. The question of being, grasped in its localization, cannot be distinguished or separated out through any ideal articulation. In *Molloy* we find this peremptory anti-Cartesian statement: 'I think so, yes, I think that all that is false may more readily be reduced, to notions clear and distinct, distinct from all other notions'.

Here the Cartesian criterion of self-evidence is inverted, and we can see why: if the black–grey localizes being, then attaining the true of being demands thinking the un-separated, the in-distinct. On the other hand, that which separates and distinguishes, separates, for example, black from light, thus constitutes the site of non-being and the false.

Last, localization in the black–grey entails that the being of being cannot be uttered as some isolable singularity but uniquely *as void*. When there is a fiction that proceeds to merge the black of wandering and the black of motionlessness, we observe that this site presents a form of being that can be called the nothing, or the void, and that has no other name.

This maxim, which from the localization of being in the black–grey attains the void as the name of *what* is localized, is basically established from the time of *Malone Dies*. Malone's voice begins by warning us that what is at stake is a fearsome phrase, one of those phrases that 'pollute the whole of speech'. This phrase is: 'Nothing is more real than nothing'.

The cardinal statement about being pollutes the whole of speech with its inconceivable truth. Many variations will follow, but the most accomplished can be found in *Worstward Ho*. In this text, we find, for example, this: 'All save void. No, Void too. Unworsenable void. Never less. Never more. Never since first said never unsaid never worse said never not gnawing to be gone'.

Such is the ultimate point to which the merged fictioning of the place of being enables us to attest: that being as void in-exists in language, because it is subtracted from every *degree*. But it is precisely its being subtracted from language that sets it in between the first two categories, that is, movement and rest, and the third, speech or logos.

That being *qua* being is subtracted from language is said by Beckett in many ways, but above all, perhaps, by the always possible equivalence between 'said' and 'missaid'. This equivalence does not form an opposition between saying (something) well and saying (it) badly, instead it inheres in the missaid as the essence of saying; it claims that being inexists in language, and that, as a consequence, as Molloy puts it, 'all language is a gap of language'.

The principal effect of this conviction involves severing being and existence. Existence is that whereof one can talk, whereas the being of existence remains subtracted from the network of significations and inexists in language.

Despite only being deployed in its veritable fictional operator (the black–grey) quite late in Beckett's work, this scission between being and existence with regard to language is visible in it very early on. Already in his *First Love* from 1945 we come across this: 'But I have always spoken, no doubt always shall, of things that never existed, or that existed if you insist, no doubt always will, but not with the existence I ascribe to them'.

This fine line separating the thing that does not exist and the same thing that, as embraced by speech, exists but always in a *different* existence, returns us to the equilibrium of the Heraclitean *mirlitonnade*: the 'let's speak about it' must operate in the site of being, in the site of the black–grey, which maintains an undecidable distinction between existence and the being of existence.

The clearest formulation of this question is perhaps to be found in *Watt*. Following an ontological tradition that Beckett revived in his own way, we may call 'Presence' being as it inexists in language, and more generally what of being remains unpresented in the existent. If being is presented in the black–grey site where existence is indistinguished, then we can decree that this Presence is neither illusion (the sceptical thesis), nor a veritable and utterable comprehension (the dogmatic thesis), but a certitude without concept. Here is what Beckett said about it:

> So I shall merely state, without enquiring how it came, or how it went, that in my opinion it was not an illusion, as long as it lasted, that presence of what did not exist, that presence without, that presence within, that presence between, though I'll be buggered if I can understand how it could have been anything else.

This text tells us three things. First, presence, which is the givenness (*donation*) of being of that which is not in a position to exist, is not an illusion. Second, it is at once distributed inside and outside, but its chosen place is doubtless rather the 'between', the interval. And, third, it is impossible to say more than that it is subtracted from existence, and, so as a result, presence does not infer any meaning. This impossible, moreover, is really also an interdiction, which points crudely to the vocabulary of castration.

We understand clearly why there can be no clear and distinct idea of presence. Because what thereof is left to us is a pure proper name, the void or the nothing. This name is the beam of the Heraclitean scales; it clearly suggests, in its absence of sense, a genuine being, not an illusion but actually a non-being, since what it refers to is the inexistence of being, which is inherent to its unsayable givenness.

If the fictional apparatus of the black–grey was all there was, the virtues of which we have exhausted, then we would have to agree with a comment often made about Beckett's work, that we are very close to a negative theology. But there is an underneath of the localization of being, something that cannot be reduced to the being of the inexistent, and that is reflection as such, the cogito. Since the one for whom there is the black–grey, and unsayable presence, does not cease to reflect and phrase both localization and its impasse.

In a certain sense, this movement from the void to the cogito is itself very Cartesian, despite the anti-Cartesian statements I have cited (concerning the criterion of self-evidence), and we know that Beckett indeed drew nourishment from Descartes. This referral back to the cogito is explicit in numerous texts, and is set out in an entirely rational fashion in the argument of *Film*, even if it is with an ironic take on this rationality.

Film is a film, indeed the film, about a single character played by Buster Keaton. It is about a man – an object O, said Beckett – who flees because he is being pursued by an eye whose name is OE. Hence the film is the story of the pursuit of O by OE, and not until the end of the film do we realize that the pursuer and the pursuant, eye and man, form an identity. When he published the script, Beckett introduced it with a text entitled *Esse est percipi*, in which we find this:

> All extraneous perception suppressed, animal, human, divine, self-perception maintains in being.
>
> Search of non-being in flight from extraneous perception breaking down in inescapability of self-perception.

Here we find the argument of the cogito, save for the ironical nuance that is involved in replacing the search for truth by the search for non-being, and the inversion of values of 'the inescapability of self-perception', which for Descartes was a foremost victory of certainty, but that here appears as a failure. What exactly is this a failure to do? Precisely to extend the Whole, the subject included, to the general form of being, which is the void. The cogito causes this extension to fail: there is something that exists whose being *cannot* inexist, and that is the subject of the cogito.

This brings us into the vicinity of the second question, after that of the site of being: the question of the subject such as it is caught in the closure of the cogito, which is also actually that of enunciation submitted to torture by the imperative of the statement.

3. OF THE SOLIPSISTIC SUBJECT AS TORTURE

The fictional apparatus that deals with the closure of the *cogito* organizes the best-known part of Beckett's work. This apparatus is that of the motionless voice, of the voice that is *assigned to residence* by a body. This body is mutilated and captive, reduced to being no more than the fixed localization of the voice. It is enchained, nailed to a hospital bed, or planted in a jar that serves as publicity for a restaurant opposite some abattoirs. It is a doubly enclosed I – in the fixity of the body and in the persistence of a voice without either echo or response – that endlessly strives to find a way to its identification.

What does identification consist in for this repetitious (ressassante)[4] voice of the *cogito*? It involves producing, with a stream of statements, fables, narrative fictions and concepts, the pure and silent point of enunciation itself. Of course, this pure point of enunciation, this always anterior, or presupposed, 'I', being that by which the voice and statements are possible, being the site of being of the voice, is itself subtracted from all naming. The unrelenting stake of the solipsistic voice, or the voice of the cogito, is to arrive at this originary *silence* in which the being of enunciation inheres, and that is the subjective condition of statements. Being identified necessitates entering this silence in which all speech finds its support. This was the hope of the hero of *The Unnamable*: 'there were moments I thought that would be my reward for having spoken so long and so valiantly, to enter living into silence . . .'

This entering silence, which holds death at bay ('still living'), was perfectly described by Maurice Blanchot as a repetition (*ressassement*) of writing, which at once effectuates its point of enunciation, and wants to capture it, to signify it.

Beckett, of course, would proceed to observe that this point of identification – the silent being of all speech – cannot be accessed via the statement at all. But it would be too simple to think that this inaccessibility derives from a formal paradox, that is, from a necessity according to which the condition of being of all naming is itself unnameable. The figure of the impossible, or of the unnameable is more tortuous; it brings together two determinations that are engaged in Beckett's prose with an insistence without hope.

The first is that the conditions of this operation, the cogito's conditions within the sole means of its capture by a fixed voice, are very precisely *intolerable*, fraught as they are with anguish and mortal exhaustion.

The second is that upon close examination we start to see that the situation of the cogito is far more complex than simple reflection. In effect, it involves not just two but three terms. The schema of *Film*, which contains the eye and the object, is inadequate.

The conditions of the cogito, or of a thought of thought, are terribly demanding, since the voice is never repetitious or mobile enough, but equally never insistent, or motionless, enough. That would require that a regime of voice be found that is simultaneously located at the heights of vehemence and the vociferant multiple, and in a state of restraint, of the almost-nothing, the out of breath. The voice does not succeed in attaining this point of equilibrium, and the unnameable, which would be just in the caesura of these two contrary registers, escapes it.

This is because, to attain it, an internal violence is necessary, a superego fury, that is capable of submitting, in the proper sense, the subject of the *cogito* to the question, to torture. That would necessitate that the avowal of its silence be *extorted*. Beckett stressed that if the 'I think' comes to mark its own thinking-being, if thinking wants to grasp itself as the thinking of thought, then a reign of terror begins. This is not without echoes of the famous letter in which Mallarmé, in a paroxystic state of crisis and anguish, declared: 'My thought has thought itself, and I am perfectly dead'. Beckett, for his part, pointed to suffering rather than to death: 'I only think [i.e. the hero of The Unnamable], if that is the name for this vertiginous panic as of hornets smoked out of their nest, once a certain degree of terror has been exceeded'.

The 'I think' presupposes terror, which alone constrains the voice to over-extend (*se sur-tendre*) towards itself in order to withdraw, as much as possible, towards its point of enunciation. As with all terror, it is also given as an imperative without concept; it imposes a repetitious insistence that does not let up and admits of no way out. This imperative, which is indifferent to all possibility, this terrorist commandment to have to maintain what cannot be, concludes *The Unnamable*: 'I must go on, I can't go on, I'll go on'.

Here what is necessary is exactly what is impossible, the continuation of the repetitious insistence of the voice is also the voice of intolerable torture. Throughout *The Unnamable* the speaker's face streams with tears.

The cogito's heroism marks an impasse. Next, after *The Unnamable*, follow the *Texts for Nothing*, which very precisely occupies the place of death: the place in which the temptation to abandon the imperative to write insists, the temptation to have a rest from the cogito's torture. This is the moment in which the relation between 'I must go on' and 'I can't go on' is so tense that the writer is not certain to be able to sustain it any longer.

CONDITIONS

In *Texts for Nothing* Beckett proceeds in a fashion that is more theoretical and less bound to the fearsome fictional apparatuses of the solipsistic subject. Apart from its torturing and intolerable conditions, their principal discovery is that, because identification is impossible, the *cogito* is ultimately without finality. The imperative addressed to the I concerning the naming of *its* founding silence is object-less. The cogito is in effect not an instance of reflection, a Two – the couple of the statement and the enunciation – it delineates a triplicity. The 'I' has three instances, which cannot be reduced to One, except under conditions of total exhaustion, of the subject's total dissipation.

On this point, the key text is twelfth *Text For Nothing*, one of Beckett's densest and most purely theoretical texts. The passage from it here performs an analytic decomposition of the *cogito*:

> one who speaks saying, without ceasing to speak, Who's speaking?, and one who hears, mute, uncomprehending, far from all [. . .]. And this other [. . .] with his babble of homeless mes and untenanted hims [. . .]. There's a pretty three in one, and what a one, what a no one.

What is the distribution of this infernal three-in-one?

1. First, there is the subject of enunciation, the 'Who speaks', a so-called reflexive subject of enunciation, one also capable of asking Who speaks, of enunciating the question himself. This is the subject the hero of *The Unnamable* strives in terror to identify.
2. Second, there is the subject of passivity, who hears without understanding, who is 'far from all' in that he is like the other side, the obscure matter of the one who speaks, the passive being of the subject of enunciation.
3. Last, there is the subject who upholds the question of identification, the one who, by means of enunciation and passivity, insists on the question concerning what he is, and who, in so doing, submits himself to torture.

The subject is thus pulled between the subject of enunciation, the subject of passivity and the questioning subject. The third is basically the one for whom the relationship of the first two, the *relationship* between enunciation and passivity, is a question.

Enunciation, passive reception, question: such is the 'pretty three in one' that makes up the Beckettian subject. Yet, if we try to conjoin them, to count all three as One, all we find is the void of being, a nothing that is worthless. Why it is worthless? Because the void of being does not claim to be the question of its being. Whereas, in the case of the subject, we have the terrorizing divagation of the question, which would turn identifying torture into a bitter buffoonery were it to resolve into the pure and simple void. Every question entails a regime of values (of what *value* is the response?), and if in the end we finish by simply rediscovering what was there well prior to every question, in other words, being as the black–grey, then the inferred value is nil.

Obviously, it might then be thought that all questions are to be abandoned. Does rest, serenity, the end of the torturing question of identity, not reside in a pure and simple coincidence with the place lof being, with this unquestionable black–grey? Why prefer the silence of the point of enunciation to silence such as it is, and has always been, in the anti-dialectical identity of being? Can the subject not rejoin the place where every question is absent, and leave aside, leave off the dead-end path of its identity?

Well, no, it cannot. The question, because it is one of those instances of the subjective trio, irrevocably insists. Beckett said expressly, in *Ill Seen Ill Said*, that it is impossible to return to a place, or a time, in which the question is abolished:

> Was it ever over and done with questions? Dead the whole brood no sooner hatched. Long before. In the egg. Long before. Over and done with answering. With not being able. With no being able not to want to know. With not being able. No. Never. A dream. Question Answered.

The idea that the subjective trio can be disarticulated by suppressing its questioning instance is impracticable. One can never return to the immemorial peace of the black–grey; there never was a time, or a place, where the questions were 'dead the whole brood no sooner hatched'.

We are in a complete deadlock. The *cogito* is literally intolerable and yet also ineluctable. Solipsism engaged in the process of identification is interminable and futile; it can no longer sustain writing, but the place of being cannot welcome us any longer either. This is the reason why Beckett's texts are *texts for nothing*. They express, with extraordinary lucidity, the 'nothing' of the attempt underway. They report not that there is nothing (Beckett was never a *nihilist*), but that writing has nothing more to assert. This text tells us of the truth of a situation, namely, Beckett's at the end of the 1950s: what he had written until this point could not *go on any further*. It was impossible to go on alternating without any mediation between the neutrality of the black–grey of being and the interminable torture of the solipsistic cogito. Writing could no longer be sustained by this alternation.

And yet Beckett did go on. So, unless we understand his continuation as a mere obsession, or as some servility to an imperative of acknowledged vacuity, then we must inquire into the point *through* which it passed. It passed, I am convinced, through a veritable intellectual and artistic mutation, and more precisely through a modification in his *orientation of thought*.

4. THE MUTATION OF BECKETT'S OEUVRE AFTER 1960

Beckett's undertaking cannot be said to have progressed from its initial parameters in a linear fashion. Contrary to commonly held critical opinion, it is quite erroneous to argue that it became ever deeper engulfed in 'despair', in 'nihilism', in the undermining of sense.

In the medium of prose, what Beckett dealt with were *problems*; his oeuvre is by no means the *expression* of a spontaneous metaphysics. Once these problems became stuck in an apparatus of prose that did not admit, or no longer did, of any solution, this apparatus and its corresponding fictions were displaced, transformed, and even destroyed by Beckett.

No doubt this is what occurred at the end of the 1950s following the *Texts for Nothing*. *How It Is*, ultimately a little-known work, marks a major mutation in the way that Beckett fictioned his thought. This text breaks with the confrontation between the torturing cogito and the neutrality of the black–grey of being. Beckett attempted to set out from entirely different categories, namely, that of the 'what happens' (which was present in his work from the beginning but is reworked here), and that, above all, of alterity, of the encounter, of the figure of the Other, which fissures and displaces solipsistic imprisonment.

To maintain conformity with these categories of thought, Beckett's literary montage itself also underwent a series of major transformations. The canonical form of the 'first' Beckett fictions alternates, as we saw, between trajectories, or wanderings and fixities, or constrained monologues. This was slowly replaced by what I would like to call *the figural poem of postures of the subject*. Prose was no longer able to sustain its usual 'novelist' functions, that is, description and narration, not even when reduced to their bare bones (the black–grey that does not describe being, and a pure wandering that recounts only itself). Such is the disposition of the fictive functions of prose that leads me to speak of the poem. And the stakes of this poetics, as regards the subject, no longer concern the question of its identity, in the torturing way it was executed in the monologue of *The Unnamable*. At issue are rather occurrences of the subject, of its possible positions, of the enumeration of its figures. Rather than by the never-ending and futile fictive reflection on self, the subject is now indicated by the variety of the dispositions it enters in dealing with encounters, with the 'what is happening', with all that supplements being in the instantaneous surprise of the Other.

To pursue the discontinuity of the figure of the subject, which is contrasted with the insistent repetition of the Same such as it is beset by its own speech, Beckett's prose became more segmented, and adopted the paragraph as a musical unity. The subject's apprehension in thought was to be carried out in a thematic frame: recurrences, repetitions of the same statements in context that slowly alter, re-takes, loops and so on.

This evolution, I believe, is typical of what I have tried to think under the name of the writing of the generic. From the moment that what was involved was a generic truth of humanity, the narrative model, even when reduced to the line of a pure trajectory, was insufficient, as was the 'internal' solipsistic monologue, even one productive of fictions and fables. Neither the technique of *Molloy*, nor that of *Malone Dies*, which remained quite close to Kafka's procedures, could bend prose sufficiently enough to what there is of indiscernible in a generic truth.

In order to grasp the lacunary intricacies of the subject, that into which it is split up, the triplet monologue–dialogue–narrative must be deposed. Yet, we cannot thereby speak of the poem in any strict sense: the operations of the poem, always affirmative, do not fiction anything. I should rather say that the prose is, in its paragraph-by-paragraph segmentation, governed by a *latent or implicit poem*. The latent poem holds the givens of the text together, but without itself being given. What appears at the text's surface are thematic recurrences and their slowed movement – a movement that is fundamentally regulated, or unified, by a latent poetical matrix.

CONDITIONS

The latent poem either moves closer to or further away from the text's surface. In *Lessness*, for example, it is almost given, while in *Imagination Dead Imagine* it is deeply buried. In all cases, there is a sort of subversion of prose and its destiny of fiction by the poem that never actually enters into poetry. It is this subversion without transgression that Beckett finely honed, with many regrets, between 1960 and his death, as the sole regime of prose adequate to a generic intention.

From a more abstract viewpoint, Beckett's evolution passed from a programme of the One – the relentlessness of a trajectory or an interminable soliloquy – to the fecund theme of the Two, by which it opens to the infinite. This discovery of the multiple then leads to combinations and hypotheses that can be likened to a cosmology, and that are grasped in their literal or given objectivity not as suppositions but as situations. Last, there is a passage from an apparatus of fictions, which sometimes also includes allegorical stories, to a semi-poetic apparatus that works to construct situations. These situations make possible an enumeration of the misfortunes and the fortunes of the subject.

On the question of the Other, this new project comes to oscillate between reports of failure and victorious insights. It can be argued that in *Happy Days*, in *Enough* and in *Ill Seen Ill Said*, there is, under the signifier of 'happiness' – which not even twists of irony can abolish – an inflexion of a predominately positive tone. By contrast, in *Company*, which finishes with the word 'alone', there is a final deconstruction of what, in the sublime of night, will, along the way, have been only the fiction of a Two. But this oscillation is itself a principle of opening. In fact, the second part of Beckett's oeuvre *opens up to chance*, and chance disposes of equal possibilities of success and lack thereof, of the encounter and the non-encounter, of alterity and solitude. Chance is what saved Beckett from falling back on the secret schemas of predestination that were still very evident in *Watt* and *How It Is*.

In the earlier part of Beckett's work, we certainly find many traces of this rupture with the schema of predestination, of an opening to the hazardous possibility that there is not only what there is, that is, traces related to the mute presentation of the schema itself. I am thinking for example of the moment when Molloy declares: 'One is what one is, at least in part'. This 'in part' concedes a point of non-self-identity, in which the peril of a freedom is lodged. This concession makes room for the judgement of *Enough*: 'Stony ground but not entirely'. There is a breaching (*ébrèchement*) of being, a subtraction from the indifferent ingratitude of the black–grey. Or to use one of Lacan's concepts, there is some not-whole, as much in the coincidence of self to self that speech is exhausted in situating, as in the ingratitude of the earth.

What is the gap in the whole of being and of the self? What is it that is held there, that something that is simultaneously the not-whole of the subject and the grace of a supplement to the monotony of being? This is the question of the event, of the 'what-is-happening'. We no longer ask: 'what is being insofar as it is?', nor 'can the subject beset by speech rejoin his silent identity?'. We ask: 'Is something happening?' and, more precisely: 'Can we name an emergence, an incalculable advent which detotalizes being and wrenches the subject from the predestination of its identity?'

5. EVENT, SIGNIFICATION, NOMINATION

Some of Beckett's earliest writings are animated by an interrogation into 'that which happens', and into the possibility of thinking the event *insofar as it comes forth*. In a book written in the 1940s, *Watt*, it is central. But it was largely obliterated by the works that made Beckett known, which, apart from *Waiting for Godot*, basically include the trilogy of *Molloy*, *Malone Dies* and the *Unnamable*. What was retained from these works was that, precisely, in the end nothing happens. Godot will never come; he is nothing but the promise of his coming. And, in this sense, the event is akin to the woman in Claudel: a promise that cannot be kept.

In *Watt*, by contrast, we come across the crucial problem of what the hero calls 'incidents', which however are very real.

Watt disposes an allegorical, structural place, which is the house of Mr. Knott. This place is immemorial and invariant, and it is being as the Whole and as Law.

> nothing could be added to Mr Knott's establishment, and from it nothing taken away, but that as it was now, so it had been in the beginning, and so it would remain to the end, in all essential respects, any significant presence, at any time, and here all presence was significant, even though it was impossible to say of what, proving that presence at all times . . .

267

CONDITIONS

Mr. Knott's house binds together presence and signification so tightly together that there can be no thinkable breaching of its being, by means of either supplement or subtraction. All one can do is reflect the Law of invariance of the place of being: how does the house function in time? Where is Mr. Knott to be found at such and such a given moment? In the garden, or in the upper stories? These are questions relative to pure knowledge, to the science of the place and that work to rationalize a sort of 'Waiting for Mr. Knott'.

But, in addition to the law of place and its doubtful science, there is – and this is what arouses Watt's passion as a thinker – the problem of incidents. Of these incidents, Beckett said, in a wonderful expression, that they are 'of brilliant formal clarity and of impenetrable content'. What are these incidents? Among the most remarkable, we might mention the visit of a piano tuner and his son, or the dumping on his doorstep of slops destined for dogs whose origins are themselves an 'impenetrable' question.

What solicits thought is the contradiction between the formal brilliance of the incident, its isolation, its exceptional status and the opacity of its content. Watt does his utmost to form hypotheses about the said content, and therewith is his thought genuinely aroused. Here there is no question of a *cogito* that is held under the voice's torturing strictures, but of surmises and of appreciations aimed at bringing the content of the incidents up to the brilliance of their form.

In *Watt*, however, a limit is set to this investigation, a limit that Beckett only crossed much later on: the hypotheses about the incidents are *bound up in a problematic of signification*. Here we remain within an attempt of a hermeneutical type, the stakes of which are to relate, through a well-conducted interpretation, the incident to the established universe of significations. Here is the passage in which the hierarchy of possibilities are laid out as they appear to Watt as an interpreter of incidents, or hermeneut:

> the meaning attributed to this particular type of incident, by Watt, in his relations, was now the initial meaning that has been lost and then recovered, and now a meaning quite distinct from the initial meaning, and now a meaning evolved, after a delay of varying length, and with greater or less pains, form the initial absence of meaning.

The hermeneut has three possibilities: if he assumes that there is a signification to the incident, he can recover it, or propose an entirely other one. If he assumes that it has no meaning, he can bring one forth.

Of course, only the third hypothesis, which posits that the incident is void of all signification, and that therefore it really is separated from the closed universe of sense (Mr. Knott's house), awakens thought with any lasting effect ('after a delay . . .') and requires it to go to work ('with greater or less pains'). However, if this were the only issue, if the interpreter were a giver *of meaning*, we would remain in thrall to meaning as law, as imperative. The interpreter does nothing except create a connection between the incident and that from which it was initially separate: the established universe of meanings, Mr. Knott's house. In *Watt*, it is always entirely possible that something has happened, but this 'that-which-happens', captured and reduced by the hermeneut, is not maintained in its character as supplement, or breaching.

Beginning with the theatre play *Endgame*, Beckett will dissociate the that-which-happens from any even invented connection to meanings. He will posit that simply because there is an event that does not enjoin us to find its signification:

> Hamm: What is happening?
> Clov: Something is taking it's course.
> Hamm: Clov!
> Clov: What is it?
> Hamm: We're not beginning to . . . to . . . mean something?
> Clov: Mean something! You and I, mean something! Ah that's a good one!

Beckett came to replace the hermeneutics with which he began, trying to pin the event to the network of meanings, with a wholly different operation, and which is that of *naming*. As regards a hazardous supplementation of being, naming will not look for meaning, but instead propose to draw an invented name from the void itself of what happens. After interpretation we then arrive at a nominal poetics whose whole stake is to fix the incident, to preserve in language a trace of its separation.

The poetics of naming is central to *Ill Seen Ill Said*, starting with the very title. For what does 'ill seen' mean? It means that what happens is necessarily outside the laws of visibility of the place of being. What *really* happens cannot be well seen (or looked well upon, including in the moral sense of the expression), because the well-seen always comprises that which is framed by the black–grey of being, and therefore does not have the capacity of isolation and of surprise of the incident–event. And what does 'ill said' mean? Saying-well is precisely the order of established meanings. Yet, if we arrive at producing the name of what comes insofar as it comes, the name of the ill seen, this name could not then be encompassed by significations attached to the monotonousness of the place. It is therefore of the register of the ill said. 'Ill seen ill said' designates the possible agreement between that which, being ill seen, is subtracted from the visible, and that which, being ill said, is subtracted from significations. It is therefore question of the agreement between an event and the poetics of its name.

On this point consider the following decisive passage:

> During the inspection a sudden sound. Startling without consequence for the gaze the mind awake. How explain it? And without going so far how say it? Far behind the eye the quest begins. What time the event recedes. When suddenly to the rescue it comes again. Forthwith the uncommon common noun collapsion. Reinforced a little later if not enfeebled by the infrequent slumberous. A slumberous collapsion. Two. Then far from the still agonizing eye a gleam of hope. By the grace of these modest beginnings.

The passage, essentially, speaks of itself. 'The inspection' is accorded with visibility; it is the well-seen, which is moreover presented as a kind of torture. During this torturing subordination to the law of the place there is – in a classic 'suddenness' indicative of evental supplementation – a noise. This noise is an outside-place, is isolated in its formal clarity, is in-visible, ill seen. The whole problem here is to invent a name that suits it, Beckett rejecting in due course the hypothesis, in appearance more ambitious, in reality less free, of an explanation that would consists in a saying-well of the ill seen.

That the name of event–noise is a poetic invention, is signified by Beckett by means of the paradoxical alliance between 'collaspion' and 'slumberous', the one 'uncommon', the other 'infrequent'. This naming appears suddenly from the void of language, as a saying-ill adequate to the ill seen of the noise.

Still more important is that, when 'slumberous collapsion' is expressed as the suddenness of a noise, as a poetic wager on the ill seen, then, and only then, is there a 'gleam of hope'.

What hope can one have here? The hope of a truth. Of a truth that comes to make an incision in the black–grey, suspended from the naming of an event that will eclipse itself. A moment of grace, the 'grace of these modest beginnings'. A truth can have no other beginning than one wherein a poetic name, a name without signification, is granted to a separable supplement that, obscure as it may be, ill seen as it is said to be, is nevertheless subtracted from the black–grey of being, is 'of brilliant formal clarity'.

Thus, the field of truth is opened, which in its separable origin is a field of alterity. The nomination keeps under its watch a trace of an Other-than-being, which is also an Other-than-self.

With this the subject is dis-closed (*dé-clôt*) from its enclosure, and enters the perils of the Other, of its occurrences and its figures. It does so marked by the hope opened up by ontological alterity, by the breach of being that crystallizes the suddenness of the event, the brilliance of the ill-seen.

6. FIGURES OF THE SUBJECT AND FORMULAS OF SEXUATION

In the texts written after 1960, Beckett was continuously occupied with putting figures of the subject into the form of a tale. The most significant montages are the – very 'structuralist' – *The Lost Ones* published in 1970, and *How It Is*.

In both cases, the fiction brings together an abstract place that connotes no established figure of the sensible. There are no longer any forests or flowers of wandering, nor the enclosure of an asylum-like room. Space is homogeneous, regulated, subject to strict parameters, one has the premonition an exact science could be at work. Such coded spaces evoke a portable cosmology, but also Dante's hell. Their bareness makes it possible to focus attention on the subject's figural dispositions.

In *The Lost Ones*, this place is a great cylinder made of rubber in which precise, empirically observable, but conceptually unknown laws govern variations in light, sounds and temperatures. It is a simple, purified cosmos, reduced to a complex made of an enclosure and a legality. Inside of it is a small people comprising persons busily obeying a single imperative: search for your lost one. This persistent imperative is no longer, as in *The Unnamable*, one of identification; at issue is no longer to say oneself or to return to oneself at the pure point of silence. The imperative consists in finding the other, or more precisely in looking for one's other.

CONDITIONS

The story starts thus: 'Abode where lost bodies roam each searching for its lost one'.

A Lost One is one who, because it is one's *own* lost one, singularizes one, extracts one from the anonymous status of those who are only lost among the people of searchers. To be 'a lost one' is to come to oneself in the encounter with one's other.

The quest for the other is constant and varied. One runs around just about everywhere in the cylinder, one climbs up ladders to find out if the lost ones might not be in one of the niches placed at different heights, which is a very tricky exercise, whose mishaps are described by Beckett in great detail. But, ultimately, we are able to identify four figures of the search, and therefore four figures of the subject, four possible figures for 'each one' who seeks his lost one.

Grosso modo, there are two criteria for the typology of figures. The first criterion contrasts those who search and those who have given up searching. That is, those who still live their lives according to the sole imperative and those who have given up on this imperative, which is the same thing as giving up on one's desire, since there exists no other desire than that of finding one's lost one. These defeated searchers Beckett calls the *vanquished*. To be vanquished, let us remark, is never to be vanquished by the other, it is to renounce the other.

The second criterion originates in the Platonic categories of rest and movement, whose importance for Beckett's thought I have already signalled. There are searchers who are perpetually in motion, there are others who sometimes pause, and others again who stop frequently, and even some who move no longer.

So that in the end we have four kinds of subject:

1. Searchers who move are perpetually in motion, who could be called nomads, and who comprise the 'initial' living, for example, babies. Babies never cease moving, naturally while on their mother's backs, but without stopping at all. Mothers are also in this category; they cannot be motionless for a single instant.
2. Searchers who sometimes stop, who pause to 'rest'.
3. Searchers who are definitively motionless, or have been for a long time, but who – and this is very important – continue to look with their eyes for their lost one. Nothing of them moves

apart from their eyes, which move about without respite in all directions.

4. Non-searchers, the vanquished.

Those who are permanently motionless or have been for a long time are called the sedentaries. The junction of the criterion of the imperative (seek) and the criterion of movement radically distinguishes the two figures at the extremities, that is, on the one hand, the totally nomadic living, and, on the other, the vanquished. Between these two figures, there is partial and total sedentariness.

The principle underlying this distribution of figures is the following: from the moment that the law of desire is the search for the other, this search can never be interrupted, except in the approximation of death that is irreversibility. The moment that one gives up on one's desire it is *for good*. The one who stops getting around enters into a state of sedentarization, then into the figure of the vanquished.

This is so if one takes things from the side of life, from the side of the imperative to search for the lost one. For, taking things from the other side, that of sedentariness, there exist many possibilities, ranging from partial to total motionlessness. More, and herein is contained all of Beckett's paradoxical optimism, there can even come about this miracle: the return (rare, almost never, but there are some cases) of one of the vanquished to the arena of the search. There is a twist in the set-up here: giving up on the imperative is irreversible, but the result (or the punishment) of this defeat, which is apathetic motionlessness, is not irreversible. And again: irreversibility is a law of decision, of the moment – it does not regulate a state of affairs. Grasped in its consequences, in its figures, and not in its pure moment, irreversibility is not irreversible.

The maxims of the subject can therefore be stated thus: to give up is irreversible, but there exists all the possibilities even when nothing is there to attest to them, internal to the figures of sedentariness. Beckett said so in an extraordinarily concise passage, very abstract and very profound concerning the link between an imperative and the field of possibles in which the imperative is carried out: 'in the cylinder what little is possible is not so it is merely not longer so and in the least less the all of nothing if this notion is maintained'.

CONDITIONS

The least failure is total (since less = nothing), but no possible is eliminated (since not-possible = provisionally no longer possible).

The ethics of the cylinder knows no *eternal* damnation, but nor any adaptation to the imperative of the Other. A figure of the subject is that which *distributes* the two variants of this ethics.

In *How It Is* the description of the figures of the subject accords with a different fictional montage, a montage that will take us closer to the crucial problem of the Two.

Beckett did, of course, maintain that there exist four major figures. There are always four figures, one cannot get outside of these four, the problem is to know which are *nameable*.

A passing remark: no doubt you are aware of Lacan's thesis about what can be said of the truth. A truth is not able to be said in full; it can only be half-said (*mi-dite*). The portion of truth Beckett stated can be said regarding the truth of subjective figures is a little different. Because only three of the four figures can be named, in this matter the saying of truth is increased to three-quarters: 'of the three quarters of our total life only three lend themselves to communication'.

The four figural postures of the subject in *How It Is* are the following:

1. Wander in the dark with a bag.
2. Meet someone in the active position, come down on top of him in the dark. This is the position of the so-called 'executioner'.
3. Be abandoned motionless in the dark by the one encountered.
4. Be encountered by someone in the passive position (this someone comes down on top of you while you are motionless in the dark. This is the position called 'victim'. It is this fourth figure that the voice does not contrive to say, which leads to the axiom of three-quarters concerning the relation between truth and speech.

Such are the generic figures of everything that can befall a member of humanity. It is important to note that these figures are egalitarian. There is no particular hierarchy in this apparatus, nothing that might indicate that such or such of the four figures must be desired, preferred or distributed in a fashion different to the others. The words 'executioner' and 'victim' should not mislead us on this matter. Besides, Beckett took care to inform us that there is something exaggerated in these conventional denominations, something falsely pathetic. We shall see, moreover, that the position of the victim, like that of the executioner, designates everything that by way of happiness may exist in life. No, the figures are only the generic avatars of existence, they are equal to one another and this intrinsic equality of destiny legitimates the following remarkable statement: 'In any case, one is within justice, I have never heard said the contrary'? The justice mentioned here, which is a judgement on collective being, obviously is not related to any sort of finality. It uniquely concerns the intrinsic ontological equality of the figures of the subject.

In this typology, we are nevertheless able to group together, on the one hand, the figures of solitude and, on the other, the figures of the Two.

The figures of the Two are the executioner and the victim, postures that follow a chance encounter in the dark, and that are tied together in the extortion of speech, in the violent incitement of a narrative. This is 'life in stoic love'.

The two figures of solitude are: wander in the dark with one's bag; and be motionless because one has been abandoned.

The bag is very important. In fact, it lends weight to the best proof I know of the existence of God: every traveller finds his bag, more or less filled with tins of conserve, and God is the best hypothesis as to why this is so; all the others – Beckett drew up the list – are extraordinarily complicated.

Let us note that travel and motionlessness, as the two figures of solitude, are the results of a separation. Travel is that of a victim who abandons his executioner, and motionlessness in the dark that of an abandoned executioner. It is clear that these figures are sexuated, but only implicitly. Beckett did not state the words 'man' and 'woman', precisely because they all too easily lead back to a structural, permanent Two. Well, the Two of the victim and the executioner, of their travels and motionlessness, suspended from the chance of the encounter, do not fulfil any pre-existing duality.

Actually, the figures of solitude are sexuated by means of two great existential theorems whose self-evidence is woven together in *How It Is*:

- first theorem: only a woman travels;
- second theorem: whoever is motionless in the dark is a man.

I shall leave these theorems for your mediation. What must be clearly seen is that this doctrine of the sexes, which states that a woman is *defined by* wandering, and that, if you encounter a motionless mortal in the dark, it is necessarily a man, is that this sexuation is, therefore, in no way empirical or biological. The sexes are distributed *as results* on the basis of an encounter in which the active position, said 'of the executioner', and the passive position, said 'of the victim', are tied together in 'stoical love'. The sexes *emerge* when a mortal crawling in the dark encounters another mortal who is, like everyone else, also crawling in the dark with a bag full of tins of conserve. Obviously, the number of tins slowly shrinks, but one day one will find another bag: God sees to it that we do not cease to crawl.

But neither do the active position and the passive position provide the final word on sexuation. In order to get to the bottom of it, it is necessary to examine Beckett's final thought in itself, which establishes the power of the Two as truth.

7. LOVE AND ITS NUMERICITY: ONE, TWO, INFINITY

One point remains the unchanged throughout all the variations of the tale in Beckett: love is inaugurated in the pure encounter, nothing destines it but the chance of two trajectories. Before this chance, there is nothing but solitudes. No Two pre-exists the encounter, in particular no duality of the sexes. To the extent the duality of the sexes is thinkable, it is so only from the vantage point of the encounter, in the process of love, without it being possible to presuppose that the encounter was conditioned or oriented by any prior difference. The encounter is the originary power of the Two, and so of love, and this power that nothing precedes in its own order is practically unparalleled. In particular, it is neither commensurable with sentiment nor with the sexual and desiring power of the body. The encounter's immeasurable excess is asserted already in the 1930s in *Murphy*: 'To meet [. . .] in my sense exceeds the power of feelings, however tender, and of bodily motions, however expert'.

Beckett would never reduce love to those mixtures of sentimentality and sexuality that opinion confects together in this word. Love *in truth* (and not in opinion) depends on a pure event, an encounter whose force radically exceeds both sentimentality and sexuality.

The encounter is founding of the Two as such. In the figure of love, as it originates in the encounter, the Two unexpectedly arrives, including the Two of the sexes or of sexuated figures. Love is in no way (such is its romantic version, which Beckett did not tire of ridiculing) that which makes One from a prior Two, love never being a fusion nor an effusion. It is a condition, often laborious, of the Two's being able to exist as Two. For example, in *Malone Dies*, when Malone contrives the encounter between Macmann and his guardian, Moll, we get an admirable tale of love, of a love that, as the love of elderly persons, or of dying persons, takes on an extraordinary lyrical intensity. Malone comments upon the truth effects of this love thus: 'But on the long road to this what flutterings, alarms, and blackful fumblings, of which only this, that they gave Macmann some insight into the meaning of the expression, Two is company'.

The Two inaugurated by the encounter, whose truth is effectuated by love, does not remain self-enclosed. It is a passage, a pivotal point, *the first numericity*. The Two creates a passage, or authorizes the pass, between the One of solipsism, which is the initial fact, and the infinite of being and of experience. The Two of love is a hazardous mediation for alterity in general. It is inductive of a rupture or of an effraction of the One of the cogito, but by this very means it cannot keep to itself, and so opens out onto the limitless multiple of Being. We may also say that the Two of love brings forth the advent of the sensible. Where there was nothing but the black–grey of being, the sensible inflection of the world comes to establish itself, within the effect of the truth of the Two. Yet, the sensible and the infinite are identical, since the infinity of the world is, along with the One of the cogito, the *other logical thesis*. Between these two presentative positions, the Two of love is a force of effraction and constitution.

Indeed, that the One and the Infinite are the two coherent theses of ontology is an axiom of *How It Is*. The protagonist, who crawls in the dark, says indeed: 'in simple words I quote on either I am alone and no further problem or else we are innumerable and no further problem either'.

But the Two of love establishes the sensible version of this abstract axiom, which jointly validates the thesis of the One and the thesis of the Infinite. Love releases beauty, nuance, colour. It releases what could be called the nocturnal other, the second nocturne, which is not that of the black–grey of being, but of the rustling night, of the night of leaves and plants, of the night of stars and of water. On the very strict conditions of hard work and the encounter, the Two of love effectuates the scission of the black into, on the one hand, the black–grey of being, and, on the other, the infinitely varied black of the sensible.

And this is why in Beckett's prose we come across those unexpected poems in which, under the sign of the founding figure of the Two, something is unfurled in the night of presentation, an unfolding of the multiple as such. Above all else that is what love is: a giving of permission to the multiple, under the threat, never abolished, of the black–grey in which an original One sustains the torture of its identification.

Here I want to cite three of these implicit poems of prose, to make that other Beckett heard, a Beckett of the giving and the happiness of being.

The first is from *Krapp's Last Tape*; it is the moment when the dying man, who is the play's protagonist, launches into interminable operations of anamnesis (he is listening to recordings of his own voice from each different period of his life), has himself return to the central moment, that in which the Two of love has burst open the multiple:

> upper lake, with the punt, bathed of the bank, then pushed out into the stream and drifted. She lay stretched out on the floorboards with her hands under her head and her eyes closed. Sun blazing down, bit of a breeze, water nice and lively. I noticed a scratch on her thigh and asked her how she came by it. Picking gooseberries, she said. I said again I thought it was hopeless and no good going on and she agreed, without opening her eyes. I asked her to look at me and after a few moments – after a few moment she did, but the eyes just slits, because of the glare. I bent over her to get them in the shadows and they opened. Let me in. We drifted in among the flags and stuck. They way they went down, sighing, before the stem! I lay down across her with my face in her breasts and my hand on her. We lay there without moving. But under us all moved, and moved us, gently, up and down, and from side to side.
>
> Past midnight. Never knew such silence.

This, as you see, is the poem the opening onto waters, the multiple of the absolute moment, the one in which love, even when in the statement of its end, suggests the infinite of the sensible.

The second quote is taken from *Enough*. This short text is wholly devoted to love. In it precise connections are established between love and infinite knowledge. The two lovers, walking along bent over in a world of flower-covered hills, are never so close as when they are speaking about mathematics or astronomy:

> His talk was seldom of geodesy. But we must have covered several time the equivalent of the terrestrial equator. At an average speed of three miles per day and night. We took flight in arithmetic. What mental calculations bent double hand in hand! While ternary numbers we raised in this way to the third power sometimes in downpours of rain. Graving themselves in his memory as best they could the ensuing cubes accumulated. In view of the converse operation at a later stage. When time would have done its work.

And next we have another very beautiful passage, also from *Enough*, in which the beloved man becomes that instance of knowledge in which the sky is given in its own order:

> On a gradient of one in one his head swept the ground. To what this taste was due I cannot say. To love of the earth and the flower' thousand scents and hues. Or to cruder imperatives of an anatomical order. He never raised the question. The crest once reached alas the going down again.

> I order from time to time to enjoy the sky he resorted to a little round mirror.

> Having misted it with his breath and polished it on his calf he looked in it for the constellations. I have it! He exclaimed referring to the Lyre or the Swan. And often he added that the sky seemed much the same.

Love is when we can say that it is we that have the sky, and the sky seems much the same. The multiple of Constellations is held together, then, in the opening of the Two.

The last poem comes from *Company*, and is probably the one that is most tied to the metaphor of a division of the dark, of the advent of a second nocturne:

> You are on your back at the foot of an aspen. In its trembling shade. She at right angles propped up on her elbows head between her hands. Your eyes opened and closed have looked in hers looking in yours. In your dark you look in them again. Still. You feel on your face the fringe of her long black hair stirring in the still air. Within the

tent of hair your faces are hidden from view. She murmurs, Listen to the leaves. Eyes in each other's eyes you listen to the leaves. In their trembling shade.

These are citations on the Two of love as the passage from the One of solipsism to the multiple infinite of the world, and nocturnal re-splitting of the black–grey of being.

But in them there is further a weaving of the Two, an insistence as fidelity. In Beckett's work this fidelity organizes four functions, which are also figures of the subject *in* love, and which are, I maintain (though without being able to establish it here), the functions that organize of every generic procedure, of the duration of love, naturally, but also of scientific accumulation, of artistic innovation and of political tenacity.

The first of these functions is wandering, travel, with or without the aid of a bag, the voyage in the dark, which presents the infinite chance of the faithful trajectory of love, the crossing without stopping point that it creates in a world henceforth *exposed* to the encounter's effects. This function of wandering, which *How It Is* gave us an abstract variant of, is also the continuous walking of the lovers through flowers and through the hills in *Enough*. It inaugurates the duration of the Two; it founds a time subject to the injunction of chance.

The second function is inverse; it is the function of motionlessness, which stands in guard, holds, confines the fixed point of the initial naming, the naming of the event–encounter, which we saw pinned the 'incident' to its absence of signification, and establishes its supernumerary aspect for ever in a name. That is the mad (*insensé*) 'I love you', 'we love each other' or whatever takes its stead, and which, in each of its occurrences, is always pronounced for the first time. This motionlessness is that of the second nocturne, that of the punt caught in the flags, that of gazes that let in the eyes of the other.

The third is the function of the imperative: always go on, even in separation, and prescribe that separation itself is a mode of continuation. The imperative of the Two here takes over from that of the soliloquy (*I must go on, I'll go on*), but takes away from it the futile torture; it commands a rigorous law of happiness, whether one is a victim or an executioner.

The fourth is the function of narrative, which, from the vantage point of the two, releases the latent infinity of the world, recounts its improbable unfolding, writes as it goes along, in a kind of archiving that escorts the wandering, everything that is uncovered in what Beckett refers to as '*the blessed days of blue*'.

Love (but also all the other generic procedures, despite being in different orders), weaves in its singular duration these four functions: wandering, motionlessness, imperative and narrative.

Now, for the sexes: Beckett constructed the Idea of the two sexes in the evental hypothesis of love by combining these four functions. He thereby determined the masculine and feminine polarities of the Two independently of any empirical or biological sexuation.

The masculine polarity combines the function of motionlessness and the function of imperative. To be a man is to remain motionless in love guarding the founding name, and prescribing a law of continuation. But since the tale function is missing, this prescriptive motionlessness is silent. A man, in love, is the silent guardian of the name. And as the function of wandering is also missing, to be a man in love is also to do nothing that attests to that love, it means keeping, motionless in the dark, to its powerful abstract conviction.

The feminine polarity combines wandering and the tale. It does not accord with the fixity of the name, but with the infinity of its unfolding in the world, with the tale of its interminable glory. It does not make do with the sole prescription without proof; it organizes a constant enquiry, the verification of a power. To be woman, in love is to move under a guarding of sense, rather than of the name. And this guarding involves the errant chance of enquires, at the same time as its continual deposition in a tale.

Love exists as a determination of this polarity, *supporting* the four functions, distributing them in a singular fashion, and that is why love alone compels the acknowledgement that there really exists man (motionlessness of the imperative, safekeeping of the name) and woman (wandering of a truth, consequences of the name in a speech). Without love, nothing would attest to the Two of the sexes. There would be One, then another One, and not Two. There would not be man *and* woman.

All this leads us to a crucial doctrine, which concerns all generic procedures, and which is that of their *numericity*.

In love, there is first the One of solipsism, which consists in the confrontation or the body-to-body of the cogito and the black–grey of being in the infinite repetition (*ressassement*) of speech. Then there is the

CONDITIONS

Two, which occurs in the event of the encounter and in the incalculable poem of its naming. And, last, there is the Infinite of the sensible which the Two traverses and develops, and in which it little by little deciphers a truth of the Two itself. This numericity – one, two, infinity – is specific to the amorous procedure. It can be shown that the other truth procedures, science, art and politics, have different numericities, that each numericity singularizes the type of procedure and makes clear that truths belong to totally heterogeneous registers.

The numericity of love (as one, two, infinity) is the place of what Beckett, quite rightly, called happiness. Happiness also singularizes the amorous procedure, there is only happiness in love; it is the reward specific to this type of truth. There is pleasure in art, joy in science and enthusiasm in politics, but in love there is happiness.

Gathered in a subject, joy, pleasure, enthusiasm and happiness all concern the void of being in its advent in the world. In happiness, there is the singular aspect that this void is intervallic; it is captured in the between-the-Two, in that which creates the actual character, of the two, and which is separation, the differences of the sexes as such. Happiness is not at all linked to the One, to the myth of fusion; on the contrary, it is the subjective index of a truth of difference, of the difference of the sexes, which love alone makes effective.

And, on this point, at the heart of happiness, we again come across, of course, sexuation, which is its site and stake. In happiness, man is the one who is the blind guardian of separation, of the between-two. The heroin of *Enough* will say: 'We were severed, if that is what he desired'. The masculine polarity in effect supports a desire for scission. It is not at all a desire to return to solipsism; it is a desire for the Two to manifest itself in the split of the between-two. There is some Twoness (*de Deux*) only if there is this between-two in which the void is localized as the Two's principle of being. 'Man's' desire takes on form in the void, or through the void. We might say that man desires the *nothing* of the Two. Whereas the feminine polarity desires *nothing but* the Two, that is to say the infinite tenacity, in which the Two continues as such. This instance of woman is magnificently stated at the very end of *Enough*, when in the nothing of the Two, to the void that internally affects the Two, and that is symbolically indicated by the fact that the man has gone off to die, the woman contrasts the persistence, the insistence of the 'nothing but the

Two', were it simply in its memorial tracing (*trace*), in the tale of wandering that is always re-done all over again:

> This notion of calm comes from him. Without him I would not have had it. Now I'll wipe out everything but the flowers. No more rain. No more mounds. Nothing but the two of us dragging through the flowers. Enough my old breasts feel his old hand.

Happiness is woman and man indistinctly; it is at once the separating void and the conjunction that reveals it. As happiness, as a tracing of happiness, it is the nothing of the Two and nothing but the Two, and it is its undivided sexuation – motionless and errant, imperative and narrative.

In *Ill Seen Ill Said* this happiness is all that fundamentally happens, from beginning to end. The entire beginning pivots around the word 'unhappiness', whereas the end tends towards the word 'happiness'. And what happens between the two is that if, at the start, we set out in the reign of visibility and the rigidity of seeing in the nocturnal grey (in limbo between life and death), at the end a sort of light void readies in the second nocturne. What else to do but listen to *what happens*? Here is the beginning, which to my mind is one of the most beautiful passages of our language, and which captures the brilliance of unhappiness:

> From where she lies she sees Venus rise. On. From where she lies when the skies are clear she sees Venus rise followed by the sun. Then she rails at the source of all life. On. At evening when the skies are clear she savours its star's revenge. At the other window. Rigid upright on her old chair she watches for the radiant one. Her old deal spindle-backed kitchen chair. It emerges from out of the last rays and sinking ever brighter is engulfed in its turn. On. She sits on erect and rigid in the deepening gloom. Such helplessness to move she cannot help. Heading on foot for a particular point often she freezes on the way. Unable till long after to move on not knowing wither or for what purpose. Down on her knees especially she finds it hard not to remain so forever. Hand resting on hand on some convenient support. Such as the foot of her bed. And on them her head. There then she sits as though turned to stone fact to the night. Save for the white of her hair and faintly bluish white of face and hands all is black. For an eye

having no need of light to see. All this in the present as had she the misfortune to be still of this world.

And now to the end, where the instant of happiness is reached in the very brief, laborious time of the visitation of the void:

Decision no sooner reached or rather long after than what is the wrong word? For the last time at last for to end yet again what the wrong word? Than revoked. No but slowly dispelled a little very little like the last wisps of day when the curtain closes. Of itself by slow millimetres or drawn by a phantom hand. Farewell to farewell. Then in that perfect dark foreknell darling sound pip for end begun. First last moment. Grant only enough remain to devour all. Moment by glutton moment. Sky earth the whole kit and boodle. Not another crumb of carrion left. Lick chops and basta. No. One moment more. One last. Grace to breathe that void. Know happiness.

This is also what I should like to call the writing of the generic: presenting in art the passage from the misfortune of life and of the visible to the happiness of a veridical incitement of the void. It requires the immeasurable power of the encounter; it requires the wager of a nomination; it requires the combinations of wandering and fixity, of the imperative and the tale. It requires the framing of all this in the division of the night, and, then, under rare conditions, we can again say with Beckett: 'Stony ground but not entirely'.

Notes

Preface

[1] *What is philosophy?* in collaboration with Félix Guattari, 1991 (abridged title: *WP*. References to the French editions of the works Francois Wahl cites are given in square brackets).

[2] *Being and Event*, 1998 (abridged title: *BE*); *Manifesto for Philosophy*, 1989 (abridged title: *M*).

[3] *WP*, p. 5 [10].

[4] *WP*, p. 33, 21 [36, 26].

[5] *WP*, p. 23 [28].

[6] *WP*, p. 36 [39].

[7] *WP*, p. 40 [43].

[8] *BE*, p. 13 [32].

[9] *BE*, p. 59 [72].

[10] *BE*, p. 155 [174].

[11] *BE*, p. 11.

[12] *BE*, p. 3 [9].

[13] *BE*, p. 133 [152]. Translation modified. On the concept of the ordinal, cf. also *Number and numbers, II*, 7 and 8.

[14] *WP*, p. 49 and 60 [50 and 59].

[15] *BE*, p. 113 [130].

[16] *BE*, p. 116 [116].

[17] *M*, p. 37 [18].

[18] *M*, p. 38 [19].

[19] *BE*, p. 288 [319].

[20] *BE*, p. 175 and 176 [196 and 197].

NOTES

[21] *BE*, p. 179 [200].

[22] *BE*, p. 232 [257].

[23] For a demonstration of the constant excess of subsets (inclusion of parts) over elements (belonging), or of the 'theorem of the point of excess', cf. Meditations 7, 8 and 26.

[24] *BE*, p. 85 [99].

[25] *BE*, p. 190 [212].

[26] *BE*, p. 179 [200].

[27] *WP*, p. 118 [111].

[28] *WP*, p. 118 [112].

[29] *WP*, p. 126 [120].

[30] *WP*, p. 144 and 140 [137 and 133].

[31] *BE*, Meditations 11 and 12.

[32] *BE*, p. 210 [232].

[33] *BE*, p. 209 [231].

[34] *BE*, p. 210 [232].

[35] *BE*, p. 210 [232].

[36] *BE*, p. 210 [232].

[37] *WP*, p. 152 [144].

[38] By focusing on this encounter between two definitions of philosophy that agree on a series of crucial statements, but that differ radically on the meaning to give to them, and even on the framework in which they are to be grounded, I do not mean to grant particular attention to the brief discussion Deleuze held of Badiou's work. There certainly seems to be a misunderstanding involved in it: Deleuze's reconstruction of Badiou makes it impossible to recognize him. This sort of blind spot, unusual with Deleuze, and that explains his awkwardness, obviously does not in the least prevent there from being arguments in Deleuze's books that are of crucial interest to the debate with Badiou.

[39] *BE*, p. 182 [203].

[40] *BE*, p. 206 [228].

[41] *BE*, p. 206 [229]. Cf. also *M*, p. 82 and 89 [63 and 70].

[42] *M*, p. 104 [86].

[43] *M*, p. 81 [61].

[44] *M*, p. 106 [89].

[45] *M*, p. 107 [90].

[46] *M*, p. 80 [60].

[47] *BE*, p. 341 [376].

[48] It is P.J. Cohen's construction in which Badiou sees the completion of set theory, insofar as it must renounce the 'task of systematically deploying the entire body of multiples' (p. 15 [22]) – and, for the philosopher, a resolution of the problem of indiscernibles. If, earlier, I allowed myself to paint broad brush strokes, this time I will have to get across a Maginot line in a tank.

[49] *BE*, p. 370 [406].

[50] *BE*, p. 376 [413].

[51] *BE*, p. 387 [425].

[52] *BE*, p. 6 [12].

[53] *BE*, p. 318 [353].

[54] Cf. The entire Meditation 30, 'Leibniz'.

[55] See Badiou's review of Deleuze's *The Fold*, in his *Annuaire philosophique 1988–1989*, p. 166.

[56] *WP*, p. 20 [25].

[57] *WP*, p. 153; cf. also p. 122 [pp. 144–45; cf. also p. 116].

[58] *WP*, pp. 128–129 [122].

[59] *Annuaire*, p. 167.

[60] *BE*, p. 392 [430].

[61] *BE*, p. 391 [429].

[62] *BE*, p. 399 [438].

[63] The formulation is Badiou's, see the *Annuaire*.

[64] *WP*, p. 211 [199].

[65] *BE*, p. 417 [457].

[66] *BE*, p. 401 [440]. The concept of 'forcing' is borrowed from the second version of the construction from Cohen; it permits the mathematician to connect the indiscernible and the undecidable in demonstrating the errancy of the quantitative excess; and the philosopher to found the ontological possibility of the subject.

[67] *BE*, p. 416 [455].

[68] *BE*, pp. 408–409 [446–447].

[69] *BE*, p. 423 [463].

[70] *BE*, pp. 419–420 [459].

[71] *BE*, p. 410 [449].

[72] *BE*, p. 410 [449].

[73] *BE*, p. 430 [470].

[74] *BE*, p. 429 [469].

[75] Différence et Répétition, p. 286 sq.

[76] Cf. *Manifesto*, Chapter 6.

[77] *M*, p. 103 [85].

[78] Cf. *Le Nombre et les nombres*, Introduction [abridged title: *Nn*].

[79] Cf. *Nn*, I, the chapters devoted to Dedekind and Cantor; and II, Chapter IX.

[80] This, as ought to be known, is the title of a book published in 1985, *Can Politics be Thought?*, in which almost all of Badiou's instruments for thinking this field were already present, apart from their articulation within an ontology of the multiple.

[81] Badiou has further occasion to reprise this argument with Lacan in the essay on *Philosophy and Psychoanalysis*.

[82] This expression is Badiou's in a commentary on Lacan.

[83] Cf. In *Le Nombre et les nombres, I*, what Badiou raises as being a pre-orientation and stumbling block, particularly in Frege and Dedekind.

[84] On the operators of philosophy even the *Manifesto* (pp. 35–36 [17–18]) remains elliptical: philosophy 'seeks to gather together all the additional names', it 'configures a place for truths', 'it configures the generic procedures, in a reception, a shelter, edified with regard to their disparate simultaneity'.

[85] *M*, p. 16 [36].

[86] *BE*, p. 523 [549].

[87] *BE*, p. 8 [14].

[88] *Encore: The Seminar of Jacques Lacan. Book 20. On Feminine Sexuality; the limits of love and knowledge, 1972–1973*. Edited by Jacques-Alain Miller. Translated with Notes by Bruce Fink. New York and London: W.W. Norton & Company, 1998, p. 103.

[89] In the lines to follow, I base myself on my correspondence with Alain Badiou during the summer of 1991, naturally with his consent.

[90] *BE*, pp. 428–429 [468–469].

[91] Translator's note: I here follow Bruce Fink (cf. *Écrits: The First Complete Edition in English*, p. 783) who translates Lacan's use of the French verb *scander* with the neologism 'to scand'. The French verb *scander*, which this renders, is the verb form of scansion (the metrical scanning of verse; the division of verse into metrical feet; an example of this), and is usually translated as 'to scan'. But it important here to distinguish the more common contemporary uses of this verb (to look over rapidly, to run through a list quickly, to cause an object or image to be

systematically traversed by a beam or detector, etc.), from Lacan's idea
here of cutting, punctuating or interrupting something.

92 *Écrits, The First Complete Edition in English.* Trans. Bruce Fink, in collaboration with Héloïse Fink and Russell Grigg. New York and London: W.W Norton & Company, 2002, p. 307 [367] ('On a Purpose').

93 *L'Envers de la psychanalyse*, p. 58.

94 Ibid., p. 69.

95 Ibid., pp. 75–77.

96 Here we encounter the question Claude Imbert raises in her *Phénoménologies et Langues Formulaires*, namely that of an inaugural, insurmountable *disjunction* between formal and categorial logic, of a disjunction between two logics supported by two different syntaxes that are, respectively, and *exclusively*, that of mathematics and that of experience. It is tempting to say that one corresponds to the signifying chain and the other to the *a*, as object and cause – and so to what Badiou refers to as Lacan's 'linear doctrine'. In using both logics haphazardly – let the reader consult *Logique du fantasme* and *Encore* – Lacan seems for once not to have noticed what resided in there of the impossible. Badiou shelters himself further from objection, insofar as his discourse limits itself to considering what can be *thought* – which he posits is only mathematical – of existence.

CHAPTER ONE

This text has composite origins, which I have re-worked here to make it almost new. It initially developed from a talk given in Italy in the spring of 1990 for a colloquium organized by the philosophy department of the University of Pavia. The title then was *The End of the End*. I revised that version for a paper I was to give at a conference in Spain, to which I had been invited by the Catalan Association *Acta*, located in Barcelona. But taking into account the nature of the audience, I opted at the last moment not to deliver this paper and gave something completely different instead. Lastly, I reworked it several more times during the first semester of my 1990–1991 Seminar at the *Collège international de philosophie* (Paris).

1 Translator's note: Badiou is referring of course to the interview in *Der Speigel*.

2 I devoted a good part of my seminar of the year 1989–1990 to examining this in Plato's works, and singularly in the *Republic* and the *Laws*. One day the question of non-academic, or active, uses of Plato must be deployed in detail. Because it is still true that every philosophical decision is a decision on, or on the basis of, Plato – something that indicates the temporal arch of philosophy that makes us contemporaries of the Greeks.

3 In *Being and Event,* trans. Oliver Feltham (London: Continuum Press, 2006 [*l'Être et l'événement*, Paris: Seuil, 1998]) the void is conceived as a suture of the situation to its being *qua* being, or as the joining of the multiple to its own inconsistency. I also claim that the 'void' is called the 'proper name of being'. The matheme of this naming is the theory (or the deducible properties) of the empty set as it is given in the existential consignment (*envoi*) of set theory. If need be, the reader might want to consult meditations 4 and 6 of *Being and Event* to complete the clarificatory remarks given in the preface by Francois Wahl.

4 These formal borrowings from science and art, which only concern philosophical construction, that is, the fictional structure of philosophy, should not be confounded with the status of art and science as *conditions* of philosophy. Because, in a second sense, art and science are not reservoirs of forms, but sites of thinking. And what they initiate is not a construction bound in the resources of fiction; it is the philosophical *act* as an act of second thought.

5 On the modalities of the subtractive, the reader can consult the essays in this book entitled 'Definition of Philosophy' and 'On Subtraction'.

6 That Nietzsche is referred to as a sophist here might give cause for surprise. Nevertheless, it is fair to say that in his work the critique of philosophy and of Truth, the theory of the sign, the genealogical argumentation, the function of etymology, the recourse to life and power, the rhetoric of parables and metaphors, the fury to persuade, the conceptual psychology, the polemical exposition, the fragmentary – that all this simultaneously paves the way for the suture of philosophy to the poem and for a radical confusion between philosophy and sophistry. The greatness of Nietzsche's endeavour makes him what one might call the Prince (seeing 'principle' in Prince) of modern sophistry. Seeing things in this way sheds a completely different light on the key question of the relationship between Nietzsche and Heidegger. Heidegger wanted to maintain a suture to the poem and re-delimit

philosophy from sophistry. It is in this paradoxical element, in which he reworked sophistic operations in a philosophizing way, that Heidegger came to situate Nietzsche at the terminal edge of metaphysics, which is in my view an untenable but symptomatic argument. In this collection I had intended to include an essay on Nietzsche entitled precisely *The Mad Prince*, dealing with the limit of the furious Nietzschean trajectory between spring 1988 and January 1889. In this essay, the thesis I put forward is that Nietzsche was the supreme sophist – but this essay remains unfinished, since it has not yet been submitted to the test, which is always crucial for me, of its public or oral exposition.

[7] On this point, the reader might want to consult the essay in this book entitled 'Philosophy and Politics'.

CHAPTER TWO

In this text I develop the definition of philosophy given in the preceding text. The text was written for, and distributed to, the attendees of my seminar of Spring 1991.

[1] For more on the modalities of the subtractive, the reader can consult the 'gamma schema', which is reproduced in the essay entitled 'On Subtraction'.

CHAPTER THREE

With some minor touch-ups, this text is the same given as a paper at a colloquium in 1989, through which the *Collège international de philosophie* later emerged. Today, due to constant reforms and the the aporias of what we call 'Europe', the question of institutions has come to impassion a good many philosophers. I would not say it impassions me but, since the injunction exists, I shall uphold it and propose a concept of it.

[1] Translator's note: PTT is the abbreviation of *Poster, Téléphone et Télécommunications* the state service coordinating delivery and maintenance of these services.

[2] Translator's note: '*maison de passe*' is literally a 'house of passage', a house to which prostitutes can take clients. I left it in the French because of the other, more spiritual connotations a house of passage has in English.

CHAPTER FOUR

This text's first kernel was a written contribution, requested by Jacques Poulain, for a colloquium on Heidegger organized in 1989 by the *Collège international de philosophy*. Some further elements came from a paper delivered, at the invitation of Christian Descamps, in a seminar of philosophy devoted to 'Philosophy and Literature' at Beaubourg in 1990. Its final reorganization was the result of a lecture I gave, again in 1990, as part of a philosophy seminar in Lyon under the responsibility of Lucien Pitti. I have somewhat revised it for this publication.

[1] I first proposed the category of an 'age of poets' in *Manifesto for Philosophy* (trans. Norman Madarasz, Albany: SUNY Press, 1999/1989). I've since had occasion to develop it in the framework of Jacques Rancière's seminar at the *Collège international de philosophie*, a seminar entitled 'The politics of poets'. This text was published in spring 1992 under the title *L'Age des poètes* along with all the other contributions to this seminar (*La Politique des poètes*, Albin Michel).

[2] Cf. my essay entitled 'Mallarmé's method' in this volume.

[3] This point obviously recalls the brilliant analyses of 'conceptual personae' proposed by Deleuze and Guattari in their *What is Philosophy?*, which was published after the present essay. My distance to this analysis should all the same be noted. For me, philosophical theatricality designates that the essence of philosophy (the seizing 'in Truth') is an act. For Deleuze and Guattari, everything is as always related to movement and description: the conceptual persona is the nomad of the plane of immanence.

CHAPTER FIVE

The third section of this essay, which focuses on the speculative function of 'purity' in Mallarmé's poems, was originally a fragment of a book project entitled *La Déliaison* that I ultimately decided not to publish. The reason for abandoning the project was that I was convinced by Francois Wahl that the book's full development presupposed more wide-ranging investigations, in particular into the category theory of mathematics. I am currently pursuing this work and will one day integrate it into a book that I regard as the second volume of *Being and Event*, a work that will have to the first volume the same relation, relatively speaking, that the *Phenomenology of Spirit* has to *The Science of Logic*.

In 1989, I turned this fragment into a paper entitled *Mallarmé: Thinker and/or Poet*, which was given at Grenada University in Spain at the invitation of the French Department.

In the present collection, I wanted to give a larger glimpse of my studies on Mallarmé, because for twenty years now I have taken Mallarmé to be emblematic of the relationship between philosophy and poetry. And I was determined to give this glimpse by engaging in the materiality of singular poems, and not by means of some over-arching hermeneutical view. It also seemed to me somewhat one-sided to do this only using the poem entitled *Prose*, which, being an exemplary case of the operator of isolation, is not such a good example of the prodigious operators that Mallarmé invented.

In the end I resolved to provide a new version, which sometimes bears little change, of my analysis of his poems in *Théorie du Sujet* (Paris: Le Seuil, 1982). Ten years have gone by since the publication of this transitional book, which is at once too complex and too open to attack. The concepts developed in *Being and Event* have enabled me to clarify what was awkwardly clothed in the hope of regenerating dialectical thinking. The resultant *discrepancy* has reorganized my reading of the poems, although the basis on which they were deciphered remains the same.

Let this be an occasion for me to say once again all that I owe to Gardner Davies, who, alas, has since passed away, but without receiving the praise that his work – which has become that memorable absent of which his books are, in Mallarmé's sense, the real tomb – has deserved.

[1] Translator's note: Badiou cites many poems throughout the course of this essay, so rather than include the original French poems in the body of the text, which would have made for a rather disruptive reading experience, I have included them in the endnotes for interested readers. All translations are taken from *Stéphane Mallarmé: Collected Poems and Other Verse* (trans. by E.H. and A.M. Blackmore, Oxford: Oxford University Press, 2006). In addition, Badiou often quotes, without referencing, from various texts of *Divagations*. Translations of these come from Barbara Johnson (*Stéphane Mallarmé: Divagations*, Cambridge, MA: The Belknap Press of Harvard University Press, 2007).

> *A la nue accablante tu*
> *Basse de basalte et de laves*
> *A même les échos esclaves*
> *Par une trompe sans vertu*
>
> *Quel sépulcral naufrage*
> *(tu Le sais, écume, mais y baves)*
> *Suprême une entre les épaves*
> *Abolit le mât dévêtu*
>
> *Ou cela que furibond faute*
> *De quelque perdition haute*
> *Tout l'abîme vain éployé*
>
> *Dans le si blanc cheveu qui traîne*
> *Avarement aura noyé*
> *La flanc enfant d'une sirène*

2 Translator's note: In French this clarification is obviously important as 'tu' can also mean 'you'.

3 The theory of evental naming is established in 'Meditation 13' of *Being and Event*. The term employed is intervention, a term that refers back to what I called, in a previous book entitled *Can Politics Be Thought?* (Paris: Le Seuil, 1985), the 'interpretation-cut', a term that still remains slightly caught up in a hermeneutical orientation. It was Jean-Francois Lyotard who brought to my attention the fact that it actually involves only one *act*, that is, an act of naming.

4 There are further developments concerning the unnameable in the essays 'On Subtraction' and 'Truth: Forcing and the Unnameable'. See also the precious critical remarks given by Francois Wahl in the preface.

5

> *Ses purs ongles très hauts dédiant leur onyx,*
> *L'Angoisse ce minuit, soutient, lampadophore*
> *Maint rêve vespéral brûlé par le Phénix*
> *Que ne recueille pas de cinéraire amphore*
>
> *Sur les crédences, au salon vide: nul ptyx,*
> *Aboli bibelot d'inanité sonore,*
> *(Car le Maître est allé puiser des pleurs au Styx*
> *Avec ce seul objet dont le Néant s'honore).*

Mais proche la croisée au nord vacante, un or
Agonise selon peut-être le décor
Des licornes ruant du feu contre une nixe,

Elle, défunte nue en le miroir, encor
Que, dans l'oubli fermé par le cadre, se fixe
De scintillations sitôt le septuor.

Hyperbole! de ma mémoire
Triomphalement ne sais-tu
Te lever, aujourd'hui grimoire
Dans un livre de fer vêtu:

Car j'installe, par la science
L'hymne des cœurs spirituels
En l'œuvre de ma patience
Atlas, herbiers et rituels.

Nous promenions notre visage
(Nous fûmes deux, je le maintiens)
Sur maints charmes de paysage,
Ô sœur, y comparant les tiens.

L'ère d'autorité se trouble
Lorsque, sans nul motif, on dit
De ce midi que notre double
Inconscience approfondit

Que, sol des cent iris, son site,
Ils savent s'il a bien été
Ne porte pas de nom que cite
L'or de la trompette d'Été.

Oui, dans une île que l'air charge
De vue et non de visions
Toute fleur s'étalait plus large
Sans que nous en devisions.

Telles, immenses, que chacune
Ordinairement se para

> *D'un lucide contour, lacune*
> *Qui des jardins la sépara.*
>
> *Gloire du long désir, Idées*
> *Tout en moi s'éxaltait de voir*
> *La famille des iridées*
> *Surgir à ce nouveau devoir,*
>
> *Mais cette sœur sensée et tendre*
> *Ne porta son regard plus loin*
> *Que sourire et, comme à l'entendre*
> *J'occupe mon antique soin.*
>
> *Oh! sache l'Esprit de litige,*
> *A cette heure où nous nous taisons,*
> *Que de lie multiples la tige*
> *Grandissait trop pour nos raisons*
>
> *Et non comme pleure la rive,*
> *Quand son jeu monotone ment*
> *A vouloir que l'ampleur arrive*
> *Parmi mon jeune étonnement*
>
> *D'ouïr tout le ciel et la carte*
> *Sans fin attestés sur mes pas,*
> *Par le flot même qui s'écarte,*
> *Que ce pays n'exista pas.*
>
> *L'enfant abdique son extase*
> *Et docte déjà par chemins*
> *Elle fit le mot: Anastase!*
> *Né pour d'éternités parchemins,*
>
> *Avant qu'un sépulcre ne rie*
> *Sous aucun climat, son aïeul,*
> *De porter ce nom: Pulchérie!*
> *Caché par le trop grand glaïeul.*

[7] This is the title of Gardner Davies' last collection *Mallarmé ou 'la couche suffisante d'intelligibilité'* (Paris: José Corti, 1988). Prior to its publication, Gardner Davies wrote to me that it was an attempt to give a

'faithful' explanation of the poem called *Prose*. This is entirely correct, when it is understood that, concerning Mallarmé, such loyalty is a feat that most commentators are barely ever capable of.

[8] Here it would be necessary to engage (but I had already written this essay) in a vast and complex discussion with the detailed reading of Mallarmé given by Philippe Lacoue-Labarthe in his *Musica Ficta* (Christian Bourgois, 1991). Lacoue-Labarthe's central idea is that Mallarmé fails in the last analysis, in his rivalry with the Wagnerian project, to subtract himself from the prescription of an ontological impress, whereby art, 'grand art', remains in thrall to its metaphysical consignment. All Mallarmé would have succeeded in achieving is a radical purification of onto-typology, which reduces it to the pure 'impress' of the 'there is' of language as such.

My differend with Lacoue-Labarthe must be stated on two heterogeneous levels:

1. I fully agree that the historical assemblage that turns on the theme of 'great art' is inherently criticizable. For, to the extent that it does touch a real, this real is not of the poem, but *alone* that of a certain philosophical seizing of (German? Romantic?) art. Lacoue-Labarthe constantly (for poetry, and incidentally also for politics) folds the effectiveness of the (poetic or political) truth-procedure, as a locus of autonomous thinking, back onto the singular operators of philosophical seizing of these procedures. Yet the categorical procedures by which a poem–thought is identified *for itself* are not the same as those by which a philosophical–thought seizes them.

In preparing Mallarmé for this folding back, instead of entering into the thrust of the poems, Lacoue-Labarthe *apprehends his prose as that which yields the very essence of poetry in the form of a programme for thought.* Or again, Lacoue-Labarthe proceeds as if the prose renderings yielded the thought–programme of poems.

I believe neither that such is the relation between Mallarmé's prose and his poems, nor, more generally, that the essence of real thinking can be passed on in the form of a programme of thought.

What is thought in Mallarmé's poetry *is not*, in general, what his prose says *ought* to be thought in it. The reason being that the relation between 'thinking' and 'the thought of thought' cannot be exhausted by a programmatic announcement.

In fact (and this is my method), the *relation* must *be inverted*. It is the poems that shed light on the prose, and the effectiveness of the thought–poem of the event and of the undecidable retroactively authorizes the multi-faceted formulation of a programme. It is from thought to the thinking of thought that we go, and not the other way round. And, in this movement, there is a perceptible change of terrain. I shall state it bluntly: every programme of thought comes after thinking, and works to alter its field of exercise.

At bottom, the ultimate figure issuing from Heidegger's work, and thus from historicism, in view of which history no longer promises us anything, consists in re-programming thought, thus making the thinking of thought the destinal essence of thought.

2. Concerning the pure, purification: I do not think that the stakes here involve releasing the onto-typology of 'great art' from its mythical charge, all the while conserving its schema (in the sense that Mallarmé would be a Wagner devoid of an explicit mythology). I posit instead that the stakes of the pure are to understand how – in the pure chance of a vanished event, of a non-original facticity – the regulated effect of a singular truth can be suspended. The issue is, then, to think 'outside of relations' (*hors lien*), in the shelter opened up by the cut of a chance.

This discussion ought to be much tighter and be continued. It shall.

CHAPTER SIX

[1] Translator's note: All translations of Rimbaud's poems are taken from *Rimbaud Complete Works, Selected Letters: A Bilingual Edition*. Translated with an introduction and notes by Wallace Fowlie. Updated, revised and with a foreword by Seth Whidden (Chicago and London: The University of Chicago Press, 2005).

I have also included the original French of each poem Badiou quotes for interested readers: *L'eau Claire; comme le sel des larmes d'enfance,/ l'assaut au soleil des blancheurs des corps de femmes;/ la soie, en foule et de lys pur, des oriflammes/ sous les murs dont quelque pucelle eut la défense;/ l'ébat des anges.*

[2] *non . . . le courant d'or en marche/ meut ses bras, noirs, et lourds, et frais surtout, d'herbe. Elle/ sombre, ayant le Ciel bleu pour le ciel-de-lit, appelle/ pour rideaux l'ombre de la colline et de l'arche.*

³ *L'haleine/ des peupliers d'en haut est pour la seule brise./ Puis, c'est la nappe, sans reflets, sans source, grise:/ un vieux, dragueur, dans sa barque immobile, peine.*

⁴ *Plus pure qu'un louis, jaune et chaude paupière/ le souci d'eau – ta foi conjugale, ô l'Epouse ! – / au midi prompt, de son terne miroir´, jalouse/ au ciel gris de chaleur la Sphère rose et chère.*

⁵ *Il nous a connus tous et nous a tous aimés. Sachons, cette nuit d'hiver,/ de cap en cap, du pôle tumultueux au château, de la foule à la plage, de/ regards en regards, forces et sentiments las, le héler et le voir, et le/ renvoyer, et sous les marées et au haut des déserts de neige, suivre ses/ vues, ses souffles, son corps, son séjour.*

⁶ *Mais, saints du ciel, en haut du chêne,/ Mât perdu dans le soir charmé,/ Laissez les fauvettes de mai/ Pour ceux qu'au fond du bois enchaîné,/ Dans l'herbe d'où l'on ne peut fuir,/ La défaite sans avenir.*

⁷ *Plutôt, se garder de la justice. – La vie dure, l'abrutissement simple,–- /soulever, le poing desseché, le couvercle du cerceuil, s'asseoir,/ s'étouffer. Ainsi point de vieillesse, ni de dangers. La terreur n'est pas/ francaise.*

⁸ *Ô mes petites amoureuses/ Que je vous haïs!/ Plaquez de fouffes douloureuses/ Vos tétons laids.*

⁹ *Mais, ô Femme, monceau d'entrailles, pitié douce,/ Tu n'es jamais la sœur de charité, jamais.*

¹⁰ *Nous sommes Ouvriers, Sire! Ouvriers! Nous sommes/ Pour les grands temps nouveaux où l'on voudra savoir,/ Où l'Homme forgera du matin jusqu' au soir,/ Chasseur des grands effets, chasseur des grandes causes,/ Où, lentement vainqueur, il domptera les choses/ Et montera sur Tout, comme sur un cheval.*

¹¹ *Il n'aimait pas Dieu; mais les hommes, qu'au soir fauve,/ Noirs, en blouse, il voyait rentrer dans le faubourg/ Où les crieurs, en trois roulements de tambour,/ Font autour des édits rire et gronder les foules.*

¹² *A quatre heures du matin, l'été,/ Le sommeil d'amour dure encore./ Sous les bosquets l'aube évapore/ L'odeur de soir fêté.*

¹³ *Mais là-bas dans l'immense chantier/ Vers le soleil des Hespérides,/ En bras de chemise, les charpentiers/ Déjà s'agitent.*

¹⁴ *Ah! Pour ces Ouvriers charmants/ Sujets d'un roi de Babylone,/ Vénus! laisse un peu les Amants,/ Dont l'âme est en couronne.*

¹⁵ This time a debate should be had with the beautiful interpretation Jean-Luc Nancy proposes of the end of *A Season in Hell* in his essay *Posséder la vérité dans une âme et un corps* (in *Une pensée finie*, Galilée, 1990).

NOTES

The basic idea in it is that to 'possess truth in one body and soul' designates that 'truth' is the thing itself, or – and I quote Nancy – 'this "real" insofar as it cannot be appropriated, not even through possession'. We are to understand that the poem must deposit us on that edge (*bord*) at which its in-apparent underside (*envers*) would release us from speaking. 'Words end as they started, and as they will start: by writing beyond words, in the thing, the truth, on the other side of their writing'. And again: 'This truth *will*, by bringing me the last words, words which are always the last, liberate me from speaking'. The 'to possess', clearly, names the impropriety of words such as they ex-write (*ex-crive*) the thing itself.

Certainly Nancy confirms the epiphanic desire that one can make out on the other side of interruption. But his aim is too general. Giving the best deal to words (and to words without words, to what he terms the 'adieu of words to words'), he misses the *figures* that alone weave Rimbaud's singularity. Words are no more than an avatar (*one* of his follies). Equally decisive, and capable of justifying a re-thinking of the operations of poetry, are the workers, women, science, Christ.

Here, too, my misgiving is that the poem has been reduced to a general programme, and the second reduction of this first reduction is to a destinal and enveloping programme of thought, of which Rimbaud is in the end a (proper) name, and of which philosophy (or the impossible philosophy) is the holder.

At bottom, the disagreement bears on this: for Lacoue-Labarthe and Nancy *there is only one thinking*. I maintain, by contrast, the multiplicity and heterogeneity of sites of thinking. And I would readily suspect that it is for having excluded science (mathematics) from thinking that they make this identification, an identification in which politics is an ontology, poetry is a prose of thought and philosophy a desire for thinking. It is as though (has it always been so? Since Plato?) it turns out to be possible to think the multiplicity of thought only under the condition of the matheme.

16 *Elle est retrouvée./ Quoi? . . . L'Éternité./ C'est la mer allée/ Avec le soleil.*

17 *Si je désire une eau d'Europe, c'est la flache/ Noire et froide où vers un crépuscule embaumé/ Un enfant accroupi plein de tristesse, lâche/Un bateau frêle comme un papillon de mai.*

18 *J'aime autant, mieux même,/ Pourrir dans l'étang,/ Sous l'affreuse crème,/ Près des bois flottants.*

[19] Patrice Loraux devoted his paper in the colloquium from which this essay is drawn to the significations of the exclamatory 'ô' in Rimbaud.

[20] *Quand tu n'auras plus mes bras sous ton cou, ni mon cœur pour t'y/ reposer, ni cette bouche sur tes yeux. Parce qu'il faudra que je m'en/ aille très loin, un jour. Puis il faut que j'en aide d'autres: c'est mon/ devoir. Quoique ce ne soit guère ragoûtant . . . , chère âme . . .*

[21] *Ah! La poudre des saules qu'une aile secoue! / Les roses des roseaux dès long-temps dévorées ! / Mon canot, toujours fixe; et sa chaîne tirée/ Au fond de cet œil d'eau sans bords, – à quelle boue?*

[22] *Jouet de cet oeil d'eau morne, je n'y puis prendre,/ ô ! canot immobile! Oh! bras trop courts! ni l'une / ni l'autre fleur: ni la jaune qui m'importune,/ là; ni la bleue, amie à l'eau couleur de cendre.*

[23] Jacques Rancière developed this point in his paper at the colloquium.

[24] *Commerçant! colon! Médium!/ Ta rime soufra, rose ou blanche,/ Comme un rayon de sodium,/ Comme un caoutchouc qui s'épanche.*

[25] *Oh! la science! [. . .] Et les divertissements des princes et les jeux qu'ils/ interdi-saient! Géographie, cosmographie, mécanique, chimie! . . . La / science, la nouvelle noblesse! Le progrès. Le monde marche!/ Pourquoi ne tournerait-il pas? C'est la vision des nombres.*

[26] *Mon esprit, prends garde. Pas de partis de saluts violents. Exerce-toi!/ – Ah! la science ne va pas assez vite pour nous!*

[27] *J'ai tant fait patience / Qu'à jamais j'oublie;/ Craintes et souffrances/ Aux cieux sont parties.*

[28] *Qu'on patiente et qu'on s'ennuie/ C'est trop simple. Fi de mes peines./ Je veux que l'été dramatique/ Me lie à son char de fortune.*

CHAPTER SEVEN

This text is the outcome of a paper given at a colloquium jointly organized by the *Collège international de philosophie* and the University of Paris VIII in 1989. It has also been published in a volume entitled *Lieux and Transformations de la philosophie*, which gathers the proceedings of the colloquium (Presses universitaires de Vincennes, 1991).

[1] The current state of the relation between philosophy and mathematics is dominated by three tendencies:

- – The logical and grammatical analysis of statements, for which the ultimate stake of philosophy involves discriminating between meaningful and meaningless statements. Mathematics, or rather formal logic, serves as its paradigm (as the example of a 'well-formed language').

– The epistemological study of concepts, most often grasped in terms of their history, with a pre-eminent role granted to original mathematical texts. Philosophy here is a sort of latent guide for a genealogy of the sciences.

– Commentaries of current 'results', using analogical generalizations whose categories are borrowed from classical philosophemes.

In neither of these three cases is philosophy *as such* put under the conditions of mathematical eventality.

I see four French philosophers as having set themselves apart from these tendencies: Jean Cavaillès, Albert Lautmann, Jean-Toussaint Desanti and myself. Although operating from very different viewpoints, and on 'discontinuous' philosophical ground, these four authors have pursued intellectual endeavours that treat mathematics neither as a model language nor as an (historical and epistemological) object, nor as a matrix for 'structural' generalizations, but as a singular site of thinking, the procedures and the events of which must be re-traced *within* the philosophical act.

[2] Plato, *Republic*, Book VI, 511, c–d. From the translation by the author.

[3] *Hegel's Science of Logic*, trans. A.V. Miller (Alantic Highlands, NJ: Humanities Press, 1989), Vol. 1, Book 1, Section 2, Chapter 2, (c), pp. 241–3.

[4] Ibid., p. 240.

[5] Ibid., p. 242. Translation modified.

CHAPTER EIGHT

This paper was presented in 1991, at the invitation of the board of directors of the *École de la Cause freudienne*, in the lecture hall of that institution. It was published in the journal *Actes* – whose subtitle is *Revue de l'École de la Cause freudienne* – at the end of 1991. It has also appeared in the Italian translation in the journal *Agalma*, published in Rome.

CHAPTER NINE

This essay was originally delivered in Montpellier in autumn 1991 at the invitation of the Department of Psychonalysis of the Paul-Valéry University, chaired by Henri Rey-Flaud.

CHAPTER TEN

This text has complex origins and is a reorganization of materials that initially had completely distinct aims.

The core of the text comes from a paper given in Strasbourg at the start of 1991, in the framework of a seminar organized by Jean-Jacques Forté and Georges Leyenberger. This essay was published along with the other interventions of the seminar in a book entitled *Politique et Modernité* (Paris: Osiris, 1992).

However, wanting to give a more comprehensive argument, I included some short developments resulting from my contribution to the colloquium on the oeuvre of Louis Althusser, which, on Sylvain Lazarus' initiative, was organized at the University of Paris VIII in spring 1991. Then, together with this complex, I articulated some ideas on right whose own origins are various. In effect, they developed out of a text requested by Jean-Christophe Bailly and Jean-Luc Nancy for the first issue of a journal *Alea*, which ultimately remained unpublished. However, displaced and re-grounded, this text found its way into a small essay called *D'un désastre obscur*, published in autumn 1991 in a collection edited by Denis Guenoun at *éditions de l'Aube*. It was translated into English as 'Of an Obscure Disaster' trans. by Barbara P. Fulks, *Lacanian Ink*, no. 22, 2004.

That said, the substantial part of this text is unpublished, and it seems to me in its ensemble to provide coherent perspectives on what mattered to me here: to think the link between philosophy and politics in the act of a desuturing, and in respecting the conviction that, from where I stand, politics *as such* is a site of thought independent of philosophy.

[1]   Cf. *La Fiction du politique* (Paris: Christian Bourgois, 1990). Translated in English as *Heidegger, Art, and Politics: The Fiction of the Political*, trans. Chris Turner (Oxford: Blackwell, 1990).

[2]   On this point the reader should consult the interpretation of the encounter between Celan and Heidegger proposed by Lacoue-Labarthe in *Poetry as Experience*, trans. Andrea Tarnowski (Stanford: Stanford University Press 1999/1986). I have sketched a different interpretation in *Manifesto for Philosophy*, trans. Norman Madarasz (Albany: SUNY Press, 1999/1989).

[3]   Maurice Blanchot, *The Unavowable Community*, trans. Pierre Joris (New York: Station Hill Press, 1988/1984).

4 Giorgio Agamben, *The Coming Community*, trans. Michael Hardt (Minneapolis: University of Minnesota Press, 1993/1991).
5 Full recognition of this point is far from being commonly accepted. We owe to Sylvain Lazarus, for the most part, the categorical elaboration authorizing politics to be considered as a form of immanent thought, or thought in interiority, *without confusing it with 'political philosophy'*. It is thanks to him that we know that there is a singular thought of Saint-Just, a thinking pertaining to an effective modality of politics, and that can in no way be identified by its 'Rousseauist' sources. Similarly, we can think Lenin's thought completely other than as a consequence of Marxism. However little Lazarus' doctrine has been disseminated, not to mention 'written', to this day, it should be impossible in the long-run to avoid all consideration of someone who has foregrounded – by forging the categories for this identification – politics as the site of a singular thinking, on the same footing, although absolutely irreducible to them, as art and science, and intransitive to philosophy. The available writings of Sylvain Lazarus are: *Peut-on penser la politique en intériorité?*, Ed. des Conférences du Perroquet, 1986; *La Catégorie de révolution dans la révolution francaise*, ibid., 1989; *Lénine et le Temps*, ibid., 1990; and *L'Anthropologie du Nom* (Anthropology of the Name) (Paris: Editions du Seuil, 1996).
6 The tension, the 'uncoupling', internal to a procedure of political thought as to every other generic procedure, between thought and the thought of thought, is one of the fundamental theses in Sylvain Lazarus' *L'Anthropologie du Nom* (cf. the previous note).
7 The numericity of a generic procedure is the 'ciphering' of its relation to the disposition of the void (ontological figure), of the One (figure of the count *and* of the event), and of the infinite (figure of the total situation *and* of truth). Each type of generic procedure admits of a particular numericity. Further on, in the essay entitled 'What Is Love?' the reader will come across the numericity of the amorous procedure, and that is: one, two, infinity. There can be no question of establishing it here, but I should like to say that the numericity of the political procedure is: Infinity-1 (the situation), Infinity-2 (the State), an ordinal (that fixes 'eventally' the excess of Infinity-2 over Infinity-1) and the One (that is the number of equality). You will see that politics starts at the point where love finishes, but also that love begins at the point where politics finishes.

8 On the unnameable cf. note 17. Every type of generic procedure admits a specific unnameable. Thus, the unnameable specific to love is sexual enjoyment; that of politics is the collective; that of the poem is language; that of mathematics is consistency.

9 Nevertheless, one will give recognition to philosophy as a power that provides an 'indirect service' to generic procedures in general and to politics in particular. In stating the 'there is' of truths, philosophy establishes a thinking that *turns* people's minds towards their existence, and shows the conditions on the basis of which thought can be contemporary to its time *without reneging on eternity*. Philosophy is in no way a politics, but it is a form of *propaganda for politics*, inasmuch as it designates its effectiveness as the non-temporal value of that time.

10 The reader again encounters here the categories of disaster such as they were formally presented in the first text of the book. But I have let the apparent repetition stand, since on this occasion ecstasy (of the site), sacredness (of the name) and terror (of having-to-be) are considered in terms of their specific appropriation by *a* specific truth procedure: politics.

11 Translator's note: the *PCF* is the French Communist Party.

12 The precarious and sequential dimension of politics, that is, its rareness, is a crucial consequence of its only existing as thought, or as a report of the configuration to its thinking. These are the founding themes of Lazarus' theory. In 1982, in *Théorie du Sujet* Paris (Editions du Seuil), I provided the properly philosophical version of this point in: Every subject is political. That is why there is little of the subject and little of politics. Today, I should not say that 'every subject is political', which is a maxim of suture. I should rather say: 'Every subject is induced through a generic procedure, and therefore depends upon an event. As a result, the subject is rare'.

13 The ontology of the State is presented (under the name of state of the situation) in meditations 7, 8 and 9 of *Being and Event*, trans. Oliver Feltham (New York: Continuum, 2005/1998). The State (in its politico-historical sense) is analysed as an example of this figure of being. The central point is that the state of a situation (its re-presentation) is in excess over the situation (over its presentation). Here 'excess' is a rigorous concept. See also François Wahl's preface.

[14] The specificity of Cantor's invention, its radicality, which he himself found fearsome, is not to have mathematized the infinite, but to have pluralized it, and therefore unequalized it. That there are different infinities (and this goes well and truly beyond the 'dialectical' opposition between the discrete and the continuous) obviously presupposes that it is possible to make sense of the equality of two infinites. This is indeed what the impetus of pluralization consists in: two infinite sets are equal (i.e., have the same power) if there exists between them a bi-univocal correspondence. They are unequal if such a correspondence does not exist. It will be seen that it is equality here that, for its existence, refers to an existence, and inequality to a negation of existence. Hence also the function of proof by contradiction. Since there are no positive ways to demonstrate an inexistence. Existence must first be posited and then a contradiction deduced from it. This link between equality, existence and proof by contradiction forms the matrix underlying all philosophical thinking on emancipation: to show that a philosophically adverse politics is absurd, one must first suppose that it bears equality, and then show that this leads to a formal contradiction. There is no better way of doing it than to underscore that equality is not a programme, *but an axiom* – as Jacques Rancière has done *with great talent* in *The Ignorant Schoolmaster,* trans. with an introduction by Kristin Ross (Stanford: Stanford University Press, 1991/1987).

[15] A debate with Jean-Claude Milner needs to be had on this point. In his *Les Noms indistincts* (Le Seuil, 1985), he argues with particular elegance that politics essentially revolves around the word 'freedom' in its dimensions of the real (the 'unauthorized' [*sauvage*] freedom of revolutions), the imaginary (that captures the links that glue together a 'political vision of the world') and the symbolic (formal freedoms). To be sure, Milner considers it preferable to defend firmly the latter by contrast to the 'chance' of the first and the 'abjection' of the second. However, in his more recent work, Milner seems to have had to revive the theme of possible correlation between thought and rebellion, by a means that, in touching on the infinite, cannot be subordinated to the symbolic 'touché' alone. And that implies one needs to go beyond the homonyms of freedom. Is it under the mark of equality that the maximum of rebellion is axiomatically (accord) with a maximum of thought? In his most recent work (*Constat*, Paris: Verdier, 1992) Milner

concludes on a self-enclosed pessimism, not allowing any decision to be made. The debate shall continue.

16 On the 'generic' as the predicate of truth, the reader may consult Francois Wahl's preface, as well as the essay included in this book entitled 'On Subtraction'. The complete elaboration of the concept can of course be found in *Being and Event*, trans. Oliver Feltham (London: Continuum Press, 2006 [*l'Être et l'événement*], Paris: Seuil, 1998).

17 On this point, which is central to Jean-Luc Nancy's current mediation, I would like to mention the magnificent text entitled 'Le Coeur des choses' [the Heart of Things] in *Une Pensée Finie*, 1990. The proximity between this and what I call the generic is patent in expressions such as 'the thing's nondescriptness constitutes its most inherent affirmation' or 'in the heart of things there is no language'. On the other hand, I cannot concur either with his eventalization of the thing ('the event is the taking-place of the being-there of the heart of things'), which cancels ('structuralizes') the chance of the occurrence, or with the doctrine of sense to which this 'ontologization' of the event inevitably leads (accordingly: 'once there is some thing, the thing and its coming are liable to sense.') For me, the event cannot (not without hermeneutical resorption) be 'the coming to presence of the thing'. This logic remains a Hegelian logic of the historicity of presence. The essence of the event is pure disappearing, and the thing, as truth, happens to infinity *as non-sense*.

18 Lacoue-Labarthe makes the argument that Nazism was a kind of humanism in *The Fiction of the Political*.

CHAPTER ELEVEN

This essay is a reworked version of a paper I gave at a colloquium in 1990 called 'Exercice des savoirs et difference des sexes.' The colloquium took place at the *Collège international de philosophie* and was organized by Geneviève Fraisse, Monique David-Ménard and Michel Tort. The paper was at the time called 'L'amour est-il le lieu d'un savoir sexué?'. L'Harmattan (1991) published it as part of the conference proceedings.

1 On forcing, the reader can consult Francois Wahl's preface to this book 'The subtractive' and of course *Being and Event* (final mediations).

CHAPTER TWELVE

This text was delivered in 1989 at a conference devoted to the topic of consent (*assentiment*) organized by the journal *Littoral*. It was published in the journal the following year as part of the conference proceedings.

CHAPTER THIRTEEN

This essay was originally given as a paper at a conference in Marseille, at the invitation of Dr. M. Dugnat. The original title of this essay, which remains unpublished, was 'The Position of the Infinite in the Split of the Subject'.

[1] Translator's note: In English in the original.
[2] Translator's note: In English in the original.
[3] For a sketch of the attributes of the humanity function, and its difference – concerning the sexes – with the phallic function, the reader can consult the essay in this book entitled 'What is Love?'
[4] Translator's note: The original French is from the poem called *Toast funèbre: . . . le maître a sur ses pas/ Apaisé de l'éden l'inquiète merveille.*

CHAPTER FOURTEEN

This text is an abridged and slightly reworked version of a paper I gave at a colloquium organized in 1990 by the *Collège international de philosophie* called 'Lacan with the Philosophers'. The first version was published in the conference proceedings (Albin Michel, 1991) under the title 'Lacan and Plato: Is the matheme an Idea?' I've made some alterations here to take into account the importance of the theme of antiphilosophy

[1] Translator's note: 'hontologie' is a neologism formed by the French words 'ontologie' that is, ontology, and 'honte', meaning 'shame' or 'disgrace'.

CHAPTER FIFTEEN

This text was delivered in 1989 in the cycle of the *Conferences du Perroquet*. It was published as a booklet of these conferences, and is today nowhere to be found. It should be noted that since the publication of this essay

Samuel Beckett has died. And that *Worstward Ho* has been admirably translated by Edith Fournier with the title *Cap au pire* (Minuit, 1991).

[1] Translator's note: A 'vers de mirliton' is an expression referring to a piece of 'bad' poetry where artistic merit is sacrificed for the sake of getting something to rhyme. The expression comes from the practice of writing short verse on the paper that spiralled round an instrument known as the 'mirliton'.

[2] Translator's note: This is my translation of the original French poem, which Beckett left untranslated. Here is the original French *mirlitonnade*: *Flux cause / Que toute chose / Tout en étant, / Toute chose, / Donc celle-là,/ Même celle-là / Tout en étant / N'est pas. / Parlons-en.*

[3] Translator's note: The French term here is *'noir grise'*, which I have literally translated as 'black–grey' because these terms fit in better with Badiou's proposal. It should be noted, however, that Beckett himself translated *'noir grise'* as 'ash grey'.

[4] Translator's note: the adjective 'ressassante' has no English equivalent. According to the *Grand Robert*, the verb *ressasser* originally meant 'to act anew', 'to examine carefully many times over', before it took on its current sense of 'to dwell on', 'to brood on', 'to go over the same things'. Hence, it now also connotes a sense of the repetition whereby something becomes 'ressassé' or 'hackneyed'. The reference to the insistent, repetitious examination of questions characteristic of the Beckettian subject evidently draws on both the older and newer senses.

Index of Concepts

INDEX OF CONCEPTS

Index of Names

INDEX OF NAMES